Mastering VMware Horizon 7.8
Third Edition

Master desktop virtualization to optimize your end user experience

Peter von Oven
Barry Coombs

BIRMINGHAM - MUMBAI

Mastering VMware Horizon 7.8
Third Edition

Copyright © 2019 Packt Publishing

All rights reserved. No part of this book may be reproduced, stored in a retrieval system, or transmitted in any form or by any means, without the prior written permission of the publisher, except in the case of brief quotations embedded in critical articles or reviews.

Every effort has been made in the preparation of this book to ensure the accuracy of the information presented. However, the information contained in this book is sold without warranty, either express or implied. Neither the authors, nor Packt Publishing or its dealers and distributors, will be held liable for any damages caused or alleged to have been caused directly or indirectly by this book.

Packt Publishing has endeavored to provide trademark information about all of the companies and products mentioned in this book by the appropriate use of capitals. However, Packt Publishing cannot guarantee the accuracy of this information.

Commissioning Editor: Vijin Boricha
Acquisition Editor: Meeta Rajani
Content Development Editor: Deepti Thore
Technical Editor: Sayali Thanekar
Copy Editor: Safis Editing
Project Coordinator: Nusaiba Ansari
Proofreader: Safis Editing
Indexer: Manju Arasan
Graphics: Jisha Chirayil
Production Coordinator: Jyoti Chauhan

First published: March 2015
Second edition: October 2016
Third edition: March 2019

Production reference: 1280319

Published by Packt Publishing Ltd.
Livery Place
35 Livery Street
Birmingham
B3 2PB, UK.

ISBN 978-1-78980-237-5

www.packtpub.com

mapt.io

Mapt is an online digital library that gives you full access to over 5,000 books and videos, as well as industry leading tools to help you plan your personal development and advance your career. For more information, please visit our website.

Why subscribe?

- Spend less time learning and more time coding with practical eBooks and Videos from over 4,000 industry professionals

- Improve your learning with Skill Plans built especially for you

- Get a free eBook or video every month

- Mapt is fully searchable

- Copy and paste, print, and bookmark content

Packt.com

Did you know that Packt offers eBook versions of every book published, with PDF and ePub files available? You can upgrade to the eBook version at www.packt.com and as a print book customer, you are entitled to a discount on the eBook copy. Get in touch with us at customercare@packtpub.com for more details.

At www.packt.com, you can also read a collection of free technical articles, sign up for a range of free newsletters, and receive exclusive discounts and offers on Packt books and eBooks.

Contributors

About the authors

Peter von Oven is an experienced technical consultant and has spent the past 25 years working with customers and partners designing technology solutions. During his career, Peter has presented at key IT events, such as VMworld, IP EXPO, and various VMUGs and CCUG events. He has also worked in senior presales roles and presales management roles for Fujitsu, HP, Citrix, and VMware, and has been awarded VMware vExpert four years running.

In 2016, Peter founded his own company, Droplet Computing, where he works today as the Founder and Chief Technology Officer.

Peter got his first taste for writing when assisting with some of the chapters in *Building End-User Computing Solutions with VMware View*, which then lead to five other Packt titles.

> *First and foremost, I would like to thank my wife and two daughters for putting up with me while I'm writing. I couldn't do it without their support.*
> *This book wouldn't have happened without support from key EUC vendors. Special thanks to Kevin Cooke at Liquidware for assisting with end user life cycle management, and thanks to Adam Gleeson at Computerworld for providing insight into the new features of Horizon and giving me access to the EUC demo lab.*

Barry Coombs is the Operations Director for Computerworld Systems LTD, a UK-based, virtualization-focused, value-added reseller. He has been focusing on virtualization, storage, and end user computing technologies as a customer, consultant, and architect for the last nine years. Barry is responsible for identifying new technologies as well as speaking and hosting customer-focused events associated with virtualization, storage, and end user computing. Barry has been awarded VMware's vExpert award for contributions to the VMware community every year since 2010. He is also part of the VMUG leadership team for South West UK. Barry has been a co-author of two VMware Horizon books.

About the reviewers

Mathias Meyenburg has been the managing director of vleet GmbH since January 1, 2019. He has more than 15 years' experience in the IT industry. Starting as a system administrator, his career has progressed to operating and administering large-scale international data centers. He has constantly updated and expanded his know-how and acquired advanced certifications, such as CCNA, MCP, and VCP. vleet GmbH sought him out in 2016 as a solution architect for the whole VMware SDDC stack, Horizon desktop virtualization, Horizon Cloud on Azure, and VMC on AWS.

I would like to express my gratitude to my wife, Andrea, who had to carry the burden while I was occupied with this book and my career, and who lovingly looked after our kids while studying herself.

Fady Fawzy Abdelmalek is a senior system engineer and solution architect working at Equinox International (EquinoxME) in Egypt. He specializes in VMware technologies, and has more than 8 years of extensive experience with vSphere, Horizon, NSX, VMware Cloud Automation Infrastructure, and complex SDDC infrastructure. He has participated in many mega-projects as an SME, architect, advisor, implementer, and technical team delivery lead. He has also worked as a freelance consultant. He has been working in IT for more than 10 years. He is known on the web as VMFCore.

Packt is searching for authors like you

If you're interested in becoming an author for Packt, please visit authors.packtpub.com and apply today. We have worked with thousands of developers and tech professionals, just like you, to help them share their insight with the global tech community. You can make a general application, apply for a specific hot topic that we are recruiting an author for, or submit your own idea.

Table of Contents

Preface — 1

Section 1: Installation and Configuration

Chapter 1: Introducing VDI and VMware Horizon 7 — 11
- **What is VDI?** — 12
  - VDI high-level architecture – how does it work? — 12
  - VDI versus server-based computing (SBC) – what are the differences? — 14
- **The benefits of deploying Horizon** — 16
- **The history of VMware and VDI** — 18
- **VMware Horizon 7** — 20
  - VMware Horizon 7 timeline — 20
- **VMware Horizon 7 product editions** — 23
  - Horizon for Linux — 23
  - Horizon Standard Edition — 23
  - Horizon Advanced Edition — 24
  - Horizon Enterprise Edition — 24
  - Horizon Apps Standard — 25
  - Horizon Apps Advanced — 25
  - Horizon editions overview and comparison — 26
  - Horizon user licensing models — 27
- **Summary** — 27

Chapter 2: Understanding Horizon 7 Architecture and Components — 29
- **Introducing the key Horizon components** — 30
- **High-level architectural overview** — 31
  - The Horizon View Connection Server — 32
    - How does the connection server work? — 32
    - Minimum requirements for the connection server — 35
      - Hardware requirements — 35
      - Supported OS — 36
  - The Horizon View security server — 36
    - How does the security server work? — 37
  - The Horizon View replica server — 37
    - How does the replica server work? — 38
  - The Horizon View enrolment server and True SSO — 39
  - VMware Unified Access Gateway — 41
- **Persistent or non-persistent desktops?** — 42
- **Horizon View Composer and linked clones** — 44
  - What is cloning? — 44
  - What is a full clone? — 45

Table of Contents

What are linked clones? — 45
How do linked clones work? — 47
Creating linked clones — 49
    Linked clone disk — 49
    Persistent disk or user data disk — 49
    Disposable disk — 50
    Internal disk — 51
Understanding how the linked clone process works — 52
    Creating and provisioning a new virtual desktop — 52
    Customizing the desktop — 53
Linked clone features and functionality — 54
    Recomposing a linked clone — 54
    Refreshing a linked clone — 56
    Rebalancing operations with View Composer — 58
Instant Clones — 59
    Instant clone build process — 61
    Instant clone benefits — 62
View Persona Management — 62
    Why do we need to manage user profiles differently in VDI? — 63
    The benefits of View Persona Management — 63
VMware UEM — 64
    UEM or Persona Management? — 66
Printing from a virtual desktop machine — 67
Managing USB devices — 67
    Filtering supported USB devices — 68
    Managing multi-function USB devices — 68
ThinApp application virtualization — 69
    How does application virtualization work? — 69
Antivirus software for virtual desktops — 71
Protocols – Delivering the virtual desktop experience — 72
    PCoIP — 72
        PCoIP host rendering — 73
        Multi-codec support with PCoIP — 74
        Controlling the image quality — 74
        Dynamic networking capabilities — 74
        PCoIP offloading with the Teradici PCoIP Hardware Accelerator — 75
        Teradici host card for physical PCs — 76
        How the PCoIP connection process works — 76
    Blast Extreme — 77
        How the Blast Extreme connection process works — 79
    Alternative display protocols — 80
        RDP — 80
        ICA protocol — 81
    Which protocol should you use – Blast Extreme, PCoIP, or RDP? — 81
Horizon View Hardware-accelerated graphics — 82
    vSGA — 83
        vSGA-supported graphics cards — 85

How many virtual desktops are supported by vSGA? ... 85
vDGA ... 86
How many virtual desktops are supported with vDGA? ... 87
vDGA-supported graphics cards ... 88
vGPU ... 88
How many virtual desktops are supported with vGPU? ... 90
Unified communications support ... 90
How do unified communications work now? ... 92
Support for Microsoft Skype ... 92
Real-Time Audio-Video (RTAV) ... 94
The issue ... 94
How does RTAV fix this issue? ... 94
URL Content Redirection ... 95
Horizon clients ... 95
Summary ... 95

Chapter 3: Design and Deployment Considerations ... 97
  Phase I – Project definition ... 99
    Step 1 – Identifying business drivers – understanding your needs and requirements ... 99
    Step 2 – Building the business case ... 100
    Step 3 – Assessment ... 100
      User experience and desktop analysis tools ... 101
      Understanding what do your users really do ... 103
      Applications ... 103
      Performance ... 104
      End user experience ... 105
      Floor walks, interviews, and department champions ... 105
      What are department champions? ... 106
    Step 4 – Defining the success criteria ... 106
  Phase II – Proving the technology ... 108
    Proof of concept (POC) ... 109
    Proof of technology (POT) ... 109
    Pilot ... 110
      Step 1 – Pilot design ... 111
      Step 2 – Deploying the pilot ... 112
      Step 3 – Testing the pilot ... 112
      Step 4 – Reviewing the pilot ... 112
  Phase III – Designing a production environment ... 113
  Technology choices ... 113
    Use case example – Scenario 1 ... 114
      Solution recommendation ... 114
    Use case example – Scenario 2 ... 114
      Solution recommendation ... 114
    Use case example – Scenario 3 ... 115
      Solution recommendation ... 115
    Use case example – Scenario 4 ... 116

Table of Contents

Solution recommendation ... 116
Conclusions ... 116
Preparing for production ... 117
Horizon View pod and block architecture ... 117
Cloud Pod Architecture ... 122
vSphere design for Horizon View ... 124
Configuration maximums ... 125
ESXi host servers ... 126
CPU and memory requirements for ESXi ... 126
Overcommitting CPU and memory resources ... 126
CPU and memory sizing ... 127
Networking ... 128
Graphics ... 128
Storage ... 129
Storage capacity ... 129
Storage performance ... 131
Horizon View design specifics ... 134
The Horizon View Connection Server ... 135
The Horizon View Replica Server ... 135
The Horizon View Security Server ... 135
The Horizon View Enrolment Server ... 136
The Horizon View Composer ... 136
vCenter Servers ... 136
VMware Access Point ... 137
Configuration maximums ... 138
Networking ... 138
Load balancing ... 140
Remote Desktop Session Host (RDSH) design considerations ... 142
Supporting infrastructure design ... 144
Database requirements ... 144
File servers ... 144
IP addressing ... 145
Antivirus ... 146
Active Directory Group Policy ... 146
Functionality ... 146
Lockdown ... 147
Performance and management ... 147
Key Management Server (KMS) ... 147
Printing ... 148
Thin clients and other endpoint devices ... 149
Desktop design considerations ... 149
Pool design ... 149
Sizing the virtual desktop machines ... 150
Sizing the host server's CPU requirements to run virtual desktops ... 150
Light user ... 151
Medium user ... 152
Heavy user ... 152

Table of Contents

Sizing the host server's memory requirements to run virtual desktops 153
Linked Clone, Instant Clone, or Full Clone 153
Persistent versus non-persistent 154
Building a composite desktop 155
    Base layer 156
    Applications 156
    User profiles and user environment management 156
Disaster recovery and backup 157
    Backup and recovery options 157
    Disaster recovery options 158
Example solution scenario 160
    End user requirements 161
        Application developers 161
        Office workers 162
        Contractors 162
        Engineering 162
        Sales 162
    Desktop pool design 163
    Sizing the desktop blocks 164
    Sizing the storage requirements 166
    Sizing the management blocks 167
    Network sizing and requirements 167
Summary 168

Chapter 4: Installing and Configuring Horizon 7 - Part 1 169
Welcome to the lab environment 169
    What you need for the example lab 170
Preparing AD 172
    AD user accounts 173
    vCenter user accounts 173
    View Composer user account 180
    View desktop Organizational Units (OUs) 180
    IP addressing and DNS requirements 181
Installing Horizon View Composer Server 182
    Configuring SQL Server for a View Composer database 183
    View Composer installation 191
Installing the Horizon View Connection Server 206
Initial configuration of the Horizon View Connection Server 214
    Adding a license to the Connection Server 216
    Adding vCenter Server to View Administrator 219
    Configuring the View events database 226
Summary 228

Chapter 5: Installing and Configuring Horizon 7 - Part 2 229
Installing a Horizon View Replica Server 230
Installing a Security Server 234

Preparing View Administrator for the Security Server install	235
Security Server software installation	237
Installing an Enrollment Server	244
Configuring Cloud Pod Architecture	246
Initializing the Cloud Pod	247
Connecting the second pod to the Cloud Pod	251
Entitling users to the Cloud Pod	254
Configuring View for GPU-enabled virtual desktops	260
Configuring the ESXi host servers	261
Summary	264

Section 2: Building and Delivering the Virtual Desktop Experience

Chapter 6: Securing Horizon View with SSL Certificates	267
Horizon View and SSL certificates	267
What is a CA?	268
Why do I need SSL certificates for Horizon View?	268
Installing SSL certificates for Horizon View	269
Installing a root CA	269
Root CA post-deployment configuration tasks	274
Installing an SSL certificate on the View Connection Server	285
Post-certificate enrollment configuration tasks	294
Horizon View True SSO	298
Preparing AD for True SSO	298
Creating a certificate template for TrueSSO	303
Issuing the TrueSSO certificate template	313
Certificate deployment	318
Configuring True SSO on the Connection Server	330
Summary	333
Chapter 7: Building and Optimizing the Virtual Desktop OS	335
Best practices for building virtual desktop images	336
Technical requirements	337
Creating a Windows 7 virtual desktop machine	338
Creating the virtual desktop machine container	339
Updating the virtual desktop machine BIOS	354
Operating system installation options	357
Installing the guest operating system	357
Installing VMware Tools	358
Installing applications for the parent image	364
Installing the Horizon Agent	364
Optimizing the guest operating system	371
Post-optimization tasks	375
Creating a Windows 10 virtual desktop machine	375
Creating the virtual desktop machine container	376

Completing the Windows 10 build	378
Creating a GPU-enabled virtual desktop machine	379
Creating the virtual desktop machine container	379
Installing the operating system for GPU-enabled desktops	383
Completing the GPU-enabled desktop build	385
Creating a Linux virtual desktop machine	385
Completing the Linux virtual desktop build	388
Installing the Horizon Agent	389
Optimizing the guest operating system	392
Preparing virtual desktops for delivery	393
Pool design – a quick overview	393
Creating a snapshot for linked clones	394
Creating a snapshot for instant clones	398
Creating a template for full clones	398
Summary	401
Chapter 8: Configuring and Managing Desktop Pools - Part 1	403
Types of desktop pools	403
Automated desktop pools	404
Creating dedicated, Linked Clone desktop pools	405
Using the Horizon View Administrator Console	406
General settings	412
Remote Settings	414
Remote Desktop Protocol settings	417
Adobe Flash Settings	420
Desktop Pool Sizing	426
vCenter Settings	432
Advanced Storage Options	442
Horizon Console method	450
Creating dedicated, Full Clone desktop pools	472
Summary	485
Chapter 9: Configuring and Managing Desktop Pools - Part 2	487
Creating floating, Linked Clone desktop pools	488
Creating floating, Full Clone desktop pools	492
Creating floating, Instant Clone desktop pools	496
Configuring the Instant Clone domain administrator	496
Creating the Instant Clone desktop pool	498
Creating a manual desktop pool	507
Adding end user entitlements	511
Adding user entitlement using the Horizon View Administrator Classic console	512
Adding user entitlement using the new Horizon console	516
Managing Linked Clone desktop pools	520
Recomposing a Linked Clone desktop pool	525
Refreshing a Linked Clone desktop pool	529
Rebalancing a Linked Clone desktop pool	531

Managing persistent disks	534
Detaching a persistent disk	534
Attaching a persistent disk	536
Reviewing the infrastructure post-deployment	540
Summary	541
Chapter 10: Fine-Tuning the End User Experience	**543**
Configuring and preparing AD	544
Importing and applying Horizon View ADMX templates	545
Creating an organizational unit (OU)	546
Creating Group Policy Objects (GPO) for Horizon View	548
Enabling the loopback policy	553
Configuring Horizon View policy settings	555
PCoIP Client Session Variables	555
PCoIP Session Variables	557
VMware Blast	558
VMware Horizon Client Configuration	559
Scripting definitions	560
Security Settings	560
View USB Configuration	561
Settings not configurable by Agent	561
VMware Horizon URL Redirection	561
Horizon View Agent Configuration	562
Agent Configuration	563
Agent Security	563
Collaboration	563
Persona Management	564
Desktop UI	565
Folder Redirection	565
Logging	566
Roaming and Synchronization	566
Troubleshooting	567
Scanner Redirection	567
Serial COM	567
PortSettings	568
Smartcard Redirection	568
Local Reader Access	569
True SSO Configuration	569
Unity Touch and Hosted Apps	570
View Agent Direct-Connection Configuration	570
View RTAV Configuration	571
View RTAV Webcam Settings	572
View USB Configuration	572
Client Downloadable only Settings	572
VMware Client IP Transparency	573
VMware Device Bridge	573
VMware Flash MMR	574
VMware HTML5 Features	574
VMware Geolocation Redirection	574
VMware HTML5 Multimedia Redirection	575

VMware Virtualization Pack for Skype for Business	575
VMware View Common Configuration	576
Log Configuration	576
Performance Alarms	577
Security Configuration	577
VMware View Server Configuration	578
PCoIP tuning tool	578
Activate Profile	579
Manage Profiles	580
Clear Profile Settings	580
Show Session Stats	580
Show Session Health	580
Teradici support tools for PCoIP	581
Monitoring the end user experience	581
Summary	583

Section 3: Advanced Features, Troubleshooting, and Upgrading an Environment

Chapter 11: Delivering Published Apps with Horizon 7 — 587

Architectural overview	588
Application connection sequence	589
RDSH sizing guidelines	592
Installing and configuring View-hosted apps	593
Configuring the RDS server role	594
Testing with the standard remote applications	601
Installing additional applications	606
Installing the Horizon Agent for RDSH	615
Configuring published apps in the View Administrator	622
Creating an application pool for published apps	628
Entitling users to application pools	631
Load-balancing published apps in Horizon View	636
Summary	645

Chapter 12: Horizon Client Options — 647

VMware Horizon Clients	648
Horizon Client for Windows	648
Horizon Client for Android	651
Horizon Client for iOS	653
Horizon Client for Linux	656
Horizon Client for macOS	658
Horizon Client for Chrome OS	660
Hardware clients	661
Thin clients	662
Zero Clients	663
Repurposed PCs (software-defined thin clients)	664

Table of Contents

Accessing the desktop using a browser	665
Summary	669
Chapter 13: Upgrading to a New Version of Horizon	**671**
Upgrading compatibility	671
Upgrading Horizon Composer	673
Before you begin the upgrade	673
Completing the View Composer upgrade	676
Verifying the upgrade	676
Upgrading the Horizon View Connection Server	681
Before you begin the upgrade	681
Completing the Connection Server upgrade	681
Alternative View Connection Server upgrade method	683
Upgrading the View Security Server	684
Before you begin the upgrade	684
Completing the View Security Server upgrade	685
Upgrading group policy templates	686
Upgrading the VMware Horizon Agent	687
Upgrading the Horizon Client	687
Summary	688
Chapter 14: JMP and VMware Horizon 7 Deployment Considerations	**689**
How does JMP work?	690
VMware Workspace ONE	691
VMware App Volumes	692
How does App Volumes work? Step 1 – app capture	694
How does App Volumes work? Step 2 – app delivery	695
Installing and configuring JMP	696
Prerequisites	696
VMware JMP component requirements	696
VMware JMP hardware requirements	696
VMware JMP software requirements	697
Installing the JMP Server	697
Syncing the time with Horizon Connection Server	700
Adding JMP Server and its components to Horizon	701
JMP assignments	711
Summary	713
Chapter 15: Troubleshooting	**715**
General troubleshooting tips	715
Look at the bigger picture	716
Is the issue affecting more than one user?	716
Performance issues	717
When a user reports performance issues	717
Non-VDI related issues	718

Bandwidth, connectivity, and networking	719
Compute resources	721
Disk	722
Troubleshooting Horizon View issues	723
Horizon View general infrastructure issues	724
View infrastructure component issues	725
Fixing View Composer issues with the ViewDBChk tool	725
vRealize Operations for Horizon	727
Liquidware Stratusphere UX	729
Getting further help	729
Summary	730
Chapter 16: What is New in Horizon 7	731
Operating system and infrastructure updates	731
Horizon management updates	732
Horizon console updates	732
View Administrator updates	732
Help Desk Tool updates	732
Scalability	733
Enhancements to the end user experience	733
Linux virtual desktop machine updates	734
Platform updates	734
Horizon Console updates	734
Scalability	735
RDSH improvements	735
Horizon with VMware Cloud on AWS	736
Horizon Agent updates	736
Windows Agent	736
Linux Agent	736
Horizon Client	737
Summary	738
Other Books You May Enjoy	739
Index	743

Preface

VMware Horizon View, part of the VMware digital workspace, is the platform for delivering centralized, virtual desktop machines and applications, hosted on servers running on a hypervisor in the data center. End users connect remotely to their virtual desktop machines and apps from their endpoint device, such as a Windows laptop, Apple Mac, or tablet device.

This technology was first introduced by VMware in 2002, and has developed and matured to become the mainstream technology that we know today as **Virtual Desktop Infrastructure (VDI)**. VDI provides users with the freedom to work in a way that suits them, by freeing them from the restrictions of not having to be in the office, but also allowing them the choice of device they use for making them more productive, and ultimately your business more agile.

From an IT administrator's perspective, it allows you to centrally manage your desktop environment, from being able to manage desktop images, to the ease of adding and removing user entitlements, all controlled from a single management console.

VMware Horizon 7 and Horizon View version 7.7 is VMware's latest virtual desktop solution, designed to centralize and virtualize your desktop environment using the market leading virtualization features and technology within VMware's **Software Defined Data Center (SDDC)** portfolio.

Horizon View 7 builds upon this technology platform, and today goes far beyond just VDI in delivering a rich user experience, enabling BYOD, flexible working, enhanced security, application delivery, and end-to-end management. Delivering an end user experience requires a different approach from other infrastructure-based initiatives, and getting this right is the key in terms of a project having a successful outcome, and this book will show you how to succeed.

Who this book is for

If you are a desktop administrator or part of a project team looking at deploying a virtual desktop and/or application delivery solution, or taking advantage of some of the latest Horizon features, then this book is perfect for you and your ideal companion in helping to deploy a solution to centrally manage and virtualize your desktop estate using Horizon 7.

Preface

You will need to have some experience in desktop management using the Microsoft Windows desktop and server operating systems, and general Windows applications, as well as be familiar with the Active Directory, SQL, and VMware vSphere infrastructure (ESXi and vCenter Server) technology.

What this book covers

Chapter 1, *Introducing VDI and VMware Horizon 7*, covers an introduction to VDI, explaining what it is, and how it compares with other VDI-type technologies. We will then cover a brief history of the VMware VDI story, followed by an overview of the latest solution.

Chapter 2, *Understanding Horizon 7 Architecture and Components*, introduces you to the architectural components that make up the core VMware Horizon solution, concentrating on the virtual desktop elements of Horizon View and the functionality of brokering virtual desktop machines.

Chapter 3, *Design and Deployment Considerations*, introduces you to design and deployment techniques to take into consideration when undertaking your VMware Horizon project. We will discuss techniques for proving the technology and understanding how it will work inside your business, methods for assessing your user's existing workload, and how to use
this information to help design your VMware Horizon Solution.

Chapter 4, *Installing and Configuring Horizon 7 – Part 1*, covers the installation process of the core Horizon View components, these being the Connection Server and View Composer in this first part.

Chapter 5, *Installing and Configuring Horizon 7 – Part 2*, completes the installation of the Horizon environment by installing the Security Server, Replica Server, Enrollment Server, as well as the Cloud Pod Architecture feature. Following installation, we will start to configure the base elements of a Horizon View installation.

Chapter 6, *Securing Horizon View with SSL Certificates*, covers the aspect of VMware Horizon View and, in particular, how we deliver secure communication to the end user client, and also the different infrastructure components within the data center. The first half of this chapter will comprise an overview of what an SSL certificate is, and then look at how to create and issue a certificate before configuring Horizon View to use it. In the second half of the chapter, we will look at configuring the VMware True SSO feature.

Chapter 7, *Building and Optimizing the Virtual Desktop OS*, covers how to create and configure the virtual desktop machines after building the Horizon View infrastructure and its components, and then build the desktop operating system on them, configuring it so that it is running at its optimum performance level to run in a virtual environment.

Chapter 8, *Configuring and Managing Desktop Pools – Part 1*, covers how Horizon View uses the concept of desktop pools to create a collection of virtual desktop machines for specific use cases, which, in turn, are allocated to the end users. In this chapter, we will look at the process for configuring the different types of desktop pools.

Chapter 9, *Configuring and Managing Desktop Pools – Part 2*, completes the process of managing desktop pools, focusing on Linked Clones, Manual Desktop Pools, and some of the day-to-day management tasks.

Chapter 10, *Fine-Tuning the End User Experience*, covers one of the key tasks in building the best user experience possible, which is to start fine-tuning the performance and experience for the end user's session with their virtual desktop machine. In this chapter, we will look at the tuning techniques and the pre-built group policy objects that can be applied to create that experience.

Chapter 11, *Delivering Published Apps with Horizon 7*, dives deeper into the key features of Horizon Advanced Edition, and looks at how Horizon View publishes an application directly in the Horizon View Client, without the need to launch a full virtual desktop machine. We will walk through the installation and configuration process to get our first set of Horizon View published applications available to end users.

Chapter 12, *Horizon Client Options*, covers how the Horizon Client is used to receive and display the virtual desktops and applications on the end user's device. In this chapter, we will look at the options for the Horizon Client, both hardware and software, and discuss the various options and why you would choose one method over another.

Chapter 13, *Upgrading to a New Version of Horizon*, covers all the things you need to consider before upgrading, and will then take you through the upgrade process. This chapter is designed for those individuals who are currently running a previous version of Horizon View and are looking to upgrade to the latest version.

Preface

Chapter 14, *JMP and VMware Horizon 7 Deployment Considerations*, covers the new just-in-time management platform feature in Horizon 7 and how this brings together UEM, App Volumes, and Instant Clones to deliver desktops on demand. This chapter discusses the architecture and walks you through installation and configuration.

Chapter 15, *Troubleshooting*, covers a number of troubleshooting techniques and methods to adopt within Horizon View, rather than going through a list of problems and issues.

Chapter 16, *What is New in Horizon 7*, discusses the latest features in the newest version of Horizon 7.

Chapter 17, *Managing the End User Environments in Horizon*, introduces you to Horizon View Persona Management, what it is, and why you would want to deploy it. We will then examine how it is driven by standard active directory group policy, finishing with an in-depth look at the policies available. The second part of this chapter introduces you to VMware UEM and how to get up and running.

For this chapter refer to: https://www.packtpub.com/sites/default/files/downloads/Managing_the_End_User_Environment_in_Horizon.pdf.

Chapter 18, *Delivering Published Desktops with Horizon 7*, covers the other half of View's publishing capabilities and looks at how Horizon View can deliver session-based desktops from a Microsoft RDSH infrastructure.

For this chapter refer to: https://www.packtpub.com/sites/default/files/downloads/Delivering_Published_Desktops_with_Horizon_7.pdf.

To get the most out of this book

To get the most out of this book, you should have some experience of working as a desktop administrator with skills and knowledge associated with building and designing Microsoft Windows-based desktop environments. You should also be familiar with the VMware vSphere platform (ESXi and vCenter Server) and be comfortable with building and configuring virtual machines as well as configuring storage and networking for use in a virtual infrastructure.

Throughout this book, you will have the opportunity to follow step-by-step practical guides in deploying Horizon View in an example lab environment. If you want to work through the practical examples, you will need the following software:

- VMware Horizon 7 or version 7.6, 7.7, or 7.8
- vSphere for Desktop (ESXi and vCenter Server 6.5)

You can download a trial copy of Horizon 7 from the following link (you will need to have a VMware account):

`https://my.vmware.com/en/web/vmware/evalcenter?p=horizon-7`

You will also need the following software to build virtual machines and deploy applications:

- Microsoft Windows Server 2016 64-bit
- Microsoft Windows 7 Professional 32-bit or 64-bit
- Microsoft Windows 10
- Microsoft SQL Express 2012
- Microsoft Office 2016

Download the color images

We also provide a PDF file that has color images of the screenshots/diagrams used in this book. You can download it here: `https://www.packtpub.com/sites/default/files/downloads/9781789802375_ColorImages.pdf`.

Conventions used

There are a number of text conventions used throughout this book.

`CodeInText`: Indicates code words in text, database table names, folder names, filenames, file extensions, pathnames, dummy URLs, user input, and Twitter handles. Here is an example: "This second instance of the Connection Server is going to be installed on the virtual machine with the hostname `hzn7-cs2.pvolab.com` that was built at the start of this chapter."

Preface

Any command-line input or output is written as follows:

```
net stop certsvc
net start certsvc
```

Bold: Indicates a new term, an important word, or words that you see on screen. For example, words in menus or dialog boxes appear in the text like this. Here is an example: "In the **Select Database Owner** box, click **OK** to accept the database owner."

Warnings or important notes appear like this.

Tips and tricks appear like this.

Get in touch

Feedback from our readers is always welcome.

General feedback: If you have questions about any aspect of this book, mention the book title in the subject of your message and email us at customercare@packtpub.com.

Errata: Although we have taken every care to ensure the accuracy of our content, mistakes do happen. If you have found a mistake in this book, we would be grateful if you would report this to us. Please visit www.packt.com/submit-errata, selecting your book, clicking on the Errata Submission Form link, and entering the details.

Piracy: If you come across any illegal copies of our works in any form on the internet, we would be grateful if you would provide us with the location address or website name. Please contact us at copyright@packt.com with a link to the material.

If you are interested in becoming an author: If there is a topic that you have expertise in, and you are interested in either writing or contributing to a book, please visit authors.packtpub.com.

Reviews

Please leave a review. Once you have read and used this book, why not leave a review on the site that you purchased it from? Potential readers can then see and use your unbiased opinion to make purchase decisions, we at Packt can understand what you think about our products, and our authors can see your feedback on their book. Thank you!

For more information about Packt, please visit `packt.com`.

Section 1: Installation and Configuration

The chapters in this section describe the architecture components, how to design and deploy an environment, and the installation of a Horizon environment.

The following chapters are included in this section:

Chapter 1, *Introducing VDI and VMware Horizon 7*
Chapter 2, *Understanding Horizon 7 Architecture and Components*
Chapter 3, *Design and Deployment Considerations*
Chapter 4, *Installing and Configuring Horizon 7 - Part 1*
Chapter 5, *Installing and Configuring Horizon 7 - Part 2*

Introducing VDI and VMware Horizon 7

n the first chapter of this book, we are going to start by discussing what we mean when we talk about **Virtual Desktop Infrastructure** (**VDI**) and define exactly what this means. Once we have defined this, we will go on to discuss the specifics of it in the context of the VMware Horizon solution.

Throughout this book we have used a number of screenshots to demonstrate installation and configuration of Horizon, using the example lab environment. These screenshots are taken from Horizon 7 version 7.6, however, the latest 7.8 version is exactly the same with the exception of the version number shown on the screenshot, and in some cases the Horizon logo. The process and steps shown remain exactly the same.

Horizon provides the foundation to VMware's **End User Computing** (**EUC**) solution for delivering desktops and applications. VMware first entered the VDI market about 16 years ago, when they demonstrated the concept of virtualizing a desktop operating system by using their success in the server virtualization market that is now becoming a more mature and prevalent technology. Taking some of the very same principles that are used in server virtualization, and instead applying them to a desktop operating system, VMware was able to create a centrally-managed, virtualized desktop solution that would lower the overall cost of desktop computing and increase security.

In this chapter, we are going to cover the following topics:

- What is VDI, and how does it work?
- A history of VMware and VDI
- VMware Horizon editions and licensing options

Before we get into discussing specific product features and functionality, let's define what we mean when we talk about VDI. We'll then take a brief stroll down memory lane and look at where and how it all started for VMware.

What is VDI?

When we talk about VDI, we are typically describing a solution whereby a desktop PC's operating system is hosted as a virtual machine that is running on a hypervisor, with the hypervisor hosted on a server that is part of the data center infrastructure, either on-premises or cloud-based.

This VDI model is also sometimes referred to as a **hosted virtual desktop (HVD)**, given that the virtual desktop is hosted as a virtual machine, with an end user that has access to their own instance of a full desktop. This is not to be confused with server-based computing, which only delivers a desktop session to the end user. We will discuss this in the *VDI versus server-based computing (SBC) – what are the differences?* section later in this chapter.

VDI high-level architecture – how does it work?

How does VDI work? Let's start with the end user and how they access a virtual desktop machine. From their endpoint device (a PC, thin client, or mobile device), the end user launches the client software, which is the Horizon client in the case of VMware, or they simply open a browser. Either way, this connects them to a connection broker using its hostname or URL. The job of the connection broker in the first instance is to authenticate the end user and then to manage the available resources and connect the end user to the appropriate virtual desktop. The desktop that's delivered to them could be based on their physical location or on a departmental basis where there are different desktop configurations depending on the context of that user.

The following diagram describes, at a high level, how VDI works:

[Diagram: Data Center containing Virtual Machines running Desktop OS, Hypervisor, x86 Servers, connecting via Connection Broker through Delivery Protocol over Internet LAN/WAN to End Point Device, with Mouse & Key Strokes sent back]

In the first VDI solutions that came to market, there was no concept of a connection broker and instead, an end user would connect directly to a virtual desktop machine on a 1:1 basis. It was like picking up their desktop and moving it to the data center.

Once an end user is connected to a virtual desktop machine, the screenshots, or the display of the virtual desktop machine, are sent over the network to the client software or browser on the endpoint device using an optimized delivery protocol. To enable the end user to interact with the virtual desktop, the mouse movements and keystrokes are then sent back to the virtual desktop machine over the network via the same protocol.

Therefore, VDI desktops are more secure as no data leaves the data center, but instead, just the screenshot updates or pixel changes are sent over the network. As per the previous analogy, it's like picking up your PC and putting it in a data center that's miles away from your home and then having your keyboard, mouse, and screen at home with very long cables back to the data center.

That's VDI from a connectivity perspective, but let's focus on the virtual desktop itself for a moment and look at how the architecture differs from a desktop in the physical world. VDI desktops are typically built on demand, that is, when a user logs in and requests a desktop resource. To help manage costs, you would typically deploy a non-persistent desktop model (as discussed in Chapter 2, *Understanding Horizon 7 Architecture and Components*) whereby users don't own their desktop and would have a new desktop built for them each time they log in. Therein lies one of the key differences between virtual and physical desktops.

As we just discussed, a virtual desktop typically gets built on demand, bringing together the different components that make up a full desktop environment. The operating system, user profile, desktop policies, and applications are all treated as separate, individual components, abstracted from the underlying machine, and then delivered back together to create the end user's desktop experience.

This is referred to as the composite desktop model, which is shown in the following diagram:

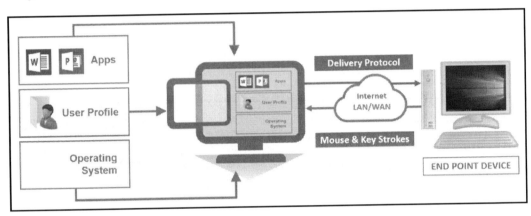

The key take away here is that virtual desktop machines need to be treated differently from physical desktops, and to reap all the benefits that virtual desktop machines offer, they should be built from the ground up and managed as virtual machines from day one, using some of the components that have been specifically designed for the management of VDI. We will discuss this in the next chapter.

VDI versus server-based computing (SBC) – what are the differences?

So, what are the differences between these technologies and VDI, if any at all?

SBC is a technology that has been around for some time. In fact, you could probably trace its roots back as far as the 1950s, to the mainframe technology that was designed to deliver centralized compute power to run a set of applications, with users connecting to the applications using a green-screen terminal, which was pretty much just a screen with a keyboard.

Chapter 1

Fundamentally, SBC has not changed that much and still runs applications centrally, albeit today, it runs on servers rather than a mainframe, and end users connect using some form of end point terminal. So, in that case, it's not that different to VDI in that you are connecting remotely to applications that are running on server infrastructure hosted in the data center. Or is it?

Let's look at delivering applications first. The difference between VDI and SBC is that with SBC, the applications are installed and run on the actual servers themselves, using a multi-user version of the application to create individual application sessions for each unique end user. The end user would connect to their own individual, separate, and protected session of that application, instead of connecting to an instance of an operating system containing the applications, as they would with VDI. Since everything is running in the data center, users would connect to the session via a terminal or thin client. In fact, SBC is sometimes referred to as thin-client computing.

The following diagram provides an overview of how applications are delivered using SBC/ **Remote Desktop Services (RDS)**:

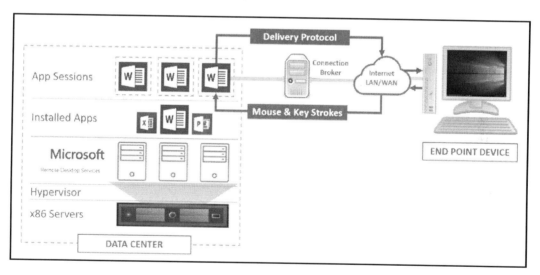

Using the SBC model, you can also deliver hosted desktop sessions in the same way. This time, instead of connecting to a separated, protected individual application session, the user now connects to a separated, protected individual session of the server's operating system. One thing to note here is that the end user is essentially running a server-based operating system session such as Windows Server 2016, rather than a Windows 10 desktop session.

At the end of the day, which technology you choose to deploy comes down to your use case, and which technology makes the most sense from both a feature and cost perspective. You may well end up with a hybrid, with the different methods delivering desktops and applications based on different departments within your organization, all of which have distinct requirements.

The benefits of deploying Horizon

By virtualizing your end user desktop estate into a centrally-managed service, you can deliver benefits not only to the IT administrators, but also to the users. Some of these are highlighted as follows:

- **Security and compliance**: No data leaves the data center unless the IT department has specifically configured a policy to allow it. Equally, end users cannot introduce malware or other malicious content. All that gets transmitted to the client devices are the screenshots of the virtual desktop, with keyboard and mouse interactions being sent back to the virtual desktop. It's a bit like having a remote control for your desktop.

- **Centralized and simplified management**: Centralized desktops means centralized management. With desktops being virtualized and hosted in the data center, it is much easier to perform tasks such as updating and patching an operating system or installing new applications en masse, rather than individually. Virtual desktops are created from a single gold or master image that is maintained and updated centrally. You can simply update the image, recreate the virtual desktops with a few mouse clicks, and hey presto – all of your users will get the new updated version. Troubleshooting the environment and user issues become easier, and all without the need for a desk visit. The worse-case scenario is that you just rebuild a new desktop for the end user from scratch or have them log on to a new one.

- **Scalability, flexibility, and agile working**: Having desktops hosted on a virtual platform allows you to scale up and scale down much more easily, without the need to purchase more physical desktops. Time to deployment is much quicker and costs are reduced. Desktops or even complete environments can be spun up quickly and taken down just as easily to accommodate seasonal workers, contractors working on specific projects, or even to deliver DR and business continuity. Costs can further be reduced with end user devices, and they can now take advantage of thin client devices, or even connect using their own personal devices. As resources are now moved to the data center server infrastructure and accessed remotely, end users have access to their virtual desktops wherever they are and no longer need to be in the office, at a desk, or require a PC to access their corporate desktop and applications. They can continue to be productive, even when experiencing bad weather, bad traffic, or other events that usually prevent them from getting into the office.

- **Mobile and BYOD from anywhere**: Virtual desktop clients enable mobile devices, tablets, and non-corporate-owned devices to connect securely to corporate virtual desktops. Following the flexible working theme, users can now choose a device that suits their needs so that they can access their corporate desktop. Whether it be a tablet, a smartphone, or a non-Windows platform, users can still access their corporate desktop securely from remote locations.

- **Cost savings**: Implementing a virtual desktop environment and adopting operational best practices around image, patch, and profile management with centralized application deployment can result in saving **operational expenditure (OPEX)**, compared to traditional desktop management. **Capital expenditure (CAPEX)** is still required to support the virtual desktop environment and get it up and running. One of the things I hear all the time is that deploying VDI will reduce costs. The point to make here is that yes, it will reduce OPEX, but typically, the CAPEX at the beginning of a VDI project will be higher as you deploy the infrastructure. Having said that, there are cost savings to be made here too, with repurposing endpoints into thin clients, for example. Overall though, these costs will reduce through savings in the ongoing management of the solution, and you will not be caught in the typical three-year desktop-hardware refresh-cycle trap with OS and application updates, which are now deployed centrally to virtual machines.

The history of VMware and VDI

The concept of virtualizing Windows desktops has been around since as early as 2002 when VMware customers started virtualizing desktop operating systems and hosting them on servers running the ESXi hypervisor from the data center. At that time, there was no concept of a connection broker, and the phrase VDI was never commonly used. End users simply connected, using the RDP protocol, directly to a dedicated desktop virtual machine running Windows XP. This was the same as how you would manage a server remotely, that is, by making an RDP connection directly to the desktop of the server. From there, the journey began. The following timeline highlights the key milestones of that journey:

- **2005**: VMware demonstrated the concept of a connection broker.
- **2006**: VMware launched the VDI alliances program.
- **2007**: A prototype connection broker was introduced to customers, before being released as a product called **Virtual Desktop Manager** (**VDM**) version 1.0. VMware acquired Propero for $25 million.
- **2008**: VDM 2.0 was released in January 2008. VMware View 3.0 released and Citrix entered the VDI market, releasing XenDesktop 2.0.
- **2009**: VMware View 4.0 released—the first version with PCoIP.
- **2010**: VMware View 4.5 was released with new features such as local mode (offline desktops), PCoIP enhancements, Windows 7 support, and the ability to tier storage. This was also the year that VMware talked publicly about the biggest VDI reference case to date with Bank of Tokyo Mitsubishi, who deployed 50,000 virtual desktop machines.
- **2011**: VMware view 4.6 released with the iPad client, and the PCoIP Secure Gateway function for the View Security Server, which allows users to connect to their virtual desktop without needing a VPN connection. View 5.0 released with the introduction of Persona Management. View 5.0 also introduced 3D graphics support by using the latest vSphere 5.0 platform, as well as some major enhancements to the PCoIP protocol.
- **2012**: View 5.1 released with View Storage Accelerator, View Composer Array Integration, the ability to scale the hosting infrastructure up to a 32-node cluster when using NFS storage, radius two-factor authentication, improved USB device support, a standalone View Composer, and the ability to support profile migration from XP to Windows 7, as well as from physical desktops to virtual desktops, with Persona Management.

- **2013**: View 5.2 released, and to bring it in line with VMware's launch of the new Horizon brand (launched at the same time), it was renamed Horizon View 5.2. This included support for unified comms with Microsoft Lync 2013, hardware-accelerated graphics with **Virtual Shared Graphics Acceleration (vSGA)**, Windows 8 support, and a feature pack that allowed a user to access their desktop in an HTML5 browser using the VMware Blast protocol. View 5.3 introduced **Virtual Dedicated Graphics Acceleration (vDGA)**, which allowed a virtual desktop to have dedicated access to a GPU that was installed on the host server. Support for Windows Server 2008 R2 was added to the virtual desktop machine to get around the fact there is no **Service Provider License Agreement (SPLA)** for Windows 7.
- **2014**: This was the final 5.x release with Horizon View 5.3.1, which added support for **Virtual SAN (VSAN)**. Horizon 6.0 was released, adding View-hosted apps, and was the first time that VMware supported hosted apps and desktops using RDS. View 6.0 also introduced the Cloud Pod Architecture, and the ability to span the View infrastructure across multiple data centers for DR and scalability. Removal of View Local Mode was also included. In the 6.0.1 release, USB 3.0 support was added, as well as extended printing, HTML access for Windows 8.x, and system tray redirection for hosted applications. This was followed by the 6.0.2 release, which included a new feature pack that added new versions of the View Agent, HTML access, MMR redirection, and scanner redirection.
- **2015**: View 6.1 was released with support for NVIDIA GRID vGPU. It also added support for IPV6, Virtual SAN 6.0, Virtual Volumes, and Windows Server 2012 R2 running as the virtual desktop operating system. 6.1.1 then launched, adding features such as client drive redirection, support for Linux desktops, MMR for RDS desktops, and HTML support for accessing hosted apps. Horizon 6.2 added support for Windows 10 desktops, Access Point integration, AMD vDGA, 4K monitors, and Virtual SAN 6.1, along with several enhancements to the Cloud Pod Architecture, admin console, and Linux desktops. A maintenance release was included 6.2.1 in December 2015, and 6.2.2 in February 2016.

To summarize, this timeline is shown pictorially in the following diagram:

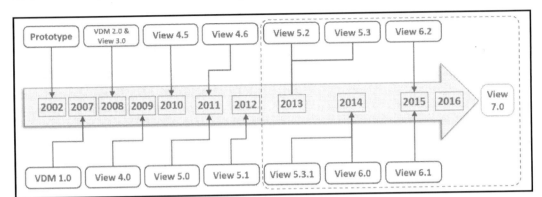

That brings us right up to date and to the latest version of Horizon, VMware Horizon 7.

VMware Horizon 7

VMware Horizon 7 is the next generation of VMware's EUC vision and strategy to deliver the digital workspace. In the previous sections, we discussed some of the differences between VDI and SBC/RDS, and the advantages of the two solutions. However, with Horizon 7, you can deliver VDI desktops, published applications, and session-based desktops, all from a single platform.

VMware Horizon 7 timeline

VMware Horizon 7 was released on March 22, 2016, and included some brand new features, as well as some ones. The full release notes can be found at https://bit.ly/2O3ZYoG, with the highlights listed as follows:

- Instant Clones for faster desktop provisioning
- Cloud Pod Architecture for 25 pods, across 5 sites, and up to 50,000 sessions
- Smart policies
- VMware Blast Extreme protocol with both TCP and UDP transport support
- True SSO
- Access Point integration

- A tech preview of Windows Server 2016 running as an RDS server for remote desktops and apps
- Broader support for Linux operating systems

The initial Horizon 7 release was then followed up with three minor update releases; 7.0.1 (https://bit.ly/2QkCrBA) added enhancements to Blast and the Linux-based virtual desktop; Horizon 7.0.2 (https://bit.ly/2NvorGw) added Client Drive Redirection, Horizon PowerCLI, RTAV for session-based desktops and apps, support for Windows 10 Build 1507, 1511, and 1607, plus support for vSphere 6.5; and Horizon 7.0.3 (https://bit.ly/2QfsTaZ) removed the View PowerCLI and replaced it with the Horizon PowerCLI. There were also Horizon Agent updates, particularly for Linux desktops, which added vGPU support, Persona Management support for V6 profiles, and updated Horizon clients.

Next came the VMware Horizon 7.1 release on March 16, 2017 (https://bit.ly/2Mj462g). The View Connection Server received numerous updates, along with new features for Blast Extreme and published apps and desktops, Instant Clones, and Cloud Pod Architecture. The ADM template files in the Horizon GPO bundle were deprecated and replaced with ADMX template files.

After 7.1 came VMware Horizon 7.2, which was released on Jun 20, 2017 (https://bit.ly/2QjAVzj). This version again concentrated on Connection Server updates, including Workspace ONE Access Policies, Instant Clone enhancements, Cloud Pod Architecture, which now supports 120,000 sessions, and the addition of the Horizon Help Desk Tool. Connection Server limits were also increased, now supporting 4,000 clones per vCenter server. Skype support was added to the Horizon Agent, along with an update for the Horizon Client.

The 7.3 release in October 2017 was found to have a few issues and so it was removed from the download page with a jump straight to VMware Horizon 7.3.2, which was released on November 20, 2017 (https://bit.ly/2QhM8Ax). This release included updates for the Horizon Help Desk Tool and Instant Clones, and an increase in regards to the scale of the Cloud Pod Architecture to 140,000 sessions across 7 sites. Again, more features were added to the Horizon Client, particularly the Linux version, along with a new Horizon Client release, version 4.6.

There were similar updates in VMware Horizon 7.4, which was released on Jan 04, 2018 (https://bit.ly/2BFJE6q), which also added session collaboration, a host of new ADMX templates, and an update to Horizon Client version 4.7.

Introducing VDI and VMware Horizon 7

Released on May 29, 2018, VMware Horizon 7.5 (https://bit.ly/2lBvrBU) concentrated on a number of new features for the connection server, adding the Horizon Console web interface that is now integrated the Horizon Help Desk Tool, and integration of the new workflow features for the just-in-time Management Platform, including the Horizon JMP Server installer. This release also added support for vSphere 6.7, along with the ability to deploy desktop pools that contain full virtual machines on VMware Cloud on AWS.

The Cloud Pod Architecture saw another increase in scale, and it now supports 200,000 sessions across 10 sites. Finally, there were several Horizon Agent enhancements and a new Horizon Client release with Horizon Client 4.8.

A maintenance release came next with Horizon 7.5.1 on July 19, 2018 (https://bit.ly/2oVxKS2). This fixed an issue with the insecure logging of credentials, as described in CVE-2018-6971 (https://cve.mitre.org/cgi-bin/cvename.cgi?name=2018-6971).

That brings us right up to date with the latest release, VMware Horizon 7.6, which was released on Sep 6, 2018. This minor release incorporated updates for the connection server, the Horizon Agent, additional features for the Horizon GPO bundle, and a new Horizon Client, version 4.9.

To summarize, this timeline is shown pictorially in the following diagram:

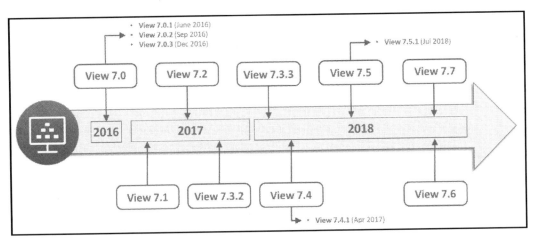

In the next section, we will look at the different Horizon 7 product editions.

VMware Horizon 7 product editions

There are six different product editions within the Horizon 7 solution portfolio, each one adding different functionality and features. Each edition can also be categorized based on the role it plays in the overall solution. These categories can be described as follows:

- Virtual desktop and application delivery
- Workspace environment management
- Operations management
- Infrastructure and hosting

As for the six product editions, these are described in the following sections of this chapter.

Horizon for Linux

As the name implies, **Horizon for Linux** allows you to centralize Linux-based virtual desktop machines and deliver them with Horizon View. The big advantage of Linux desktops is that you can move away from other, costlier, operating systems, further reducing the cost of deployment. Horizon for Linux supports several Linux distributions, including Ubuntu, RHEL, and CentOS, and it also takes advantage of some of the other features that View has to offer, such as NVIDIA graphics solutions.

Horizon Standard Edition

Horizon Standard Edition delivers the core VDI components and features to allow for the delivery of Windows-based virtual desktop machines to end users. Included in this edition is the licensing for the hosting infrastructure, vSphere, and vCenter for desktops. Also included is ThinApp, VMware's application virtualization and packaging solution, which allows you to extract applications from the underlying OS and deliver them back independently.

Horizon Advanced Edition

Horizon Advanced Edition is all about virtual desktop and application delivery and management. Advanced Edition is the first edition that includes application publishing as part of the View solution, allowing an application running on a Microsoft RDSH backend to be published via the View client using the PCoIP protocol, HTML, or VMware Blast Extreme. This feature means that a user can now just have an individual application delivered to their client device, rather than a full-blown desktop.

Also included in the Advanced Edition is a unified workspace solution that delivers a unified workspace, so that users can select applications from a catalog of entitled applications. These applications can be ThinApp packages, SaaS-based applications, XenApp published applications, and anything from Microsoft Office 365.

The Advanced Edition also used to include VMware Mirage, so that you could deliver centralized image management for physical desktops. However, that product is now at its end-of-life, along with Horizon Flex. Although you can no longer purchase these products, VMware are still offering technical support up until June 30, 2020 for those customers who have them deployed.

Finally, Advanced Edition includes support for Skype, VMware Identity Manager, and VSAN.

Horizon Enterprise Edition

Horizon Enterprise Edition builds on the previous versions and adds features to deliver operations management by using vRealize Operations for Horizon. This, coupled with the Horizon Help Desk Tool, gives IT admins the ability to monitor the health and performance of the environment, as well as capacity-planning capabilities for ensuring the most optimal configuration as you scale.

Also included in the Enterprise Edition is VMware App Volumes, which allows you to deliver just-in-time applications to a virtual desktop. This works alongside the just-in-time delivery with Instant Clone Technology to build and deliver desktops and apps on demand. These are then configured for end users using the VMware User Environment Management solution. For a detailed overview of VMware App Volumes, you can read *Learning VMware App Volumes*, by Peter von Oven and published by Packt.

Enterprise Edition also added support for delivering Linux-based desktops and session collaboration, which allows users to easily work together.

Horizon Apps Standard

Horizon Apps Standard is all about delivering published applications and published desktops, and as such does so without the ability to deliver full virtual machine-based desktops. It also includes VMware ThinApp, support for VMware Identity Manager, session delivery using the Blast Extreme Protocol, and VMware User Environment Management.

Horizon Apps Advanced

Horizon Apps Advanced builds on the standard edition by adding features such as the Virtualization Pack for Skype for Business, VMware App Volumes with just-in-time delivery, and the Horizon Help Desk Tool.

Horizon editions overview and comparison

The following table details the features that are available in each of the different Horizon editions:

Desktop and App Delivery	Horizon for Linux	Horizon Standard	Horizon Advanced	Horizon Enterprise	Horizon Apps Standard	Horizon Apps Advanced
Windows Virtual Desktops		✓	✓	✓		
Linux Virtual Desktops	✓			✓		
Unified Workspace with VMware Identity Manager Std.			✓	✓	✓	✓
Published apps and dekstops			✓	✓	✓	✓
Application virtualization/packaging with ThinApp		✓	✓	✓	✓	✓
Blast Extreme protocol	✓	✓	✓	✓	✓	✓
Support for Skype for business			✓	✓	✓	✓
SSO with VMware Identity Manager Std.			✓	✓	✓	✓

Workspace Management	Horizon for Linux	Horizon Standard	Horizon Advanced	Horizon Enterprise	Horizon Apps Standard	Horizon Apps Advanced
Image management for desktops with VMware Mirage			✓	✓		
Real-time app delivery with VMware App Volumes				✓		✓
User profile management with VMware UEM				✓	✓	✓
Just in time delivery with Instant Clones				✓		✓

Operations Management	Horizon for Linux	Horizon Standard	Horizon Advanced	Horizon Enterprise	Horizon Apps Standard	Horizon Apps Advanced
Horizon Help Desk Tool				✓		✓
Operations dashboard - vRealize Operations for Horizon				✓		
Capacity planning with vRealize Operations for Horizon				✓		

Infrastructure Components	Horizon for Linux	Horizon Standard	Horizon Advanced	Horizon Enterprise	Horizon Apps Standard	Horizon Apps Advanced
Virtual storage with VSAN Advanced for Desktop			✓	✓		
vSphere for Desktop						
vCenter for Desktop	✓	✓	✓	✓	✓	✓

Horizon user licensing models

Horizon is available in two different licensing models, which are also based on the edition you deploy:

- **Concurrent user**: Available for all Horizon editions where the license is based on the number of simultaneous users accessing apps and desktops.
- **Named user**: Available for all Horizon editions, with the exception of Horizon for Linux and Horizon Standard Edition. With a named user, the license is assigned to specific users.

Summary

In this chapter, we looked at what VDI is, described how it works, and how it compares to other, similar technologies. Next, we covered the history of where it all began for VMware, demonstrating that VMware was—and still is—at the forefront of virtual desktop and application delivery, which today is more commonly referred to as the digital workspace.

We then went on to discuss the latest release, VMware Horizon 7, and the different editions that are available, with an overview of each edition and its core set of features.

In the next chapter, we will take a deep dive into the technology of Horizon View and start looking at the architecture and the different components that make up the solution.

Understanding Horizon 7 Architecture and Components

In the previous chapter, we introduced you to virtual desktop infrastructure and, in particular, the VMware solution, VMware Horizon. As part of that introduction, we took a high-level view of some of the different components that make up the complete solution. In this chapter, we will start to take a deeper dive into these architecture and infrastructure components, concentrating on how they work together to make up the complete solution.

Throughout the sections of this chapter, we will discuss the role of each of the Horizon View components, explaining where each one fits into the overall infrastructure, and its role. Once we have explained the high-level concept, we will then take a deeper dive into how each individual component works. As we work through the sections, we will also highlight some of the best practices, as well as some useful hints and tips along the way.

Along the way, we will also cover some of the third-party technologies that integrate and complement VMware Horizon, such as antivirus solutions, storage acceleration technologies, and high-end graphics solutions, which all help deliver a complete end-to-end solution from the data center to the end user. After reading this chapter, you will be able to describe each of the Horizon components, such as the following:

- Connection server
- Security server
- Replica server
- Security and the VMware Unified Access Gateway
- Managing end user profiles in **View Persona Management** (**VDI**) and **User Environment Manager** (**UEM**)

Understanding Horizon 7 Architecture and Components

- Display protocols
- Linked, instant, and full clones
- Hardware-accelerated graphics (vSGA, vDGA, and vGPU)

We will discuss what part each one plays within the overall solution, and why you would use them, along with how to configure them and the prerequisites for installation.

Introducing the key Horizon components

To start with, we are going to introduce you to, at a high level, the core infrastructure components and the architecture that make up the Horizon View solution. We will start with a top-level overview, as shown in the following diagram, before we start to drill down into each component in greater detail:

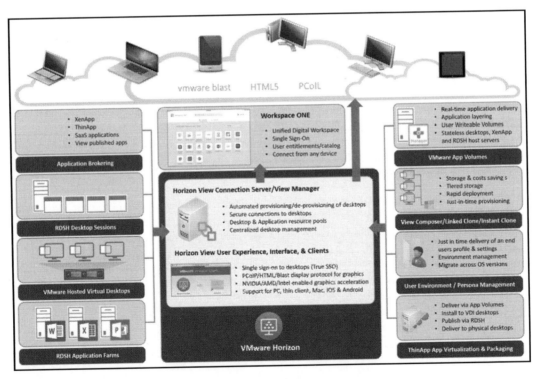

All the VMware Horizon components described in the preceding diagram are part of the overall Horizon solution, but, don't forget, some of the features available are dependent on which edition you have purchased.

It's also worth remembering that Horizon licensing includes the relevant vSphere components, ESXi hypervisor and vCenter Server licensing, to enable you to deploy the core hosting infrastructure. You can deploy as many ESXi hosts and vCenter servers as you require to host the desktop infrastructure.

High-level architectural overview

In this section, we are going to discuss the core Horizon View features and functionality for brokering virtual desktop machines that are hosted on the VMware vSphere platform.

The Horizon architecture is straightforward to understand, as its foundations lie in the standard VMware vSphere products (ESXi and vCenter). So, if you have the skills and experience of working with this platform, then you are already halfway there.

Horizon View builds on the vSphere infrastructure, taking advantage of some of the features of the ESXi hypervisor and vCenter Server, adding a number of virtual server machines to perform the various View roles and functions.

An overview of the View architecture for delivering virtual desktops is shown in the following diagram:

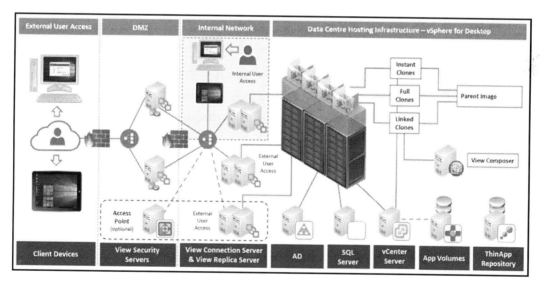

Horizon View infrastructure components run as applications that are installed on the Microsoft Windows Server operating system, except for the Unified Access Gateway, which is a hardened Linux-based appliance. In theory, these infrastructure components could run on physical machines; however, there are a great number of benefits when you run them as virtual machines, such as delivering HA and DR, as well as the typical cost savings that can be achieved through virtualization.

The following sections will cover each of these roles and components of the View architecture in greater detail, starting with the Horizon View Connection Server.

The Horizon View Connection Server

The Horizon View Connection Server is also referred to as a connection broker or a view manager. It is the primary component of the View infrastructure. Its primary role is to connect a user to their virtual desktop by means of performing user authentication and then delivering and managing the appropriate desktop resources based on the user's profile and entitlement. When logging on to your virtual desktop, it is the connection server that you are communicating with.

How does the connection server work?

A user will connect to their VDI desktop using their endpoint device by first launching the Horizon Client, but, equally, they could use browser-based access. We will cover the Horizon clients and other access methods in `Chapter 12`, *Horizon Client Options*.

So, what happens next, and how does the login process work? Once the Horizon client has launched, the end user enters the address details of the View Connection server they want to connect to (1), which in turn responds (2) by asking them to provide their network login details, their Active Directory domain username, and their password.

It's worth noting that Horizon View now supports the following different AD Domain functional levels:

- Windows Server 2003
- Windows Server 2008 and Windows Server 2008 R2
- Windows Server 2012 and Windows Server 2012 R2
- Windows Server 2016

The end users' credentials are authenticated with Active Directory (3) and, if successful, the user can continue the login process. Depending on what resources they are entitled to, the end user will see a launch screen that displays a few different virtual desktop machine icons that are available for them to log in to. These desktop icons represent the desktop pools that the user has been entitled to use. They may well also see application icons representing published applications.

A desktop pool is basically a collection of similar virtual desktop machines. For example, it could be a pool for the marketing department where the virtual desktop machines contain specific applications and software for that department. We will discuss desktop pools in more detail in `Chapter 8`, *Configuring and Managing Desktop Pools – Part 1*.

Once authenticated, the view manager or the connection server makes a call to the vCenter server (4) to create a virtual desktop machine, and then vCenter makes a call (5) to either View Composer (if you are using linked clones), or it will create an instant clone using the VM fork feature of vSphere to start the build process of the virtual desktop if there is not one already available for the user to log in to.

As part of the overall build process, at this point, if configured, VMware UEM will load the end user's profile, personalizing and customizing the virtual desktop to that individual user. The same applies to VMware app volumes, which, if configured, will now deliver any layered applications at the same time.

When the build process has completed, and the virtual desktop machine is available to the end user, complete with their profile and applications, it is displayed or delivered within the Horizon Client window (**6**) or browser, using the chosen display protocol PCoIP, Blast Extreme, or RDP. This process is described pictorially in the following diagram:

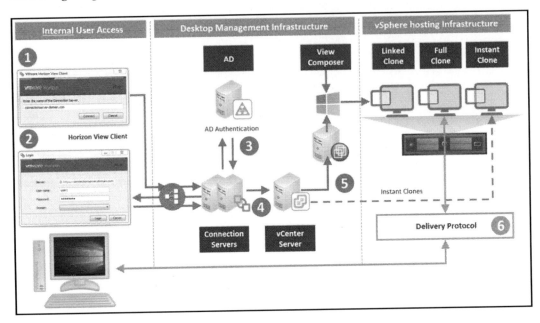

There are other ways to deploy VDI solutions that do not require a connection broker, although you could argue that, strictly speaking, this is not a true VDI solution. As we discussed in the introduction and history, this is what the first VDI solutions looked like, allowing an end user to connect directly to their own virtual desktop via the RDP protocol. If you think about it, though, there are still some specific use cases for doing it this way.

For example, if you have a large number of remote branches or offices, you could deploy a subset of the infrastructure, hosting it on the local site, allowing users to continue working in the event of a WAN outage or poor network communication between the branch and head office.

It just so happens that VMware also thought of this as a use case and has a solution that's referred to as a **Brokerless View**, which uses the VMware Horizon view agent DirectConnection plugin to connect directly to a virtual desktop machine without needing the connection server. This was originally part of the Desktone **Desktop as a Service (DaaS)** solution that VMware acquired in October 2013. However, don't forget that in a Horizon View environment, the view connection server provides greater functionality and does much more than just connect users to desktops, as we will see later in this chapter.

Along with brokering the connections between the end users and the virtual desktop machines, the view connection server also works with the vCenter server to manage the virtual desktop machines. For example, when using linked clones or instant clones and powering on virtual desktops, these tasks are initiated by the connection server, but they are executed by the vCenter server.

Now that we have covered what the connection server is and given you an overview of how it works, in the next section, we are going to look at the requirements you need in order for it to run.

Minimum requirements for the connection server

To install the connection server, you need to meet the following minimum requirements to run on physical or virtual machines.

Hardware requirements

The following table shows the hardware required for installing the connection server:

Hardware Required	Required	Recommended
Processor	Pentium IV 2.0GHz processor or higher	4 x CPU's
Networking	100Mbps Network Card	1Gbps Network Card
Memory	4GB RAM or Higher	At least 10GB RAM for 50 or more Desktops

Supported OS

The view connection server must be installed on one of the operating systems listed in the following table:

Operating System	Version	Edition
Windows Server 2008 R2 SP1	64-bit	Standard, Enterprise, Datacenter
Windows Server 2012 R2	64-bit	Standard, Enterprise
Windows Server 2016	64-bit	Standard, Enterprise

Windows Server 2008 R2 without a service pack is no longer supported.

In the next section, we are going to look at the Horizon View security server.

The Horizon View security server

The **Horizon View security server** is another individual component of the architecture and is another role performed by the connection server. The key differences are that firstly, it sits within your DMZ, and therefore is not joined to your domain. This allows it to be used for end users to securely connect to their virtual desktop machine from an external network or the internet without the need for a VPN. As it is paired with one of your connection servers, the internal connection server it is paired with takes care of knowing about the users and desktop pools, and so on. Secondly, it does not hold a copy of the ADAM database. As you will see in Chapter 5, *Installing and Configuring Horizon 7 – Part 2*, the installation process is the same as installing the view connection server, but, instead, this time, you select the security server role from the drop-down menu at the start of installation.

You cannot install the view security server on the same machine that is already running as a connection server or any of the other Horizon View components.

How does the security server work?

To start with, the user login process at the beginning is the same as when connecting to a view connection server, essentially because the security server is just another version of the connection server running a subset of the features, with the exclusion of the ADAM database. The difference is that you connect to the address of the security server. The security server sits inside your DMZ and communicates with a connection server sitting on the internal network that it is paired with. So, now we have added an extra security layer, as the internal connection server is not exposed externally, with the idea being that users can now access their virtual desktop machines externally without needing to first connect to a VPN on the network.

 The security server should not be joined to the domain.

This security server connection process is described pictorially in the following diagram:

When the user logs in from the Horizon client, they now use the external URL of the security server to access the connection server, which, in turn, authenticates the user against Active Directory. If the connection server is configured as a PCoIP gateway, then it will pass the connection and addressing information to the Horizon client. This connection information will allow the Horizon client to connect to the security server using PCoIP. This is shown in the diagram by the green arrow (**1**). The security server will then forward the PCoIP connection to the virtual desktop machine (**2**), creating the connection for the user. The virtual desktop machine is displayed/delivered within the Horizon client window (**3**) using the chosen display protocol (PCoIP, Blast Extreme, or RDP). We will cover this process and the different ports View uses for connecting later in this chapter.

The Horizon View replica server

The Horizon View replica server, as the name suggests, is a replica or a copy of a view connection server and serves two key roles.

The first role is to enable high availability for your Horizon view environment. Having a replica of your view connection server means that, if a connection server fails, a replica server will take over the management of connection requests so that end users are still able to connect to their virtual desktop machines.

Secondly, adding replica servers allows you to scale up the number of users and virtual desktop connections. An individual instance of a connection server can support 2,000 connections, so adding additional connection servers allows you to add another 2,000 users at a time, up to the maximum of five connection servers and 10,000 users per Horizon view pod. We will discuss the Pod and Block architecture in Chapter 3, *Design and Deployment Considerations*.

> When deploying a replica server, remember that you will need to change the IP address or update the DNS record to match this server if you are not using a load balancer.

As with the security server, you will see that the installation process is again almost the same as the connection server, but this time, you select the replica server role from the drop-down menu during installation.

How does the replica server work?

The first question is: what gets replicated? The connection broker stores all its information relating to the end users, desktop pools, virtual desktop machines, and other View-related objects, in an ADAM database. Then, using the **Lightweight Directory Access Protocol** (**LDAP**) (it uses a method similar to the one AD uses for replication), this View information gets copied from the original connection server to the replica server.

As both the connection server and the replica server are now identical to each other, if your connection server fails, then you essentially have a backup that steps in and takes over, so that end users can continue to connect to their virtual desktop machines. Also, as the replica server is another instance of a connection server within your environment, you can scale up and manage additional end users.

As with the other Horizon components, you cannot install the replica server role on the same machine that is running as a connection server or any of the other Horizon View components.

The Horizon View enrolment server and True SSO

The **Horizon View Enrollment Server** is the final component that is part of the Horizon View connection server installation options, and is another installation option from the connection server installation process and is selected from the drop-down menu. So, what role does the enrolment server perform?

Horizon 7 saw the introduction of a new feature, called **True SSO**. True SSO is a solution that allows a user to authenticate to a Microsoft Windows environment without them having to enter their AD credentials. It integrates into another VMware product, **VMware Identity Manager** (VIDM), which forms part of both Horizon 7's advanced and enterprise editions.

Its job is to sit between the connection server and the Microsoft CA to request temporary certificates from the certificate store.

This process is described pictorially in the following diagram:

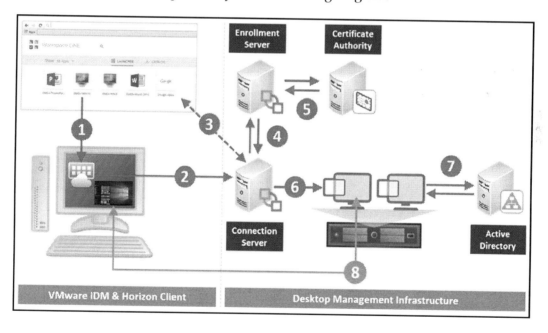

[39]

Understanding Horizon 7 Architecture and Components

A user first logs into VIDM, either using their credentials or another authentication method such as the following:

- RSA SecurID
- Kerberos
- RADIUS authentication
- RSA Adaptive Authentication
- Standards-based, third-party identity providers

Once successfully authenticated, the end user will be presented with the virtual desktop machines or hosted applications that they are entitled to use. They can launch any of these by simply double-clicking, which will launch the Horizon client, as shown by the red arrow (1) in the previous diagram. The user's credentials will then be passed to the connection server (2), which, in turn, will verify them by sending a **Security Assertion Markup Language (SAML)** assertion back to the identity manager (3).

If the end user's credentials are verified, then the connection server passes them on to the enrolment server (4). The enrolment server then makes a request to the Microsoft **Certificate Authority (CA)** to generate a short-lived, temporary certificate for that user to use (5).

With the certificate now generated, the connection server presents it to the operating system of the virtual desktop machine (6), which, in turn, validates with Active Directory to confirm whether the certificate is authentic (7).

When the certificate has been authenticated, the end user is logged on to their virtual desktop machine, which is then displayed/delivered to the Horizon client using the chosen display protocol (8).

True SSO is supported by all Horizon 7-supported desktop operating systems, as well as Windows Server 2008 R2 and Windows Server 2012 R2. It also supports PCoIP, HTML, and Blast Extreme delivery protocols.

VMware Unified Access Gateway

The **VMware Unified Gateway** performs the same role as the view security server and is shown in the following diagram, but there's one key difference. Instead of being a Windows application and another role in the connection server, the Unified Access Gateway is a separate virtual appliance that runs a hardened, locked-down Linux operating system:

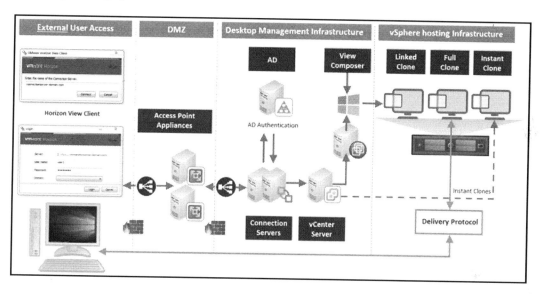

Although the Unified Gateway appliances deliver pretty much the same functionality as the security server, they do not yet completely replace it, especially if you already have a production deployment that uses the security server for external access. In that event, you can continue to use this architecture.

If you are using the secure tunnel function, PCoIP Secure Gateway, or the Blast Secure Gateway features of the connection server, then these features will need to be disabled on the connection server if you are using Unified Access Gateway. They are all enabled by default on the Unified Gateway appliance.

A key difference between Unified Access Gateway Appliances and the security server is in the way Unified Access Gateway scales. Before, you had to pair a security server with a connection server, which was a limitation, but this is no longer the case. As such, you can now scale to as many Unified Access Gateways as you need for your environment, with the maximum limit being around 2,000 sessions for a single appliance. Adding additional appliances is simply a case of deploying the appliance, as appliances don't depend on other appliances and do not communicate with them. They communicate directly with the connection servers over a load balancer.

Persistent or non-persistent desktops?

In this section, we are going to talk about the different types of desktop assignments and the way a virtual desktop machine is delivered to an end user. This is an important design consideration, as the chosen method could potentially impact on the storage requirements (covered in the next section), the hosting infrastructure, and which technology or solution is used to provision the virtual desktop machines to the end users.

One of the questions that often gets asked is whether you should deploy a dedicated (persistent) assignment or a floating desktop (non-persistent) assignment. Desktops can either be individual virtual machines, which are dedicated to a user on a 1:1 basis (as we have in a physical desktop deployment, where each user effectively owns their own desktop), or a user has a new, vanilla desktop that gets provisioned, built, personalized, and then assigned to them at login. The virtual desktop machine they access is chosen at random from a pool of available desktops that the end user is entitled to use.

The two options are described in more detail as follows:

- **Persistent desktop**: End users are assigned a desktop that keeps all their documents, applications, and settings between sessions. The first time the user connects to it, the desktop gets statically assigned and is further used for all subsequent sessions. No other user is permitted access to the desktop.
- **Non-persistent desktop**: End users might be connected to different virtual desktops each time they connect. Environmental applications or user data does not persist between sessions and is instead delivered as the user logs on to their desktop using the composite desktop model we discussed back in Chapter 1, *Introducing VDI and VMware Horizon 7*. The desktop is refreshed or reset when the user logs off and is then ready for the next user.

In most use cases, a non-persistent configuration is the best option; the key reason is that using this model, you don't need to build all the desktops upfront for each user. You only need to power on a virtual desktop as and when it's required. All end users start with the same basic desktop, which then gets personalized before delivery. This helps with concurrency rates. For example, you might have 5,000 people in your organization, but only 2,000 ever log in at the same time; therefore, you only need to have 2,000 virtual desktops available. Otherwise, you would have to build a desktop for each one of the 5,000 users that might ever log in, resulting in more server infrastructure, more storage capacity, and more software licensing.

One of the things that used to be a bit of a showstopper for non-persistent desktops was regarding how to deliver the applications to the virtual desktop machine, and whether this would mean you had to install applications each time an end user logged in. Now that application layering solutions, such as VMware App Volumes or Liquidware FlexApp, are becoming a more mainstream technology, the applications can be delivered on demand as the desktop is built and the user logs in.

Another thing that we often see some confusion over is the difference between persistent and non-persistent desktops, and how cloning fits in. Just to make it clear, linked clones, full clones, and instant clones are not what we are talking about when we refer to persistent and non-persistent desktops. *Cloning operations* refers to how a desktop is built and provisioned, whereas the terms *persistent* and *non-persistent* refer to how a desktop is assigned to an end user.

Persistent and non-persistent desktops are purely about user assignment and whether an end user has a dedicated desktop, or one allocated from a pool on demand each time they log in. Cloning is a feature of Horizon View, which uses either View Composer and/or vCenter to create the desktop images for each user from a master or parent image. This means, regardless of having a persistent or non-persistent desktop assignment, the virtual desktop machine could still be a linked clone, full clone, or instant clone.

In the next sections, we are going to cover an in-depth overview of the cloning technologies available in Horizon 7, starting with Horizon View Composer and linked clones, and the advantages the technology delivers.

Horizon View Composer and linked clones

In this section, we are going to discuss how virtual desktop machines are built, created, and scaled using cloning techniques. We will describe the different cloning options, what they deliver, and how they impact disk storage requirements.

What is cloning?

Starting at a high level, a clone is a copy of an existing or parent virtual machine. This parent virtual desktop machine is your gold build from which you want to create new virtual desktop machines. When a clone is created, it becomes a separate, new virtual desktop machine with its own unique identity. This process is not unique to Horizon View. It's actually a function of vSphere and vCenter, and in the case of Horizon View, we add in another component, View Composer, to manage the desktop images. There are three types of clone that can be deployed: a full clone, a linked clone, or an instant clone.

One of the main reasons a virtual desktop project fails to deliver or doesn't even get out of the starting blocks is because of the heavy infrastructure and storage requirements. The storage requirements are often seen as a huge cost burden, which can be attributed to the fact that people are approaching a VDI project in the same way they would approach a physical desktop environment. This would mean that each user gets their own dedicated virtual desktop and the hard-disk space that comes with it, albeit a virtual disk. This is then scaled out for the entire user population, with each user being allocated a virtual desktop with some storage.

Let's discuss an example. If you had 1,000 users and allocated 250 GB disk space per desktop, you would need 1,000 * 250 GB = 250 TB of disk space just for the virtual desktop environment. That's a lot of storage just for desktops and could result in significant infrastructure costs, which could possibly mean that the cost to deploy this amount of storage in the data center would render the project cost-ineffective compared to physical desktop deployments. This would be described as the **Full Clone** approach.

What is a full clone?

As the name implies, a full clone disk is an exact, full-size copy of the parent virtual machine or gold image template. Once the clone of the gold image has been created, the virtual desktop machine is unique, with its own identity, and operates as a fully independent virtual desktop in its own right and is not reliant on the gold image from which it was created.

However, as it is a full-sized copy, be aware that it will take up exactly the same amount of storage as the gold image, which leads back to our discussion earlier in this chapter about storage capacity requirements. Using a full clone will require larger amounts of storage capacity and will possibly lead to higher infrastructure costs.

But before you completely dismiss the idea of using full clone virtual desktop machines, there are some use cases that rely on this model. For example, if you use VMware Mirage to deliver the operating system as a base layer, it only works today with full clones and dedicated Horizon View virtual desktop machines.

With VDI, a new approach to deploying storage is needed, and this is where linked clone and instant clone technology comes into play. In a nutshell, linked and instant clones are designed to reduce the amount of disk space required, and to simplify the deployment and management of images to multiple virtual desktop machines, making it a centralized, and much easier, process.

What are linked clones?

Having discussed full clones, we are going to talk about deploying virtual desktop machines using linked clones.

In a linked clone deployment, a delta disk is created and then used by the virtual desktop machine to store the data differences between its own operating system and the operating system of its parent virtual desktop machine. Unlike the full clone method, a linked clone is not a full copy of the virtual disk. The term *linked clone* refers to the fact that the linked clone will always look to its parent in order to operate, as it continues to read from the replica disk. Basically, the replica is a copy of a snapshot of the parent virtual desktop machine.

The linked clone itself could potentially grow to the same size as the replica disk if you allowed it to. However, you can set limits on how big it can grow, and should it start to get too big, then you can refresh the virtual desktops that are linked to it. This essentially starts the cloning process again from the initial snapshot.

Immediately after a linked clone virtual desktop is deployed, the difference between the parent virtual machine and the newly-created virtual desktop machine is extremely small, and therefore reduces the storage capacity requirements compared to that of a full clone. This is how linked clones are more space-efficient than their full clone brothers.

The underlying technology behind linked clones is more like a snapshot than a clone, but with one key difference—View Composer. With View Composer, you can have more than one active snapshot linked to the parent virtual machine disk. This allows you to create multiple virtual desktop images from just one parent.

Best practice would be to deploy an environment with linked clones (or instant clones) to reduce the storage requirements. However, as we previously mentioned, there are some use cases where you may need to deploy full clones.

One thing to be aware of, which still relates to the storage, is that, rather than capacity, we are now talking about performance. All linked clone virtual desktops are going to be reading from one replica and will, therefore, drive a high number of **Input/Output Operations Per Second (IOPS)** on the storage where the replica lives. Depending on your desktop pool design, you are likely to have more than one replica, as you would typically have more than one data store. This, in turn, depends on the number of users who will drive the design of the solution. We will cover this in greater detail in `Chapter 3`, *Design and Deployment Considerations*.

With Horizon View, you can choose the location where the replica lives. One of the recommendations is that the replica should sit in fast storage, such as a local or shared SSD.

An alternative solution would be to deploy some form of storage acceleration technology to drive the IOPS. Horizon View also has its own integrated solution, called **View Storage Accelerator (VSA)** or **Content Based Read Cache (CBRC)**. This feature allows you to allocate up to 2 GB of memory from the underlying ESXi host server, which can be used as a cache for the most commonly read blocks. As we are talking about creating and booting up desktop operating systems, the same blocks are required; as these can be retrieved from memory, the process is accelerated.

View Storage Accelerator is enabled by default when using instant clones and cannot be configured.

Another solution is **View Composer Array Integration (VCAI)**, which allows the process of building linked clones to be offloaded to the storage array and its native snapshot mechanism, rather than taking CPU cycles from the host server.

There are also several other third-party solutions that resolve the storage performance bottleneck, such as ThinScale's ThinIO (`https://www.thinscale.com/products/thinio/`) solution, which delivers software-defined storage acceleration to actively reduce disk I/O.

In the next section, we will take a deeper look at how the linked clone process works.

How do linked clones work?

The first step, before you even start to build clones, is to create your master virtual desktop machine image, which should contain not only the operating system, core applications, and settings, but also the Horizon View Agent components. This virtual desktop machine will become your parent VM or your gold image from which all other virtual desktop machines will be created. We will cover the build process in `Chapter 7`, *Building and Optimizing the Virtual Desktop OS*. Linked clones are built and managed using View composer and the vCenter server.

 The gold image or parent image cannot be a virtual machine template.

Once the parent VM has been built, then you can start to build virtual desktops and virtual desktop pools using that image. An overview of the linked clone creation process is shown in the following diagram:

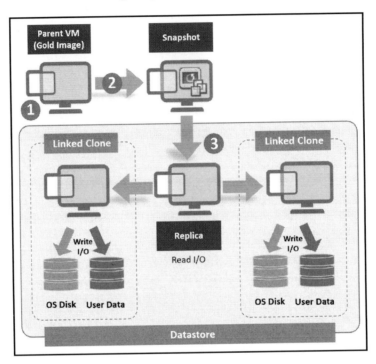

Take your gold image (**1**), and take a snapshot of it (**2**). When you create your desktop pool, this snapshot is selected and will become the replica (**3**) and will be set to be read-only. Each virtual desktop is linked back to this replica, hence, the term *linked clone*. When you start creating your virtual desktops, you create linked clones that are unique copies for each user.

 Try not to create too many snapshots for your parent VM. I would recommend having just a handful; otherwise, this could impact the performance of your desktops and make it a little harder to know which snapshot is which.

Creating linked clones

During the image-building process, and once the replica disk has been created, View Composer creates several other virtual disks, including the linked clone (operating system disk) itself. These are described in the following sections.

Linked clone disk

The main disk that is created is the linked clone disk itself. This linked clone disk is basically an empty virtual disk container that is attached to the virtual desktop machine as the user logs in and the desktop starts up and boots.

This disk will start off small but will grow over time depending on the block changes that are requested from the replica disk by the virtual desktop machine's operating system. These block changes are stored in the linked clone disk, and this disk is sometimes referred to as the **delta disk**, or **differential disk**, since it stores all the delta changes that the desktop operating system requests from the parent VM. As mentioned before, the linked clone disk can grow to the maximum size, equal to the parent VM, but, following best practice, you would never let this happen. Typically, you can expect the linked clone disk to only increase to a few hundred MBs. We will cover this in the *Linked clone features and functionality* section later in this chapter.

The replica disk is set as read-only and is used as the primary disk. Any writes and/or block changes that are requested by the virtual desktop are written/read directly from the linked clone disk.

Recommended best practice is to allocate tier-1 storage, such as local or shared SSD drives, for storing and hosting the replica, as all virtual desktop machines within the cluster will be continually referencing this single read-only VMDK file as their base image. Keeping it high in the stack improves performance, by reducing the overall storage

Persistent disk or user data disk

The persistent disk feature of View Composer allows you to configure a separate disk that contains just the user data and user settings and not the operating system. This allows any user data to be preserved when you update or make changes to the operating system disk, such as a recompose action.

It's worth noting that the persistent disk is referenced by the VM name and not the username, so bear this in mind if you want to attach the disk to a different VM.

The data disk is also used to store the end user's profile. You, therefore, need to size it accordingly, ensuring that it is large enough to store any user profile type data, such as Virtual Desktop Assessments. This is another reason why it's a good idea to run a desktop assessment, as we will cover in Chapter 3, *Design and Deployment Considerations*, so that you can build up a picture of what your user desktop profiles and user data requirements look like.

Disposable disk

With the **disposable disk** option, Horizon View creates what is effectively a temporary disk that gets deleted every time the user powers off their virtual desktop machine.

If you think about how the Windows desktop operating system operates and the files it creates, there are several files that are used on a temporary basis. Files such as temporary internet files or the Windows pagefile are two such examples. As these are only temporary files, why would you want to keep them? With Horizon View, these types of files are redirected to the disposable disk and then deleted when the VM is powered off.

Horizon View provides the option to have a disposable disk for each virtual desktop. This disposable disk is used to contain temporary files that will get deleted when the virtual desktop is powered off. These are files that you don't want to store on the main operating system disk, as they would consume unnecessary disk space. For example, files on the disposable disk are things such as the pagefile, Windows system temporary files, and VMware log files.

It's worth pointing out that we are talking about temporary system files and not user files. An end user's temporary files are still stored on the user data disk so that they can be preserved. Many applications use the Windows temp folder to store installation CAB files, which can be referenced post-installation. Having said that, you might want to delete the temporary user data to reduce the overall desktop image size, in which case you could ensure that the user's temporary files are directed to the disposable disk.

Internal disk

Finally, we have the internal disk. The internal disk is used to store important configuration information, such as the computer account password, which would be needed to join the virtual desktop machine back to the domain if you refreshed the linked clones. It is also used to store the **Sysprep** and **Quickprep** configuration details. We will cover Quickprep in `Chapter 7`, *Building and Optimizing the Virtual Desktop OS*.

In terms of disk space, the internal disk is relatively small, averaging around 20 MB. By default, the user will not see this disk from their Windows Explorer, as it contains important configuration information that you wouldn't want them to delete.

The following diagram shows you an outline of the different disk types created:

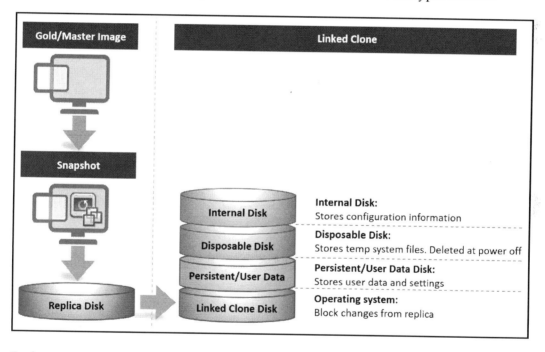

In the next section, we will take a deeper dive into how the linked clone process works.

Understanding how the linked clone process works

There are several complex steps performed by View Composer and View Manager that initiate when a user requests a virtual desktop machine. So, what's the process of building a linked clone desktop, and what goes on behind the scenes? When a user logs into Horizon View and requests a virtual desktop machine, View Manager, using vCenter and View Composer, will create a virtual desktop machine if there is not already one available to the end user.

This process is described in the following sections.

Creating and provisioning a new virtual desktop

The first step in the process is to create and provision the virtual desktop machine as described in the following steps:

1. An entry for the virtual desktop machine is created in the **Active Directory Application Mode (ADAM)** database before it is then put into provisioning mode.
2. The linked clone virtual desktop machine is created by View Composer.
3. A machine account is created in Active Directory with a randomly generated password.
4. View Composer checks for a replica disk and creates one if one does not already exist.
5. A linked clone is created by the vCenter Server API call from View Composer.
6. An internal disk is created to store the configuration information and machine account password.

The virtual desktop machine has been created and is now ready for the next step of the process—customization.

Customizing the desktop

Now that the new linked clone virtual desktop machine has been built, the next step in the process is to customize it.

To customize the virtual desktop machine, follow these steps:

1. The virtual desktop machine is switched to customization mode.
2. The virtual desktop machine is customized by vCenter Server using the `customizeVM_Task` command and is joined to the domain with the information you entered in the View Manager console.
3. The linked clone virtual desktop is powered on.
4. The View Composer Agent on the linked clone virtual desktop machine starts up for the first time and joins the machine to the domain, using the `NetJoinDomain` command and the machine account password that was created on the internal disk.
5. The linked clone virtual desktop machine is now Sysprep'd or Quickprep'd. Once complete, View Composer tells View Agent that the customization has finished, and View Agent tells View Manager that the customization process has finished.
6. The linked clone virtual desktop machine is powered off and a snapshot is taken. If you use Quickprep, then you don't need to restart the virtual desktop machine following customization.
7. The linked clone virtual desktop machine is marked as provisioned and is now available for use.

When an end user connects and powers on a linked clone virtual desktop machine, the View Composer agent installed on that virtual desktop is able to track changes to the machine account password. If there is a change, then the new updated password will be stored on the linked clone internal disk. The machine account password is often changed, depending on password policies, so if the View Composer agent detects this change of password, then it will update the machine account password on the internal disk that was created when the linked clone desktop was created. This is a key feature when refreshing linked clone disks, as the linked clone virtual desktop machine reverts back to the snapshot taken after the virtual desktop machine has been customized. This means that the View Composer agent can reset the machine account password to the latest one.

The linked clone process is depicted in the following diagram:

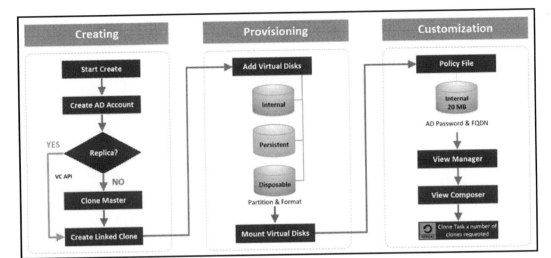

In the next section, we are going to look at some of the additional features and functions of using linked clones.

Linked clone features and functionality

There are several other management functions that you can perform on a linked clone disk using View Composer. These functions are outlined in this section and are used to deliver the ongoing management of the virtual desktop machines.

Recomposing a linked clone

Recomposing a linked clone virtual desktop machine or desktop pool allows you to perform updates to the operating system disk, such as updating the image with the latest patches, or software updates. You can only perform updates on the same version of an operating system, so you cannot use the recompose feature to migrate from one operating system to another, such as going from Windows 7 to Windows 10.

As we've covered in the *What does View Composer Build?* section, we have separate disks for items such as a user's data. These disks are not affected during a recompose operation, so all user-specific data on them is preserved.

When you initiate the recompose operation, View Composer essentially starts the linked clone building process over again; thus, a new operating system disk is created, which then gets customized, and a snapshot, such as the ones shown in the preceding sections, is taken.

During the recompose operation, the Mac addresses of the network interface and the Windows SID are not preserved. There are some management tools and security-type solutions that might not work due to this change. However, the UUID will remain the same.

Before you perform the recompose operation, you will need to create your new image and then take the initial snapshot. The recompose process is described in the following steps:

1. View Manager switches the linked clone to maintenance mode.
2. View Manager calls the View composer resync API for the linked clones being recomposed, directing View Composer to use the new base image and the snapshot.
3. If no replica for the base image and snapshot exist, then, in the target datastore used by the linked clone, View Composer will create the replica in that same target datastore, that is, unless you have configured View to use a separate datastore for storing replicas.
4. For the linked clone, the current OS disk is deleted by the View composer. It then creates a new OS disk that is linked to the newly created replica.
5. The remainder of the recompose cycle follows the customization phase of the provisioning and customization cycles.

The following diagram shows a graphical representation of the recompose process. Before the process begins, the first thing you need to do is update your gold image (1) with the patch updates or new applications you want to deploy as the virtual desktops:

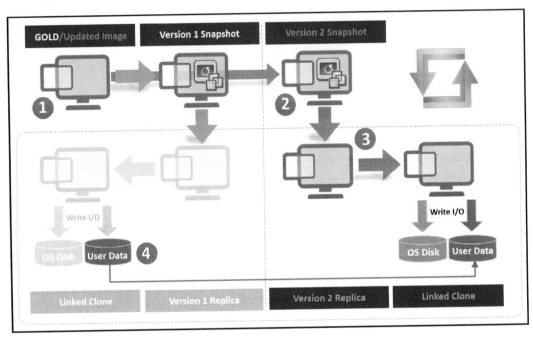

As described in the preceding steps, the snapshot is then taken (2) to create the new replica, Replica V2 (3). The existing OS disk is destroyed, but the user data disk (4) is maintained during the recompose process.

Refreshing a linked clone

By carrying out a refresh of the linked clone virtual desktop, you are effectively reverting it to its initial state, when its original snapshot was taken after it had completed the customization phase. This process only applies to the operating system disk and no other disks are affected.

An example use case for refresh operations would be recomposing a non-persistent desktop two hours after logoff, to return it to its original state and make it available for the next user.

The refresh process performs the following tasks:

1. The linked clone virtual desktop is switched to maintenance mode.
2. View Manager reverts the linked clone virtual desktop to the snapshot taken after customization was completed: `- vdm-initial-checkpoint`.
3. The linked clone virtual desktop starts up, and the View Composer agent detects whether the machine account password needs to be updated. If it doesn't, and the current password on the internal disk is newer than the password currently stored in the registry, then the View Composer agent updates the machine account password using the password that is on the internal disk.

One of the reasons you would perform a refresh operation is if the linked clone OS disk starts to become bloated. As we previously discussed, the OS-linked clone disk could grow to the full size of its parent image. This means it would be taking up more disk space than is necessary, which kind of defeats the objective of linked clones. The refresh operation effectively resets the linked clone back to a small delta between it and its parent image.

The following diagram shows a representation of the refresh operation:

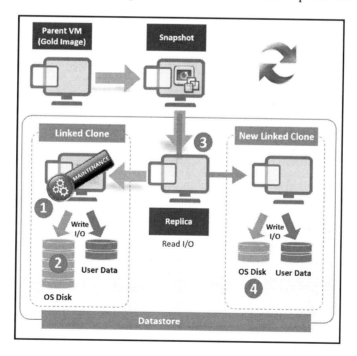

The linked clone disk on the left-hand side of the diagram has started to grow (2). Refreshing the first places the virtual desktop machine in maintenance mode (1). The virtual desktop is then reverted to the original snapshot (3). The new linked clone desktop has now been reset to the same size as when it was first created (4).

Rebalancing operations with View Composer

The rebalance operation in View Composer is used to evenly distribute the linked clone virtual desktop machines across multiple datastores in your environment. You would perform this task if one of your datastores was becoming full while others have ample free space. It might also help with the performance of that datastore. For example, if you had 10 virtual desktop machines in one datastore and only 2 in another, then running a rebalance operation would potentially even this out and leave you with 6 virtual desktop machines in each datastore.

> You must use the View Administrator console to initiate the rebalance operation in View Composer. If you simply try to Storage vMotion any of your virtual desktop machines, then View Composer will not be able to keep track of them.

On the other hand, if you have six virtual desktop machines on one datastore and seven on another, then it is highly likely that initiating a rebalance operation will have no effect, and no virtual desktop machines will be moved, as doing so has no benefit. A VDI desktop will only be moved to another datastore if the target datastore has significantly more spare capacity than the source:

1. The linked clone is switched to maintenance mode.
2. Virtual machines to be moved are identified based on the free space in the available datastores.
3. The operating system disk and persistent disk are disconnected from the virtual desktop machine.
4. The detached operating system disk and persistent disk are moved to the target datastore.
5. The virtual desktop machine is moved to the target datastore.
6. The operating system disk and persistent disk are reconnected to the linked clone virtual desktop machine.
7. View Composer resynchronizes the linked clone virtual desktop machines.

8. View Composer checks for the replica disk in the datastore and creates one if one does not already exist, as per the provisioning steps covered earlier in this chapter.
9. As per a recompose operation, the OS disk for the linked clone gets deleted and a new one is created and then customized.

The following diagram shows the rebalance operation. It started with two virtual desktop machines in datastore A, and four virtual desktop machines in datastore B. The rebalance operation in this example evened out the datastores so that there are four virtual desktop machines in each of the two datastores:

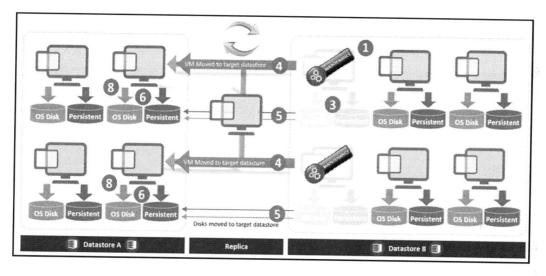

In the next section, we are going to look at the Instant Clone feature for creating virtual desktop machines.

Instant Clones

The **Instant Clones** feature is functionality built into the vSphere platform rather than a specific Horizon feature, and was made available from the vSphere 6.0 U1 release when it became a supported feature as part of Horizon.

It uses the VMware VM Fork technology to very quickly provision virtual desktop machines. An instant clone is created from an already powered on and running virtual desktop machine, called the parent virtual desktop machine, which is quiesced before the instant clone is created. This is what makes instant clones quicker to provision than linked clones and View Composer.

Understanding Horizon 7 Architecture and Components

The instant clone shares its memory and its disk with the parent virtual desktop machine for read operations and is created immediately, and in an already powered-on state, unlike with View Composer-based linked clones that must power on as part of the creation process. As well as sharing the memory and disk with the parent virtual desktop machine, the instant clone has its own unique memory and delta disk file. The following diagram shows the instant clone's architecture:

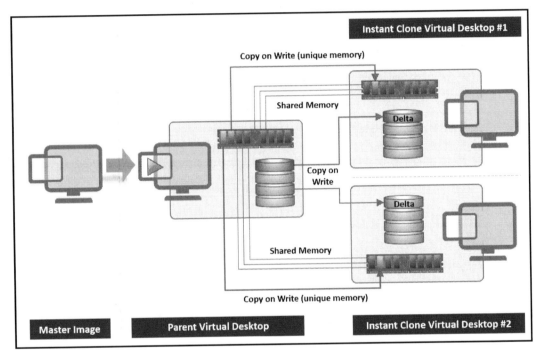

When the end user logs off the instant clone virtual desktop machine, it is destroyed, and when the user logs on again, they will have a new instant clone created. If they need any data to persist, then they would use the Writeable Volume feature of App Volumes to deliver that functionality and UEM to manage their personalization settings.

 To take advantage of instant clones, the virtual desktop machines will need to be running virtual machine hardware version 11 or higher.

Instant clone build process

Previously, when we talked about linked clones, we looked at what the build process looks like and what gets built, so let's now look at that again from an instant clone perspective.

As always, we start with the master image, the virtual desktop machine that all other desktops are built from. The first thing that happens is that a snapshot of the master virtual desktop machine is taken. Next, an internal template is created that is a linked clone of the master virtual desktop machine based on the virtual desktop machine snapshot taken in the previous step.

Next, we have the replica virtual desktop machine, which is a thin-provisioned, full clone of the internal template virtual desktop machine. View Storage Accelerator uses a CBRC digest of this virtual desktop machine. After the replica virtual desktop machine, the running parent virtual desktop machine is created using a linked clone of the replica virtual desktop machine, which, in turn, is based on a replica virtual desktop machine snapshot.

Finally, the instant clone desktop is created and is ready for the end user. The following diagram describes this process pictorially:

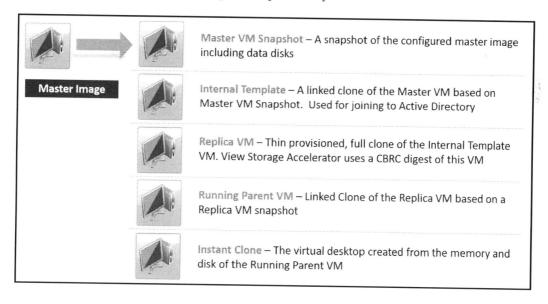

Instant clone benefits

There are several benefits to using instant clones, compared to linked clones:

- Instant clones provision in seconds, whereas linked clones take a lot longer (typically minutes).
- There are no longer any boot storms, as the parent desktop is already powered on, and therefore all instant clones get created in an already powered-on state.
- There is no requirement to perform a refresh or recompose operation, as desktops have a short life cycle.
- Patching the operating system requires you to just update the parent VM, rather than running a recompose operation, resulting in an end user receiving the updated virtual desktop machine on their next login, automatically.
- They lessen the load on the vCenter server.
- There is no requirement for SE Spare Disk or CBRC.

In the next section, we are going to look at how these newly built virtual desktop machines are customized and personalized.

View Persona Management

Let's start with a little bit about the background and history behind **View Persona Management**. View Persona Management was originally a technology product called **Virtual Profiles**, and was acquired by VMware from RTO Software in 2010.

View Persona Management was then introduced with **View 5.0**, and it allows you to configure user profiles so that they dynamically synchronize with a remote profile repository that is located on a file server in the data center. Its purpose is to manage user profiles centrally within a virtualized desktop environment as part of the composite desktop model we discussed in `Chapter 1`, *Introducing VDI and VMware Horizon 7*.

Why do we need to manage user profiles differently in VDI?

In a VDI solution, one of the key benefits is the way the virtual desktop is either built on demand or delivered from a pool of prebuilt, non-persistent desktops and then delivered back to the user. The typical deployment model is the non-persistent model, which basically means that the user doesn't own their own desktop or have personal files, data, or settings stored on it either. It's these settings that form their user profile.

When they log in, they could have any desktop delivered to them from a pool of available virtual desktop machines. This means that the virtual desktop that is delivered would not be personalized to that user. It would just be a standard vanilla build of the operating system and applications.

This is where View Persona Management comes into play and delivers the user's profile to that non-persistent virtual desktop machine they have been assigned to, effectively making it their own.

When we talk about the desktop being built on demand, we are again referring to the composite desktop model and how a desktop is put together from several different components. As a reminder, the desktop can be broken down into three components: the operating system, applications, and the user's personalization or profile, essentially, the bit that makes the desktop yours. As a user logs in, all these pieces come together to deliver the end user desktop experience. With View Persona Management, we are talking about the user's profile.

In this section, we will introduce you to View Persona Management and its benefits for managing user profiles. A deeper dive into the technical details and configuring View Persona Management can be found in `Chapter 17`, *Managing the End User Environment in Horizon*.

The benefits of View Persona Management

At a high level, View Persona Management provides the following features:

- Fast loading of user personalization settings, with just-in-time retrieval of user profile data
- Little or no infrastructure is required—just a file share or the use of an existing folder redirection structure
- Profile consistency maintains personalization between sessions

- Efficient architecture with no dependency on Windows roaming user profiles
- Multiplatform support for Windows XP, Windows Vista, Windows 7, Windows 8.x, and Windows 10

In addition to the listed features, View Persona Management also helps reduce virtual desktop TCO by enabling the move to a stateless virtual desktop environment. In some deployments, users were placed in dedicated pools solely to retain their profile settings, which added to the cost and complexity in management. When it comes to cost, as persona management is an integrated part of Horizon View; you don't need to purchase additional third-party products, unless you need additional functionality above and beyond the basics.

On the subject of management, there are no additional components to set up or install, since everything is driven by the Active Directory Group Policy. In terms of scalability, again, as there are no infrastructure overheads such as databases, so scalability is not an issue, as it scales with your active directory.

VMware UEM

The **VMware UEM** product is one of the newest editions to the Horizon portfolio and was added when VMware acquired the Dutch company Immidio back in February 2015. Immidio was a software company that created products that were aimed at helping their consultants out in the field, with the core product being called **Flex+**.

UEM adds additional functionality over and above the standard persona management solution, providing a central management console, to deliver personalization of the end user's virtual desktop machine as well as the ability to dynamically configure policies. It works across several different environments, such as virtual desktop machines, physical PCs, as well as cloud-based Windows desktop environments or DaaS. It's all about managing Windows profiles regardless of where or how the operating system runs.

To manage a virtual desktop machine with UEM, you will need to install the FlexEngine components onto the virtual desktop machine. Make sure you include this as part of your master image or parent virtual desktop machine.

There are five key use cases that UEM can be used with:

- **Application Configuration Management**: Allows you to configure an application's initial settings rather than deploying the application's own default settings. You can configure predefined settings as one-time defaults, fully enforced (application starts with the user's personalized settings every time), or partially enforced (application starts as configured, but allows the user to perform limited personalization), using the VMware UEM Application Profiler to capture predefined settings for an application.
- **User Environment Settings**: Allows you to centrally manage user environment settings such as the following:
    - Application blocking
    - Application shortcuts and file type associations
    - Drive and printer mappings
    - Environment variables
    - Files, folders, and registry settings
    - Folder redirection
- **Personalization**: Abstracts user-specific desktop and application settings from the underlying OS and then makes these settings available across multiple devices, Windows versions, and applications. It also supports operating system migration such as Windows 7 or Windows 10.
- **Application Migration**: Allows an end user to effectively have roaming application and personalization settings so that they can move between different operating system versions, such as from Windows 7 to Windows 10.
- **Dynamic Configuration**: Using condition sets allows you to combine conditions based on variables such as user, location, and device, to deliver dynamic delivery of content and appearance, for example, delivering access to a network printer based on an end user's location, or to create drive mapping that is based on the user's identity.

SmartPolicies is a feature of Horizon and uses UEM to deliver a set of policies that are specific to virtual desktop machines.

To use SmartPolicies, it is recommended that you run View Connection Server Version 7.2 or later and is required for using Smart Policies with RDSH-published applications. You also require UEM 9.0 or later, but UEM 9.2 or later is recommended.

With Smart Policies, administrators have a more granular level of control over an end user's virtual desktop machine. Horizon 7 features can be dynamically enabled, disabled, or controlled based on the end user as well as other variables, such as the client device type, IP address, and desktop pool name. With SmartPolicies, you can configure the following:

- USB redirection
- Printing
- Clipboard behavior
- Client drive redirection
- HTML access file transfer
- Bandwidth profile

 If you are using UEM 9.1 or later, along with the Horizon Agent 7.0.1 or later, this setting applies when users are using either the Blast Extreme display protocol or the PCoIP display protocol.

UEM or Persona Management?

The question is which solution should you use? UEM is available as part of Horizon Enterprise Edition or as a standalone product, so that means higher or additional costs, unless, of course, you planned on purchasing Enterprise Edition in the first place.

UEM delivers a far greater set of configuration variables and features, as well as having a central management console that makes it far easier to manage and deploy. However, you may already have a more comprehensive UEM solution in place. If you are using a lesser edition of Horizon, then Persona Management may well deliver your requirements, and, if not, then maybe it's worth considering a third-party product, such as Liquidware ProfileUnity.

Printing from a virtual desktop machine

A question that often comes up when deploying a VDI solution is "*How do you manage printing?*" As your virtual desktop is now effectively running on a server in the data center, does that mean that when you hit the print button, your print job comes out there? What about printer drivers? Typically, your desktop has the driver installed for the printer that is nearest to you, or it might be a locally-attached printer. Does that mean you need to install every possible printer driver on to your virtual desktop machines? Luckily, the answer to these questions is no, and, in this section, we will briefly cover how VMware Horizon View manages printing.

Bundled within Horizon View is an OEM virtual printing solution, **ThinPrint**, for which a company called Cortado is the OEM. ThinPrint allows your end users to print either to a network-based printer or to a local printer that is attached from the user's endpoint device to their virtual desktop machine via USB redirection. We will cover USB device management in the next section.

To answer the question about the printer drivers that must be installed, ThinPrint uses a single, virtual print driver that replaces all other print drivers. You can still install a specific print driver, if necessary, for use cases where your printer has some additional features or functionalities. However, the virtual print driver provides support for most multifunctional printers, supporting features such as double-sided printing.

The other question is regarding location and where your print job prints are also addressed with ThinPrint, which provides a location-based printing feature that allows you to map to a printer that is nearest to your endpoint device. There are, of course, third-party solutions available such as UniPrint.

Managing USB devices

There isn't a list that details every single device that works within Horizon View, as that would be one very long list, and it would be impractical to test everything out there, given the number of USB devices on the market.

Most USB devices should work in a Horizon View environment, as all it essentially does is redirect the USB traffic from the View client running on the endpoint device to the View agent running on the virtual desktop machine. A complete list of validated devices does not exist, as it would be a very long list and impossible to test every device on the market. If there are any questions about the functionality of a device, you should contact the USB device's manufacturer.

There might be some devices that will not work, purely due to the nature and the behavior of the device itself; for example, some security devices that check the physical properties of the machine or device they are plugged into. We used to classify USB webcams as unsupported devices. However, with the introduction of **Real Time Audio Video (RTAV)**, these devices are now supported. In the next section, we will talk about how you can select which USB devices get redirected by using USB filtering.

Filtering supported USB devices

In some circumstances, you might not want to allow users to have the ability to plug in external USB devices and redirect them to their virtual desktop machine. The question is whether you allow users to plug USB devices into their physical desktops?

Horizon View has a feature that can prevent USB devices from being redirected to the user's VDI desktop. You can apply this using a policy on the endpoint device, the virtual desktop, or by means of an Active Directory Group Policy. For example, your organization might want to prevent USB memory sticks from being used, as this would give the user the ability to copy data from the virtual desktop machine (one of the reasons for the deployment of VDI is so that data is centralized and doesn't leave the data center).

You can create specific filters to include devices (by the manufacturer or by device type) that you want to allow, but block all others. So, if you have a corporate, standard-type device, it will be allowed. You could even go to the next level and choose a specific model of a device while blocking any other devices, even though they are from the same vendor.

Managing multi-function USB devices

In your environment, you might have USB devices that have several different functions, while still using a single USB connection. For example, a multimedia keyboard could have a touchpad mouse, speakers, a fingerprint reader, and the keyboard itself.

Horizon View supports a function known as **device splitting**. This allows you to just redirect certain components of that device rather than the entire device. With our multimedia example, you might want to leave the mouse as a local device on the endpoint, while redirecting the fingerprint reader to allow secure login to the virtual desktop.

ThinApp application virtualization

ThinApp is an agentless application virtualization or application packaging solution that decouples applications from their underlying operating systems. It's designed to eliminate application conflict, streamline application delivery, and improve management. ThinApp licenses are included with the Horizon View license and can be used on both physical and virtual desktops, therefore providing a mechanism to deliver applications across your entire desktop estate.

How does application virtualization work?

ThinApp encapsulates applications into a package consisting of a single .exe or .msi file and abstracts them from the following:

- The host operating system
- Any traditionally installed applications already running on the system
- All other virtual applications running on the system

Applications then run in their own isolated virtual environment, with minimal or zero impact on the underlying operating system, virtual filesystem, or virtual registry.

When you create a ThinApp package, you are basically capturing all the application files, registry settings, and filesystem changes that an application requires for it to run. It also captures its own agent as part of the process, so the endpoint device requires nothing to be installed.

Once packaged, the application can be deployed (either streamed or installed) on to the virtual desktop machine or even a physical desktop. The only requirement ThinApp packages have to run is an underlining Windows operating system, either physical or virtual. When running, it's important to note that the package makes no changes to the OS of the machine it's running on.

Understanding Horizon 7 Architecture and Components

There are no requirements for additional backend infrastructure components, as all your ThinApp-packaged applications are stored in a file share on a file server. This means that you can centrally manage and easily update your packages so that all users will receive the updates the next time they launch the application. The following diagram shows a high-level ThinApp architecture:

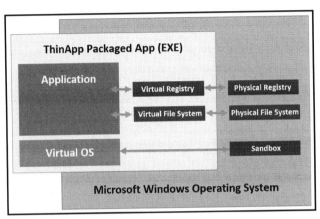

To summarize, ThinApp delivers the following:

- Allows Windows applications to be packaged, distributed, and executed as single .exe or .msi files on either physical or virtual desktop machines
- Builds process links, a Virtual OS (VOS) with a compressed embedded filesystem, and registry, in a single file
- Requires no pre-installed software on the end user machine.
- Provides a zero footprint on the underlying OS
- Necessitates no traditional installation or changes to the local OS registry or filesystem
- Requires no backend server infrastructure, other than a file share to store your ThinApp packages

To learn more about ThinApp and how to use it in your environment, read *VMware ThinApp 4.7 Essentials*, by Peter Bjork, Packt Publishing.

Antivirus software for virtual desktops

In a traditional desktop model, an antivirus agent is installed, runs on every desktop, and is responsible for the performance of antivirus detection scans, while maintaining and updating the definition files containing information about the latest malware.

This model works well in the physical desktop world, but presents some challenges when running in a virtual desktop environment. When a detection scan starts, every virtual desktop's resource usage will increase significantly. This will result in end user performance degradation, and the desktop host server will become resource-bound. That's fine on a physical desktop, but now, in VDI, it's the servers hosting the desktops that are going to become resource-bound. When recomposing desktops or building them on demand, the desktops will have to download the definitions file each time, taking up network bandwidth and storage capacity. One last thing you need to take into consideration is the memory footprint of the typical desktop AV software that gets installed on each virtual desktop. You will need to allocate more memory to run the agents and scanning process.

Let's say you have a vSphere host server running maybe 100 virtual desktops or so; what if, at 12:00 on Thursday, they all kick off a virus scan? That host is likely to become 100% utilized very quickly, both for CPU and storage I/Os, with the result being unresponsive desktops. Instead of affecting one user's desktop, you have now affected 100 users, desktops. You could schedule the scans so that they don't all happen at once, but, ideally, you need to look at alternative methods that are designed to work more specifically with a virtual desktop infrastructure.

Secondly, if we are recomposing desktops or building them on demand, we must download the definitions file every time, which not only takes up network bandwidth, but also unnecessary storage capacity.

So, what is required is a new approach to antivirus protection, specifically designed for virtual desktop infrastructure. With VMware vSphere 5.5, VMware introduced a product called **vShield Endpoint**, which has now been superceded by VMware NSX that addresses the problems inherent in antivirus scanning in large-scale virtual desktop implementations. It does this by offloading all antivirus operations into one centralized appliance. The scanning is then done at the hypervisor level and not on each of the virtual desktop machines.

Although VMware provide the engine to help deliver the scanning process, they have also worked alongside and partnered with some of the leading antivirus software vendors to deliver the knowledge around how to identify and protect against viruses, malware, and other threats. They work with partners including the following:

- Bitdefender
- Kaspersky
- McAfee
- Sourcefire
- Symantec
- Trend Micro

Protocols – Delivering the virtual desktop experience

One of the most important elements of a virtual desktop solution is how you get the screen contents of the virtual desktop machine, which is running in the data center, delivered to the end user's device they are connecting from, and how they interact using the keyboard and mouse. To do this, VMware Horizon View has the option to use several displays or delivery protocols: PCoIP, Blast Extreme, or RDP. In this section, we are going to cover each protocol, how it works in delivering the end user experience, and some more advanced technical details.

PCoIP

PCoIP is a high-performance display protocol designed and developed by Teradici (http://www.teradici.com/). It has been purpose built to deliver virtual desktops over the LAN or WAN and to provide end users with the best feature-rich desktop experience.

With PCoIP, the entire screen content is compressed, encrypted, and encoded in the data center before transmitting only the pixels across a standard IP network to PCoIP-enabled endpoint devices (such as zero clients) that use the hardware-based Teradici Terra 1 or Terra 2 chipset, or to Windows, macOS, or tablet devices running the software-based Horizon Client. The key thing to remember is that no data ever leaves the data center.

PCoIP supports high-resolution, full-frame rates, 3D graphics, HD media, multiple displays (up to four, depending on the endpoint device), and high-definition audio. PCoIP also supports USB peripheral redirection.

Unlike some legacy display protocols that were built just to deliver applications, PCoIP was designed and built from the ground up, specifically to deliver a full desktop experience, taking advantage of Teradici-based zero clients with an integrated graphics acceleration technology built into the silicon on these devices, or software-based clients. PCoIP ensures the best user experience, regardless of the end user location, whether that is on the LAN or even across a WAN. It adapts, dynamically adapts based on network conditions and user policy.

PCoIP host rendering

So, let's start by looking at how the different rendering models work. With a desktop PC, the applications, operating system, and graphics drivers work together locally to deliver the best performance on that PC. This is local client rendering.

If we move to a client rendering model, we now introduce a network between the components. Images are now sent across the network to the endpoint device, where they are processed locally using the resources of that endpoint device. Using this model introduces degradation of the application performance as it travels across the network from the host server to the client, and you would still need a powerful Windows-based endpoint device.

So, what about host rendering? In a host rendering scenario, the desktop PC environment that we previously described is pretty much the same. However, the PC is now running as a virtual desktop machine. This means that applications will work as they normally would on a physical desktop PC and the rendering is done at the host end. PCoIP then works by encrypting just the pixels on the virtual desktop machine running the View agent, and then sends them to the endpoint device running the View client, or to a zero client device running Teradici hardware, where the decoding takes place.

Using this model, you can easily deploy lower powered, non-Windows devices such as zero clients, as the applications have no dependencies on the endpoint on which they run.

Multi-codec support with PCoIP

If you look at how an image is built up and how the content is rendered, some of the components of the image might require the use of different codecs to display the image, depending on what type of image it is. For example, you would use a different codec to display text from one that you would use to display videos.

PCoIP can analyze these different media image components and apply the appropriate codec for each pixel before compressing, encrypting, and sending the pixels to the endpoint device for decoding. Working in this way allows PCoIP to transmit the pixels more efficiently, which ultimately means less bandwidth and better performance. It also means that you can control the image content quality that is being delivered. We will talk about it in the next section.

Controlling the image quality

The quality of the image that PCoIP delivers can be controlled through the AD Group Policy or SmartPolicies to deliver the appropriate image quality, depending on the use case. The image is built progressively from what is termed a **perceptually lossless image** to a **lossless image**, with the latter delivering a high-fidelity, pixel-perfect image. For example, would you really need to build a pixel-perfect image if you were just running Microsoft Word?

The important thing to remember is that the quality of the image will have an impact on the bandwidth required to deliver it. We will cover these controls in more detail in `Chapter 10`, *Fine-Tuning the End User Experience*.

Dynamic networking capabilities

To manage the use of bandwidth, PCoIP employs adaptive encoders that automatically adjust the image quality on networks that are congested. The level of network congestion can be defined via policies that allow you to configure this based on use case, location, and so on. So, maybe the limits are different for those users based in the HQ on the main network, versus those in satellite/branch sites. When the network is no longer congested, then the maximum image quality is restored. PCoIP doesn't transfer any user data over the network. It just transmits pixels, and therefore uses a real-time **User Datagram Protocol (UDP)**, rather than using a TCP protocol (used for **Voice over IP (VoIP)**, to ensure a responsive and interactive end user experience. This will reduce the overall bandwidth requirement and deliver the best interactive user experience, based on the network bandwidth available at any particular time.

UDP does not employ error checking or correction, and therefore removes any overheads in processing the checking and correcting. The lack of retransmission delays that you would find with a TCP protocol means that it's ideal for streaming media. For the end user experience, these delays translate to jerky movements, most commonly experienced when watching video content.

PCoIP offloading with the Teradici PCoIP Hardware Accelerator

In addition to the software solutions discussed in the previous sections, Teradici also offers a server offload card called the **Teradici PCoIP Hardware Accelerator**. This PCI card is installed in the servers that are hosting the virtual desktop machines.

The first thing to say about this card is that it is not a **Graphics Processing Unit (GPU)** card. I often hear some confusion around this, and users assume that, by adding an accelerator card, you would get the OpenGL and DirectX capabilities, but this is not the case. You might improve the overall experience and performance, but you won't be adding additional GPU features.

The objective of this card is purely to take the load away from the CPU of the host server when it is processing image encoding operations. Offloading the image encoding to a specialized hardware solution reduces CPU utilization, which, in turn, delivers a consistent end user experience, thereby allowing applications to run more smoothly as they have the resources they require. If you compare it to something such as TCP Offload Engine or the TOE card used in the IP storage world for iSCSI, it's much better to use hardware-based cards than it is to use software initiators.

Freeing up CPU cycles and the overall load on the servers' CPU will potentially result in better consolidation ratios of the virtual desktops, that is, more virtual desktops per host server. Typically, you will see a 1.2 fold increase.

The accelerator card can also be used in conjunction with a GPU. In this scenario, the card efficiently encodes the extra pixels that are generated by the GPU, ensuring the end user has all the benefits that the local GPU can deliver.

Teradici host card for physical PCs

Teradici also has a solution for physical workstations to leverage the PCoIP protocol: the **PCoIP Remote Workstation card**. This card is not actually for virtual desktop sessions, but, instead, it allows you to add a Teradici host card to a physical workstation, connect to your workstation, and send remote graphics, audio, and USB from the workstation to a PCoIP-enabled endpoint device, such as a zero client. Think of it as picking up your desktop PC and putting it in the data center, and then running a very long video, mouse, and keyboard cable to it. This use case is typically deployed for high-powered rack mount workstations or PCs.

So, how does that fit in with Horizon View? Quite simply, the connection to the physical desktop from the client device is managed using Horizon View and the connection server brokers the session in the same way it would when connecting to a virtual desktop machine. The pixels and keyboard and mouse strokes are sent over the network using the PCoIP protocol.

How the PCoIP connection process works

The following describes how the PCoIP connection process works when an end user logs in and requests a virtual desktop machine:

1. The Horizon Client sends the end user's credentials for authentication via HTTPS to the external URL of the PCoIP External URL that you configured on the security server or Unified Access Gateway. To do this, it uses the XML-API.
2. HTTPS authentication data is passed through from either the Unified Access Gateway or the security server to the connection server. The security server uses IPsec protected AJP13-forwarded traffic, from the security server to the connection server that it is paired with. The desktop pools and apps that the user is entitled to are read from the connection server and then displayed as available resources displayed in the Horizon Client.
3. The end user launches either a virtual desktop or published app session. This connection is initiated on TCP port `4172` (PCoIP port) to the Unified Access Gateway or the security server. This session initiation process is called the **PCoIP session handshake**.

4. A bi-directional PCoIP connection is established using UDP port `4172` (ensure that this port is not being blocked) to send the session data from the Horizon client and the configured `pcoipExternalUrl` to the Unified Access Gateway or the security server. Details of the PCoIP session are then forwarded from the Unified Access Gateway or the security server back to the Horizon Agent running on the virtual desktop machine and then to the client.

 `pcoipExternalUrl` is only used for the Unified Access Gateway. If you are using security servers for external access, then the PCoIP external URL on the paired connection server will be used instead.

This process is shown in the following diagram:

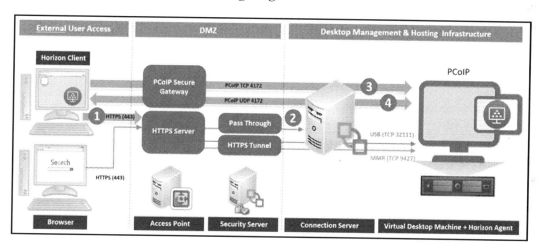

In the next section, we are going to look at the **Blast Extreme** protocol in more detail.

Blast Extreme

Blast Extreme is a new VMware developed protocol that uses the H.264 video codec as an option if you have the appropriate GPU acceleration resources available in the host servers, allowing it to deliver the user experience to H.264-enabled client devices. H.264, or MPEG-4 part 10, is an advanced video coding, or MPEG-4 AVC, solution. It is a standard of video compression that is block-oriented, motion compensation-based. It's a commonly used video format, and an example of where it is used is in the delivery of DVD video content.

Blast as a VMware protocol has been around for a while and was first seen in Horizon 5.2 a few years ago, where it was used to deliver HTML5 access to virtual desktop machines. Now, however, it's not just limited to delivering HTML5 access; it can also deliver the user experience to the latest client devices using standard HTTPS ports.

The Blast Extreme delivery method is also on feature parity with PCoIP and supports similar functionality, such as client drive redirection, USB, unified communications, and local printing. Where they start to differ is in resource consumption, with Blast using far fewer CPU cycles, and delivery protocols, and more flexible.

Like PCoIP, Blast Extreme can compensate for an increase in latency or a reduction in bandwidth and dynamically adjust; however, it can also leverage both TCP and UDP, whereas PCoIP is UDP only.

You can also connect multiple monitors. Depending on the endpoint device, up to four monitors are supported, each one running at 2,560 x 1,600. Or you can run three 4K monitors running at 3,840 x 2,160 for Windows 7 remote desktops with Aero disabled.

Some of the other features of Blast Extreme are detailed in the following list:

- **Blast Adaptive UX**: Delivers end user access to Horizon View virtual desktop machines and hosted applications via the Horizon View Client or browser-based clients, using either Blast Extreme, PCoIP, or RDP. It automatically adapts to network conditions, delivering the best experience possible, through either.
- **Blast Multimedia**: Delivers rich video playback for Flash, HTML5, QuickTime, Microsoft Silverlight, and Windows Media.
- **Blast 3D Services**: Built on the broadest virtualized graphics capabilities in the industry, including hardware-accelerated graphics with NVIDIA GRID vGPU technology. With Blast 3D enabled, Horizon View supports either up to two monitors running up to 1,920 x 1,200, or a single 4K monitor running at 3,840 x 2,160.
- **Blast Live Communications**: Delivers full access to communications tools such as headsets and webcams, for rich audio and video. Supports applications such as Skype, Google Hangouts, and Cisco WebEx.

- **Blast Unity Touch**: Delivers a more intuitive interface, allowing you to use Windows desktops, applications, and files from a mobile device.
- **Blast Local Access**: Supports connecting peripheral devices such as USB flash drives, printers, smart card devices, and smartphones to your virtual desktop machine.
- **Blast Horizon Clients**: Blast-enabled clients for delivering a high-end user experience to endpoint devices.

How the Blast Extreme connection process works

The following steps describe how the Blast Extreme connection process works:

1. As with PCoIP, with Blast Extreme, the Horizon Client sends the end user's credentials for authentication via HTTPS to the external URL of the PCoIP external URL that you configured on the security server or Unified Access Gateway.
2. HTTPS authentication data is passed through from either the Unified Access Gateway appliance or the security server to the connection server. The security server uses AJP13-forwarded traffic from the security server to the connection server it are paired with. The desktop pools and apps that the user is entitled to are read from the connection server and then displayed as available resources displayed in the Horizon client.
3. The end user launches either a virtual desktop or published app session from the Horizon client. A session handshake occurs over HTTPS on TCP port 443 to the Unified Access Gateway Appliance or the security server.
4. A secure WebSocket is established on TCP port 443) to allow the session data between the Horizon client and the Unified Access Gateway Appliance or the security server.
5. The Blast Secure Gateway Service (either Unified Access Gateway Appliance or security server-based) will attempt to establish a UDP WebSocket connection on port 443. If the connection fails, or is blocked for some reason, then the Blast Secure Gateway Service will revert to the initial WebSocket TCP port 443 connection.

This process is shown in the following diagram:

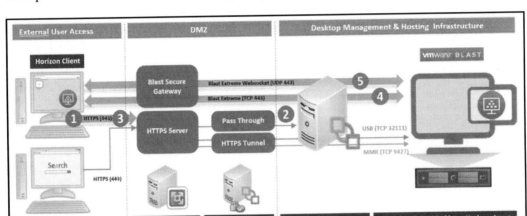

For more detailed port settings, follow this link:

https://techzone.vmware.com/resource/network-ports-vmware-horizon-7.

Alternative display protocols

There are a couple of other mainstream desktop protocols available on the market, some that work with VMware Horizon, and others that are used by Horizon's competitors. The main protocols available today are Microsoft **Remote Desktop Protocol** (RDP) and Citrix **Independent Computing Architecture** (ICA). These are described in the following sections.

RDP

The RDP was developed for Microsoft and is used primarily to connect to a remote machine, server, desktop, or virtual machine using TCP IP. The RDP is now more commonly known as the **Remote Desktop Connection**. You probably use it daily to connect remotely to your server infrastructure in order to manage servers remotely.

When you connect to the remote desktop or machine, you are essentially connecting to a terminal service component, which then relays the screen content back to the client, along with keystrokes and mouse movements.

ICA protocol

ICA is another display protocol that is used by Citrix in its products, XenDesktop and XenApp. It is similar in design to other protocols in that it is used to deliver screen content and keyboard strokes to a client device over a TCP IP network connection.

You connect using an ICA client, such as **Citrix Receiver**, installed on your endpoint device. This loads an ICA file containing the details of the remote system you are connecting to and any properties to apply to that session.

What about **High Definition Experience (HDX)**? HDX is not a protocol or a technology, but rather a marketing brand for HDX. HDX encompasses a number of Citrix technologies that describe the entire user experience rather than concentrating on just the protocol element. You will also see some sub-brands fall under HDX, such as HDX MediaStream, HDX RealTime, and HDX 3D.

Which protocol should you use – Blast Extreme, PCoIP, or RDP?

Now that we have a good understanding of PCoIP, Blast Extreme, and RDP, which one would you choose?

The most compelling reason to go with PCoIP is the fact that it uses the UDP protocol, which is much better suited to streaming media and therefore lends itself perfectly to the characteristics of virtual desktop delivery, but, as discussed, Blast can also use UDP as the delivery protocol. Just to highlight this again, UDP is not concerned with how the data ends up on the endpoint device; it's only concerned with the speed of delivery and how quickly it gets there.

On the other hand, RDP uses TCP as its protocol, which is widely used across the internet. The key difference with TCP is that it is concerned with how the data is being received. TCP requests an acknowledgment from the endpoint device as to whether it has received all of the packets successfully. If the endpoint device does not receive what it was expecting, then it replies, asking TCP to either stop sending packets or to narrow the amount that it receives. UDP just keeps sending and is much speedier, simply because there is no acknowledgment packet back from the endpoint device.

This is where Blast Extreme would come in, as it can use either TCP or UDP as the delivery protocol and is able to determine what network capacity it has available to it and adjust accordingly.

Blast Extreme will also use fewer resources on the endpoint device, especially if you offload the decoding using the NVIDIA GRID technology. However, the only point to be aware of is that when using TCP as the delivery protocol, it could potentially consume more bandwidth, as it compensates for packet loss.

There are some cases where PCoIP won't be the appropriate protocol and Blast Extreme or RDP would need to be used. The one we see most often is when the required network ports are being blocked by corporate policy, or from remote locations that lock down internet connections.

When your desktop is displayed back to you, PCoIP uses UDP port 4172 to send the pixels. This port is sometimes blocked, as it's not typically used. The result of this port being blocked is that, even though you will be able to log on to your virtual desktop via the View client and everything looks OK' you will just receive a black screen. The black screen is due to the pixels being blocked as they are sent. In this example, the workaround is to access the desktop from an HTML5-enabled browser using Blast Extreme, which uses standard HTTPS ports. We will cover this in `Chapter 10`, *Fine-Tuning the End User Experience*.

The key takeaway here is to engage with your networking and security teams when planning how users connect to their virtual desktop machines and look at how the users are working and from what locations. It may well be that you don't need external access, and therefore WAN limitations are no longer a consideration.

Now that we have talked about how to deliver graphics via the delivery protocol, in the next section, we are going to look at the options for enabling high-end graphics in virtual desktop machines.

Horizon View Hardware-accelerated graphics

Early versions of virtual desktop technology faced challenges when it came to delivering high-end graphical content, as the host servers were not designed to render and deliver the size and quality of images required for such applications.

Let's start with a brief history and background. The technology to support high-end graphics was released in several phases, with the first support for 3D graphics released in vSphere 5, with View 5.0 using software-based rendering. This gave us the ability to support things such as the Windows Aero feature, but it was still not powerful enough for some of the high-end use cases due to this being a software feature.

The next phase was to provide a hardware-based GPU virtualization solution that came with vSphere 5.1 and allowed virtual machines to share a physical GPU by allowing virtual machines to pass through the hypervisor layer to take advantage of a physical graphics card installed inside the host server.

If we had this conversation a couple of years ago and you had a use case that required high-end graphics capabilities, then virtual desktops would not have been a viable solution. As we just discussed, in a VDI environment, graphics will be delivered using a virtualized, software-based graphics driver as part of the hypervisor.

Also, don't forget that, as we are now using servers to host the virtual desktops, we are using the power of the graphics card in the server, and servers aren't renowned for their high-end graphics capabilities and have limited GPU power, as typically, all a server needs to do is display a management console.

That has all changed now. With the release of View 5.2 back in 2013, the ability to deliver hardware-accelerated graphics became a standard product feature with the introduction of **Virtual Shared Graphics Acceleration** (**vSGA**), which was then followed by the launch of **Virtual Dedicated Graphics Acceleration** (**vDGA**).

We will discuss these two technologies in the following sections of this chapter. We will also discuss the latest installment of graphics capabilities in Horizon View, with **Virtual Graphics Processing Unit** (**vGPU**).

vSGA

The vSGA implementation allows for multiple virtual desktop machines to share a physical GPU card, which is installed inside the ESXi host server that is hosting those virtual desktop machines.

Understanding Horizon 7 Architecture and Components

In this model, the virtual desktop machines do not have direct access to a dedicated physical GPU card. Instead, the standard VMware SVGA 3D graphics driver that is part of VMware Tools is installed on the virtual desktop's operating system. The SVGA driver is a VMware driver that provides support for DirectX 9.0c and OpenGL 2.1.

In this configuration, the driver supplied by the graphics card manufacturer (VIB) is installed on the ESXi hypervisor rather than the virtual desktop machine's own operating system. Graphics commands from user sessions are intercepted by this driver and sent to the hypervisor, which controls the GPU in the ESXi server.

Delivery to the user's endpoint works in the same way, where DevTAP encodes the user experience to PCoIP or Blast Extreme, and delivers it to the end user's device, either in an HTML5 browser or Horizon Client. The following diagram shows an overview of the vSGA architecture:

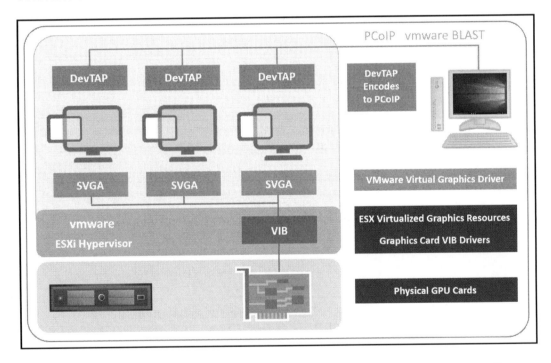

There are several configurations and support options to consider, which we will cover in the next sections.

vSGA-supported graphics cards

vSGA will support OpenGL 2.1- and DirectX 9-based applications running either on Windows 7 or 8 virtual desktop machines, virtualized on VMware vSphere 5.1 and greater, using one of the following manufacturer's GPU cards:

- Intel HD Graphics P4700, and Intel Iris Graphics
- Tesla
- NVIDIA GRID
- AMD FirePro

For the latest compatibility guide and supported graphics cards, please click on the following link: http://www.vmware.com/resources/compatibility/search.php?deviceCategory=vsga.

How many virtual desktops are supported by vSGA?

This is a question that often gets asked when talking about delivering hardware-based graphics within a Horizon View environment, so let's spend some time understanding this. Within Horizon View, you can create different desktop pools depending on the use case, as we will cover in Chapter 8, *Configuring and Managing Desktop Pools – Part 1*, where one of the desktop pools will be configured to use high-end graphics. Typically, you would not want to give all users access to a hardware-based GPU, hence the reason you would create a desktop pool for this use case.

So, to answer the question, the number of virtual desktops you can allocate to a GPU is dependent on the amount of video memory (VRAM) that you allocate to each virtual desktop. The thing to bear in mind is that the resources are shared, and therefore normal VMware virtualization rules apply. The first thing to note is how memory is shared.

Half of the video memory allocated to a virtual desktop machine is allocated from the GPU card's memory, and the other half is from the host server's memory. When sizing your host servers, you need to ensure that you have enough memory configured in the server to allocate this as video memory.

Based on this, and on the number of virtual desktops supported being based on the amount of allocated VRAM, let's look at how that works out.

The default amount of VRAM allocated to a virtual desktop machine is 128 MB. So, in this example, 64 MB will come from the GPU and the other 64 MB from the host server. If you then take a GPU card that has 4 GB of VRAM on board, you will be able to support 64 virtual desktops (4 GB or 4,096 MB divided by 64 MB from the GPU = 64 virtual desktop machines).

With Horizon View, you can allocate a maximum of 512 MB of VRAM per virtual desktop machine. If you apply this to the preceding example using the same 4 GB GPU card, you now reduce the number of supported virtual desktops to 16 (4 GB or 4,096 MB divided by 256 MB from the GPU = 16 virtual desktop machines).

With the AMD graphics solutions, the maximum number of supported desktops is 15 desktops per GPU.

We stated previously that normal VMware virtualization rules apply, so let's explain exactly what that means. Basically, what happens when you can't fulfil a virtual desktop machine's specification and there are insufficient resources? It won't boot or power on, right? It's the same for GPU configuration. If you configure a desktop pool with more virtual desktop machines than you can support on that GPU, they will not boot.

If you do happen to configure more virtual desktop machines in a pool where you probably cannot guarantee the GPU resources to be available, set the Hardware 3D setting in the View Administrator console to Automatic. Doing this allows Horizon View to revert to the software-based 3D rendering to deliver the virtual desktop machines.

vDGA

While vSGA works on a shared basis, vDGA allows for an individual VM to have its own dedicated access to a physical GPU card installed in the ESXi host server. This allows the virtual desktop machine to have a higher level of graphics performance, making it perfect for such use cases as CAD/CAM applications, as it supports DirectX (9, 10, and 11), OpenGL 4.4, and NVIDIA CUDA.

The following diagram shows the architecture for vDGA:

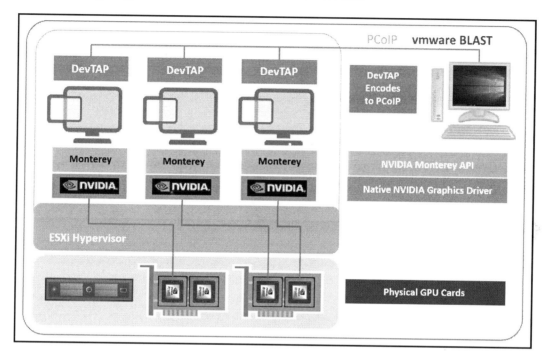

The vDGA solution makes use of a feature called **VMDirectPath I/O pass-through**, sometimes referred to as **PCI pass-through**, which allows the virtual desktop machine to pass through the hypervisor layer and directly access the hardware in the host server. In this case, the hardware in question is the NVIDIA GPU cards.

As a VDI Desktop is mapped directly to a GPU on a one-to-one basis, you cannot use vSphere features such as HA, DRS, or vMotion.

How many virtual desktops are supported with vDGA?

Unlike vSGA, which is limited by the amount of memory on the GPU card, vDGA is limited purely by the number of GPUs or GRID cards you can physically fit into the host server. This is dependent on your server vendor and what they support.

Server vendors offer NVIDIA GRID-enabled servers that are prebuilt, and therefore this technology is only available from the OEM channel. The primary reason is that servers require additional power and cooling components to drive the GRID cards.

For example, an NVIDIA GRID K2 GPU card has two GPUs on board, which would mean that you can allocate four virtual desktop machines to this card. Depending on your server hardware platform, you could install more than one card, thereby increasing the number of users that have access to a hardware-enabled GPU in their virtual desktop.

vDGA-supported graphics cards

The following are some of the GPU cards that are supported with vDGA:

- NVIDIA GRID, NVIDIA Tesla, and NVIDIA Quadro
- AMD FirePro

For the latest compatibility guide and supported graphics cards, please click on the following link: `http://www.vmware.com/resources/compatibility/search.php?deviceCategory=vdga`.

vGPU

In the previous sections, we have talked about two different models for delivering high-end graphics. However, there are a couple of limitations to each of these solutions.

With vSGA, you get the scalability in terms of the number of users that can use the GPU card; however, because it does not use the native driver provided by the GPU vendor, then some of the ISVs will not certify their applications running on this solution. They would need to certify the VMware SVGA driver, as that's the driver that's used.

So, the answer to tackle the ISV support issue is to use vDGA, which does use the native GPU vendor's graphics driver, but now you are limited in terms of scalability and the high cost. Having a virtual desktop machine dedicated to a GPU, with only a handful of GPUs available in each host server would make for quite an expensive solution. Having said that, there may be a use case where that would be the correct solution.

What we need is a solution that is the best of both worlds; a solution that takes the shared GPU approach for scalability, yet uses the native graphics drivers. That solution is called vGPU, and was launched as part of Horizon 6 and the 6.1 release.

The following diagram shows the architecture for vGPU:

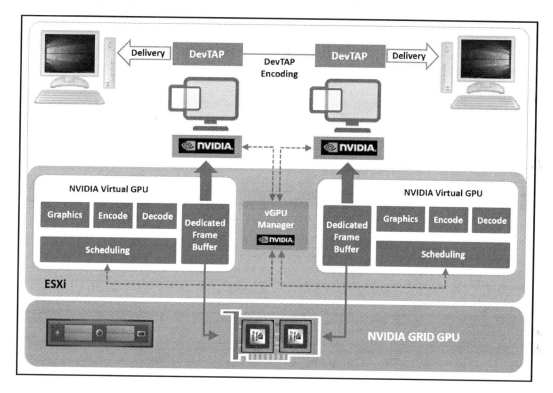

In this model, we have the native NVIDIA driver installed in the virtual desktop machines, which then has direct access to the NVIDIA GRID card in the host servers. The GPU is then effectively virtualized and time-sliced, with each virtual desktop machine having a slice of that time.

 vGPU is only available with VMware vSphere 6 and Horizon View 6.1 and later.

How many virtual desktops are supported with vGPU?

With vGPU, the number of supported users/virtual desktop machines is based on different profiles. These profiles are detailed in the following diagram and give you the number of users, number of supported monitors, and so on:

NVIDIA GRID K2	vGPU Profile	Video Memory	Max Displays	Max Resolution	Maximum No. Users
	K280Q	4GB	4	2560 x 1600	2
	K260Q	2GB	4	2560 x 1600	4
	K240Q	1GB	2	2562 x 1600	8
	K220Q	512MB	2	2560 x 1600	16

NVIDIA GRID K1	vGPU Profile	Video Memory	Max Displays	Max Resolution	Maximum No. Users
	K180Q	4GB	4	2560 x 1600	4
	K160Q	2GB	4	2560 x 1600	8
	K140Q	1GB	2	2562 x 1600	16
	K120Q	512MB	2	2560 x 1600	32

As with the vDGA and vSGA solutions, you need to check that you have the correct supported hardware. In addition, you should also check that your applications are supported in these configurations. You can find the current list of supported applications by following the link to the NVIDIA website: `http://www.nvidia.com/object/grid-isv-tested-applications.html`.

Unified communications support

Like high-end graphics, if we had a conversation about running a unified communications solution or VoIP session on a VDI desktop a couple of years ago, I would have described it as Kryptonite for VDI! Although it technically works, the first call might have acceptable performance, but adding more users would ultimately bring the servers to their knees with the amount of traffic generated and resources required to conduct the calls. Eventually, the experience would have become completely unusable. Unified communications was not a good use case for VDI.

However, this has all changed, and you can now happily use a unified communications solution with your virtual desktop. There was always a great use case to deploy unified communications with VDI; it's just that it never worked! Take, for example, a call center environment. with the ability to provide a DR solution or allow users to work from home during a snowy day and still be able to make and answer calls as if they were in the office.

So, why didn't it work? Quite simply, because when you placed a VoIP call from your virtual desktop, the call would go over the PCoIP protocol, causing bandwidth issues and making your desktop perform slowly, and placing an additional load on the servers in having to process the call. This is detailed in the following diagram, which shows how it was before and the result afterward:

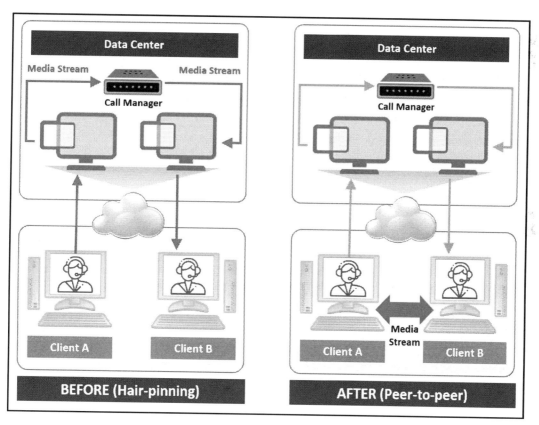

To solve these issues, and to enable a working solution, VMware concentrated on three key areas and delivered the following new features/enhancements:

- Offloading media processing to the client device by removing the load that was placed on the server in the data center
- Optimized point-to-point media delivery, eliminating the hairpin effect
- High-quality UC VoIP and video with QoS

How do unified communications work now?

A remote procedure call utilizes a virtual channel to allow the different components of a softphone, running on a VDI desktop, to communicate and pass voice and video data to other softphone components in the client device. These out-of-band communications.

The call-control stack (a **SIP stack** if using SIP signaling) communicates with the call-control server or call manager to register or establish the call.

A media engine on the client device performs the encoding and decoding of voice and video streams into native voice and video codecs and then streams the VoIP/video stream directly to the other endpoint (as directed by the call manager server), therefore setting up a peer-to-peer call and not going through the data center. This now eliminates the hairpin effect.

Currently, VMware supports solutions from Cisco, Mittal, Avaya, and Microsoft Lync 2013. We will cover the **Microsoft Skype (Lync)** solution in the next section.

Support for Microsoft Skype

Based on what we just discussed, VMware Horizon now supports Microsoft Skype with the Horizon Virtualization Pack for Skype for Business. This includes full support for VoIP and video. The following diagram shows the process of how the client works:

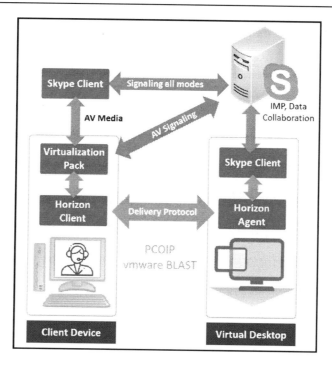

To enable Skype, you need to ensure that the Horizon Virtualization Pack for Skype for Business is installed on the endpoint device, along with the Horizon Client and Microsoft Skype client. VMware has implemented Microsoft's **Dynamic Virtual Channels** (**DVC**) inside the PCoIP protocol to enable this feature. DVC provides the communication path between the virtual desktop machine and the client endpoint.

There are some limitations to the solution that should be mentioned:

- Tuning pages are not available for the audio device and the video device.
- Multi-view video is not supported.
- The recording of conversations is not supported.
- Call delegation is not supported.
- The response group agent anonymization feature is not supported.
- Joining meetings anonymously is not supported.
- Using the Skype for Business VDI plugin with a Skype for Business Phone Edition device is not supported.

Real-Time Audio-Video (RTAV)

Following on from the unified communications support, the next question we hear concerns support for plugging in a USB webcam and using it with a virtual desktop.

The issue

Like unified communications and VoIP, using a webcam, or using audio in and audio out on a virtual desktop machine was not initially supported due to the high bandwidth requirements these types of devices require, thereby resulting in poor performance. Any redirection of these types of devices was previously handled with the USB redirection feature of the PCoIP protocol.

This is how audio-in used to work, but audio-in using a 3.5 mm jack socket did not work at all. Audio-out did work when using the PCoIP audio redirection feature, which was much better than using USB redirection. This was because the client system was unable to split a USB audio device, which resulted in the audio-out functionality remaining local, while the audio-in got redirected. This implies that using a USB headset in a VoIP solution would require the entire headset (audio-in and audio-out) to be forwarded to the guest.

How does RTAV fix this issue?

RTAV does not use a USB to forward audio and webcam devices. Instead, the USB devices remain connected to the local client, and the audio and images are taken from the local device. Audio and image data are encoded and delivered to the guest virtual desktop machine, where they are then decoded. VMware installs a virtual webcam and a virtual microphone virtual desktop machine. These devices are used to play back the audio and video. You will see these device entries in the device manager of your virtual desktop machine.

RTAV can support the following:

- Connecting webcams and audio devices simultaneously, used for VoIP-based video conferencing apps such as Skype.
- Audio-in only (no video) for VoIP (voice-only) apps
- Webcam only; used for webcam monitoring type apps (CCTV, for example), and taking photos

URL Content Redirection

The **URL Content Redirection** feature allows you to configure a URL to either open on a local browser on the endpoint device, or open on the virtual desktop machine. Which content opens in which is configured by using a **GPO**.

The use case for doing this is to separate internal browsing from internal browsing. It may be that if you want to look at secure content, then you would use the browser on the virtual desktop machine, since, if the data doesn't leave the data center, then any other browsing can happen locally. Another case may be that you want to limit bandwidth usage into the data center, and if users are browsing heavy content, they can use their local internet connection.

There are two types of URL that you can configure for redirection:

- URLs that a user enters into the address bar of the browser
- Links in an application, such as Outlook or Word, that users can click

Horizon clients

The Horizon client is basically where your virtual desktop machine's screen is decoded and displayed on an endpoint device. There are two distinct types of Horizon Clients: a software-based version, which is installed on the user's endpoint device, and a hardware-based version, which uses zero or thin clients.

We will cover the View client options in `Chapter 12`, *Horizon Client Options*.

Summary

In this chapter, we discussed the Horizon View architecture and the different components that make up the complete solution. We covered key technologies, such as how linked clones and instant clones work to optimize storage, and then we introduced some of the features that go toward delivering a great end user experience, such as delivering high-end graphics, unified communications, profile management, and how the protocols deliver the desktop to the end user.

Now that you understand all of these features and components, how they work, and how they fit into the overall solution, in the upcoming chapters, we will be taking a deeper look at how to configure them.

3
Design and Deployment Considerations

Now that we have provided a comprehensive overview of the different components of VMware Horizon in the first couple of chapters, in this chapter, we are going to concentrate on how to put those components to use by introducing you to some of the design and deployment techniques that you need to consider when undertaking your VMware Horizon project.

First, we are going to discuss techniques that you can use to prove the technology and understand how it needs to work inside your business, starting with how to assess your current environment and then how to use this information to design your Horizon deployment.

Once you fully understand what it is you need to achieve for the business, we will then take a deeper dive into the design elements of your Horizon solution, including, but not limited to, ESXi host design, memory and CPU allocations for virtual desktops, storage considerations, clients, and other best practices and tips.

Design and Deployment Considerations

We are going to look at both the business and the technical elements of a project, and then discuss each one and see how it fits into the overall project. To make this easier and more logical, we will break these down into three distinct project phases, as shown in the following diagram:

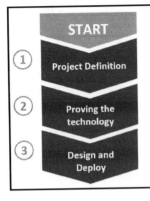

- **Phase I – Project Definition:** looks at the business elements of the project, identifying both business and use cases
- **Phase II – Proving the technology:** provides the opportunity to test the solution in your environment
- **Phase III – Design and Deploy:** for production takes the output and findings from the previous two phases and allows you to design and deploy the solution in production

In the following sections, we are going to explore and discuss these three phases in more detail.

In this chapter, we will cover the following topics:

- Phase I – Project definition
- Phase II – Proving the technology
- Phase III – Designing a production environment
- Technology choices
- Horizon View pod and block architecture
- Cloud Pod Architecture
- vSphere design for Horizon View
- Horizon View design specifics
- Supporting infrastructure design
- Printing
- Thin clients and other endpoint devices
- Desktop design considerations
- Example solution scenario

Phase I – Project definition

In this first phase, we are going to look at how you can approach a project. Phase one is broken down into four individual steps, as shown in the following diagram:

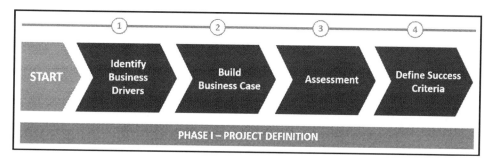

Let's look at each individual step in more detail, starting with the business drivers and understanding what your business requirements look like.

Step 1 – Identifying business drivers – understanding your needs and requirements

Before you jump headlong into your Horizon project, take a step back and ensure that you start to document what you are trying to achieve. Often, it can be very easy to get carried away with all the new, shiny, technological aspects of the solution, such as the installation and configuration of new hardware and software, which means that the end goal is either lost or is not relevant to the business.

It may be an obvious point to make, but the key to identifying the business drivers is to really understand what you want to evaluate. By this, we mean, is it a strategic decision based on the need to transform your organization with new working initiatives, or is there a more compelling event, such as the end of life of an operating system or application? It may even simply be the need to reduce costs. Whatever the case, you need to get that nailed down, written up, and documented on day one so that the project has meaning and direction, and even more importantly, provides a baseline to refer to when it comes to reviewing time in order to gauge whether the project has been successful.

Design and Deployment Considerations

Start by writing a document of requirements that lists the business needs, the current problems you need to solve, the vision, and any compromises and assumptions. As you progress through your project, you should regularly refer to this document to keep yourself focused on the end goal.

Step 2 – Building the business case

Once you have defined the drivers behind an initiative or the compelling event that's kicked off the project, and also understood the high-level objectives, the next stage is to start building the business case around these. This requires you to go to the next level of detail and start drilling into the specific areas the solution needs to address. To do this, you need to understand the business strategy and then identify the key stakeholders for the project. You can then start to define the high-level requirements of each of the areas identified as drivers and start to define user segmentation. For example, you can look at what different user types you have, how they work today, and what they need going forward. At the end of the day, it will be the end users that decide whether the project is a success, not you! This leads us into the next section, which is the assessment phase.

Step 3 – Assessment

Once you have built and validated your business case against your strategy and identified that there is a requirement for a new way of delivering a desktop environment, then the next stage is to run an assessment. Although often called a desktop assessment, what you are actually doing is on-boarding an end user so that you can map their entire life cycle through infrastructure—not just today, but by continuously monitoring them to ensure that they continue to have the best user experience possible as they move through the OS, app migrations, and updates.

So, what do we mean by an assessment, or in this instance, how do we on-board end users so that we can assess and monitor them throughout their working life cycle? What exactly is involved? It comes down to several things that we are looking for. This includes examining your current desktop landscape by gathering key metrics so that you can understand what is currently being delivered, to whom it is being delivered, and more importantly, how resource-intensive it is. The assessment is designed to build a complete and accurate picture of what the current end user environment looks like.

It's not just about an inventory report—you need to understand exactly what the end users are doing, and how they are working. Some of the key metrics we are looking for include the following:

- Which users are using which applications (when, from where, and how often?)
- Resource consumption (CPU, memory, disk, and network are key)
- Unsuitable applications/use cases for remote delivery or VDI
- Which client operating systems are being used?
- Hardware inventory of existing devices
- Machine boot times and login process breakdown
- Current delivery methods (RDSH, XenApp, VDI, physical PCs, and so on)
- User profile details

What you are ultimately looking to achieve is the creation of a baseline of what your environment looks like today. Then, as you move into defining the success criteria and proving the technology, you have a baseline as a reference point to demonstrate how you have improved current functionality and delivered on both the business case and strategy.

If you have deployed a VDI solution already, and this new project is for something like a migration, or upgrading, then you should have most of this data available. However, if this was a while ago, then it's worth re-running the assessment so that you have up-to-date data, especially around the applications in your environment. Ideally, you would have been monitoring the infrastructure continuously from day one to help plan for such events.

User experience and desktop analysis tools

There are several different third-party, complementary products on the market that you can use to conduct the analysis. You are often able to use the services of a partner to assist with this process to help you understand the information and data that's been gathered.

One of the most popular solutions is the Liquidware Stratusphere solution. Stratusphere not only provides you with a detailed breakdown of the current user environment, with highlights such as a detailed breakdown of the login process, consumption reports, and a score to easily identify which users are virtualization candidates—it also provides that complete end user life cycle picture.

Design and Deployment Considerations

Stratusphere takes the baseline data and then uses that to continuously monitor the end user experience so that you can ensure that your VDI solution is optimized, as shown in the following screenshot. We will discuss this in more detail later in this book:

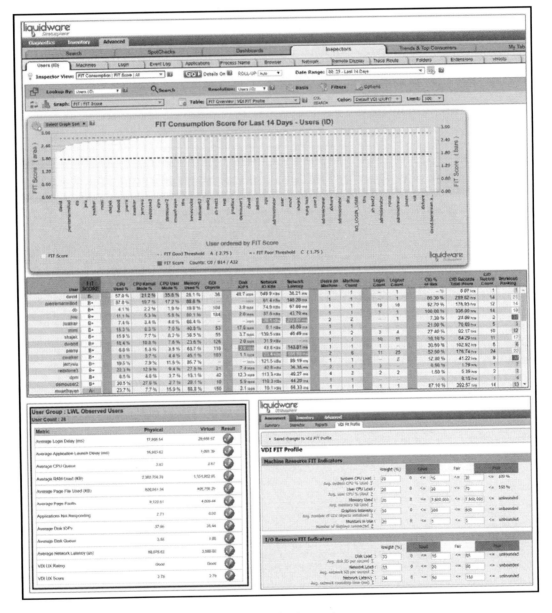

Stratusphere monitor the end user experience

One thing to ensure is that the assessment solution is designed specifically for measuring desktops and not servers. The two technologies, although both virtualization technologies, are completely different, and while you could probably use desktop assessment software to plan your server virtualization project, it simply would not work the other way around.

As well as actually collecting the assessment data, there are several other points that you should take into consideration and look at. This will help you understand what some of the raw assessment data is telling you. For example, it might tell you that a specific user is unsuitable to have a virtual desktop due to the number of resources it consumes; however, when you speak to them, you may find that whatever they are doing isn't going to be relevant in VDI.

Understanding what do your users really do

Working in an IT department will often give you a good level of understanding of the tasks that users undertake and the software that they use to achieve these tasks daily. However, this can usually be a lot more complex than it might first appear. By undertaking a desktop assessment, you gather a more granular level of understanding about the processes, applications, and experience your end users are getting from their existing desktops. This will likely include the applications they use, and those that they don't use, including the installed versions and capacity and performance requirements, as well as user experience metrics, such as login times and application load times.

Applications

Understanding your current applications is a key part of the assessment phase. Not only could this impact end user productivity—after all, it's the apps that keep the users working—it will also impact many other areas when it comes to design, including the number of pools, pool design, application virtualization, and, potentially, whether the desktop that gets assigned to the user can be non-persistent or whether you need to allocate a persistent desktop.

In some environments, you may well have legacy apps still running, and it's important to understand this as these apps may not be able to run in a virtual desktop environment and would, therefore, stall or derail your project completely. Often, when moving to virtual desktops, you would move from an older operating system as part of the project—which again would cause issues with application compatibility.

Design and Deployment Considerations

With the metrics gathered from the assessment, you will be able to fully understand the current situation of your desktop estate. It's not uncommon to find many disparate versions of software, meaning potential security risks, and in other cases, key applications crashing on a regular basis. This information will help you build a business case for change and help you prioritize your rollout to the users with the biggest security holes or the worst user experience.

Performance

Without actual performance metrics, it will be near on impossible to size your virtual desktops. If you don't have this data, then it will be likely that your desktops will be sized in one of two ways. The first would be by oversizing your desktops. Oversizing often occurs when virtualizing as it is so simple to configure a virtual machine that we sometimes get carried away and start adding more CPU and memory than we really need. The result is that we need more infrastructure to resource this and so the costs goes up. This also happens when we guesstimate the size of the desktop, and then add ten or twenty percent on top of that, just in case. Pushing the costs up could mean that the project is not financially viable.

The flipside would be to undersize your desktops, potentially causing performance issues and a poor end user experience. If you then base your infrastructure on this lower spec and you end up having to add more resources, it may be a difficult conversation to secure more budget to increase the spec of the host servers or even add more servers.

This is one to watch out for if you are looking at a Desktop as a Service solution. On paper, the desktops look like they're good value for money, maybe costing somewhere around $30 to $50 per month. But after you have signed on the dotted line and your end users start ramping up and consuming more resources, the costs start to ramp up too. We have seen many a customer invoice with a much larger monthly payment than budgeted for because of taking low-spec desktops.

By performing a desktop assessment, you will understand what the performance looks like throughout the working day. How many resources are being consumed, and when? You are likely to see many dips and spikes throughout the day, such as login storms, AV scans, logoff storms, and other metrics, such as increased internet usage during lunch breaks.

If you work in an education environment, you might see many login and logoff storms during the day. It is important to understand this, as you will need to ensure that your solution is designed to meet these requirements. This information can be used to help guide you when sizing the relevant desktop pools, but bear in mind that, potentially, you are going to be making changes to the desktops between the assessment phase and deploying VDI desktops. This may be something such as migrating from Windows 7 to Windows 10, or the upgrade of an application. In these cases, the assessment will have been performed on the previous version of the operating system and therefore may not give you 100% accurate information on the resources required. Some third-party assessment tools can take care of this and allow you to model "what if" type scenarios.

End user experience

Above all else, what matters is user experience, which is the measurement of how good or how poor the end user's experience of using their virtual desktop is. When you undertake a server virtualization project, if done correctly, the users will probably not even realize it has happened.

With a desktop virtualization or any other EUC-type project that is very focused on the end users, it is more likely that they will realize a change has happened, and you need to ensure that this is a positive experience for the project to be a success. To do this, you need to almost get inside the head of the users to see exactly how they use the environment today. The measurements of user experience will be wide, varied, and often subjective, but will include elements such as boot time, application load time, login time, page load time, app failures, and finally, how intuitive it is to use. This is something that assessment tools are unlikely to tell you.

As you are progressing through the **proof of concept** (POC), pilot, and tuning processes, you need to ensure that the user experience is constantly improving. Failing to take end user experience into consideration will result in a definite failure of the project. To do this, you need to be interactive with the end user community.

Floor walks, interviews, and department champions

As we outlined previously, while performing desktop assessments and gathering data on your environment are important parts of any EUC project, they should not replace the need to interact with your users. The benefit of human involvement is that you can pick up elements that simply would not be possible with software alone.

Design and Deployment Considerations

Start by simply walking through your office, noting what the users are doing, what applications they are using, what accessories, how many screens, whether they are using laptops or PCs, and so on.

Once you have this high level of understanding, consider booking meetings with key business leaders in each department to understand their needs, requirements, and the problems they have with their desktops today. You should also start considering who your department champions are going to be.

What are department champions?

If you are going to make a list of the key considerations from this book, then department champions should be high on your list. A department champion is an end user who is going to be the go-to person within the department for everything to do with their department's desktop, design, testing, and support. They don't need to be IT experts, but they should have a desire to help you improve the overall desktop experience. You should work with these champions to help with the design of their desktops, as they will be your first port of call for testing, and then testing again after you have listened to and implemented any of the feedback.

By working with a department champion, you will have a sponsor within the department. They will have a sense of pride over what is being rolled out and will be there to help you shape the desktop and be the user on your side to help explain why certain decisions have been made.

Step 4 – Defining the success criteria

The key objective in defining the success criteria is to document what a good solution should look like for the project to succeed and become production-ready.

You need to clearly define the elements that need to function correctly to move from POC to POT and then into a pilot phase, before finally deploying into production. You need to fully document what these elements are and get the end users or other project stakeholders to sign up to them. It's almost like creating a statement of work with a clearly defined list of tasks. If you don't have any success criteria in place, then you should not start the testing!

Another important factor is to ensure that during this phase of the project, the success criteria don't start to grow beyond the original scope, which is commonly known as "scope creep." This means that any additional elements should not get added to the success criteria, or at least not without discussing them first. It may well transpire that something key was missed; however, if you have conducted your assessment thoroughly, this shouldn't happen. This is another reason for having the success criteria in place, otherwise you won't know what is on the list, and the list will never end with things continually being added.

Another thing that works well at this stage is to, once again, involve the end users. Set up a steering committee or advisory panel by selecting people from different departments to act as sponsors within their area of business. Actively involve them in the testing phases but get them on board early to get their input in shaping the solution from the outset.

Too many projects fail when a user tries something that didn't work. However, the thing that they tried is not actually a relevant use case or something that is used by the business as a critical line of business app, and therefore shouldn't derail the project.

I once saw a VDI project failing due to the unresponsiveness of the mouse when using Microsoft Paint. This knocked the project way off course while the issue was investigated. In the end, it was shown that Paint was not used by anyone, and so was totally irrelevant to the business or use case. However, it still ended up burning precious cycles while the team tried to enhance performance. As this customer had no success criteria defined beforehand, it was difficult to move the project on. If there had of been a list and this application was not on that list, then it could simply be ignored, and the project could have moved on.

If we have a set of success criteria defined up front that the end users have signed up to, anything outside that criteria is not in scope. If it's not defined in the document, it should be disregarded as not being part of what success should look like.

Design and Deployment Considerations

Phase II – Proving the technology

In this section, we are going to discuss the approach to proving that the technology is fit for purpose. This is another very important piece of work that needs to be successfully completed once you have completed Phase I and is somewhat different to how you would typically approach an IT project. This is the same approach you should take for any end user computing type of project.

As we discussed previously, the starting point is to focus on the end users rather than the IT department. After all, these are the people that will be using the applications daily and know what they need to get their jobs done. Rather than giving them what you think they need, why not ask them what they really need and then, within reason, deliver their requirements. As the saying goes, don't try and fit a square peg into a round hole, as no matter how hard you try, it's just never going to fit.

First and foremost, you need to design the solution around the requirements of the end user rather than spending time and money on building an infrastructure only to find out at the end of the project that it doesn't deliver what the users require.

Once the previous steps have been discussed and documented, you should be able to build a picture around what's driving the project. You will understand what you are trying to achieve/deliver and, based upon hard and fast facts from the assessment phase, be able to work on what success should look like. From there, you can then move into testing the technology in some shape or form.

There are three distinct roads we can take within the testing cycle, and it might be the case that you don't need all of them. In fact, it is usually best to jump straight to the last one if you can and look at deploying a pilot to save time and cost, and get the end users engaged early. The three stages we are talking about are as follows:

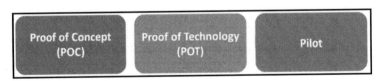

In the following sections, we are going to briefly cover what each of these stages mean and why you may or may not need them.

Proof of concept (POC)

A POC typically refers to a partial solution, which is often built and installed on any old hardware kicking about the IT department. In terms of end user testing, a POC usually involves a small number of users, who are typically those in the IT teams, acting in business roles to establish whether the solution satisfies some aspect of the purpose it was designed for and is fit for purpose.

At the end of the POC, one of two things tend to happen. Firstly, nothing happens as it's just the IT department playing with technology and there wasn't a real business driver in the first place. This is usually down to not having a defined business case. In a similar way, by not having any success criteria, it will also fail, as you don't know exactly what you are setting out to prove.

The second outcome is that the project moves into a pilot phase, which we will discuss in a later section. You could consider moving directly into this phase and bypassing the POC altogether—after all, the vendor has already proved the concept, and to be honest if it's a production-ready solution that you can buy off the shelf today, then there is nothing conceptual about it. Maybe a demonstration of the technology would suffice and using a demo environment over a longer period would show you enough of how the technology works. Most vendors these days have a cloud-based test environment that can be used for prospective customers.

Proof of technology (POT)

In contrast to POC, the objective of POT is to determine whether the proposed solution or technology will integrate into your existing environment and therefore demonstrate compatibility. POT should highlight any technical problems that are specific to your environment, such as how your bespoke systems might integrate. Similar to POC, POT is typically run by the IT department and no business users are usually involved. A POT is purely a technical validation exercise.

Design and Deployment Considerations

Pilot

A pilot refers to what is almost a small-scale rollout of the solution, in a production-like environment, to be tested by real end users. The scope may be limited by the number of users who can access the pilot system, the business processes affected, or the business partners involved. The purpose of a pilot is to test whether the system is working as it was designed to, while limiting business exposure and risk. It should also touch real users so that you can gauge their feedback from what might ultimately become a live, production solution.

This is a critical step in achieving success as the end users are the people that will use the systems daily, and are the reason why you should set up some form of working group so that you can gather their feedback. This would also mitigate project failure, as the solution may deliver everything the IT department could ever wish for, but when it goes live, and the first user logs on and reports a bad experience or performance, you may as well have not bothered.

The pilot should be carefully scoped, sized, and implemented, which breaks down nicely into the following four steps toward a successful pilot, as shown in the following workflow diagram:

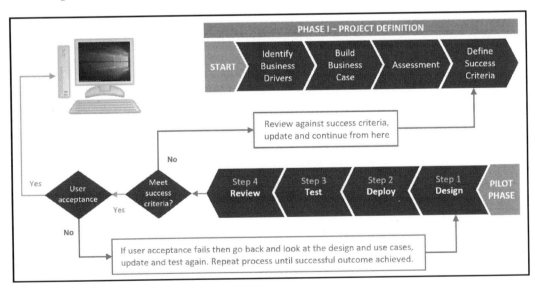

Let's have a look at these steps in a bit more detail.

[110]

Step 1 – Pilot design

The pilot infrastructure should be designed on the same hardware platforms that the production solution is going to be deployed on. For example, the same servers and storage should be used. This takes into account any anomalies between platforms and configuration differences that could affect things such as scalability, or more importantly, performance.

Even at the pilot stage, design is key, and you should make sure that you consider production design, even at this stage. Why? Basically, we do this because many pilot solutions end up going straight into production and more and more users get added above and beyond those that have been scoped for the pilot. It's great going live with the solution and not having to go back and rebuild it, but when you start to scale by adding more users and applications, you might have some issues due to the initial sizing, given that it was meant to be a pilot. It may sound obvious, but often with a successful pilot you just keep going, with end users continuing to work and IT adding more and more users. Well, until it breaks! If it's only ever going to be a pilot, that's fine, but keep this in mind and bear this in mind—if you are planning on taking the pilot straight into production, design it for production right at the very start.

It is always useful to work from a prerequisite document to understand the different elements that need to be taken into consideration in the design. Design elements include the following:

- Hardware sizing (servers—CPU, memory, and consolidation ratios)
- Pool design (based on user segmentation)
- Storage design (local SSD, SAN, and acceleration technologies)
- Image creation (rebuild from scratch and optimize for VDI)
- Network design (load balancing and external access)
- Antivirus considerations
- Application delivery (delivering virtually and/or layering versus installing in the base image)
- User profile management
- Persistent or non-persistent desktop user assignments
- Linked Clone, Full Clone, or Instant Clone desktop builds

Once you have all of this information, you can start to deploy the pilot environment.

Step 2 – Deploying the pilot

In the deployment phase of the pilot, you are going to start building out the infrastructure, deploying the test users, and building the OS images. After this, you will start the testing phase.

Step 3 – Testing the pilot

During the testing phase, you need to work closely with the end users and your sponsors, showing them the solution and how it works, closely monitoring the users, and assessing the solution as it's being used. This allows you to keep in contact with the users and give them the opportunity to continually provide real-time feedback. This, in turn, allows you to answer questions and adjust and make enhancements on the fly rather than waiting until the end of the project, only to be told it didn't work or they just simply didn't understand something.

This then leads us onto the last section, reviewing the pilot.

Step 4 – Reviewing the pilot

This final stage sometimes tends to get forgotten. You have deployed the solution, the users have been testing it, and then it ends there for whatever reason. However, there is one very important last thing to do to enable you to move into production.

You need to measure user experience and the IT department's experience against the success criteria that you set out at the start of this process. You need to get customer sign-off and agreement that you have successfully met all of the objectives and requirements. If this is not the case, you need to understand the reasons why. Have you missed something in the use case, have the user requirements changed, or is it simply a perception issue?

Whatever the case, you need to cycle around the process again. Go back to the use case, understand and reevaluate the user requirements (what it is that is seemingly failing or not behaving as expected), and then tweak the design or make the required changes and get the users to test the solution again.

You need to continue this process, repeating again and again until you get acceptance and sign-off, otherwise you will not get to the final solution deployment phase.

When the project has been signed off after a successful pilot test, there is no reason why you cannot deploy the technology in production. However, it is useful to come back and revisit this occasionally to ensure that nothing has changed.

Now that we have talked about how to prove the technology and successfully demonstrated that it delivers against both your business case and your user requirements, in the following sections, we are going to start looking at designing a production environment.

Phase III – Designing a production environment

Now that you have proved that the solution works within your environment, you can take all of the findings from both the assessment and the pilot phases and start building out a design for production. In this section, we are going to cover the main considerations for a successful design and discuss the general rules of thumb and best practices, before moving on to the specifics of sizing the storage requirement, scalability, availability, and how to architect the solution.

Before we do that, we are going to look at a few different example scenarios that could have been highlighted during the assessment and pilot phases, and look at which technology you should consider deploying.

Technology choices

With VMware Horizon, there is no one-product-fits-all solution to meet the needs of your end users, so it is important to consider the use cases carefully and match the different use cases to the different technologies that are available within the VMware Horizon portfolio. Once you have collected key information from assessments and user interaction, you will be able to make some technology solutions around which elements of the solution are going to deliver end user requirements. Choices include whether you should deliver full VDI desktops or published desktops, and how to deliver applications with ThinApp or App Volumes. You also need to consider third-party solutions, and how they are going to integrate. These technology decisions will influence your final design.

In the following sections, we will discuss some sample scenarios and the likely technology decisions that will enable you to deliver a working solution.

Use case example – Scenario 1

In this example, the end users are based in a call center that operates 24/7 and use a Windows desktop to access a customer relationship database log. They are also using a web browser to access an intranet page. These users work set hours in a shift pattern of three shifts per day across the call center, and they all work from hot desks, utilizing whichever desk and devices are available at the time they start their shift.

Solution recommendation

This would seem to be the ideal scenario for a Horizon View VDI desktop. However, with such a simple use case, it would make more sense to deliver these desktops using the Horizon View hosted desktop feature, which is done by using Microsoft RDS. This would allow for greater levels of consolidation and potential cost savings as you would only need to deliver enough sessions to cover one of the three shifts.

If they did not require any of the functionality of the underlying operating system, then you could just publish the CRM client app and a browser to allow them access to the intranet.

Use case example – Scenario 2

There are several engineering users who currently use a laptop, both online and offline. When offline, they will be utilizing bespoke software to program machinery. Often, this work is carried out in areas of poor mobile signal and no Wi-Fi. They rarely come into the office, but do work from home once or twice a week, where they have good internet access. They also need access to a job allocation system when they have access to the internet. At the time of writing this book, this is accessed via connecting to a work VPN and running a Windows client application on their laptops. They would like to be able to adopt iPads or smartphones to access the job allocation system, but are restricted by the need to use the Windows client.

Solution recommendation

This scenario highlights the exact type of user that does not suit a VDI desktop alone. Previously, if you had tried to make VDI work in this scenario, it would have led to a poor user experience, given the lack of connectivity. With the diversity now available in the Horizon Suite, you can use individual components to deliver a solution that can be seamless to the user and offer them a genuine productivity advantage.

In this scenario, you would be looking to centralize and manage laptop images using VMware Mirage. This would allow you to not only store a copy of the devices locally in the case of failure or loss, but it would also allow you to update and deliver new software when a connection to the Mirage server is available over the internet.

However, there is a key requirement, and that is that you need to access an online application in the form of a job allocation system. You could, of course, deliver this in the same way as it is delivered today, but you could also consider delivering this with Horizon View as a published application. This would give you the advantage of this application being accessible through a variety of devices, without the complexity of a second desktop that VDI would bring. You could also consider AirWatch by VMware to manage iPad and smartphone devices and add a layer of security.

Use case example – Scenario 3

In this scenario, you have a marketing department with 10 users, all using desktop PCs with dual screens running Windows 7. These desktops are typically running the same apps, but each desktop also has a few individual applications that have been installed by IT for users over the years. They are now looking to start making use of several SaaS applications and services such as WebEx and would also like to have the ability to work from home.

Solution recommendation

With the end of support for Windows 7 rapidly approaching, you are going to want to move these users to Windows 10. As such, you are going to want to check the compatibility of their applications with the new operating system version, and where possible, try and standardize the applications as much as possible without affecting the user. Where there are applications that don't support the latest operating system, you could see whether VMware ThinApp would allow them to be virtualized and run on the new operating system. As the user has no offline requirements and they actually need to be online for the SaaS apps, this would seem like a good fit for VDI, and as there is a large commonality across the desktops, you should try and see how a non-persistent Linked Clone pool would work for these users.

You could deliver these common applications by installing them in the base image and then delivering the individual bespoke applications where possible using App Volumes. Additionally, you should look at Workspace ONE for delivering a unified workspace, from where they can access all apps and desktops from a single web-based portal.

Use case example – Scenario 4

There's a small CAD and engineering department with 10 users utilizing Autodesk AutoCAD products. Their last purchase was a year ago, and was for five workstations with high-end graphics cards for half of their users. The users must be able to install their own software, and they also keep a lot of data locally while they are working on designs.

Solution recommendation

There are several options for this scenario. With Horizon and NVIDIA GRID graphics cards, it is likely that you would be able to offer these users a good experience using a virtual desktop machine. With AutoCAD, it is likely that the users will need access to a GPU, and so you need to look closely at the graphics requirements and match them to a vGPU profile or deliver a dedicated GPU with vDGA.

Since half of the workstations have recently been refreshed, you would likely recommend that these be kept in use until they are due to be replaced, but maybe use Horizon Mirage for data protection and to manage updates and software rollouts. When machines are due to be replaced, you could now consider replacing them with thin clients.

For the remaining users, you could consider virtual desktop machines that are persistent as they are saving a lot of local data and are installing their own apps. You could also consider non-persistent desktops and use App Volumes and the Writable Volume feature for them so that they can save data and install apps. Once you move to VDI for everyone, then it gives you the option for remote working.

It is recommended that this scenario is heavily tested during the POC and pilot stages so that you fully understand the type of graphics card required, along with the CPU and memory resources.

Conclusions

The scenarios that we have given demonstrate that there is no one-size-fits-all solution that can be deployed over diverse businesses requirements. If you were to try and shoehorn some of these scenarios into a single solution, it would result in a poor user experience. With the Horizon Suite, you are not only able to have commonality across the solutions for the users and administrators, but are also able to offer a diverse range of solutions to meet the differing and diverse requirements of the end users.

Preparing for production

You now have all of the necessary information about the current environment, business requirements, and goals, and have considered the different scenarios to meet the needs of the end users. You can now consider what the production environment will look like. This is where things start to get serious. You have tested your solution, proved the concept, piloted with a subset of your users, built a business case, and signed it off. Now is the time to start rolling out to your agreed user base.

This will happen in several ways, but initially, it's worth starting this slowly and gathering momentum over time. By gathering momentum in this way, you can guarantee success, and less tuning is required along the way. The big bang approach will end in a world of pain, both for the users and for you when you have so many things to consider when looking at issues.

In the next section, we are going to look at designing for production deployment.

Horizon View pod and block architecture

We are going to start by discussing the core concept of a Horizon View design: **the pod and block reference architecture.** This provides the underpinnings to all Horizon View deployments.

The Horizon View pod and block architecture provide you with a reference architecture that can support up to 10,000 users. This is achieved by taking a modular approach to infrastructure deployment by creating separate Horizon View blocks that are designed to support up to 2,000 users each. These contain all the infrastructure components that are required to support and run those 2,000 virtual desktop machines.

The management components are also deployed as a module called the management block, as well as hosts components such as the Connection Servers and Security Servers.

The blocks then scale up in multiples of 2,000 until they reach the limit of 10,000 (five blocks). This configuration of five blocks is called a pod and gives you one large, unified virtual desktop environment to manage.

If you were to then introduce the Cloud Pod Architecture into the mix, you could scale even further—up to 200,000 users in total!

Now, you might be reading this thinking, "I only have 500 desktops to create in my environment, so this pod and block architecture does not matter to me," but I would urge you to carry on and understand the design principle, since it's core to understanding how to deploy Horizon View.

If you are creating a VDI solution for 500 desktops, you will still be utilizing the concepts within the pod and block architecture but on a smaller scale, as you will only be creating one pod that contains a single block. However, if you want to add DR into the mix, then this is based on this architecture. The following diagram depicts an individual Horizon View block:

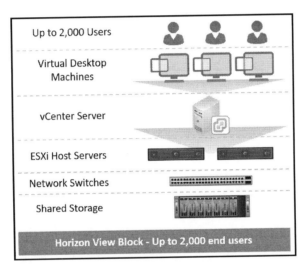

As we mentioned previously, the management block contains all of the Horizon View infrastructure components, such as the **Connection Servers** and **Security Servers** that support the desktop blocks. This is depicted in the following diagram:

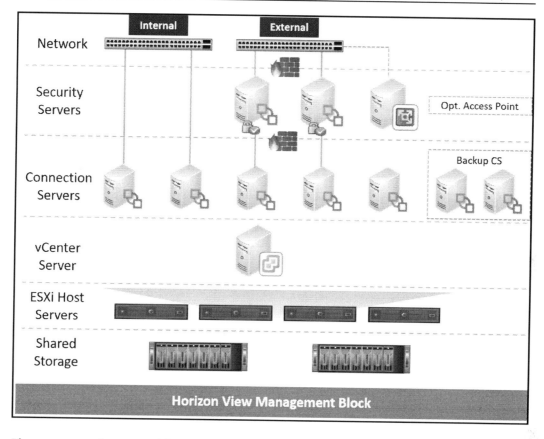

If you are starting out with one block in your pod, you will want to ensure that you still have at least two View Connection Servers for resilience.

 VMware does not support the configuration of blocks across a WAN link as the JMS that's utilized for communication is very susceptible to network latency. However, from Horizon 6 onward, VMware added support for the Cloud Pod Architecture, which allows you to further scale out and provide high availability across multiple sites.

Design and Deployment Considerations

Within each desktop block, as well as having several ESXi hosts of enough capacity to be able to accommodate the number of virtual desktop machines, there is also a vCenter Server to manage these virtual desktop machines. In addition, there are a couple of other components that are not depicted.

You will also need a View Composer server instance for deploying Linked Clone virtual desktop machines, along with a supporting SQL database that will host the View Composer database and the View Events database. This should be made highly available and should also be backed up as the Composer database keeps track of all the virtual desktop machines that are built. The final requirement is a shared storage platform that can either be exclusive to the block or shared across multiple blocks.

It's worth pointing out that, as of VMware View 5.2, it is possible to scale a block up to 10,000 users when there are multiple Connection Servers being used to overcome the 2,000-connection limit of View Connection Servers. However, this would result in a large, single point of failure in the vCenter Server itself. You should consider this risk to your business should vCenter fail and design your architecture accordingly to mitigate any failures. Would you really want to bring down 10,000 users all at once?

> It would be recommended by VMware that, where possible, you limit your pods to 2,000 users to limit the risk of failure.

With a single vCenter Server, you will also be limited to the number of concurrent operations that you are able to undertake. This will be of major significance, for example, when powering up large numbers of desktops or recomposing a large number of desktop pools. If you have multiple vCenter Servers, you will be able to further increase the number of parallel operations that could happen across the vCenter Servers rather than the serial nature of a single vCenter Server.

Inside the pod, the Horizon View Connection Servers are configured in a cluster, and they replicate their data using Microsoft's lightweight directory services and the **Java Message Service (JMS)**. VMware recommends a limit of seven View Connection Servers in a single pod. These are installed as one per block, plus two additional blocks for availability and/or external connectivity.

The following diagram shows the high-level overview of the Horizon View block and pod architecture, complete with the management block. When implemented in a production environment, the users would connect to the View Connection Servers, Security Servers, or Access Point appliance via third-party load balancers:

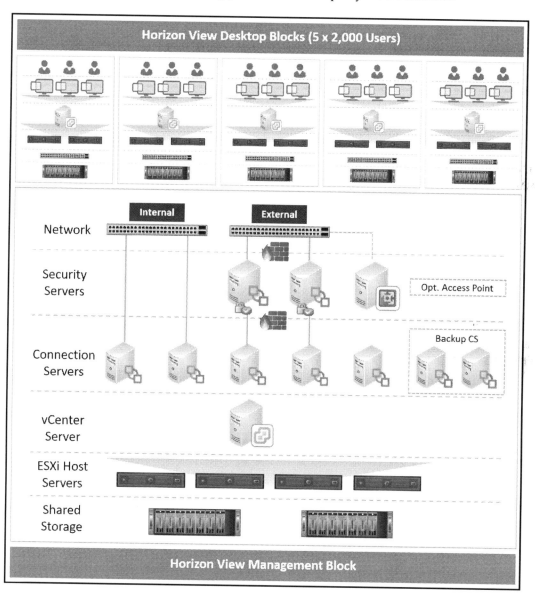

Design and Deployment Considerations

In the next section, we are going to look at how you can extend pods over multiple sites to allow for disaster recovery scenarios, and how to scale beyond the 10,000-user limit by configuring your environment with the Cloud Pod Architecture.

Cloud Pod Architecture

In the latest Horizon 7 release, the Cloud Pod Architecture extends on the scalability and feature set from the previous version. You can now federate up to 25 pods across 10 sites, allowing you to deliver a single desktop solution for up to 200,000 users.

When connecting multiple pods in this manner, you will be able to entitle users across pools on both pods and sites. So, if you have currently scaled past a single pod, either for scaling on one site or to deliver a Horizon View environment on multiple sites, you can now administer users through a global user entitlement layer. You can also deliver DR to your virtual desktops, in the event of failure, through the global user entitlement layer.

You can also configure the scope to set whether View shows a user's resources based only being local to them, on the same site but across pods, or in all pods across both sites. The following diagram depicts the Cloud Pod Architecture:

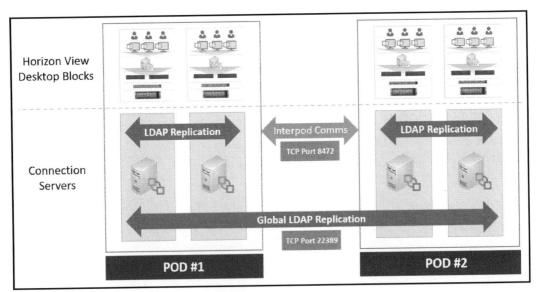

Microsoft Active Directory Lightweight Service and the new **View Interpod API** (**VIPA**) are used for interpod communications. VIPA is enabled when you enable the Cloud Pod Architecture from the command line on the View Connection Servers and is used when virtual desktops are launched to send health information and to find existing desktops.

By default, when a user connects to Horizon View, and they have a global entitlement, there will be a preference applied by the global entitlement to utilize virtual desktops at the local site rather than across a secondary site where possible. However, this is fully customizable by the administrator when creating the global entitlement.

With the scope configuration options, you can specify where the View Connection Server looks for virtual desktops or hosted applications to satisfy a request from the global entitlement. You can configure the following:

- **All sites**: View will look for virtual desktops or hosted applications on any pod within the federation
- **Within a site**: View will look for virtual desktops or hosted applications that are only on pods that are in the same site as the pod that the user is connected to
- **Within a pod**: View will look for virtual desktops or hosted applications that are only in the pod that the user is connected to

In addition to these scopes, you can configure an option called **home site.** This allows you to configure a site that acts as the end user's default site and when the user logs in, the View Connection Server will look for virtual desktops in that user's home site.

Along with configuring the Cloud Pod Architecture, you will need to utilize third-party load balancing technologies to allow the benefits of this technology to be seamless to the end users. However, this gives us a way of unifying our multiple View deployments that would have been separate entities previously. We will look at how this is configured in later chapters.

Design and Deployment Considerations

vSphere design for Horizon View

Now that we have looked at some of the reference architectures, it's time to turn our attention to some of the components that are part of that architecture, namely our vSphere virtualization platform, and look at some of the high-level considerations for your design.

In this book, we aren't going into the intricacies of how to install and configure ESXi hosts. However, we will briefly discuss the recommendations on how you should configure vCenter Server, as well as the hosts and clusters for your Horizon environment.

It is technically possible to run your Horizon View and virtual server environments from one set of infrastructures, with one vCenter Server, and one or more ESXi clusters. By doing this, you could create several points of contention and a lot of difficulty during the time of upgrades.

As we discussed previously, there are two infrastructure areas when it comes to Horizon View: the management block that runs the vCenter Server, View Composers, and View Connection Servers, and so on, and the second one, which runs the virtual desktops themselves. The recommendation is that these two components are separated physically on different ESXi hosts and clusters, minimizing any risk of there being performance issues with the server components during heavy use periods or large desktop provisioning processes. From a licensing perspective, this is covered, as it is included with Horizon is the vSphere for desktop entitlement, which allows you to deploy as many ESXi hosts and vCenter Servers as you need to support your environment.

You should also run the Horizon View components on a different vCenter Server from your production vSphere environment. Separating the Horizon View components onto a separate vCenter Server will mean fewer clashes of priorities and prerequisites when it comes to upgrading either environment.

You should also run the Horizon View components on a different vCenter Server from your production vSphere environment. Separating the Horizon View components onto a separate vCenter Server will mean less clashes of priorities and prerequisites when it comes to upgrading either environment. The following diagram shows an example of how your virtual environments could be designed:

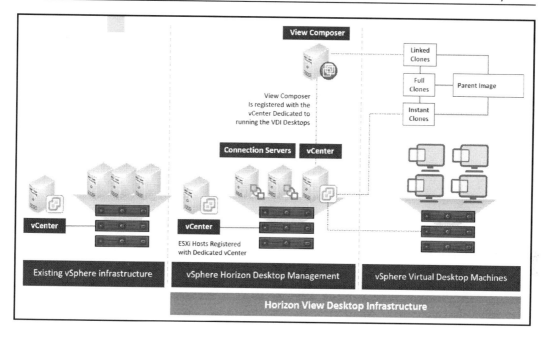

In the following section, we are going to look at the maximum values that can be configured.

Configuration maximums

When building any VDI infrastructure, you very quickly and easily hit the configuration maximums that have been set by the product vendors. When it comes to vSphere and vCenter Server, there are a few maximums that you should be aware of.

 To check out the latest configuration maximums for VMware vSphere, see the following link: `https://configmax.vmware.com/guest`.

You should also keep in mind that the Horizon View has specific maximums. We will discuss those later in this chapter. Don't forget that these maximums are not goals to try and hit, but maximum limits. When designing your architecture, you should also keep in mind the risk of losing an individual component such as a vCenter Server or a View Connection Server.

ESXi host servers

In this section, we are going to cover some recommendations on the sizing and quantities of host servers that might be required to host and support your infrastructure.

As with any virtual infrastructure, you need to ensure that redundancy is built-in as standard. This means ensuring that your chosen servers have redundant power supplies, RAID hard disks, or mirrored SD cards for ESXi, and multiple network cards for network failovers in the case of a card or switch failure.

You also need to look at how many hosts are likely to be required to support your environment, and then add the relative amount of hosts to allow for the N+ capacity that you require. In most environments, this will be N+1, meaning that you will have the number of hosts you require to run your virtual desktops, plus one additional host to allow for a host failure. This ensures that any outage does not impact your end users.

Remember that you are effectively going to be sizing for two different environment profiles; one will host the management block infrastructure, and the other will host the virtual desktop machines.

In the next section, we are going to cover some of the generic points that you should consider for your design.

CPU and memory requirements for ESXi

The next thing we are going to look at is CPU and memory configurations and recommendations.

Overcommitting CPU and memory resources

As a rule of thumb, never overcommit memory in a VDI environment. This can have many negative knock-on effects if memory is not granted when required, which will ultimately affect the end user experience.

When it comes to CPUs, while it would be nice to also not to have an overcommitment, this would simply not be affordable. CPU overcommitment, if done carefully and not pushed too far, can usually be allowed with little to no effect on the end users. However, the question is, how far is not too far? This will generally depend on the type of workload you are running within your environment. If you look at various resources on the internet, you will find different answers to this question, with some claiming figures of more than 10 **virtual CPUs (vCPUs)** per physical core. The only true way to find out what is going to be acceptable in your environment is by reviewing the CPU Ready figure; you can review this metric via vCenter, ESXTOP, or similar tools. When reviewing the CPU Ready figures, you should initially be looking to ensure that you are keeping CPU Ready below 5% per vCPU for the desktops in your environment. Your environment might be able to accept CPU Ready higher than 5%, but this should only be after testing during your POC and pilot stages. Generally, if CPU Ready is as high as 10% per vCPU, the environment is going to struggle enough so that it affects user experience considerably.

CPU and memory sizing

The number of hosts that are required for your Horizon View infrastructure is usually dictated by the number of desktops required, the amount of CPU and RAM these desktops require, what overcommit ratio you can allow for the CPU within your infrastructure, and how much CPU and memory you can physically fit into your chosen host servers.

Taking that into consideration, you should be looking to include the amount of memory and CPU cores across the infrastructure that allows you to balance these in a cost-effective way without too much wastage.

When selecting your host server platform, you should also consider what effect it would have on the business if that one host was to fail. As such, sometimes, you might consider hosts with two physical CPUs to be a better design decision than having four physical CPUs, especially as the number of cores per CPU continues to increase.

This may well become a financial consideration as well as a technical one, and introduces the scale-up or scale-out argument of should you have fewer, larger servers, or spread the load across more, lower spec servers.

Within your calculations, ensure that you are considering the overheads that the ESXi hypervisor requires to be able to run your virtual machines, as well as memory to be dedicated as graphics memory to virtual machines if required.

The following table details some typical overhead values (in MB) that are required per VM:

	1 vCPU	2 vCPU's	3 vCPU's	4 vCPU's
MEMORY OVERHEAD IN MB	20.29	24.28	32.33	48.16
	25.90	29.91	37.86	53.82
	4864	52.72	60.67	76.68
	139.62	143.98	151.93	168.60

Next, we will look at the networking considerations.

Networking

There are generally two considerations for networking in your ESXi hosts, which is whether to use 1 Gbps or 10 Gbps NICs. You could always consider a 40-Gbps network as well. No matter what, you will always want to ensure that you have at least two multiport network cards to separate your traffic, which will allow the resilient network design that you require. Regarding the speed of the network that you require, this will depend on the VM LAN traffic within your infrastructure, and that completely depends on your use case.

If you are streaming a lot of HD media into your VDI desktops, then 10 or 40 Gbps may well be required. Whatever the case, ensure that you really understand the network requirements, as getting this wrong will result in a poor end user experience.

Graphics

A lot of information has already been covered regarding the hardware and software graphics offload and accelerating options in `Chapter 2`, *Understanding Horizon 7 Architecture and Components*.

The requirements for graphics in your environment should be carefully considered and tested during the POC and pilot stages of your project. You should consider all of the elements we mentioned in the previous chapter, and then decide what is required with regard to PCI cards in your ESXi hosts. The requirement for PCI cards for graphics acceleration or offloading will affect the hardware you choose for your ESXi hosts due to the limitations of some of these cards with regard to power and cooling, along with the number of PCIe slots available.

> NVIDIA publishes a list of supported servers, with the number of cards that can be configured into specific servers. This list can be found by clicking on the following link: `http://www.nvidia.com/object/grid-partners.html`.

Storage

We could probably write a whole book on storage considerations, designs, and options regarding your VDI environment. Along with the network, storage is probably among the most important areas to get right. The most obvious reason is that you don't want to end up with insufficient storage for your planned rollout, and secondly, failure to specify a storage solution that is going to meet your performance requirements will leave you with unhappy users and a failed project. This is particularly key when deploying Linked Clone desktops, as we will now discuss.

When it comes to storage, we need to look at two aspects: performance and capacity.

Storage capacity

Your first consideration will be how much storage space you need for your Horizon View environment. You will need to consider where the relative elements of your virtual infrastructure are to be located. The first and easy bit is going to be totalling the required space for any server components. Often, the server components will live on the same storage device as the rest of your virtual infrastructure, and the desktops will live on a dedicated storage device. However, this is not compulsory and will depend on the type of storage you are utilizing and the levels of separation you desire. You will then need to understand the required storage for your desktops based upon the technologies being used to deploy the desktops, such as Linked Clones, Full Clones, or Instant Clones, not forgetting to include persistent disks for user data if you plan on using them.

Design and Deployment Considerations

An important point to remember is to think beyond just the virtual desktops. If you are planning on delivering apps with App Volumes, then you will also need space to store App Stacks.

With Linked Clones, you need to understand the growth of the Linked Clone between the refresh and recompose operations. The following diagram gives an example of some areas for consideration regarding storage for a typical desktop pool that's utilizing Linked Clones and persistent disks:

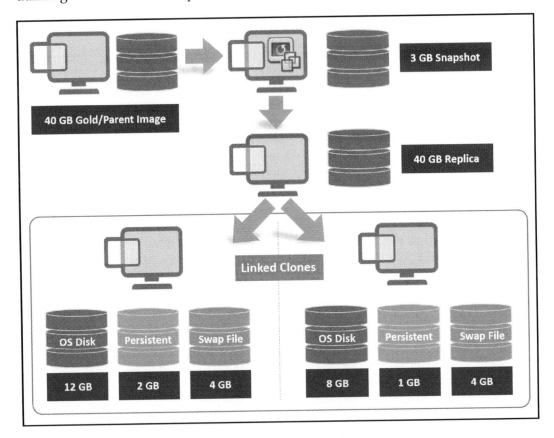

The replica from which a Linked Clone originates needs to be located on fast storage, either local to the host server or via a SAN. To enable this in Horizon View, you can choose the location of where the replica should live, and one of the recommendations is that the replica sits on fast storage, such as local SSD, for example.

The recommendation is that during your POC and pilot stages, you collect this type of storage usage information. Once you have this information, you will be able to use a spreadsheet to create a model to predict storage utilization, and then you can grow your environment. The following table depicts a sample Excel spreadsheet outlining the storage requirement across three desktop pools:

Desktop Pool	Gold Image Size	Linked Clone or Full Clone	Replica Size	Swap File	Persistent Disk per Desktop	No. of Desktops	Space per Desktop	Total Space (GB)
Administration	40 GB	Linked Clone	40 GB	2 GB		200	12 GB	2880
Managers	60 GB	Full Clone		4 GB		20	40 GB	940
Marketing	40 GB	Linked Clone	40 GB	4 GB	10 GB	30	20 GB	1100

During the POC, we have been able to understand the capacity that's required per desktop for the Linked Clones. This is a key component for understanding the overall capacity required for the solution moving forward.

This now leads to the other part of the storage story, that is, storage performance.

Storage performance

Once you have worked out how much capacity you require for your Horizon View environment, you can start considering your performance needs. As always, it is recommended that you understand your performance requirements during the POC and pilot stages and use this to size your storage. When examining your virtual environment, you are looking to keep the read and write latency as low as possible to guarantee a good user experience. The amount of latency that's acceptable will depend greatly on the workload of your users and the tolerances of the applications they are using. However, keeping your average latency as low as 25 ms will often deliver a good user experience for your users.

The question is, how do you ensure that you can deliver this type of performance? The first thing to look at would be to deploy some form of storage acceleration technology to drive the IOPS requirements. Horizon View also has its own integrated solution called the **View Storage Accelerator (VSA)** or **Content-Based Read Cache (CBRC)**. This feature allows you to allocate up to 2 GB of memory from the underlying ESXi host server, which can be used as a cache for the most commonly read blocks. As we are talking about booting up desktop operating systems, the same blocks are required, and since these can be retrieved from memory, the process is accelerated.

Design and Deployment Considerations

 Remember that CBRC is not required when using Instant Clones.

Another solution is to use **View Composer Array Integration (VCAI)**, which allows built Linked Clones to be offloaded to the storage array and its native snapshot mechanism, rather than having to take CPU cycles from the host server.

 Instant Clones does not support VCAI.

There are also several other third-party solutions that resolve the storage performance bottleneck and increase the overall storage I/O. These are software-defined solutions such as ThinScale ThinIO, or hardware-based solutions such as deploying an all-flash array. So, the question is, how many IOPS do you need?

As with the question of how many virtual desktop machines can you configure per core, the answer to the IOPS question is also "it depends!". If you read some of the guides and white papers on the subject, you will probably see something like Windows 7 needing 20 to 25 IOPS. That might be correct for a steady state, but what about for peak disk activity? The only way you will know the answer to how many IOPS you need is by analyzing your assessment report data.

The following graph depicts a sample storage environment, which shows a sample workload as the desktops are booted. Users log in and then continue to use the desktops. On the vertical axis, you can see the IOPS, and on the horizontal axis, you can see time.

As you can see, the boot storm is heavily read-intensive, with the login storm and steady state being heavily write-intensive. You need to size accordingly and based on your assessment data:

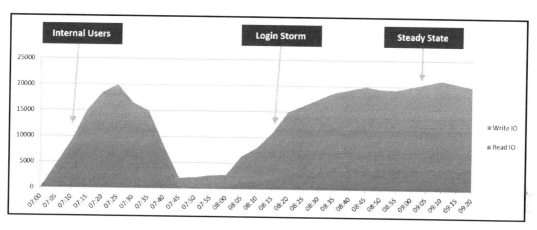

While the desktop may well drive 25 IOPS, what about any applications running on that desktop? How many IOPS will the application require? You don't want to find out the answer to this after you have deployed your solution.

There is also the debate around the split of IOPS between read and write. It is often quoted that the split is 80:20, with 80 writes and 20 reads, but this again will be dependent on your environment and the actual answer will be in your assessment data. It may well transpire that you have 70:30 or even 60:40.

As the IOPS requirements are a key part to the sizing exercise and can have a hit on the virtual desktop machine's performance, you need to get this right, so let's take a closer look at some actual sizing calculations.

One thing that gets forgotten when sizing is the RAID penalty or IOPS penalty when writing to the disks. This means that, for every read operation, there will be multiple write operations occurring, depending on the RAID level being used.

For our example, let's take RAID 5, which has a write penalty of 4, and you need to deliver 200 IOPS with a 60:40 read/write ratio. To calculate this, you can use the following formula:

$$\text{(Total Workload IOPS * Percentage of read operations)}$$
$$+$$
$$\text{(Total Workload IOPS * Percentage of read operations) * RAID IO Penalty))}$$

Going back to our example, the calculation would look something like the following:

$$\text{(200 IOPS * 60\% read operations)}$$
$$+ \quad = 600\ IOPS$$
$$\text{(200 IOPS * 60\% read operations) * 4))}$$

In this example, you would need to configure a RAID 5 array that could deliver the 600 IOPS that is required.

Once you understand what performance and capacity you require for your VDI environment, you can browse the market to find a suitable solution that will work for you.

Horizon View design specifics

Now that we have looked at some of the more general elements of your infrastructure, and the vSphere platform that is going to support your environment, it's now time to turn your attention to the Horizon View-specific components of the infrastructure.

Let's start by looking at the requirements of those components before looking at sizing the actual VDI desktops themselves.

The Horizon View Connection Server

The View Connection Server is a Windows Server with Horizon View installed as an application. In this instance, the application would be that of the View Connection Server role. This server would be hosted as a virtual machine on the management block, and has a recommended configuration, as shown in the following table:

Hardware Config	2,000 Users	10,000 Users
Processor	2 vCPUs	4 CPUs
Memory	4 GB	10 GB
Maximum desktop pool size	1,000	2,000
Hard disk space requirements	40 Gb	60 GB

Operating System	Version	Edition
Windows Server 2008 R2 SP1	64-bit	Standard, Enterprise, Datacenter
Windows Server 2012 R2	64-bit	Standard, Enterprise
Windows Server 2016	64-bit	Standard, Enterprise

As we have touched on previously, if this is purely for a POC or pilot with a limited number of users, you can lower the specification to maybe two vCPUs and 4 GB of memory. You can't resize this afterwards, which is the reason why you should size appropriately should you want to move straight into production without reinstalling.

The Horizon View Replica Server

The View Replica Server is essentially the same as the View Connection Server, as it acts as a backup to the main Connection Server. As such, it should be sized in the same way as the View Connection Server.

The Horizon View Security Server

As with the Replica Server, the Security Server is just another role of the Connection Server, meaning that it should be sized in the same way as these components.

The Horizon View Enrolment Server

Again, the Enrolment Server is another role of the Connection Server, meaning that it should be sized the same as these components.

The Horizon View Composer

The View Composer is slightly different from the Connection Server roles. It can either be installed on the same server that vCenter Server is running on or as a standalone server. You would typically install it as standalone server for performance or if you are using the vCenter Server Appliance. The configuration recommendations for View Composer are detailed in the following table:

Hardware Config	2,000 Users	10,000 Users
Processor	2 vCPUs	4 CPUs
Memory	4 GB	10 GB
Maximum desktop pool size	1,000	2,000
Hard disk space requirements	40 Gb	60 GB

Operating System	Version	Edition
Windows Server 2008 R2 SP1	64-bit	Standard, Enterprise, Datacenter
Windows Server 2012 R2	64-bit	Standard, Enterprise
Windows Server 2016	64-bit	Standard, Enterprise

vCenter Servers

With the latest version of Horizon View, you can manage all 10,000 users with a single vCenter Server. However, that is probably not the best way of doing it, as you have no failover should your vCenter Server fail. The configuration recommendations for vCenter Server are detailed in the following table:

Hardware Config	2,000 Users	10,000 Users
Processor	2 - 8 vCPUs	16 vCPUs
Memory	10 - 24GB	48 GB
Hard disk space requirements	40 GB	180 GB
Maximum provisioning operations	20	20
Maximum power operations	50	50

Operating System	Version	Edition
Windows Server 2008 R2 SP1	64-bit	Standard, Enterprise, Datacenter
Windows Server 2012 R2	64-bit	Standard, Enterprise
Windows Server 2016	64-bit	Standard, Enterprise

VMware Access Point

The VMware Access Point is a Linux-based appliance and not a Windows application. Therefore, it gets deployed via the vCenter Server. As an appliance, the configuration is fixed, and the recommendation is not to change it. You will need enough free resources to host it, as detailed in the following table:

Hardware Config	Required
Processor	2 vCPUs
Memory	4 GB
Hard disk space requirements	20 GB

In the next section, we will look at the configuration maximums for the Horizon View components.

Configuration maximums

Alongside the configuration maximums we listed earlier in this chapter for vSphere, you need to be aware of the specific configuration maximums for Horizon View. We have listed some of the more important ones to consider in the following table:

Description	Config Maximums
Maximum number of direct connections for a single connection server (PCoIP, Blast & RDS)	4,000
Maximum number of direct connections for seven connection servers (PCoIP, Blast & RDS)	20,000
Maximum Blast Secure Gateway connections for a single Connection Server	2,000 (default) / 4,000 (tested)
Maximum PCoIP Secure Gateway connections for a single Connection Server	2,000 (default) / 4,000 (tested)
Maximum number of desktops in a cloud pod	200,000
Maximum number of pods in a cloud pod architecture	25
Maximum number of sites in a cloud pod architecture	10
Maximum View Connection Servers in a cloud pod architecture	175
Maximum number of sessions per pod	10,000
Clusters per desktop pool	1
Hosts per cluster	32
Maximum monitors with PCoIP	4
Maximum monitors with 3D Rendering enabled	2
Maximum monitors with RDP 7	16
Maximum 4K monitors with	3

In the following sections, we'll look at the other supporting infrastructures that are required to host the virtual desktop machines, starting with the networking requirements.

Networking

Network optimization is important for giving the users a great experience, as this is how their virtual desktop machine is going to be delivered. You need to consider a couple of different factors when sizing the network.

First, you need to look back at your different use cases, paying close attention to where your end users will be connecting from, and whether they are connecting over a LAN, WAN, or the internet. Although there is nothing you can do from a network perspective for internet users, you can configure policies that limit some of the features and capabilities that could potentially consume more bandwidth.

On the subject of bandwidth, let's take a closer look at the things you need to think about.

When it comes to bandwidth, the question of how much bandwidth is required often pops up in conversation, and again the answer depends on what your end users are doing that, in turn, will determine how much they would consume. This is something that the assessment data will tell you, but VMware has published some guideline figures, which are shown in the following table:

		Typical Tasks	Average Bandwidth
User Types	Light user	Basic office productivity, no video or high-end graphics	50 - 150 Kbps
	Medium user	Office productivity optimized for Horizon View	250 Kbps - 1 Mbps
	Heavy user	Advanced office user with 3D graphics, Aero	400 Kbps - 2 Mbps
	Power user	High-end user running video and CAD applications	2 Mbps +

The figures in the previous table refer to the bandwidth requirements overall, but depending on the bandwidth that's available, this will also dictate the audio bandwidth and ultimately the audio quality. This is outlined in the following table:

		Available Network Bandwidth	Audio Usage
Audio Type	CD quality audio	Up to 8 Mbps	1,500 Kbps
	Stereo audio	Between 2 and 8 Mbps	400 Kbps
	Mono audio	Between 700 Kbps and 2 Mbps	90 Kbps
	Compressed mono audio	Between 125 Kbps and 700 Kbps	60 Kbps

Note that if you can't provide at least the minimum bandwidth requirements for audio, it will be disabled for that session.

You can, however, make configuration changes to enhance the end user's experience. The PCoIP protocol is completely configurable via the use of a Windows group policy so that you can tune the user experience accordingly. We will cover more on how to tune and optimize the virtual desktop machines in `Chapter 10`, *Fine-Tuning the End User Experience*.

There are two other considerations when looking at networking for your View. The first is the latency of the connection.

We previously discussed bandwidth and what is required for the different use cases, but latency can also have a big impact on the end user experience. Typically, the maximum tolerance is anything between 250 milliseconds and 300 milliseconds for acceptable performance. Anything above this may well work, but could result in a degraded user experience, but this would depend on the use case. For example, a basic office worker may work fine when compared with a heavy user. Again, this is information you would determine from your pilot with the end users.

The second is load balancing between Connection Servers, which we will discuss in the next section.

Load balancing

Another requirement for Horizon View is the need to use load balancers between View Connection Servers, both for internal and external connections. This not only allows you to scale your solution but also offers high availability, should there be a failure.

It should be noted that there is no load balancer functionality included within Horizon View. As such, you will require third-party load balancers. It is possible to make use of Microsoft **Network Load Balancing (NLB)** on small scale and POC deployments, but as your solution starts moving on from POC to the pilot stage, you should consider the need for dedicated physical or virtual load balancers.

When selecting a load balancer, you need to ensure that it is able to offer session persistence. This ensures that the connected user is already directed to the same View Connection Server or View Security Server during their session. You should also ensure that the load balancing solution that is implemented is highly available. The following diagram shows how a typical load balancing solution for Horizon View could be configured:

Chapter 3

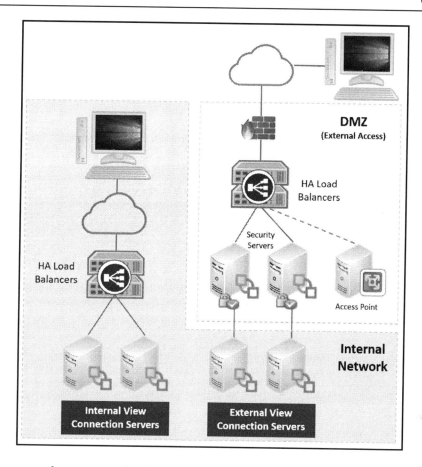

As you can see, there are multiple VMware Horizon Connection Servers being configured for internal and external connections. The internal Connection Servers are load balanced behind an HA pair of load balancers. Externally, there are also two View Connection Servers, each paired with a dedicated View Security Server. The View Security Servers are then load balanced using a dedicated HA pair of load balancers. There's also the optional Access Point that you could deploy in place of the View Security Servers.

Remote Desktop Session Host (RDSH) design considerations

Since Horizon View 6, VMware has supported Microsoft RDS as a means of delivering hosted desktop sessions rather than full virtual desktop machines. Hosted desktops have full support for PCoIP, whereas previously, while session-based desktops had been supported, they were only supported using RDP as the delivery protocol.

Along with the support for RDS as a desktop source, you also use RDS servers to present published applications to your users. This is referred to as Horizon View Hosted Applications. We will cover hosted desktop sessions and hosted applications in `Chapter 11`, *Delivering Published Apps with Horizon 7*, and `Chapter 18`, *Delivering Published Desktops with Horizon 7*. In those chapters, we will look at installing and configuring these features, but for now, let's concentrate on the design considerations for RDS-based environments.

Horizon View uses the concept of farms to place hosts that provide a common set of applications or desktops for users. When you are creating applications or desktop pools, you will point them at the specific farms that you have created. A farm might contain anywhere between 1 and 200 RDS hosts.

With Horizon View, the RDS servers are able to be either physical or virtual. An important point to consider when designing your RDS servers in a virtual environment is to ensure that you do not over commit virtual CPUs to the underlying physical CPUs. In the following diagram, we will try and illustrate why:

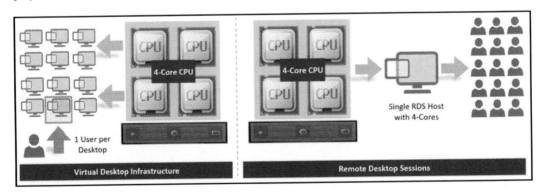

With VDI, you can achieve good levels of consolidation by over-allocating virtual CPUs to physical cores. With RDS, you can achieve good levels of consolidation by over-allocating users to physical or virtual cores. If you over-allocate virtual CPUs to physical CPUs, it will ultimately result in poor performance for your end users. As ever, you don't want to place memory over-allocation into the design as standard.

If you are utilizing RDS for published applications, you need to consider the design regarding application deployment. Will all of your applications be deployed on one server farm, or are there going to be separate server farms for different applications? You need to consider resources such as CPU, memory, and disk, which are required for each of your RDS servers, depending on their workload.

Consideration regarding how many PCoIP or Blast Extreme connections are required based on your application and desktop design should also be made. In the following diagram, you can see that the end user has a View virtual desktop and is also running an application from **Server Farm A** and another application from **Server Farm B**. In total, this user will be utilizing three connections—one for the View virtual desktop, one for the application from **Server Farm A**, and one for the application from **Server Farm B**. As a result, you will need to be sure that you understand the maximum connections for one View Connection Server and decide how you are going to scale the solution to meet your design needs:

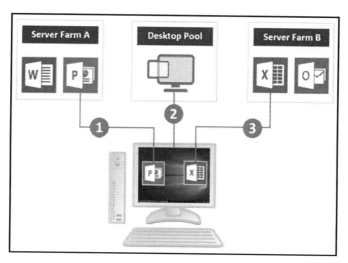

With RDS, the Connection Server supports a maximum of 150 sessions, based on a configuration of 4 vCPUs and 64 GB of memory.

Please note that you can also use Horizon Workspace ONE to deliver published applications to virtual or physical desktops. Your VDI or RDS desktops could be in a separate View environment to that of your hosted applications.

Supporting infrastructure design

Outside of the virtual infrastructure components—and by this we mean the VMware specific components—there are several other components or third-party tools and services that Horizon View is reliant on, which we will discuss in the coming sections.

Database requirements

Microsoft SQL Server or an Oracle database are key components for View Composer and the View Events database, as well as vCenter. Without the View Composer database being available, View is unable to undertake any provisioning or recompose operations. As such, you might wish to consider the availability of the database server and split the environment up as per the block architecture so that you can use multiple database servers at one per block. You should also ensure that you have regular and up-to-date backups of the View Composer database in case of loss or corruption.

 Horizon View supports several different Microsoft SQL and Oracle databases. The latest support matrix can be found at the following link: `https://bit.ly/2QyH362`.

File servers

File servers are often overlooked when it comes to creating a Horizon View environment, but often play a critical role in the overall functionality of the VDI environment.

For example, they will be storing things like ThinApp packages, user profiles, or application layers from App Volumes. First, size your file server for performance, ensure that your file server has enough RAM and CPU to meet user demands, particularly at peak times, and then continue to monitor utilization, and ensure that you add extra capacity as and when it is required.

It's not just about CPU and memory performance—the hard disk performance associated with your file server will also be critical.

With your applications and personas being saved on the file servers, we need to consider the effect of these resources being unavailable when the users are trying to use their desktops. In the case of the layered applications, App Volumes app layers may not attach or might fail midway through the user using an application if the file server goes offline. With the end user's persona stored on a file server, this could have a severe impact on the users accessing their data, or there may be unconsidered effects, such as the application data being unable to load or reduced performance of the desktop.

As such, the availability of file servers needs to be a serious consideration if you plan on using a shared storage device that supports CIFS shares. You could consider storing these files on this device; otherwise, a clustered file server or a DFS share should probably be considered to ensure availability. Of course, these decisions need to be taken alongside the business needs. If your View environment is going to be small initially, and your file server is stored on a virtual environment, the built-in HA functionality might be enough for your requirements.

IP addressing

Often overlooked in a VDI rollout are IP addressing, subnets, and DHCP requirements. Quite often, in a large company, you are going to use multiple subnets across the business as you separate areas with VLANs. When you slowly start scaling your deployment, it can sometimes be easy to forget that your subnets or DHCP scopes won't be large enough until it is too late, and you run out of IP addresses.

You should consider how you are going to configure your VDI desktops with IP schemes. By default, through the View Administrator, it is only possible to assign each pool with a single network tag. As such, when the desktops are rolled out, they will use the same network tag that the golden image is configured to use. However, it is possible to configure multiple network tags to pools via the View PowerCLI.

 Horizon 7 supports IPv6, but be aware that when you configure the Horizon View infrastructure components, such as the Connection Server, you must also use either IPv4 or IPv6 and not a mixed mode. Mixing IP versions across the Horizon View components is not supported.

Antivirus

Antivirus can often be the nemesis of a good VDI design. If the antivirus solution is not configured in a way that is understanding of the shared nature of the VDI solution, it can often be the cause of large performance issues across the environment.

The first consideration with any optimized desktop solution is to ensure that you optimize your antivirus solution to be considerate to the use cases of the users and the applications that they are using. With a VDI solution, you often want to deliver just the right amount of resources to ensure that it meets the users' needs while not over-delivering resources that can have a knock-on effect on the overall cost of the solution. We have personally seen in VDI environments with misconfigured antivirus that double the CPU, RAM, and disk resources are required. Clearly, this could have a massive effect on the cost of the overall solution and, ultimately, your ability to deliver the project on a budget.

Secondly, full desktop scans need to be considered. You need to consider whether full scans are required at all on the desktops if they are being refreshed daily. If full AV scans are a defined requirement, ensure that they are run out of hours and staggered across the desktops. Simultaneously starting scans across all the desktops will affect the RAM, CPU, and the IOPS being consumed, and potentially cause knock-on effects across the environment.

Active Directory Group Policy

As ever, group policy can have a major effect on your desktops, irrespective of whether they are physical or virtual. When designing any EUC solution, there are three main areas you should consider when designing your group policies, namely functionality, lockdown, and performance.

Functionality

Group policy can be your best friend, particularly when implementing non-persistent desktops. Correctly configured, you should be looking to use group policy to configure first-use settings for your desktops and Microsoft applications, alongside the obvious login scripts and mapped drives.

Lockdown

Using group policy to lock down virtual desktops can offer an advantage in a VDI environment, particularly for non-persistent desktops where you don't want users saving documents in areas that won't be redirected, or customizations that probably won't be saved, but there can be downsides. Our advice would be, in a new VDI environment, try not to use the implementation of your new VDI infrastructure as an opportunity to introduce new strict lockdowns while implementing VDI itself. Often, when these kinds of stringent lockdowns are implemented at the same time as VDI, the VDI solution will be blamed for any disruptions or reduction in user experience that's caused by the new lockdowns.

If a new stringent lockdown policy is required, either try to implement it on the physical desktops prior to the migration to VDI or implement the VDI solution first, before introducing the new lockdowns.

You will also find that it can be difficult to troubleshoot where a problem may reside by introducing too many changes at once, particularly when it comes to what users can and can't access. It may be one policy too far.

Performance and management

We aren't going to use this book to write about the A to Z of group policy configuration for optimal performance. There are already several resources on the internet and multiple topics on this subject. However, we recommend that you keep on top of your group policies, ensuring that old unnecessary policies are removed wherever possible. Use a functional design, where you group together GPOs into functional groups but don't take them to the nth degree by creating a GPO per setting. This will ensure ease of management and will reduce performance effects when changes are made.

Key Management Server (KMS)

To ensure seamless license activation between recompose operations of Windows and Office, a Microsoft KMS is imperative to your VDI design. Your desktop will find the KMS via DNS or via manual assignment, which you can preconfigure into the base image and will then be assigned the relevant keys to gain activation.

If you wish to activate Microsoft Office products using the KMS server, you also need to install the Microsoft Office 2013 Volume License Pack on your KMS server. This can be downloaded from the Microsoft Download Center.

Design and Deployment Considerations

Microsoft KMS is quickly and easily configured as a role within Windows Server and earlier versions of Windows. As part of the configuration, you will need your KMS license key from Microsoft. This key will be used during configuration, and your KMS will need to be activated by Microsoft over the web or via the phone. Once the role has been configured, you are ready to start rolling out and activating your desktops with KMS. However, you should be aware that there is a threshold for activations prior to KMS going live of 25 client machines. If you want to give this a try, ensure that your first pool is larger than 25 machines. Once the threshold has been reached, you will be able to activate single machines one at a time, if required.

Printing

Printing is often a tricky subject, and working with any VDI or RDS can often be even more complicated. Included with Horizon View is the ThinPrint technology that allows several configurations when it comes to printing from your desktop pools. We covered ThinPrint in some detail in `Chapter 2`, *Understanding Horizon 7 Architecture and Components*.

However, often, the simplest solution across the board is to implement a follow-me printing solution. With a solution such as PaperCut, users print to a virtual follow-me printer. They are then able to release the document to the printer from a localized **Release Station** or compatible printer, which can be explained by the following diagram:

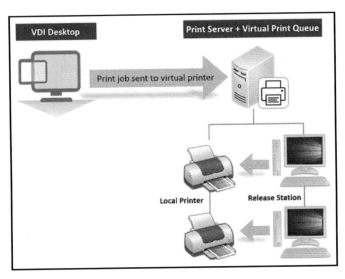

Thin clients and other endpoint devices

We will discuss thin clients and how end users will connect to their VDI desktop in `Chapter 12`, *Horizon Client Options*.

Desktop design considerations

You might think that once you have spent your time considering and designing all of the elements we mentioned earlier that the hard work is over. Realistically, it has only just begun. Your VDI solution, without the desktops, is just a virtual infrastructure, and the design and functionality of the desktops are critical to a successful implementation. There are a great number of choices we need to make around the design for the desktops within Horizon View. This will be affected by the way the users need to use the desktops and is likely to have a knock-on effect on the way you are going to manage the desktops and the resources the desktops require.

Pool design

You will want to design your desktop pools based on the similarities between the desktops, which will ultimately allow you to group desktops together. You should use information that's been collected by the desktop assessment and other sources to start designing how your desktop pools are going to look. While analyzing this data, you are going to look for similarities between the applications and use cases, and make decisions based on information regarding how you will design these pools. To make management and maintenance easier, you should create the smallest number of pools possible, but you also won't want to take this to the nth degree and have thousands of desktops in a pool, as trying to recompose ridiculously large pools with large numbers of virtual desktop machines could be difficult and will likely affect performance. As you can see, it is going to be a very careful balancing act to get the pool design correct.

Sizing the virtual desktop machines

The following table gives a list of some of the recommendations for base desktop sizing, which have been collected from several different VMware documents. Obviously, the resources that are required for the desktops will be greatly affected by the applications being used within the desktops as well:

		Recommended Initial RAM Size	Initial CPU
Operating System	Windows XP 32-Bit	1 GB	1 vCPU
	Windows 7 32-bit	1 GB	1 vCPU
	Windows 7 64-bit	2 GB	2 vCPUs
	Windows 8	2 GB	2 vCPUs
	Windows 10	2 GB	2 vCPUs

In this chapter, we have already covered some of the high-level host server considerations, but now that you have an idea of what desktop resources you need to deploy, you can go to the next level of detail and look at the clock speeds of the CPUs and determine how many hosts you will need, along with the RAM requirements.

Sizing the host server's CPU requirements to run virtual desktops

One of the most frequently asked questions when sizing the servers that are hosting the virtual desktop machines is, how many can I fit on each host server, or how many virtual desktops per core? Well, the answer is, it depends!

First, it depends on the CPU resources that your desktops are going to consume, and the answer to that question will only come from your assessment data.

Second, and more obviously, it will depend on the CPU you configure in the host servers. This is usually chosen on price/performance, as there is usually a CPU that makes more financial sense and the best cost-per-desktop model.

For this section, as we don't have any actual assessment data to work from, we will use some assumptions on the types of users and CPU requirements for each type of user, just to give you an example to work with. The users are then grouped into light usage, medium usage, and heavy usage. We will base our calculations on an industry-standard, rack-mounted server that's been configured with two Intel Xeon E5-2660 v3 CPUs that run at 2.6 GHz and have 10 cores per CPU, giving us a total of 20 cores per host server.

In the example calculations, you will also notice that we have subtracted two of the cores from the total available cores on the host server. The reason for this is that the hypervisor layer (ESXi) also needs CPU resources to run.

The following sections classify a typical user profile and then give an indication of the per-core ratio and how it was calculated.

Light user

Typical utilization is around 300 MHz of CPU resource. It's also worth adding some additional resources to cover any peaks in workload and other tasks such as sounds and USB devices. For this example, we will add 10 percent to the 300 MHz.

The profile of this user type would be somebody working in a call center, an administrator, or the basic web-browser-type user. These desktops might be suspended for long periods of time and have very low utilization, running just one or two light applications. We can work out the CPU requirements with the following quick calculation:

> (CPU Speed in MHz x (Number of Cores − 2) ÷ CPU requirements of each virtual desktop
>
> (2600 MHz x 18 Cores) ÷ 330 MHz = 141.81 (141 desktops)

In this user scenario, using the standard sever we described previously, you could host approximately 141 virtual desktop machines, which gives you approximately 17 users per core.

Medium user

Typical utilization is around 500 MHz of CPU resource, plus 10 percent. This type of user would be someone like a data entry personnel, doctors, students, Microsoft Office users, or a help desk operator. These desktops will mainly be used during business/office hours and not heavily utilized. We can work out the CPU requirements with the following quick calculation:

> (CPU Speed in MHz x (Number of Cores – 2) ÷ CPU requirements of each virtual desktop
>
> (2600 MHz x 18 Cores) ÷ 550 MHz = 85.09 (85 desktops)

In this user scenario, using the standard sever we described previously, you can host approximately 85 virtual desktop machines, giving you five users per core.

Heavy user

Typical utilization is around 750 MHz of CPU resource, plus 10 percent. This type of user would be something like a developer, system administrator, IT worker, database administrator, or engineer. These desktops will more than likely be heavily utilized throughout the day and after normal business hours. They may also be running more graphically intensive or Java-based applications that increase the utilization of the desktop. We can work out the CPU requirements with the following quick calculation:

> (CPU Speed in MHz x (Number of Cores – 2) ÷ CPU requirements of each virtual desktop
>
> (2600 MHz x 18 Cores) ÷ 825 MHz = 56.72 (56 desktops)

In this user scenario, using the standard server we described previously, you can host approximately 65 virtual desktop machines, giving you three users per core.

What we have highlighted in the previous user scenarios is based on assumptions and example use cases. This is where your assessment data becomes critical, as it will tell you the actual resource requirement figures for your own environment.

Sizing the host server's memory requirements to run virtual desktops

Sizing the memory for the servers hosting the virtual desktop machine is somewhat easier than the CPU, although you might need to play a balancing act with the chosen server. The reason for this is that, just because it can accommodate the number of desktops from a CPU perspective, it might not have the memory capacity to serve that number.

If you take a virtual desktop that requires 2 GB of memory and look at the light user scenario from the previous section as an example, you would be hosting 141 virtual desktop machines. That means that the host server will need 282 GB of memory just to host the virtual desktop machine, plus enough memory to run the hypervisor too.

Depending on your choice of server hardware, you might not be able to configure this amount of memory or it might be too expensive, in which case you might end up deploying more, but lower-configuration servers.

Don't forget that when sizing and configuring memory for the virtual desktop machines, never over-commit the memory and set the memory reservation to 100 percent. This stops the swap file from being created, saves storage capacity, and helps performance.

Linked Clone, Instant Clone, or Full Clone

As we have already discussed in `Chapter 2`, *Understanding Horizon 7 Architecture and Components*, there are three ways to build virtual desktops from golden images: Linked Clones, Instant Clones, or Full Clones. To recap briefly, Linked Clones are created by replicating a golden image into a thin provisioned replica VM. This VM will be the same size as the used space within the golden image; all reads come from this VM and, no matter how many desktops we have within the pool within limits, each desktop will have a delta disk for writes that will continue to grow until the Linked Clone is recomposed, refreshed, or deleted. With a Full Clone, it does exactly what it says on the tin and will represent a copy of the golden image itself and consume the same amount of space. Finally, Instant Clones essentially take a snapshot of the memory of a running virtual desktop machine.

As such, to save space on our storage device where possible, Linked Clones or Instant Clones are the best options. However, there are a few important use cases where using clones will simply not make sense, such as desktops where regular refresh or recompose is not possible.

As you can see, while clones are possibly the most attractive from the outside and should be able to be widely used, they are not always going to be possible or the right design choice. When your design utilizes full clone desktops, you should be considering your storage design carefully so that it is in-line with this design choice. There are many storage manufacturers that offer re-duplication, compression, and single instance storage that allows you to minimize the storage impact of this type of desktop.

Persistent versus non-persistent

Along with deciding whether you are going to use Linked Clones or full clones, you will also need to decide whether you are going to use persistent or non-persistent desktops. With persistent desktops, the user is allocated a desktop, either manually or automatically, and will always be directed to that desktop when connecting to their desktop pool. With non-persistent desktops, the users will be directed to any desktop in the given pool. In a lot of designs, Linked Clone and Instant Clone desktops will be configured as non-persistent and Full Clone desktops will be configured as persistent, but this is not always the case and will come down to your own specific use case.

The recommendation would be, wherever possible, to utilize non-persistent desktops that are built on-demand using Linked Clones or Instant Clones. The user's profile would be delivered using View Persona Management/UEM or an AD group policy to configure the desktops. Applications would be delivered using App Volumes. This offers you the easiest way to maintain and refresh the desktops with minimal effect on the users. If your design does not allow this, consider your use case carefully; if you do have to configure persistent desktops due to some value of data or a configuration held within the desktop, consider whether a Full Clone persistent desktop managed by Horizon Mirage for protection and maintenance might be a better approach.

Building a composite desktop

The key to a flexible desktop design is being able to build and customize the desktops in layers. In this context, layers are delivering the individual component parts of the desktop, such as the OS, persona, and applications.

By achieving this, the desktops can not only be more flexible to allow one base image to be used for many more users or pools, but also allow you to configure more Linked Clone or Instant Clone desktop pools. The following screenshot depicts a user's desktop and where all the key elements are being controlled and managed:

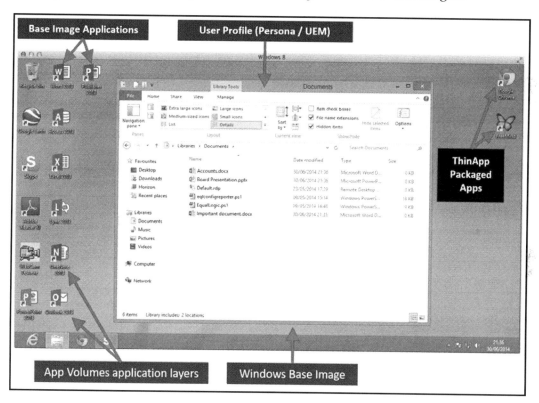

Desktop showing key components

Base layer

Your base layer will consist of an optimized operating system that's been configured to the needs of your business. Agents such as the View agent and AV will be installed into the base image, along with any applications. You will need to decide as to what applications should be installed into the base image and which ones are going to be delivered by other means. Often, the applications that will get installed into the base image will be applications that are used across the organization or a complete pool, such as the Microsoft Office suite. You will also want to consider the nature of the application; if the application is unable to be virtualized with ThinApp since it contains drivers, or integrate with the shell, these applications will also need to be installed in your base image.

You need to get the base image correct, especially if you are using Linked Clones or Instant Clones, otherwise you could end up creating hundreds of desktops very quickly that are configured incorrectly.

Applications

You need to have also built an application delivery strategy. This will detail how each application is going to be delivered to the end user. Some applications will be delivered as part of the base operating system, whereas others may be packaged using ThinApp, or layered in using App Volumes.

There is also the option of Workspace ONE, which would deliver a web-based portal containing additional application delivery methods such as Citrix XenApp or SaaS-based applications.

User profiles and user environment management

Finally, let's look at delivering the Persona, or a user's profile on top of the desktop. Think of the Persona as everything that makes the desktop personal; for example, application settings, the contents of my documents, and icons on the desktop. There are a number of ways to achieve this, including redirected profiles, group policy, View Persona Management, VMware UEM, and other third-party products, such as Liquidware Labs ProfileUnity. Wherever possible, keeping the solution as simple as possible and not having to combine third-party products is often the easiest way to reduce management overheads. However, depending on the levels of customization needed, you might need to introduce third-party solutions to achieve this level of customization.

With View Persona Management, the users' profiles are redirected by a set of group policies to a dedicated file server. When a user logs into their VDI desktop, elements of the profile are downloaded from the file server to the VDI desktop as they are required. As such, once a file has been called from the profile, it is cached on the local VDI desktop for future use. Any changes to the profile are stored locally on the VDI desktop but periodically uploaded back to the file server.

Disaster recovery and backup

As with any solution, fully understanding the backup and disaster recovery options is highly important. With Horizon View, there are multiple areas where you should understand the backup and recovery options, as well as the options that are available to you if a DR event should occur.

Backup and recovery options

There are several elements that you need to ensure are backed up when it comes to a Horizon View solution, which are as follows:

- View Connection Servers
- View Security Servers
- Microsoft Lightweight Directory Service
- View Composer Database
- vCenter Database
- vCenter Server(s)
- File servers containing ThinApp, View Persona Data, UEM, and App Stacks
- Golden images
- Full Clone and persistent desktop images

As you can see, there are several areas that you need to ensure are protected on a daily basis, if not more often.

Through the Horizon View Administrator, you can configure the scheduled backup of the LDAP repository and the View Composer Database. These will be backed up to the following location on your View Connection Servers:

`C:\Program data\VMWare\VDM\backups`

You should ensure that these backup files are regularly backed up to an external backup solution. We will investigate the configuration and restoration of the View LDAP repository and View Composer Database in `Chapter 4`, *Installing and Configuring Horizon 7 - Part 1*.

It is highly recommended that all server components are protected by some form of backup software solution, such as Veeam Backup and Replication, or VMware Data Protection. As we mentioned previously, you could consider protecting and maintaining your full clones using Horizon Mirage.

Disaster recovery options

Due to the integration of Horizon View with View Composer and vCenter Server, it is not recommended or supported to replicate View environments from production to a DR site. Likewise, Horizon View is not supported for use with VMware SRM. You need to ensure that you design a DR strategy for your Horizon View environment in a different manner. There are several ways you could consider offering DR for View, but let's just cover one of those for now.

First, we need to think of the components that are important to our View environment. Typically, these are things such as the following:

- User profiles
- ThinApp applications or app layers
- Golden images
- Full Clone desktops

If you have these components available at DR, then you can start recovering your View environment at the DR site with relative ease. The DR site will be configured with a dedicated View environment, preconfigured with all the required components such as vCenter Server, View Connection Servers, and View Security Servers. You then need to understand what you need to do to roll out the VDI solution that's been customized for your business needs during a DR event.

As the users' personas, ThinApp applications, and App Volumes AppStacks are all located on a file server, you can consider using technology such as Microsoft's **Distributed FileSystem Replication (DFSR)** or similar technology. This allows you to have a copy of this data at both the production and disaster recovery sites.

Once you have your ThinApp packages, AppStacks, and Persona at the DR site, you need to understand how you are going to deliver the desktops. Since the desktops will be rolled out from the golden images, you should consider replicating the golden image from production to DR by utilizing replication that's been integrated into the storage device. You could even do something as primitive as exporting the golden image as an **Open Virtualization Format (OVF)** and moving it to the DR site. You are then able to recompose the desktop pools from this golden image at the DR site.

When it comes to full clone desktops, as these are just standard VMs, you could simply consider replicating these directly from the SAN and utilizing SRM to mount them online at the DR site, ready to be added back into Horizon View.

Finally, you should think about how users are going to connect to your DR site in the event of a failure. This could be something as simple as getting the users to connect their client device to a different address, or you could make use of global load balancing technology to redirect the regular URL to the DR site.

As you can see, there isn't a simple solution to building a DR site for your Horizon View solution, but if you break it down to its component level, you can easily configure a solution that will work to deliver the desktops and relevant files for our users, should the need arise. You could also consider utilizing the Cloud Pod Architecture to help enable the cross-site management of users between production and DR, and deploy a global namespace and allow View to direct the user to the appropriate desktop resource.

VMware is also able to deliver desktops as a service as part of their Horizon Air Cloud-Hosted Desktops and Apps service. You could consider utilizing this technology in some way to offer DR for your on-premises Horizon View environment.

Example solution scenario

To finish up this chapter, we wanted to give you an example of a real-life scenario so that you have the opportunity to put all the elements that we've covered in this chapter into action and see how they would all fit together. You will see that we have put together a mock scenario. Read through it and make some notes about the elements that you would be configuring and how you would design the architecture for a production environment.

We are going to build an example design based on a fictitious company called PVO Engineering Inc. and their requirements for deploying a VDI solution. This is shown in the following topology diagram of their current network environment and locations:

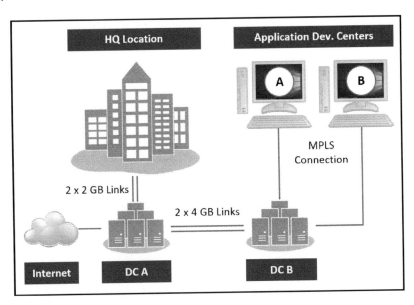

The company has three office locations: an HQ office and two remote sites for the app development teams. To serve these, they have two data centers that are running active/active. Data center A supports the mobile and HQ workers, while data center B supports the app development teams. Each data center can support the entire environment in the event of a data center failure.

End user requirements

In this example, we have conducted an assessment to gather information on the current user install base of 5,750 users, and we have built up a picture of the types of users and their requirements, along with their location. This is detailed in the following table:

User Type	No. of Users	Location	Specific Requirements
Application Developers	125	App Dev Site A	Local admin rights to install software
	125	App Dev Site B	
Office Workers	2,000	HQ	Standard Office applications
	1,500	HQ	Standard Office + Visio + Project
Contractors	250	HQ	BYOD + Local admin rights
Engineering	150	HQ	Require CAD with high-end graphics
	100	HQ	Require 3D and video
Sales	1,500	Remote/Internet	Secure remote access

We now have information on the different types of user and their requirements, and can now start to consider how we are going to deliver the requirements to the end users.

Application developers

In the example scenario, there are two remote development sites, but from the network topology, you can see that they are WAN-based and connect to data center B. They will only use their desktops from within the office and therefore do not require external access.

They do, however, need the ability to install software on their desktops. To deliver this, in this example scenario, we configured a dedicated pool with persistent desktops. The other option would be to configure floating, non-persistent desktops and use App Volumes to deliver Writable Volumes for the users to install their applications onto.

Whichever option you choose, the virtual desktops themselves need to be of a high specification in terms of memory.

Office workers

These end users are your basic task workers and require a basic desktop configuration (2 CPUs and 2 GB memory). They are also perfect candidates for non-persistent virtual desktops. The core Office applications would be installed as part of the base image, with any of the additional applications being delivered via published applications or app layering using App Volumes AppStacks.

Contractors

With contractors, it might be difficult to understand what they are coming into the business to work on, and so since one size doesn't fit all, it's probably best to err on the side of caution when it comes to the configuration. Therefore, we will size for the most intensive role they could perform. In the example scenario, this would be the application development role. That being the case, they will have the same configuration as the internal applications developers; however, they will need external access.

Engineering

There are two teams in the engineering department. Team one are heavy CAD users and design products, and team two create the engineering training material. Team one, therefore, requires a high-end graphics solution to run the CAD software, whereas team two doesn't need quite as many graphics resources; however, they still need substantially more than a standard user would need. The solution for engineering would include NVIDIA accelerated graphics technology, which requires dedicated desktops.

Sales

The sales department follows a similar work pattern to the standard office workers and therefore would use a floating, non-persistent desktop pool. The key difference is that the sales teams would need external access from the internet.

Now that we have the user requirements, we can start to look at creating a pool design based on delivering these use cases.

Desktop pool design

The pool design reflects the use cases, and any similar desktops will be included in a single pool. Based on the information we've gathered, we can start building the pool design, based on the information in the following table:

Desktop Pool	DC	Pod	No. Desktops	Pool Description
Application Developers	B	2	250	Dedicated global pool
Office Workers & Sales	A	1	5,000	Floating pool
Engineering - CAD	A	1	150	Dedicated pool with GPU
Engineering - Video	A	1	100	Dedicated pool with 3D
Contractors	A	1	250	Dedicated pool

All the office workers in the design are part of the same desktop pool, along with sales, even though they have different application requirements. We will look at delivering these applications outside of the core virtual desktop machine image using either ThinApp, the Horizon published apps, or App Volumes.

Using the pod and block architecture, we are going to deploy two View pods, one in data center A and the other in data center B. The reason for this is that it makes more sense from a network perspective to have these desktops nearer to the users; however, we will take advantage of the Cloud Pod Architecture since the developers travel between sites, and will configure a global pool for these users. Although in this example we have decided to configure a dedicated pool for the developers, we could deploy floating desktops and use App Volumes to deliver the ability for the developers to install their own software using the Writeable Volumes feature.

Now that we have an idea of the pools, we can start to shape the pod's design and size the management blocks and the desktop hosting blocks. Let's start with the desktop blocks.

Sizing the desktop blocks

In data center A with pod 1, we have 5,500 virtual desktop machines. As there are 2,000 virtual desktop machines supported per block, we would need to configure three blocks with approximately 1,800 virtual desktop machines per block.

In data center B, we have 250 virtual desktop machines, so we only need one block. The next question is, how many servers do we need to host the virtual desktop machines? For this example, we will use the users-per-core figures we previously discussed in this chapter to cover light users for the office and sales workers, and very heavy users for the developers and engineering users. This means that, for office users, we can configure 98 virtual desktop machines per host and, for the very heavy users, we can configure 50 virtual desktop machines per host.

We also need to remember that we have some distinct differences in the host server requirements, as the engineering users require access to hardware-based GPU. This would result in deploying a cluster for each. The number of hosts required for pod 1 could look something like what's shown in the following screenshot. Note that the users per core ratios in these examples are based on servers with two 3-GHz, 10-core CPUs, and user profiles of 300 MHz for light users and 1.1 GHz for power users:

Pod #1	No. of Users	Desktops per Server	No. Server Hosts	Cluster
Office & Sales	5,000	98	52 + 1 for DR	A
Contractors	250	50	5 + 1 for DR	A
GPU based CAD (K180Q)	150	8	19	B
GPU based Video (K140Q)	100	16	7	B
App Developers	250	50	5 + 1 for DR	A
TOTAL			86	

For the GPU-based virtual desktop machines, two configuration options have been used, both using NVIDIA GRID K1 graphics cards and vGPU. The CAD users will use a K180Q profile, and the video users will use a K140Q profile.

There is no DR option for the GRID-enabled servers due to the high cost of the hardware. In the event of a failure, users can continue to work, but with lower graphics capabilities.

Pod 2 in data center B contains just the virtual desktop machines for the application development users and would look something like the following:

Pod #2	No. of Users	Desktops per Server	No. Server Hosts
App Developers	250	50	5 + 1 for DR
TOTAL			6

With pod 1, we have exceeded the number of hosts we can support in a cluster, the limit being 32. Therefore, we would deploy two clusters per desktop block with the number of host servers divided across the clusters, while a separate cluster will support the graphics enabled users.

Design and Deployment Considerations

The design is now starting to look like the following diagram:

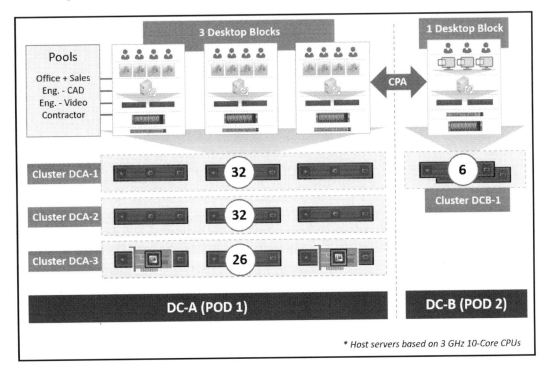

Sizing the storage requirements

Using the calculations we detailed previously, you can work out the IOPS requirements you need to deliver. In this example scenario, we will base the calculation on a requirement of 30 IOPS per virtual desktop machine, a 30/70 read/write ratio, a RAID 5 array, and a 10 GB disk capacity. Given those variables, we can work out what the storage requirements are, as shown in the following table:

Storage	No. of Users	IOPS Required	Capacity
Pod #1	5,000	412,500	55 TB
Pod #2	250	18,750	2.5 TB

These storage requirements are for hosting the desktops only. If you are using components such as App Volumes, or ThinApp for delivering applications, you will need to think about the capacity and performance requirements to support those environments.

Sizing the management blocks

Once we have configured the desktop blocks and know the pool configuration, we can look at sizing the management blocks to provide the supporting infrastructure. This infrastructure component configuration will look something like what's shown in the following table:

Component	Pod #1	Pod #2
Connection Servers	6 (2 per block)	6 (2 per block)
Security Servers	2 (external access)	0 (no external access)
View Composer Servers	3 (1 per block)	1 (1 per block)
vCenter Servers	3 (1 per block)	1 (1 per block)

The final element to look at is the network. You need to assess whether the current network configuration will support the users. If not, then you may need to look at some form of a network upgrade.

Network sizing and requirements

Now that we have our pool design, management and desktop blocks, and the storage requirements, we can look at the network requirements, as shown in the following table:

User Type	Pod Number	No. Desktops	Bandwidth per Desktop	Total Bandwidth
Office Workers & Sales	Pod #1	5,250	150 Kbps	787.5 Mbps
GPU Based Users	Pod #1	250	500 Kbps	125 Mbps
App Developers	Pod #2	250	500 Kbps	125 Mbps

Summary

In this chapter, we have covered some of the essential tasks in designing and building out our Horizon View infrastructure.

We started at a high level, discussing the approach to a VDI project and the different phases to work through to plan and test an environment. The most important of these phases is the assessment phase.

Once we worked through these, we looked at the pod and block reference architecture, before examining the sizing of the key Horizon View components, such as the View Connection Server, View Security Server, and View Composer.

Following on from the management architecture, we looked at some of the considerations for sizing and configuring the virtual desktop machines and the user assignments, before putting all of this together in a high-level example design.

You should now have a methodology for approaching a project, coupled with the knowledge to be able to start sizing an environment that's specific to your end user's requirements.

In the next chapter, we will discuss how to install all of the components that make up the Horizon View solution. We will take a deep dive into installation and follow this process using step-by-step screenshots. By the end of this chapter, we will have a fully functional View infrastructure up and running.

4
Installing and Configuring Horizon 7 - Part 1

In the previous chapters, we discussed how things work and what role they play within Horizon View. Those were the theory chapters, if you like. But now, it's time to turn to the practical side of this book, instill what we have learned so far, and install Horizon View.

In this chapter, we will cover the installation process for the core Horizon View Connection Server.

Once the installation is complete, we will then move on to configuration tasks, so that the Horizon View environment is up and running, ready to deliver to end users. To help with the installation, we are going to use an example lab, which will guide you through the whole process step by step, using real-life screenshots. With that in mind, let's get started and introduce you to the example lab environment.

In this chapter, we will cover the following topics:

- Preparing AD
- Installing the Horizon View Composer Server
- Installing the Horizon View Connection Server
- Configuring the Horizon View Connection Server

Welcome to the lab environment

In the practical parts of this book, you can follow the tasks and steps that are described using the example lab environment. If you prefer, you can use these guides to set up your own environment, whether that's for a proof of concept, a pilot, or a production deployment.

What you need for the example lab

The example lab will be used across the entire book, and so this section will get you started with the infrastructure ready so you can build your own lab as you work through the chapters. If you are not planning on installing some of the features, such as JMP, then there is no need to install the required infrastructure to support this.

We are going to start with the management block infrastructure. The example lab management block consists of the following infrastructure components (although, feel free to use different versions of the infrastructure components):

- 2 x ESXi host servers running vSphere 6.7
- 14 x Windows Server 2012 R2 Enterprise Edition virtual machines for the following roles, which we will configure in this chapter:
    - **Domain controller** (hostname: `dc.pvolab.com`)
    - **Connection Server** (hostname: `hzn7-cs1.pvolab.com`)
    - **Security Server** (hostname: `hzn7-ss1.pvolab.com`)
    - **Replica Server** (hostname: `hzn7-cs2.pvolab.com`)
    - **Connection Server for second site CPA** (`hzn7-cs1b`)
    - **View Composer** (hostname: `hzn7-cmp.pvolab.com`)
    - **Enrolment Server** (hostname: `hzn7-enroll.pvolab.com`)
    - **Certificate of authority server** (`hzn7-certs.pvolab.com`)
    - **RDSH Server for hosting desktop sessions** (`rdsh-desktops.pvolab.com`)
    - **RDSH Server for hosting applications** (`rdsh-apps.pvolab.com`)
    - **JMP Server** (`hzn7-jmp.pvolab.com`)
    - **SQL Express 2012 instance with 3 x databases** (one for View Composer, one for the events database installed on the Composer Server, and one for the JMP server)
    - **2 x vCenter Servers** (one for the management block (`vcs1.pvolab.com`), and one for the desktop block (`vcs2.pvolab.com`))

All machines should be domain-joined, except for the Security Server. The lab should look something like the following diagram:

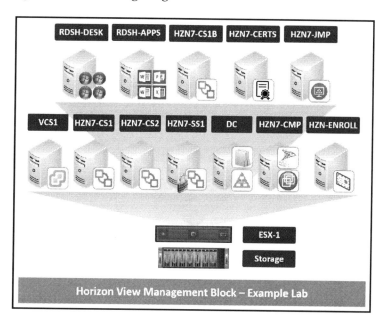

Before we get started and install anything, there are a few prerequisites that need to be in place, regardless of whether you are following the example lab or not. For this example, we will assume that you already have the virtual infrastructure components, such as the ESXi host servers, the vCenter Servers, **Active Directory** (**AD**)/domain controller, and SQL Server, in place and have created the virtual servers, ready to have their Horizon View roles installed on them.

It's probably also worth building the infrastructure for the desktop block and having the ESXi host server and vCenter Server already built.

There's no need to build virtual desktops yet, as we will cover that in `Chapter 7`, *Building and Optimizing the Virtual Desktop OS*.

The following diagram shows the desktop block configuration for the example lab:

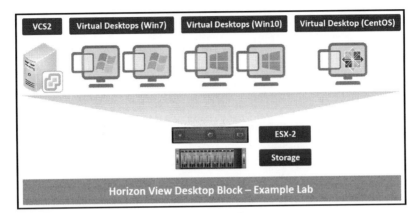

One final thing is to download the Horizon 7 software. For the example lab, all the software components and installation files were saved on a shared folder on the domain controller. You can download Horizon 7 (version 7.8) by clicking on the following link:

```
https://my.vmware.com/web/vmware/info/slug/desktop_end_user_computing/
vmware_horizon/7_8
```

With the lab infrastructure now in place, you can start the installation and configuration.

Preparing AD

Horizon View requires AD for the authentication of users and desktops, as well as to make use of group policy to control and tune many aspects of your end users' desktops. This will be covered in later chapters.

As a reminder, Horizon View is compatible with the following AD functional domain levels:

- Windows 2008 and Windows 2008 R2
- Windows 2012 and Windows 2012 R2

When deploying your View Connection Servers, they either need to be in the same domain as the desktops that you are going to deploy, or in a domain with a two-way transitive trust of the domain where your desktops will be located.

AD user accounts

We recommend that you also take this opportunity to create several user accounts, which will be needed across your installation.

These accounts will include service accounts for your View Connection Server Services and Composer Services. You need an AD account for View to use to log in and manage components within your vCenter, and a user account for View Composer to manage the creation of computer accounts in AD.

vCenter user accounts

You will need an AD user account to allow View to connect to your vCenter Server. This account should also be added as a local admin on the vCenter Server, as we will be using View Composer to create linked clone desktops. Once you have created your user account within AD, you will need to give it user permission in your vCenter Server.

Installing and Configuring Horizon 7 - Part 1

The following table lists the permissions required by this user:

Required Group	Privilege Required (1)	Privilege Required (2)
Folder	Create Folder	
	Delete Folder	
Datastore	Allocate Space	
	Browse Datastore	
	Low Level File Operation	
Virtual Machine	Configuration	All
	Inventory	All
	Snapshot Management	All
	Interaction	Power Off
		Power On
		Reset
		Suspend
	Provisioning	Customize
		Deploy Template
		Read Customization Specifications
		Clone Virtual Machine
		Allow Disk Access
Resource	Assign Virtual Machine to Resource Pool	
	Migrate Powered off Virtual Machine	
Global	Act as vCenter Server	
	Enable Methods	
	Disable Methods	
	System Tag	
Host	Configuration	Advanced Settings
Network	All	

Let's now add the user to the vCenter Server, by first creating a new role specifically for the View vCenter user, as follows:

1. Log in to the vCenter Server using the VMware vSphere client. Once logged in, from the **Home** screen, click on **Administration** (1), as shown in the following screenshot:

Installing and Configuring Horizon 7 - Part 1

2. You will now see the **Roles** screen, as shown in the following screenshot:

3. Next, create a new role by clicking on **Roles** (2) and then the **+** symbol (3). You will now see the **New Role** screen, as shown in the following screenshot:

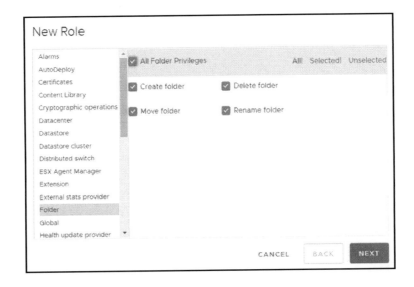

4. From the list of options on the left-hand side, select each category you want to configure, and then, in the right-hand section of the screen, select each individual privilege. These should match those described earlier so that you configure the correct roles and privileges for the Horizon View vCenter user account. Once you have completed adding privileges to the role, click the **NEXT** button to continue. You will now see the screen in which you can give the new role a name, as shown in the following screenshot:

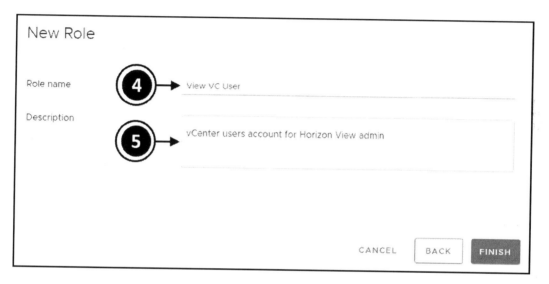

Next, we need to add permissions to the user account using the following steps:

1. From the VMware vSphere Client home screen, under the **Administration** section, click on the option for **Global Permissions** (6).

Installing and Configuring Horizon 7 - Part 1

2. Now click the **+** button (**7**), as shown in the following screenshot:

3. You will now see the **Add Permission** screen, as shown in the following screenshot:

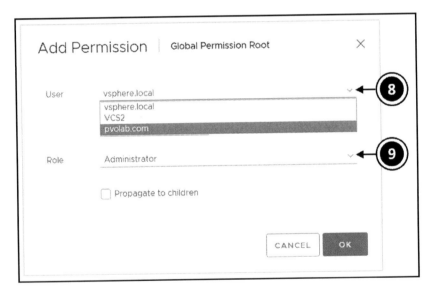

4. In the **User** section, click the drop-down arrow (**8**) and select the domain in which the user resides from the list. In the example lab, this is **pvolab.com**.

Chapter 4

5. Next, we are going to search for the user, `view-vc-user`, that we created in AD. Start to type the username into the box (**9**), next to the magnifying glass icon. This will automatically start the search. Once the username has been found, you can click on it to select it (**10**).

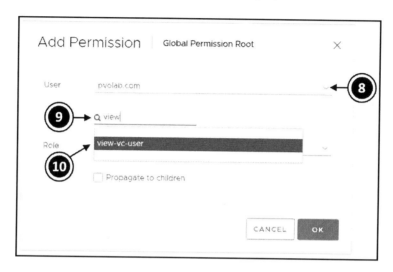

6. You then need to select the **Role** for the user, as shown in the following screenshot:

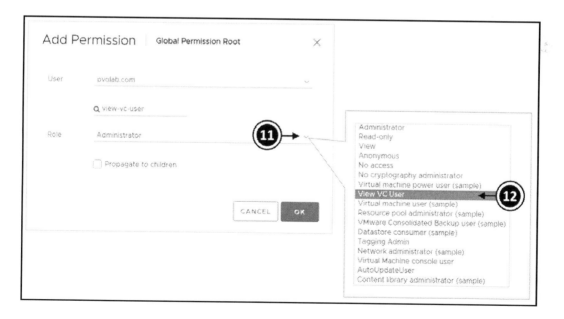

7. In the **Role** section, click the drop-down arrow **(11)**, and then, from the options list that is displayed, click on **View VC User (12)**.
8. Click **OK** to complete the configuration.

You have now successfully set up a user account for Horizon View and vCenter Server.

View Composer user account

You will also require an AD user for your View Composer account, as this account will be responsible for the addition and deletion of computer accounts for your clones that are linked to the domain. The following are the required AD permissions this user should have:

- List contents
- Read all properties
- Write all properties
- Read permissions
- Reset passwords
- Create computer objects
- Delete computer objects

The permissions for this account need to apply at the root domain level for the AD container and all child objects of the container. You will also need to ensure that you have advanced features selected when creating this user. This account will be used later to configure the View Administrator for the View Composer connection.

View desktop Organizational Units (OUs)

Although you will have OUs already in place to support your current desktop environment, now is the time that you should start considering what that looks like and whether it will work for your new virtual environment. You should think about having dedicated OUs that easily allow you to configure specific group policies based on the requirements of the desktop pool being created.

If you are planning on still having an element of physical desktops in your environment, then you will need to create new OUs for the new virtual desktops. It's not a good idea to mix and match, in case you add policies that would not suit one of the environments. For example, you wouldn't want to apply a physical desktop policy to a virtual desktop.

IP addressing and DNS requirements

For your Horizon View installation, there are several requirements for IP addresses and DNS names used by the different View components.

The typical requirements for IP addresses and DNS names are summarized for each of the components in the following table:

View Component	Internal IP Address	Internal DNS Name	External IP Address	External DNS Name	Network
vCenter Server	✓	✓	✗	✗	Production
View Composer Server	✓	✓	✗	✗	Production
SQL Server	✓	✓	✗	✗	Production
View Connection Server	✓	✓	✗	✗	Production
Interal Load Balancer	✓	✓	✗	✗	Production
View Connection Server (External)	✓	✓	✗	✗	Production
View Secutiry Server	✓	✓	✗	✗	DMZ
VMware Access Point	✓	✓	✗	✗	DMZ
External Load Balancer	✓	✓	✓	✓	DMZ

As you can see from the table, the suggestion is that load balancers are utilized to load balance connections between internal View Connection Servers as well as between external View Security Servers. In a smaller environment, you might decide to go with only one View Security Server, in which case, you would require the external DNS name rather than the load balancer.

In the next section, we are going to start installing the Horizon View components.

Installing Horizon View Composer Server

View Composer is slightly different from Connection Server roles, in that it is not installed as a Connection Server role, and so uses a separate installer. It can either be installed on the same server that vCenter Server is running on, or as a standalone server. You would typically install it as a standalone server for performance or if you are using the vCenter Server Appliance. The configuration recommendations for View Composer are detailed in the following screenshot:

Component	Recommended Supported Configuration
Operating Systems	Windows Server 2008 R2 SP1 64-bit (Std, Ent, DC Editions)
	Windows Server 2012 R2 64-bit (Std & Ent Editions)
	Windows Server 2016 64-bit (Std & Ent Editions)
Processor	2GHz or faster and 4 CPUs
Networking	1Gbps NICs
Memory	8GB RAM or higher for deployments of 50 or more
Disk Space	60 GB
Database Options	Microsoft SQL Server 2014 32-bit & 64-bit, no SP & SP1, Std & Ent
	Microsoft SQL Server 2012 32-bit & 64-bit, SP2, Express, Std & Ent
	Microsoft SQL Server 2008 R2 32-bit & 64-bit, SP2 & SP3, Express, Std, Ent & DC
	Oracle 12c Release 1 (up to 12.1.0.2) Standard One, Std & Ent

In the example lab, View Composer is going to be installed on a standalone server; however, you could install it directly onto the vCenter Server if the vCenter Server is Windows-based. A standalone Composer is used for scalability when you have deployed the vCenter Server Appliance. As the vCenter Server Appliance is Linux-based and the Composer software is Windows-based, obviously it cannot be installed on the vCenter Server Appliance.

It may seem a little odd to install View Composer before the first Connection Server is installed, but the reason it's done in this order is because, during the initial configuration of the first Connection Server, when you configure a vCenter Server, you will need to enter the details of the View Composer Server, if used, so that the View Connection Server can connect to it.

Chapter 4

You now have what you need for View Composer, but before we go ahead and start the installation, there is one other component that needs to be configured, and that's a database.

Configuring SQL Server for a View Composer database

To create a SQL database for View Composer, follow these steps:

1. Open a console to the virtual machine running SQL Server and launch the **Microsoft SQL Server Management Studio** application. In the example lab, the SQL Server is installed on the same server that we are going to install View Composer on, so the server name is `hzn7-cmp.pvolab.com`. You will see the login box, as shown in the following screenshot:

Installing and Configuring Horizon 7 - Part 1

2. Log in using an account with the appropriate permissions. In this example, we are using the SA account. Click the **Connect** button.
3. You will now see the **SQL Server Management Studio** screen. From the **Object Explorer**, expand the `Security` folder and select `Logins` (1). Right-click and select the **New Login…** option (2), as shown in the following screenshot:

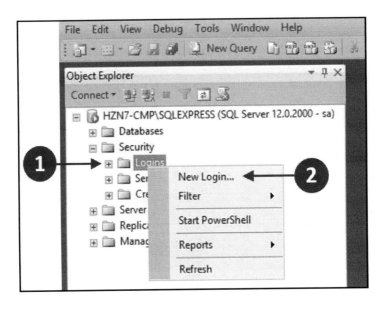

Chapter 4

4. You will then see the **Login – New** screen, as shown in the following screenshot:

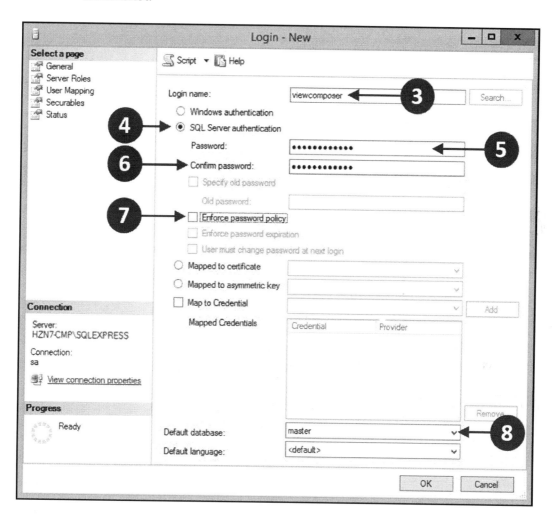

Installing and Configuring Horizon 7 - Part 1

5. In the **Login name** box (3), enter the new login name. In the example lab, the new login is going to be called `viewcomposer`. Click the radio button for **SQL Server authentication** (4), and then, in the **Password** box (5), enter a new password. Type the new password again in the **Confirm password** box (6).
6. Next, uncheck the **Enforce password policy** box (7). Finally, in the **Default database** drop-down box (8), select the **master** option. We will update this to reflect the correct database for View Composer once we create it in the next step.
7. Click **OK** once you have configured this screen. You will return to the **Object Explorer**.
8. Now that you have created the login account, you need to create a new database for View Composer. From the **Object Explorer**, select the `Databases` folder (9), right-click, and select **New Database...** (10), as shown in the following screenshot:

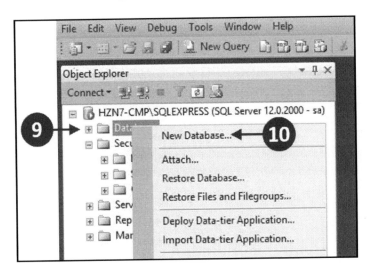

Chapter 4

9. You will see the **New Database** screen, as shown in the following screenshot:

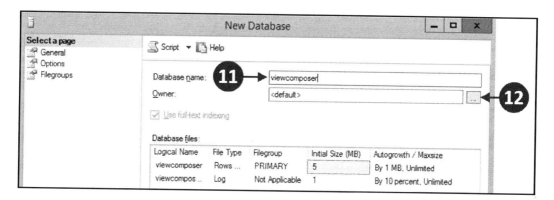

10. In the **Database name** box (**11**), type in a name for this database. In the example lab, the database is called `viewcomposer`.
11. In the **Owner** box, click the **...** box (**12**). You will now see the **Select Database Owner** screen, as shown in the following screenshot:

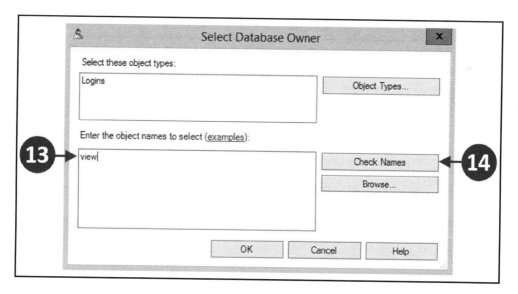

[187]

Installing and Configuring Horizon 7 - Part 1

12. Type `view` into the **Enter the object names to select** box (13), and then click the **Check Names** box (14). This will search for any entries that contain the word `view`.
13. You will now see the **Multiple Objects Found** box, as shown in the following screenshot:

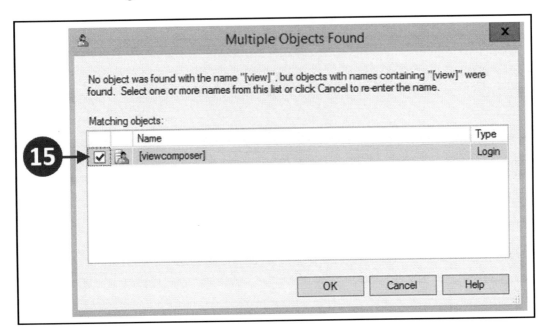

14. Check the **viewcomposer** box (15). This is the login we created previously.

15. Now click the **OK** button, and you will return to the **Select Database Owner** box, which will now show the `viewcomposer` user entered, as shown in the following screenshot:

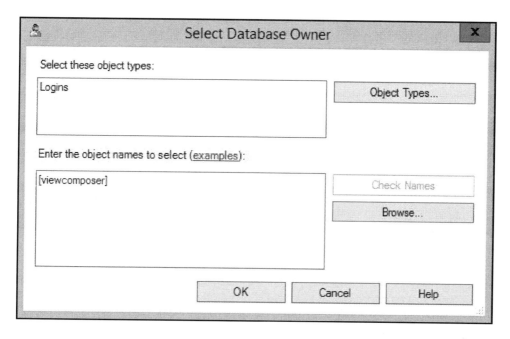

16. In the **Select Database Owner** box, click **OK** to accept the database owner.
17. You will now return to the **New Database** screen, which will show both the **Database name** and the database **Owner**, as shown in the following screenshot:

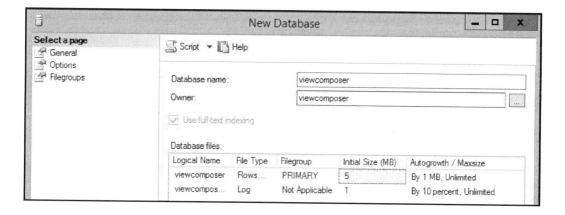

18. Click **OK** to complete the process and close the **New Database** screen. The final configuration task is to go back and edit the `viewcomposer` user login and enter the `viewcomposer` database details.

19. From the **Object Explorer**, expand `Logins` **(16)** and then select the `viewcomposer` option **(17)**. Right-click and then, from the contextual menu, select **Properties** **(18)**. In the **Default database** box, click the drop-down menu **(19)** and select the **viewcomposer** option, as shown in the following screenshot:

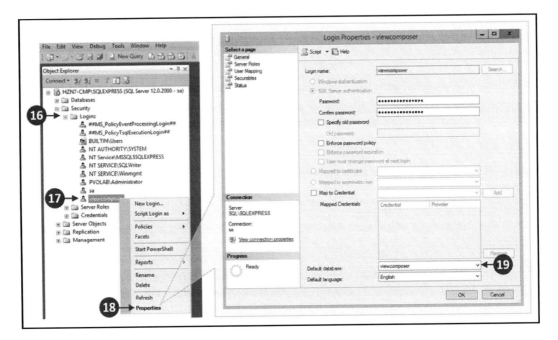

20. Click the **OK** button to complete the configuration changes.

Before you close SQL Server Management Studio, there is one other database to create; so, repeat the entire process, as previously described, and create a database and database owner for the View events database. In the example lab, both the owner and database have been called `viewevents`. We will use this later in the chapter.

With the database configuration now complete, we can go ahead and install the View Composer software.

View Composer installation

In the example lab environment, we are going to install View Composer on the vCenter Server. Before you start the installation, ensure that you have SQL Server Native Client 11.0 installed, as this will be required to configure the connection between the View Composer Server and the SQL database. To install View Composer, follow these steps:

1. Open a console to the **VCS2** vCenter Server virtual machine, and then locate the Horizon View installation software, as shown in the following screenshot:

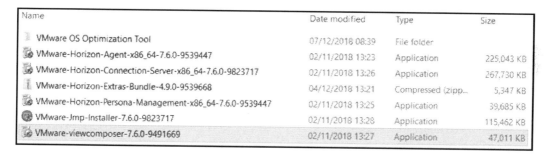

2. Launch the `VMware-viewcomposer-7.6.0-9491669` file to start the installation.
3. If you see the **Open File - Security Warning** message shown here, click the **Run** button to continue:

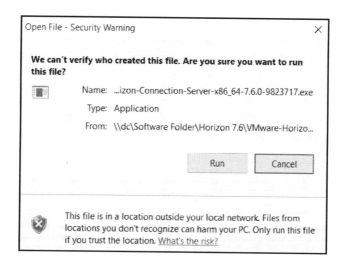

4. You will now see the **Welcome to the Installation Wizard for VMware Horizon 7 Composer** screen, as shown in the following screenshot:

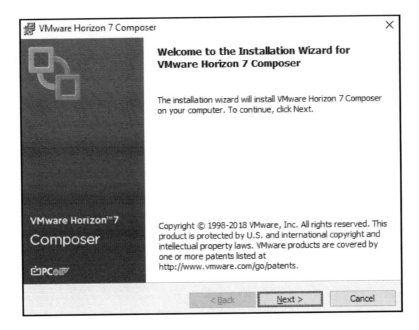

5. Click the **Next >** button to start the installation. You will now see the **License Agreement** screen, as shown in the following screenshot:

6. Click the radio button for **I accept the terms in the license agreement** (1), and then click the **Next >** button. You will then see the **Destination Folder** screen shown in the following screenshot:

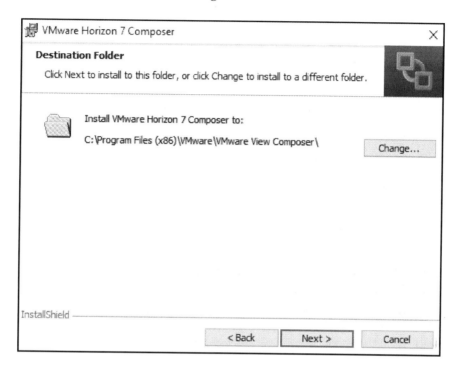

7. Leave the folder as the default and then click the **Next >** button to continue. You will now see the **Database Information** screen shown in the following screenshot:

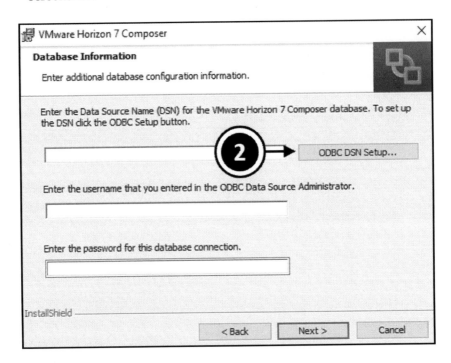

8. The first thing you need to do is to create an ODBC DSN to connect to the View Composer database.

Chapter 4

9. Click the **ODBC DSN Setup…** button (**2**). You will now see the **ODBC Data Source Administrator (64-bit)** box shown in the following screenshot:

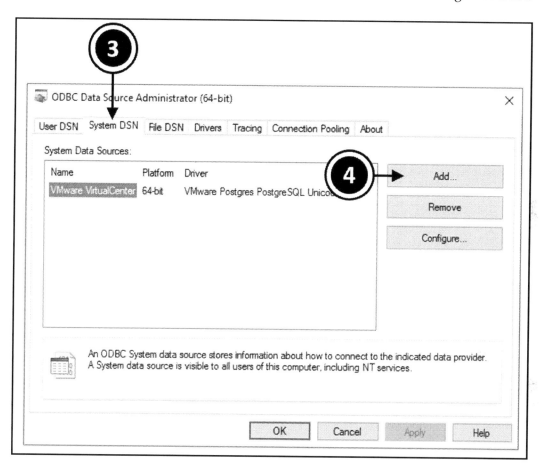

10. Click the **System DSN** tab (3), and then click the **Add...** button (4).
11. In the **Create New Data Source** box that you now see, click the **SQL Server Native Client 11.0** option (5), and then click the **Finish** button, as shown in the following screenshot:

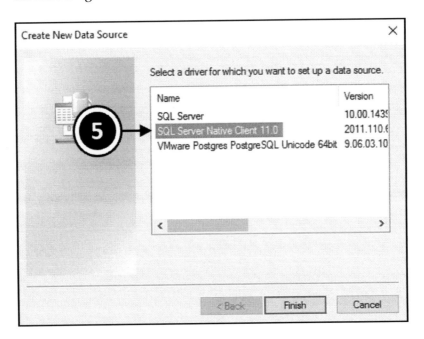

12. You will now see the **Create a New Data Source to SQL Server** box shown in the following screenshot:

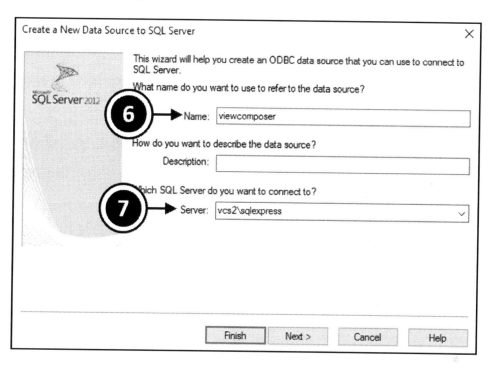

13. In the **Name** box (6), type in a name for this data source. In the example lab, this is `viewcomposer`.

14. In the **Server** box (7), click the drop-down arrow and select the SQL Server that you want to connect to. In the example lab, this is **vcs2\sqlexpress** as we are installing the View Composer in the vCenter Server.

15. Click the **Next >** button to continue.

16. Next, you need to enter the authentication details.

17. Click the **With SQL Server authentication using a login ID and password entered by the user** radio button **(8)**, and then, in the **Login ID** box **(9)**, enter the user login details. In the example lab, we are going to use the SA account. Finally, in the **Password** box **(10)**, type in the password for the SA account, as shown in the following screenshot:

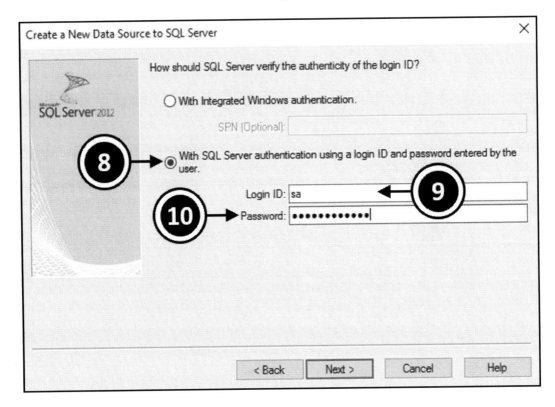

18. Click the **Next >** button to continue.
19. In the next configuration box, you need to change the default database details to reflect the database for View Composer.

Chapter 4

20. Check the **Change the default database to** box (11), and then, in the box below it, click the drop-down arrow (12) and select the **viewcomposer** option. This should automatically populate when you click the dropdown, as shown in the following screenshot:

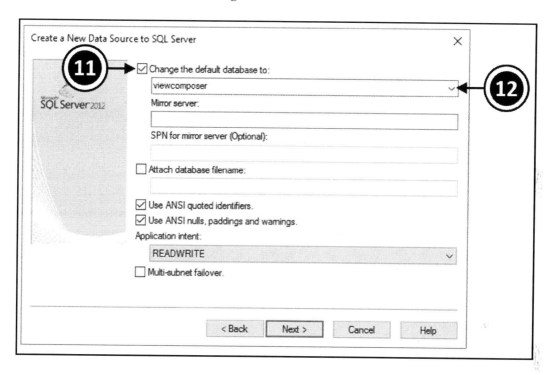

21. Click the **Next >** button to continue. You will see the final configuration box shown in the following screenshot:

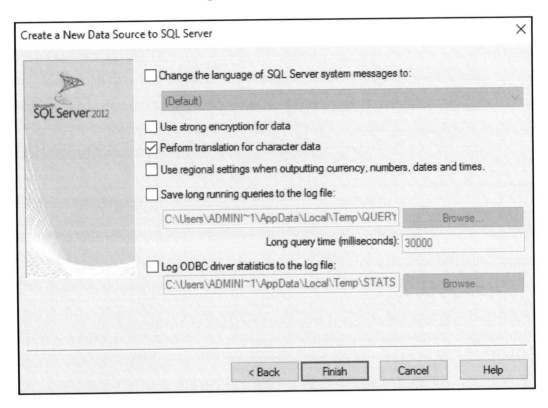

22. Leave the settings on this screen as the defaults and then click the **Finish** button to complete the configuration.

Chapter 4

23. You will now see the configuration summary shown in the following screenshot:

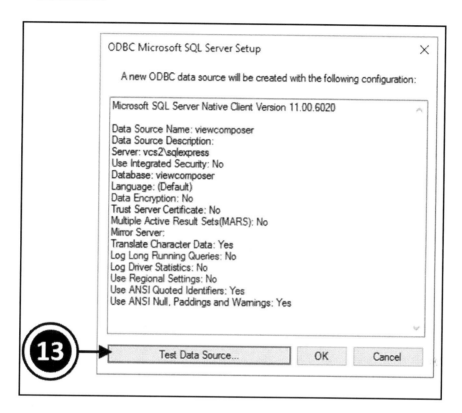

24. The final thing to do is to test the newly created connection. To do this, click the **Test Data Source…** button (**13**).

Installing and Configuring Horizon 7 - Part 1

25. You should see the **Test Results** box showing the `TESTS COMPLETED SUCCESSFULLY!` message, as shown in the following screenshot:

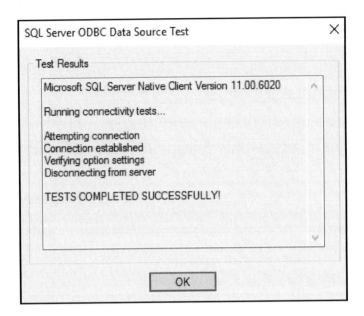

26. Click the **OK** button to complete the tests and close the **Test Results** box.
27. Next, click **OK** to close the **ODBC Microsoft SQL Server Setup** box.
28. You will now return to the **ODBC Data Source Administrator** screen, which will now show you the newly created system DSN connection to the View Composer database.

Chapter 4

29. Click the **OK** button to close the **ODBC Data Source Administrator** screen and return to the View Composer installation screen and the **Database Information** configuration screen, as shown in the following screenshot:

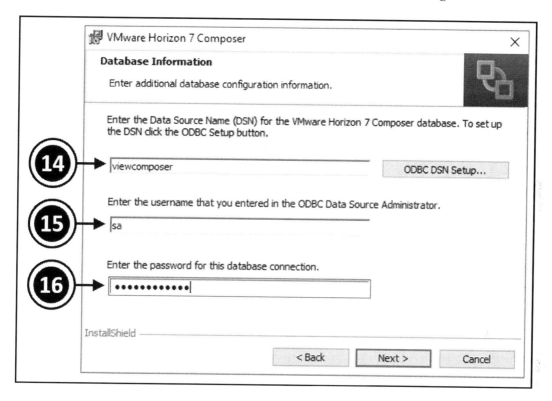

30. You can now enter `viewcomposer` in the DSN box (**14**) and in the **Enter the username that you entered in the ODBC Data Source Administrator** box (**15**), type `sa`, followed by the password for the SA account in the **Enter the password for this database connection** box (**16**).
31. Click the **Next >** button to continue.

Installing and Configuring Horizon 7 - Part 1

32. On the **VMware Horizon 7 Composer Port Settings** screen, leave the **SOAP Port** setting as the default, as shown in the following screenshot:

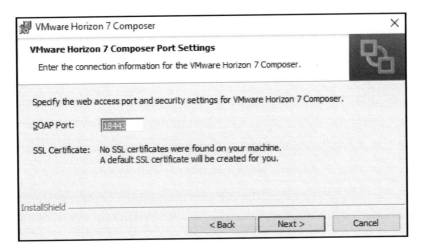

 The **Simple Object Access Protocol (SOAP)** port is used by View to communicate with Composer in XML format. The recommendation would be to leave this setting as is, unless there is a specific reason for changing it.

33. Click the **Next >** button to continue.
34. You will now see the **Ready to Install the Program** screen shown in the following screenshot:

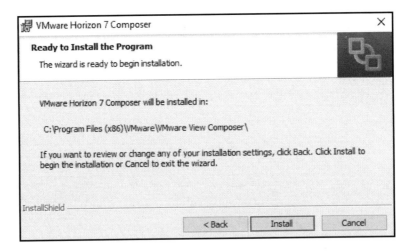

[204]

35. Click the **Install** button to start the installation.
36. Once the installation has completed, you will see the **Installer Completed** screen:

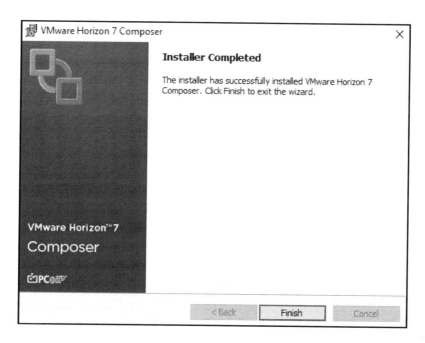

37. Click the **Finish** button to close the installer. If, for any reason, the installation of View Composer fails, installation logs are held on View Composer in the `%TEMP%\vminst.log_date_timestamp` folder. Additionally, MSI logs are also created and can be found in the `%TEMP%\vmmsi.log_date_timestamp` folder.
38. You will now be prompted to restart the virtual machine:

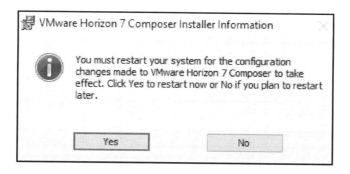

39. Click the **Yes** button to reboot the View Composer virtual machine.
40. When the View Composer virtual machine has restarted, log in, and then check that the View Composer Service is running. To do this, press the Windows key and *R* to open a **Run** dialog box. In the box, type `services.msc`. You will now see the **Services (Local)** screen. Scroll down and check that **VMware Horizon 7 Composer (17)** is running, as shown in the following screenshot:

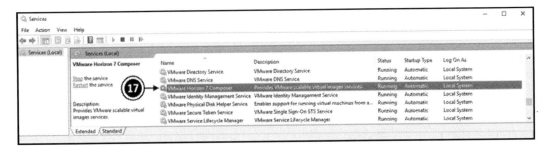

41. When you are happy that the VMware Horizon 7 Composer Service is running, close the **Services** screen.

You have now successfully installed VMware Horizon View Composer.

Installing the Horizon View Connection Server

The View Connection Server and its other roles (Security Server, Replica Server, and so on) are installed on a dedicated Windows Server. The following table lists the recommended configuration for the Connection Server:

Component	Recommended & Supported Configuration
Operating Systems	Windows Server 2008 R2 SP1 (Standard, Enterprise & Datacenter)
	Windows Server 2012 R2 (Standard & Datacenter)
	Windows Server 2016 (Standard & Datacenter)
Processor	4 CPU's
Networking	1 Gbps NIC with static IP address
Memory	10 GB RAM or higher for deloyments of 50 or more desktops
Disk space	60 GB

Chapter 4

The next step in setting up the example lab is to deploy the first Connection Server. This first instance of the Connection Server is going to be installed on a Windows Server 2016 virtual machine with the `HZN7-CS1` hostname that was built at the start of this book as part of the example lab environment. It was configured with a static IP address assigned to it, and then joined to the domain.

To install the Connection Server software, follow these steps:

1. Open a console to the `HZN7-CS1` virtual machine, and then locate the Horizon View installation software. In the example lab, this was saved to a shared folder on the Domain Controller.
2. Launch the `VMware-Horizon-Connection-Server-x86_64-7.6.0-9823717` file to start the installation.
3. If you see the **Open File - Security Warning** message, click the **Run** button, as shown in the following screenshot:

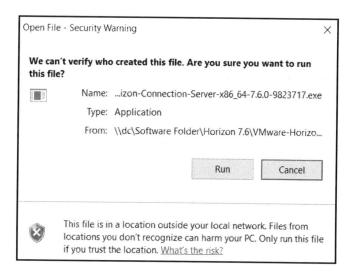

4. You will now see the **Welcome to the Installation Wizard for VMware Horizon 7 Connection Server** screen.
5. Click the **Next >** button to start the installation. You will now see the **License Agreement** screen.
6. Click the **I accept the terms in the license agreement** radio button, and then click the **Next >** button. You will then see the **Destination Folder** screen.

Installing and Configuring Horizon 7 - Part 1

7. Leave the folder as the default and then click the **Next >** button to continue. You will now see the **Installation Options** screen shown in the following screenshot:

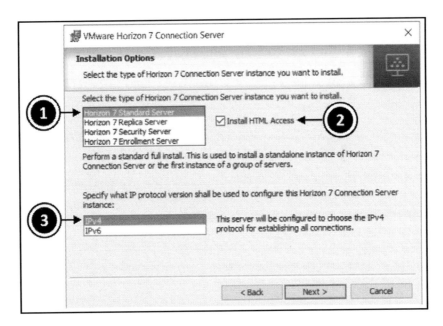

8. As this is the first View Connection Server, from the list of Horizon 7 Connection Server instances, select the **Horizon 7 Standard Server** option from the list (**1**).
9. We are also going to install HTML access, so check the **Install HTML Access** box (**2**). This will allow users to access their desktops using the Blast Protocol from an HTML 5 web browser. The final option on this screen is to select which IP protocol version to use, either IPv4 or IPv6. For the example lab, select the IPv4 option (**3**).

Chapter 4

 Remember that you cannot mix and match IPv4 and IPv6 in the same environment, so for the example lab, IPv4 is going to be used for all components.

10. Once you have selected the instance, click the **Next >** button to continue.
11. You will now see the **Data Recovery** screen shown in the following screenshot:

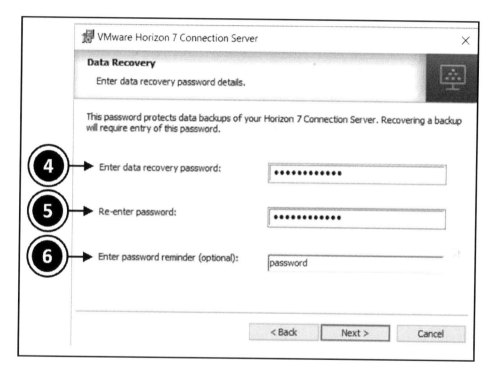

12. On the **Data Recovery** screen, you need to enter a password that will be used for the backups of the Connection Server. In the **Enter data recovery password** box (4), type in the password you want to use, and then type it again in the **Re-enter password** box (5). Finally, enter a password prompt in the **Enter password reminder (optional)** box (6).

[209]

Installing and Configuring Horizon 7 - Part 1

13. Click the **Next >** button to continue. You will now see the **Firewall Configuration** screen shown in the following screenshot:

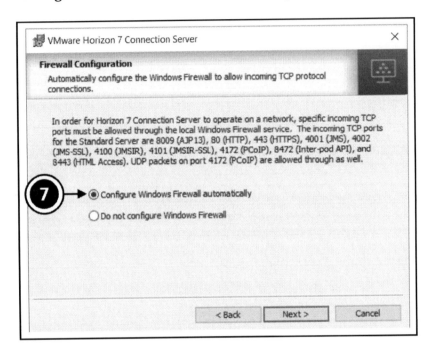

14. Click the **Configure Windows Firewall automatically** radio button, and then click the **Next >** button to continue.

Windows Firewall is a requirement for Horizon View, specifically for Security Server-to-Connection Server communications. Under no circumstances should you disable the Windows Firewall service on your Connection Servers. The recommendation is to allow Windows Firewall to be configured automatically and then note down the required ports where needed.

[210]

15. You will now see the **Initial Horizon 7 Administrators** screen shown in the following screenshot:

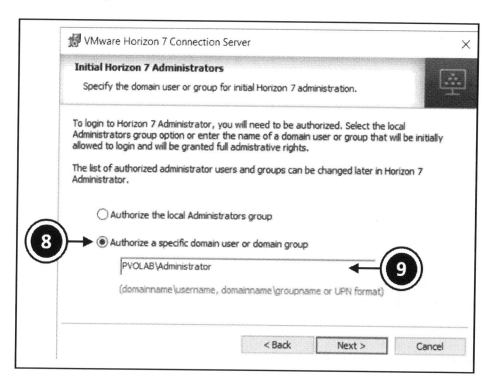

16. On this screen, you need to configure which users on your domain, or on the local server, are going to be configured as your first View Administrators. In the example lab, we are just going to use the standard Administrator account; however, it is recommended that you create a specific user and/or group of users who will have admin access to the Horizon View admin console.

17. Click the **Authorize a specific domain user or group** radio button (8), and then, in the box below, enter the user or group name. You need to enter this in the format domain name\username. In the example lab, you would type in `PVOLAB\Administrator`.

18. Click the **Next >** button to continue. You will now see the **User Experience Improvement Program** screen shown in the following screenshot:

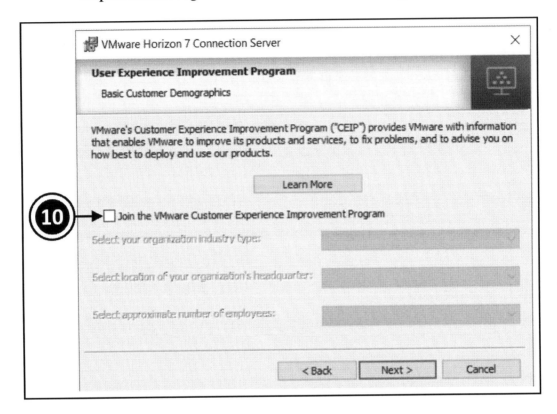

19. The **User Experience Improvement Program** is an optional program that anonymously sends product stats to VMware. It's not a licensing check! In the example lab, ensure that the box is unchecked (**10**).
20. Click the **Next >** button to continue.
21. You will now see the **Ready to Install the Program** screen shown in the following screenshot:

Chapter 4

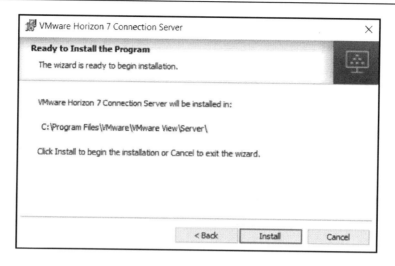

22. Click the **Install** button to start the installation process.
23. Once the Connection Server has been installed, you will see the **Installer Completed** screen shown in the following screenshot:

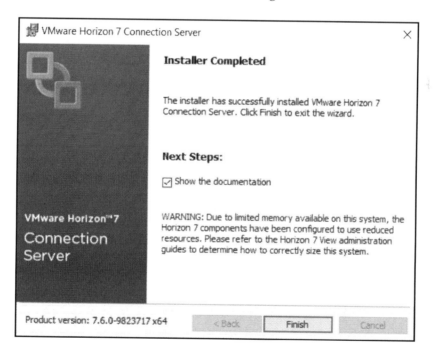

24. You have the option to check the **Show the documentation** box on this screen before you close it. It's recommended that you review this document, as it discusses the importance of valid SSL certificates in the Horizon View installation, which we will cover in more detail in `Chapter 6`, *Securing Horizon View with SSL Certificates*.
25. If the installation fails for any reason, the installation logs are held in the Connection Server at `%TEMP%\vminst.log_date_timestamp`. Additionally, there are MSI logs created, which can be found at `%TEMP%\vmmsi.log_date_timestamp`.

Finally, click the **Finish** button to complete the installation and close the installer. You will now see an icon for the **Horizon 7 Administrator Console** has been placed on the desktop, as shown:

In the next section, we are going to log in to View Administrator and complete the initial configuration tasks.

Initial configuration of the Horizon View Connection Server

With the Connection Server now installed, you can now connect to the management console, called the **View Administrator**, and complete the initial configuration tasks.

From a workstation with Adobe Flash 10.1 or higher installed, open a browser and enter the address details of the View Connection Server. In the example lab, the address to enter would be `https://hzn7-cs1.pvolab.com/admin`.

As SSL certificates have yet to be configured, you need to create a security exception to allow you to browse to the HTTPS page with an unsecured certificate. We will cover SSL certificates in `Chapter 6`, *Securing Horizon View with SSL Certificates*.

Chapter 4

You will now see the View Administrator login screen shown in the following screenshot:

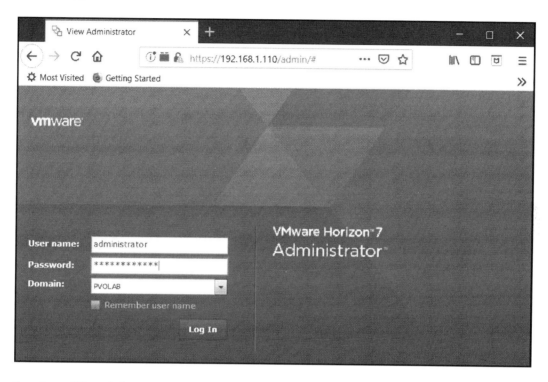

Log in to View Administrator using the Administrator account and password, ensuring that the domain is set to match your domain in the drop-down menu box. Now click the **Log In** button.

You should now be logged on to View Administrator for the first time. The first component to be configured is the product licensing.

Installing and Configuring Horizon 7 - Part 1

Adding a license to the Connection Server

In the first of the configuration tasks to complete, once the Connection Server has been installed, you need to add the product license to enable the relevant features. To do this, follow the steps described here:

1. When you first log in, as there is no license yet installed, the admin screen will default to the **Product Licensing and Usage** section of the **Inventory** pane. At the top of the page, you will see the **Licensing** box. Click the **Edit License...** button (1), as shown in the following screenshot:

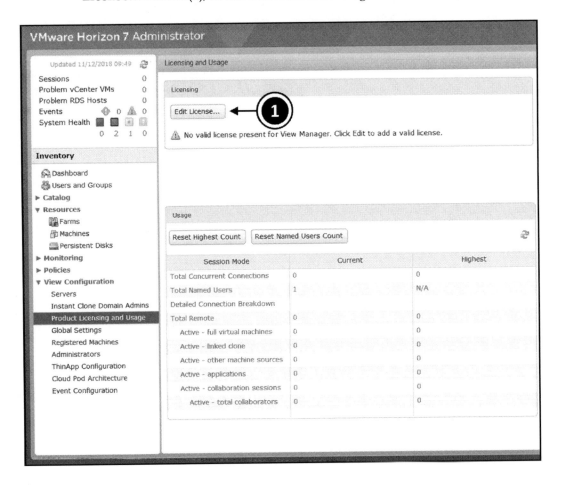

2. You will now see the **Edit License** box shown in the following screenshot:

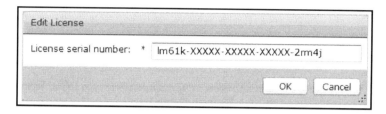

3. In the **License serial number** box, enter your license key and then click the **OK** button. In the preceding example, the license key has been partly obscured using xxxxx to hide the actual license key. When you enter the license key, it will appear letter for letter, on screen.

4. Once you have entered your license key, you will see detailed information relating to it in the **Licensing** box. It will provide a license expiry date, along with all the features that are enabled with the license. In the example lab, you can see all the features and also the usage model, **Concurrent User**, in this example:

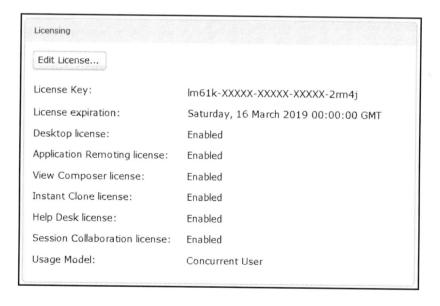

The **Licensing** page also shows you your current usage, as shown in the following screenshot:

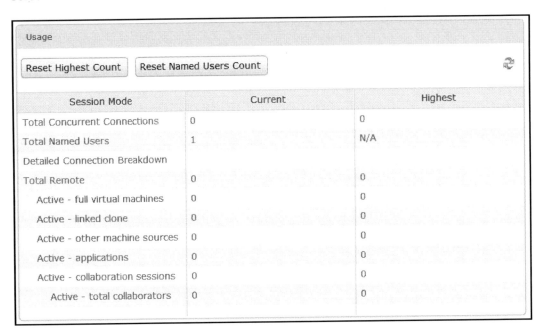

This allows you to ensure you are within the remit of your purchased licenses and also allows you to monitor your usage, so that you can preempt an upgrade before reaching your limits.

Chapter 4

Adding vCenter Server to View Administrator

The next task is to configure the connection between View Administrator and vCenter Server:

1. From the View Administrator main screen, expand the **View Configuration** option (**1**), and then select **Servers** (**2**). Next, from the **Servers** screen, ensure that the **vCenter Servers** tab is selected (**3**), and then click the **Add...** button (**4**), as shown in the following screenshot:

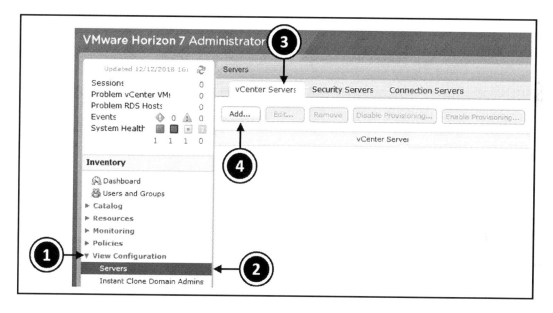

2. You will now see the **vCenter Server Information** screen shown in the following screenshot:

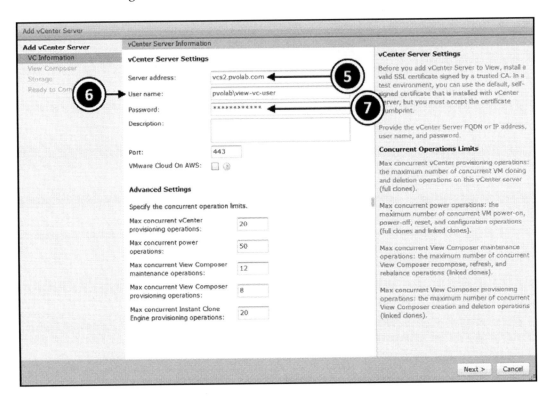

3. In the **Server address** box (5), type in the address of the vCenter Server you want to connect to the Connection Server. In the example lab, this is `vcs2.pvolab.com`, the address of the vCenter managing the virtual desktops.

4. Next, in the **User name** box (6), type in the vCenter username followed by the password for this account in the **Password** box (7). In this example, the administrator account has been used; however, you will probably want to use the specific user account for this that we created earlier in this chapter.

Chapter 4

5. You will now see the following **Invalid Certificate Detected** warning box:

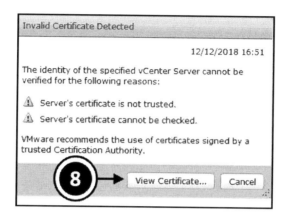

6. Click the **View Certificate...** button (8). You will now see the **Certificate Information** box.
7. Click the **Accept** button.
8. The next screen is the **View Composer Settings** screen shown in the following screenshot:

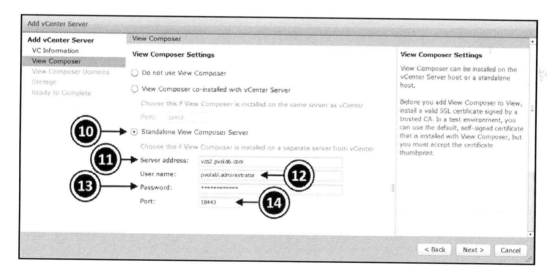

[221]

Installing and Configuring Horizon 7 - Part 1

9. You have three options to configure View Composer: **Do not use View Composer**, **View Composer co-installed with vCenter Server**, and **Standalone View Composer Server**.
10. For the example lab, View Composer is going to be installed on a standalone server, so click the **Standalone View Composer Server** radio button **(10)**.
11. Next, you need to enter the details of the View Composer Server. In the **Server address** box **(11)**, type in the server address. In the example lab, this is `vcs2.pvolab.com`. Then, type in the username for this server in the **User name** box **(12)**. Remember to add this in the format domain\username, so in the example lab, type `pvolab\administrator` followed by the password for this user account in the **Password** box **(13)**. Leave the **Port** box **(14)** at the default setting of `18443`.
12. When you have completed the details, click the **Next >** button.
13. As with adding the vCenter Server, you will again see the following **Invalid Certificate Detected** warning box:

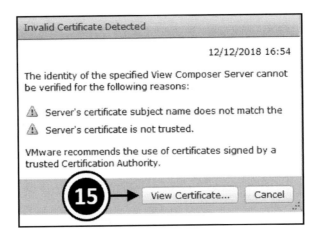

Chapter 4

14. Click the **View Certificate...** button (**15**). You will now see the **Certificate Information** box
15. Click the **Accept** button. You will now see the **View Composer Domains** configuration screen shown in the following screenshot:

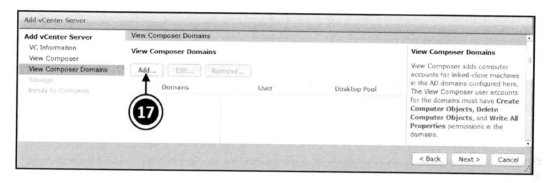

16. On this screen, we are going to configure View Composer with access to a domain account to allow it to add, create, and delete computer accounts in AD. Click the **Add...** button (**17**). You will now see the **Add Domain** configuration box shown in the following screenshot:

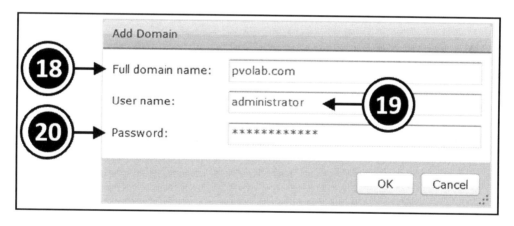

17. In the **Full domain name** box (**18**), type in the domain name. In the example lab, this is `pvolab.com`. Then, in the **User name** box (**19**), enter the username that has the ability to create and delete computer objects in AD. In the example lab, we will use the `administrator` account.

[223]

18. Finally, in the **Password** box, type in the password for the administrator account. Click the **OK** button when you have entered the information. You will now return to the **View Composer Domains** configuration screen, which now shows the configured domain details, entered as shown in the following screenshot:

19. Click the **Next >** button to continue.
20. You will now see the **Storage Settings** configuration screen. There are two main elements to configure here. The first option is to configure whether or not you want to **Reclaim VM disk space** for your virtual desktops. If this is selected, the virtual machines will be configured with space-efficient disks, which will allow the reclamation of unused space.
21. The second option is to configure **Enable View Storage Accelerator**. This allows a specific amount of memory to be utilized as a read cache to reduce the storage overheads on the shared or local storage used to run the VMs. By default, this will be set to 1024 MB of memory per server and can be increased to up to 2GB per server. Alternatively, if you check the box for **Show all hosts**, you can then select individual host servers and configure the cache size differently on each host server.
22. In the example lab, we are going to enable the options for **Reclaim VM disk space** and **Enable View Storage Accelerator**, as shown in the following screenshot:

Chapter 4

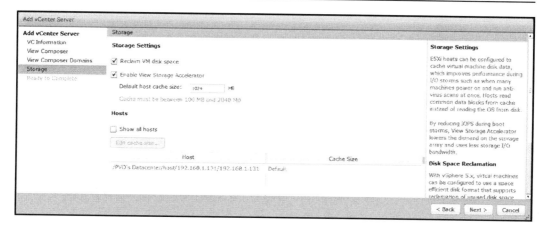

23. Click the **Next >** button to continue. You will now see the **Ready to Complete** screen shown in the following screenshot:

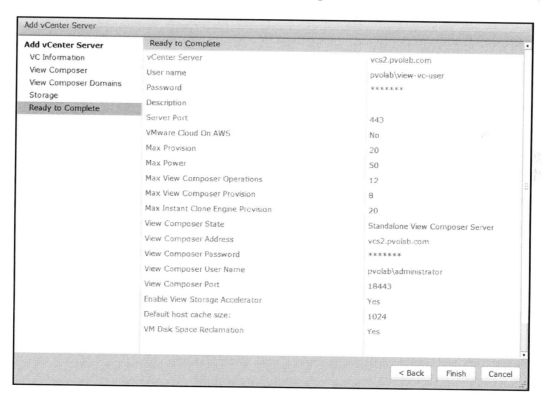

[225]

24. Finally, check the configuration details and then click the **Finish** button to complete the configuration. You will return to the View Administrator screen, which now shows the vCenter Server that was just added, as shown in the following screenshot:

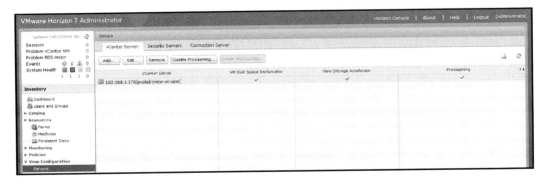

View Administrator screen

You have now added a vCenter Server to Horizon View. In the next section, we are going to configure the View events database.

Configuring the View events database

The final part of the initial configuration tasks is to configure the events database. This is where Horizon View stores all the events that take place on the Connection Server.

A database called **view-events** was created at the start of this chapter, and now we are going to use it in the configuration:

1. From the View Administrator main screen and the **Inventory** section, expand the **View Configuration** option, and then select **Event Configuration** (1). You will now see the **Event Configuration** screen shown in the following screenshot:

Chapter 4

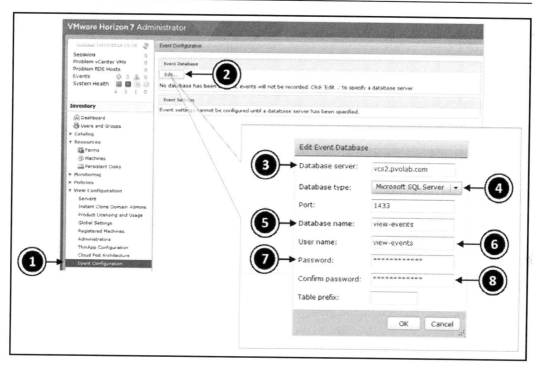

2. In the **Event Database** section, click the **Edit…** button (**2**). You will now see the **Edit Event Database** dialog box pop up, as shown in the preceding screenshot.

3. In the **Database server** box (**3**), enter the name of the SQL server that is hosting the events database. In the example lab, it's on the same server as vCenter, so enter `vcs2.pvolab.com` as the server name.

4. Ensure that **Microsoft SQL Server** is selected from the drop-down menu for the **Database type** (**4**). The other option here is to set up an Oracle database.

5. Leave the **Port** setting as the default port of `1443`.

6. In the **Database name** box (**5**), type in the name of the database. In the example lab, the database is called `view-events`.

7. In the **User name** box (**6**), type in the username for this database, and in the **Password** box (**7**), type in the password for this user, and then type it in again in the **Confirm password** box (**8**).

Installing and Configuring Horizon 7 - Part 1

8. Finally, in the **Table prefix** box, you can enter a prefix name. This allows you to use the same events database for multiple installations. Once you have entered the configuration information, click **OK**.
9. Once completed, you should see the following screenshot:

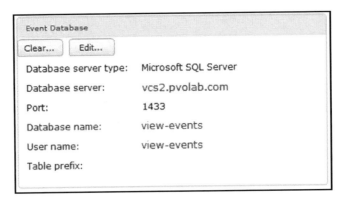

You have now successfully completed the initial Connection Server configuration tasks. In the next part of this chapter, we will move on to installing the other Connection Server roles, starting with the Replica Server.

Summary

In this first part of the chapter, we have walked you through installing and configuring the first components of the Horizon View solution, namely the View Composer and the Horizon View Connection Server.

In the second part of this chapter, Chapter 5, *Installing and Configuring Horizon 7 – Part 2*, we will continue the installation and install the Replica Server, the Security Server, and the Enrollment Server.

5
Installing and Configuring Horizon 7 - Part 2

In the previous part of this chapter, we installed the core Horizon View Connection Server. Now, in this second part, we are going to continue building out the environment and install the other server roles and components, starting with the Replica Server.

In this chapter, we will cover the following topics:

- Installing a Horizon View Replica Server
- Installing a Security Server
- Installing an Enrollment Server
- Configuring the Cloud Pod Architecture
- Configuring View for GPU-enabled virtual desktops

Installing a Horizon View Replica Server

In this section, we are going to deploy a second View Connection Server. Additional View Connection Servers are referred to as Replica Servers. This is due to the nature in which View shares its configurations between multiple View Connection Servers using the ADAM database.

Additional Connection Servers are generally deployed for availability reasons, as discussed in the previous chapters. For test purposes, you could roll out a single View Connection Server.

This second instance of the Connection Server is going to be installed on the virtual machine with the hostname `hzn7-cs2.pvolab.com`. This was built at the start of the previous chapter. It will also need a static IP address assigned to it and needs to be joined to the domain. Since the screenshots are almost identical to those from the first Connection Server install, we will only highlight and show the differences in this section:

1. Open a console to the `hzn7-cs2` virtual machine, and then locate the Horizon View installation software. In the example lab, this was saved to a shared folder on the Domain Controller.
2. Launch the `VMware-Horizon-Connection-Server-x86_64-7.6.0-9823717` file to start the installation. This is the same installer application that you used for the first Connection Server, but it will be configured differently to reflect the fact that this is a Replica Server.
3. If you see the **Open File - Security Warning** message, click the **Run** button.
4. You will now see the **Welcome to the Installation Wizard for VMware Horizon 7 Connection Server** screen.
5. Click the **Next >** button to start the installation. You will now see the **License Agreement** screen.
6. Click the radio button for **I accept the terms in the license agreement**, and then click the **Next >** button. You will now see the **Destination Folder** screen.
7. Leave the folder with its default settings and then click the **Next >** button to continue.

Chapter 5

8. You will now see the **Installation Options** screen, as shown in the following screenshot:

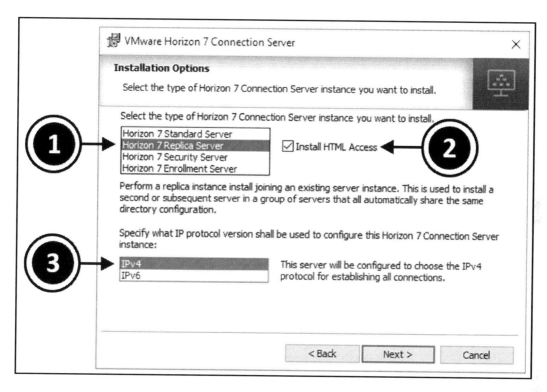

9. As this is the second Connection Server, or Replica Server, from the list of **Horizon 7 Connection Server** instances, select the option for **Horizon 7 Replica Server** from the list (1).
10. Like before, we are going to install HTML access, so check the box for **Install HTML Access** (2). This will allow users to access their desktops from an HTML 5 web browser. This setting should match that of the original Connection Server so that this server is capable of delivering the same features and functionality. Don't forget that a Replica Server could take over should the first Connection Server be unavailable.

Installing and Configuring Horizon 7 - Part 2

11. The final option on this screen is to select which IP protocol to use: either **IPv4** or **IPv6**. In the example lab, select the **IPv4** option (3). Again, as a reminder, you cannot mix the IP protocol version between the different View server instances.
12. Click the **Next >** button to continue.
13. You will now see the **Source Server** configuration screen, as shown in the following screenshot:

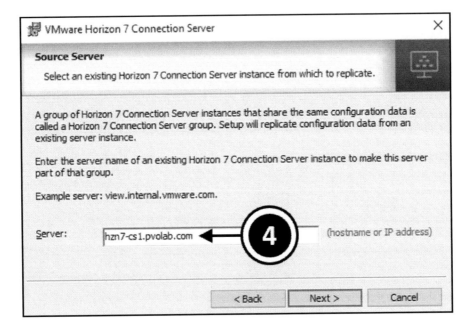

14. The Source Server is the Connection Server that you want to use as the source to replicate from, so in the **Server** box (4), type in the address of the first Connection Server. In the example lab, this is `hzn7-cs1.pvolab.com`.
15. Click the **Next >** button to continue. You will now see the **Firewall Configuration** screen.
16. Click the radio button for **Configure Windows Firewall automatically**, and then click the **Next >** button to continue. You will now see the **Ready to Install the Program** screen.

[232]

Chapter 5

17. Click the **Install** button to start the process.
18. The install will start and you will see the program filed install, and also the status of the initial replication. Once the Replica Server has been installed, you will see the **Installer Completed** screen. Click the **Finish** button on this screen to close the installer.
19. You will now see the icon on the desktop for the **Horizon 7 Administrator** console. To check that the Replica Server has been installed correctly and that it is up and running, log in to the **View Administrator**.
20. From the **Inventory** menu, expand the **View Configuration** section, and then click on **Servers** (5). Click the **Connection Servers** tab (6). You will now see the Replica Server `hzn7-cs2` listed (7), as shown in the following screenshot:

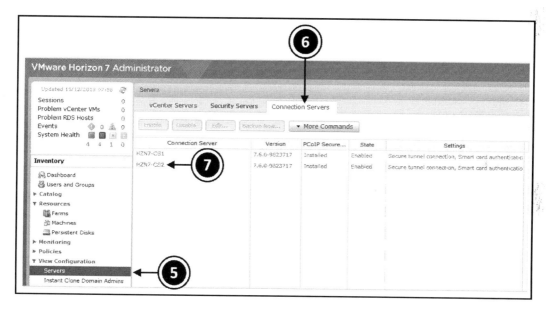

You have successfully installed and configured the Replica Server.

[233]

Installing and Configuring Horizon 7 - Part 2

Now that you have two Connection Servers, don't forget that Horizon View, as standard, includes no method to load balance Connection Servers or Security Servers. As such, you should work with the relevant documentation from your load balancing manufacturer to configure your load balancers to work with your View Connection Servers as required. This allows users to be load balanced for availability and scale.

In the next section, we are going to install a Horizon View Security Server.

Installing a Security Server

The next component that we are going to install is the Security Server so that you can allow external access to your end users.

The Security Server is another instance of the Connection Server and is going to be installed on the virtual machine with the hostname `hzn7-sec.pvolab.com`. This was built in the previous chapter. It will also need a static IP address assigned to it, but this should not be joined to the domain.

Don't forget that a Security Server has a one-to-one relationship with a Connection Server. If you wish to roll out a number of Security Servers, you will want to have multiple View Connection Servers.

It is also recommended that you have dedicated external View Connection Servers ready to pair with your Security Servers and separate View Connection Servers for internal connections. This will allow you to specify which users can access desktops from outside the organization by using the tagging functionality, which we will discuss later in this chapter and in `Chapter 8`, *Configuring and Managing Desktop Pools - Part 1*.

Chapter 5

Preparing View Administrator for the Security Server install

Before we start with the installation, we need to prepare the Connection Server for the Security Server by creating a pairing password. This password will be used to connect the two servers together securely. It's the same kind of process you would use to pair your Bluetooth cell phone to the hands-free system in your car:

1. Log in to the View Administrator. You will then see the main configuration screen, as shown in the following screenshot:

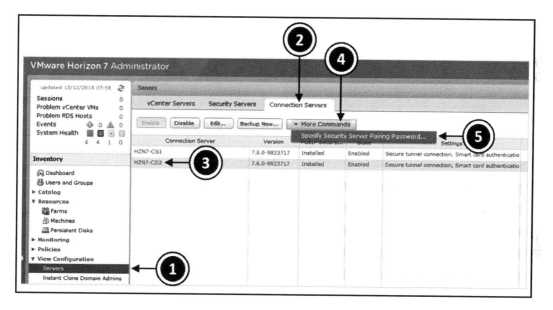

2. From the **Inventory** menu, expand the **View Configuration** section, and then click on **Servers** (**1**). Now, click the **Connection Servers** tab (**2**). You will then see the **Connection Server** within your environment. In the example lab, we have two, `hzn7-cs1` and `hzn7-cs2`.

3. Click to select the Connection Server you want to pair the Security Server with. In the example lab, we are going to pair it with the Connection Server called `hzn7-cs2` (**3**).

[235]

Installing and Configuring Horizon 7 - Part 2

4. Now, click the **More Commands** button (**4**) and select the option for **Specify Security Server Pairing Password...** (**5**). You will now see the **Specify Security Server Pairing Password** screen, as shown in the following screenshot:

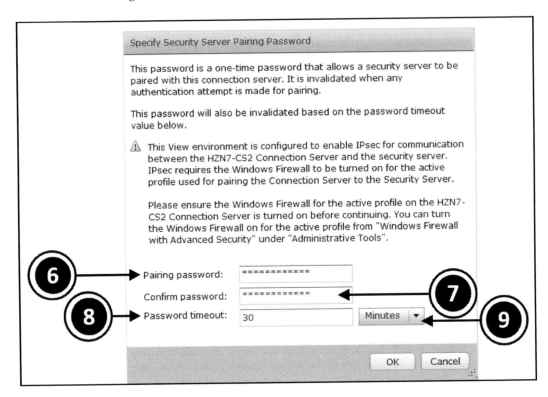

5. In the **Pairing password** (**6**) box, type in the password you want to use for pairing. You will need to remember this password as you will enter it again during the installation of the Security Server. Type the password again in the **Confirm password** box (**7**).

6. In the **Password timeout** box (8), enter a time for this password to be valid for. Make sure that the time you set will give you enough time to install the Security Server. This will save you from having to come back and set up a new pairing password. From the dropdown box (9), you can also choose whether the time to live for the password is in hours or minutes.
7. Click **OK** once you have configured the pairing password.
8. You can now go ahead and start the installation of the Security Server.

Security Server software installation

With the prerequisites in place and the pairing password set, we can now install the Security Server. As the screenshots are almost identical to those from the previous Connection Server installs, we will only highlight and show the differences in this section:

1. Open a console to the `hzn7-sec.pvolab.com` virtual machine, and then locate the Horizon View installation software. In the example lab, this was saved to a shared folder on the Domain Controller.
2. Launch the `VMware-Horizon-Connection-Server-x86_64-7.6.0-9823717` file to start the installation. This is the same installer application that you used for the first Connection Server, but it will be configured differently to reflect the fact that this is a Security Server.
3. If you see the **Open File - Security Warning** message, click the **Run** button.
4. You will now see the **Welcome to the Installation Wizard for VMware Horizon 7 Connection Server** screen.
5. Click the **Next >** button to start the installation. You will now see the **License Agreement** screen.
6. Click the radio button for **I accept the terms in the license agreement**, and then click the **Next >** button. You will now see the **Destination Folder** screen.
7. Leave the folder as the default setting and then click the **Next >** button to continue.

8. You will now see the **Installation Options** screen, as shown in the following screenshot:

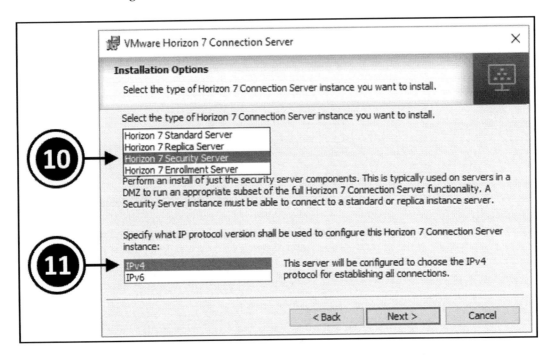

9. As this is the third Connection Server instance, or Security Server, from the list of **Horizon 7 Connection Server** instances, select the option for **Horizon 7 Security Server** from the list (**10**).
10. The final option on this screen is to select which IP protocol to use: either **IPv4** or **IPv6**. In the example lab, select the **IPv4** option (**11**). Again, as a reminder, you cannot mix the IP protocol version between the different View Server instances.
11. Click the **Next >** button to continue. You will now see the **Paired Horizon 7 Connection Server** screen, as shown in the following screenshot:

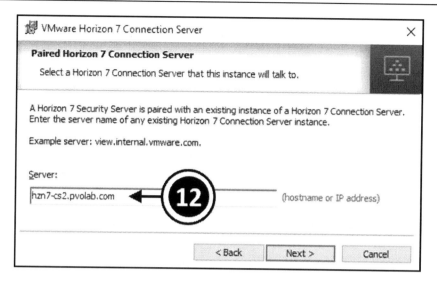

12. In the **Server** box (**12**), enter the details of the Connection Server to pair with. In the example lab, we are going to pair with the server called `hzn7-cs2.pvolab.com`, which is the Replica Server we set up in the previous section.

13. Click the **Next >** button to continue. You will now see the **Paired Horizon 7 Connection Server Password** screen:

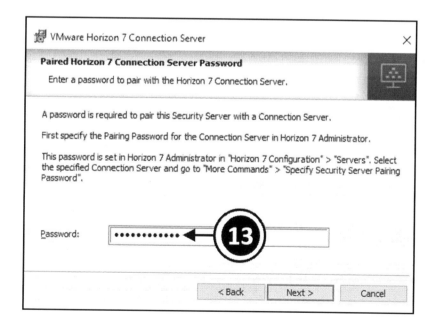

Installing and Configuring Horizon 7 - Part 2

14. In the **Password** box **(13)**, type in the pairing password that you specified when you configured it in the View Administrator.
15. Click the **Next >** button to continue.
16. You will now see the **Horizon 7 Security Server Configuration**, as shown in the following screenshot:

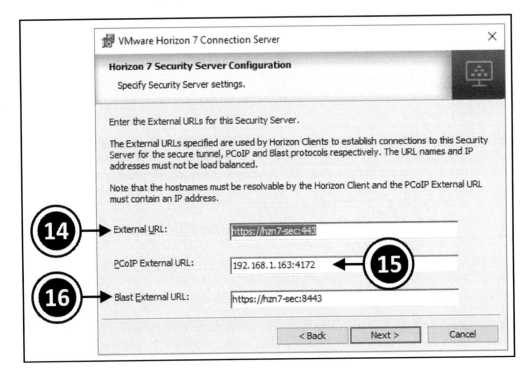

17. On this screen, you can specify the Security Server settings. First, in the **External URL** box **(14)**, enter the address that users will use to connect their Horizon client to over an internet connection. In the preceding example, this has been left as the default; however, you would probably want to change this to something more user-friendly.
18. In the **PCoIP External URL** box **(15)**, enter the IP address for the external PCoIP connection. Note that, this must contain an IP address rather than a URL, as the box suggests. The address must also have the port suffix added, so in this case, `:4172` is the default PCoIP port.

Chapter 5

19. Finally, in the **Blast External URL** box (16), enter the address for the Blast protocol. This is used for HTML5 access.
20. Click the **Next >** button to continue. You will now see the **Firewall Configuration** screen.
21. Click the radio button for **Configure Windows Firewall automatically**, and then click the **Next >** button to continue. You will see the **Ready to Install the Program** screen.
22. Click the **Install** button to start the installation process.
23. Once the Security Server has been installed, you will see the **Installer Completed** screen. Click the **Finish** button to exit.

Unlike when we installed the Connection Server and the Replica Server, no Horizon icon is placed on the desktop. The settings are managed using the View Administrator console. However, to check whether the Security Server is installed and running, on the desktop of the Security Server, launch a **Services** console, as shown in the following screenshot:

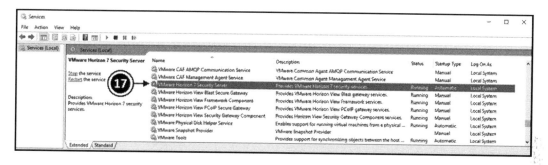

Scroll down until you see the entry for **VMware Horizon 7 Security Server** (17), and then check that it is running.

[241]

Installing and Configuring Horizon 7 - Part 2

You also need to check that the Security Server had registered with the View Administrator. To do this, perform the following steps:

1. From the **Inventory** menu, expand the **View Configuration** section, and then click on **Servers** (**18**). Click the **Security Servers** tab (**19**). You will now see the Security Server `HZN7-SEC` listed (**20**). This is shown in the following screenshot:

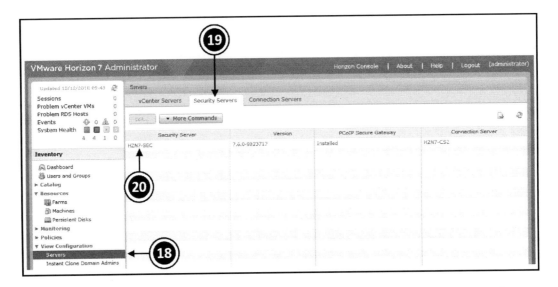

2. You have successfully installed and configured a Security Server.

As we mentioned earlier, we recommend installing Security Servers in conjunction with dedicated external View Connection Servers so that you can limit access to the virtual desktop machines from external connections by using the tagging functionality.

The first step in achieving this is by tagging your external Connection Servers. To tag a server, perform the following steps:

1. In the View Administrator, from the **Inventory** menu, expand the **View Configuration** section, and then click on **Servers** (**21**). Click the **Connection Servers** tab (**22**) and then highlight the Connection Server that is paired with the Security Server for the external connections. In the example lab, this server is called `HZN7-CS2` (**23**).
2. Right-click and then from the contextual menu, click on **Edit…** (**24**), as shown in the following screenshot:

[242]

Chapter 5

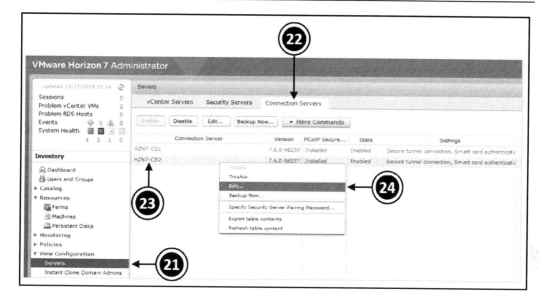

3. You will now see the **Edit Connection Server Settings** screen, as shown in the following screenshot:

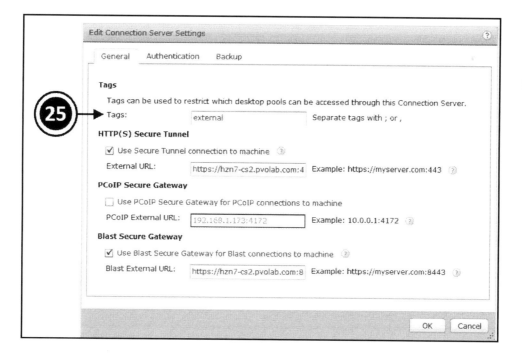

[243]

4. In the **Tags** box **(25)**, type in the name for this tag. In the example lab, this tag is called `external`. This means that only desktop pools that have also been configured with the tab named `external` can connect via this Connection Server.

Installing an Enrollment Server

The final component we are going to install is the Enrollment Server.

This FINAL instance of the Connection Server is going to be installed on the virtual machine with the hostname `hzn7-enrol.pvolab.com`. This was built in the previous chapter. It will also need a static IP address assigned to it and needs to be joined to the domain. As the screenshots are almost identical to those from the other Connection Server installs, we will only highlight and show the differences in this section:

1. Open a console to the `hzn7-enrol.pvolab.com` virtual machine, and then locate the Horizon View installation software. In the example lab, this was saved to a shared folder on the Domain Controller.
2. Launch the `VMware-Horizon-Connection-Server-x86_64-7.6.0-9823717` file to start the installation. This is the same installer application that you used for the first Connection Server, but it will be configured differently to reflect the fact that this is a Replica Server.
3. If you see the **Open File - Security Warning** message, click the **Run** button.
4. You will now see the **Welcome to the Installation Wizard for VMware Horizon 7 Connection Server** screen.
5. Click the **Next >** button to start the installation. You will now see the **License Agreement** screen.
6. Click the radio button for **I accept the terms in the license agreement**, and then click the **Next >** button. You will now see the **Destination Folder** screen.
7. Leave the folder as the default setting and then click the **Next >** button to continue.

Chapter 5

8. You will now see the **Installation Options** screen, as shown in the following screenshot:

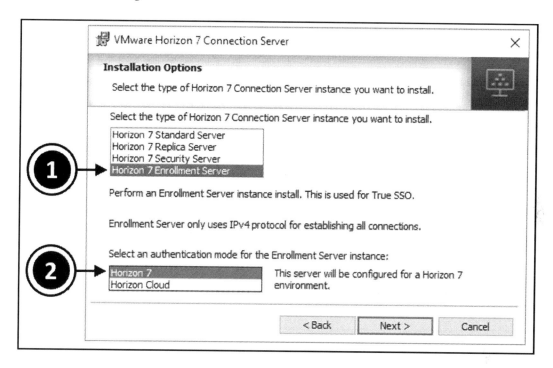

9. As this is the final Connection Server instance, or Enrollment Server, from the list of **Horizon 7 Connection Server** instances, select the option for **Horizon 7 Enrollment Server** from the list (1).
10. The final option on this screen is to select an authentication mode for this Enrollment Server instance. Horizon 7 supports both on-premises and Horizon Cloud deployments. The example lab is an on-premises environment, so click the option for **Horizon 7** (2).
11. Click the **Next >** button to continue. You will now see the **Firewall Configuration** screen.
12. Click the radio button for **Configure Windows Firewall automatically** and then click **Next >** to continue.
13. You will see the **Ready to Install the Program** screen.
14. Click the **Install** button to start the installation process. Once the Enrollment Server has been installed, you will see the **Installer Completed** screen. Click the **Finish** button to close the installer.

[245]

15. There is no user interface or console for the Enrollment Server, nor is there an icon on the desktop. To check whether or not it's running, we are going to check the Windows Services console. To do this, press the Windows key and *R* to open a **Run** dialog box. In the box, type `services.msc`. You will now see the **Services** screen, as shown in the following screenshot:

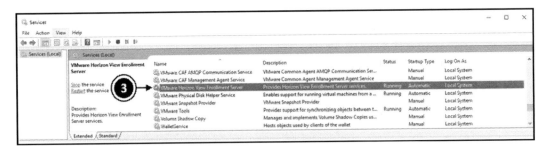

16. Scroll down, and you will see an entry for **VMware Horizon View Enrollment Server**. Check that the service is running, and then close the **Services** screen.

You have successfully installed and configured an Horizon View Enrollment Server. In the next section, we are going to complete the View Administration elements of the installation and configuration by enabling the Cloud Pod Architecture.

Configuring Cloud Pod Architecture

In `Chapter 3`, *Design and Deployment Considerations*, we discussed the Cloud Pod Architecture and its ability to deliver multi-site View deployments to allow for scalability and also disaster recovery scenarios. We are now going to look at how to set up a cloud pod by using the example lab.

In the example lab, we have built and configured another Connection Server called `hzn7-cs1b.pvolab.com`, which we will use to represent a second pod, located on a second site.

 This server is installed as a Connection Server and not a Replica Server, as it needs to be the first server in a different pod.

The following diagram illustrates the installation we are going to follow, using the example lab:

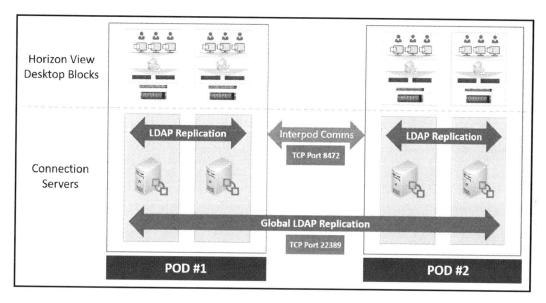

The first step of the process is to initialize the Cloud Pod from the first Connection Server.

Initializing the Cloud Pod

To initialize the Cloud Pod Architecture, perform the following the steps:

1. Log in to the **View Administrator**, and from the console screen, in the **Inventory** pane on the left, expand the **View Configuration** section and click **Cloud Pod Architecture (1)**.

Installing and Configuring Horizon 7 - Part 2

2. Now, click the option for the **Initialize the Cloud Pod Architecture** feature (2), as shown in the following screenshot:

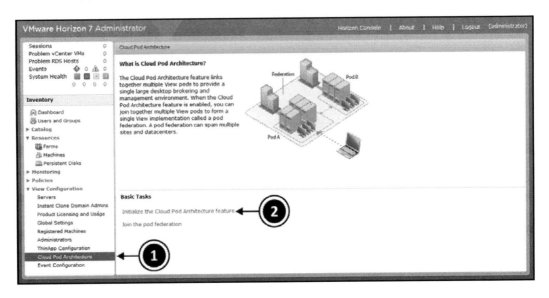

3. You will now see the **Initialize** dialog box, as shown in the following screenshot:

[248]

Chapter 5

4. Click the **OK** button to start the initialization. You will now see the initialization process start, and a visual representation of the progress displayed as a % bar across the screen. You will also see that the status is shown as **Pending**, as shown in the following screenshot:

5. Once the **Cloud Pod Architecture** feature has complete its initialization, you will see the **Reload** dialog box, as shown in the following screenshot:

Installing and Configuring Horizon 7 - Part 2

6. Click the **OK** button to reload the client. You will now see the **Cloud Pod Architecture** screen in the View Administrator, as shown in the following screenshot:

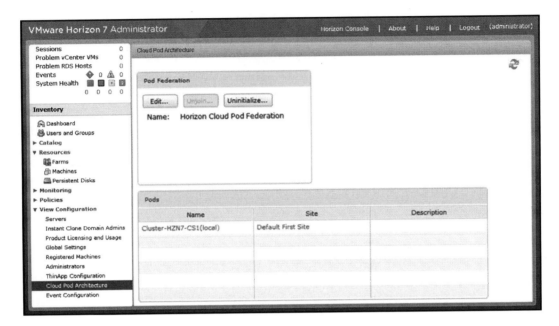

As you can see, a Pod Federation has been created called **Horizon Cloud Pod Federation**. You can change this name by clicking the **Edit…** button, should you need to.

You will also see that the pods are listed, along with the site information. In the example lab, we only have the `HZN7-CS1` Connection Server listed, as this is the first Connection Server to have the Cloud Pod Architecture installed.

The next step is to connect the Connection Server in the second pod, or second site to the federation.

Chapter 5

Connecting the second pod to the Cloud Pod

The next step in this process is to connect or join your other pods to the pod federation.

Log in to the **View Administrator** console on the second Connection Server. This is called `hzn7-cs1b.pvolab.com`. This is the first Connection Server on the second site in the example lab.

Perform the following steps to connect the second pod to the federation:

1. Log in to the **View Administrator** console. In the **Inventory** pane on the left, expand the **View Configuration** section and click **Cloud Pod Architecture** (1), but this time click the option for **Join the pod federation** (2), as shown in the following screenshot:

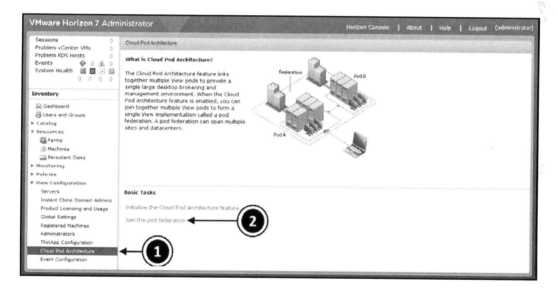

[251]

2. You will now see the **Join** dialog box, as shown in the following screenshot:

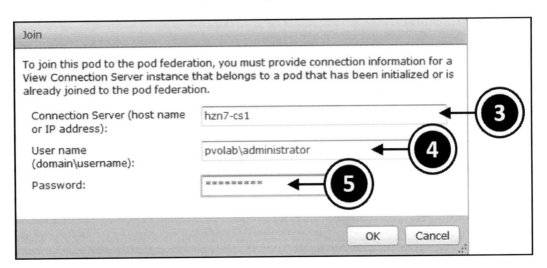

3. Here, enter the details of a **Connection Server** that is in a pod that has the Cloud Pod Architecture already initialized.
4. In the **Connection Server** box (3), enter the address of the **Connection Server** from the first site. In the example lab, this is the server called `hzn7-cs1.pvolab.com`.
5. In the **User name** box (4), enter the username that has the correct privileges for joining pods together. In the example lab, we are going to use the administrator account. Note that you need to enter the username in the format `domain\username`, so in the example lab, we are going to enter this as `pvolab\username`.
6. Click **OK** to continue.
7. You will now see the join process start, and a visual representation of the progress displayed as a % bar across the screen, as well as the status, being shown as **Pending.**

8. Once the **Cloud Pod Architecture** feature has completed the join to the pod federation, you will see the **Reload** dialog box.
9. Click the **OK** button to reload the client. You will now see the Cloud Pod Architecture screen in the View Administrator, as shown in the following screenshot:

As you can see, both pods are now listed, along with the site information. In the example lab, we now have the `HZN7-CS1` and `HZN-CS1B` Connection Servers listed.

If you were to now look at the **Sites** screen, you would see that the site is listed with the number of pods that make up that site, as well as the details of the pods in the site.

Installing and Configuring Horizon 7 - Part 2

You will also be able to see the **Global Entitlements**, as shown in the following screenshot:

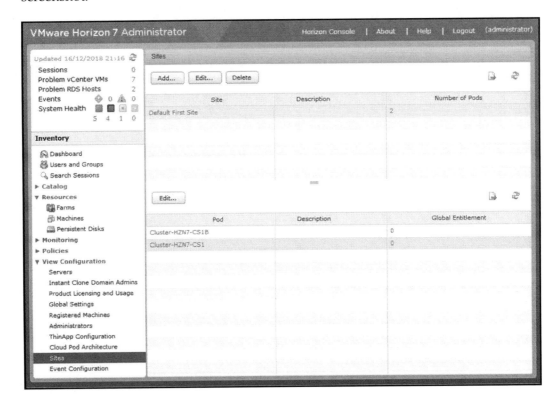

Now that you have created a pod federation by initializing the Cloud Pod Architecture feature and added a second pod to the pod federation, you can now create **Global Entitlements**, which we will cover in the next section.

Entitling users to the Cloud Pod

In this section, we are going to add a Global Entitlement by creating a desktop pool and then entitling a user to connect to desktops within the pool. To do this, follow these steps:

1. From the View Administrator console, in the **Inventory** pane on the left, expand the **Catalog** section, and then click on **Global Entitlement (1)**.

Chapter 5

2. Next, click the **Add...** button (2), as shown in the following screenshot:

3. You will now see the **Add Global Entitlement** dialog box and the first section where you choose the type of entitlement you want to create, as shown in the following screenshot:

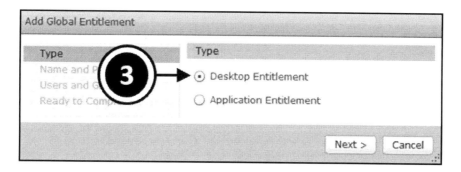

[255]

Installing and Configuring Horizon 7 - Part 2

4. In this example, we are going to create a desktop entitlement, so click the radio button for **Desktop Entitlement (3)**, and then click the **Next >** button. You will now see the **Name and Policies** configuration screen, as shown in the following screenshot:

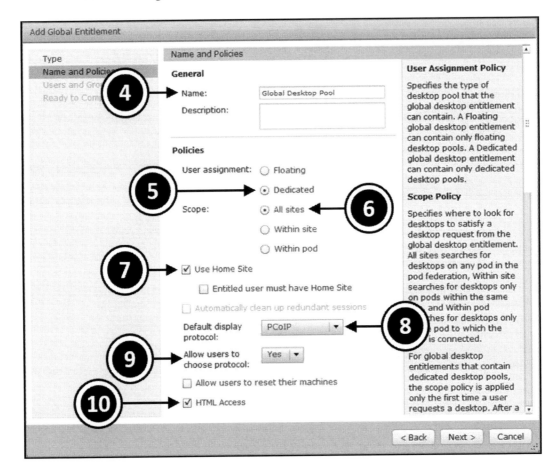

5. In the **General** section, enter a **Name (4)** for the policy name. In the example lab, we will call this `Global Desktop Pool`.

Chapter 5

6. In the **Policies** section, under **User assignment,** click the radio button for **Dedicated** (5). You can specify the user assignment and whether the desktop pool is floating or dedicated. Under **Scope**, click the radio button for **All sites** (6). You can choose from either **All sites**, **Within site**, or **Within pod**.
7. Check the box for **Use Home Site** (7).
8. You then have the option to choose the **Default display protocol**. In the example lab, we are going to select **PCoIP**, so from the dropdown menu, select **PCoIP**.
9. From the **Allow users to choose protocol** option, choose whether you want users to change protocol. In the example lab, from the dropdown menu (9), select **Yes**.
10. Finally, check the box if you want to enable **HTML Access** (10).
11. Click the **Next >** button to continue.
12. You will now see the **Users and Groups** configuration screen, as shown on the following screenshot:

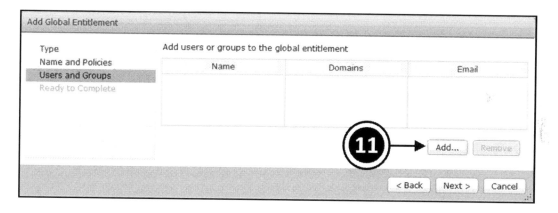

13. Click the **Add...** button (11). You will now see the **Find User or Group** configuration screen, as shown in the following screenshot:

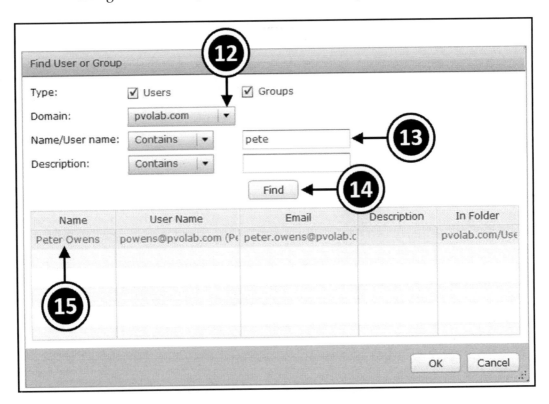

14. Click the dropdown arrow (**12**) and select the domain in which the user resides. In the example lab, this is pvolab.com. Then, in the **Name/User name** box (**13**), enter the name of the user you want to entitle to this pool, and then click the **Find** button (**14**). The details of the user are then displayed. Click to highlight and select the user (**15**), and then click the **OK** button.

Chapter 5

15. You will return to the **Users and Groups** screen, which now shows the selected user, as shown in the following screenshot:

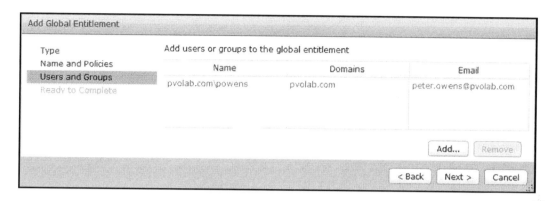

16. Click the **Next >** button to continue. You will now see the **Ready to Complete** screen, as shown in the following screenshot:

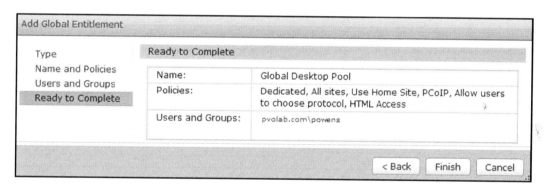

17. Check that the details have been entered correctly and then click the **Finish** button. You will return to the **Global Entitlements** screen, which will now show the **Global Desktop Pool** and the number of assigned users, as shown in the following screenshot:

You have now successfully configured a Cloud Pod federation.

In the final section of this chapter, we are going to finish off the installation by configuring the ESXi host servers with NVIDIA graphics cards.

Configuring View for GPU-enabled virtual desktops

In Chapter 2, *Understanding Horizon 7 Architecture and Components*, we discussed that Horizon View virtual desktop machines can be configured to use hardware that's been installed in the ESXi host server hosting those desktops. In this case, the hardware in question is a graphics card.

As we discussed earlier, an advanced feature of Horizon View is its ability to use dedicated hardware installed that's been on the ESXi host servers, configured with PCI pass-through so that the virtual desktop machine can see the hardware.

In this section, we will perform the initial steps to install a NVIDIA GRID GPU card into one of the host servers. Later on, in Chapter 7, *Building and Optimizing the Virtual Desktop OS*, we will create a virtual desktop machine image, which will have a dedicated assignment and access to the GPU resource.

If you are going to be using vGPU, you will need vSphere 6 installed as the hypervisor to support this.

Configuring the ESXi host servers

Before you build the virtual desktop machine, you need to have the graphics card physically installed and configured into the ESXi host in preparation to build the new virtual desktop machines that will use it.

In the example lab, we are using the NVIDIA GRID K2 card. These cards are available via the OEM route and come already configured from the server vendors due to them requiring additional power connectors, cooling fans, and specific BIOS settings.

It's worth checking these before you start, as just retrofitting the cards to an existing server might mean that they do not work. You will find the list of certified servers by clicking on the following link: http://www.nvidia.com/object/grid-partners.html.

Installing and Configuring Horizon 7 - Part 2

With the hardware installed, log in to the vSphere Web Client, select the host that the card has been installed on, and perform the following steps:

1. Login into the vSphere Web Client and then navigate to the host server that has the NVIDIA card installed. In the example lab, this is host `esx-1.pvolab.com`, as shown in the following screenshot:

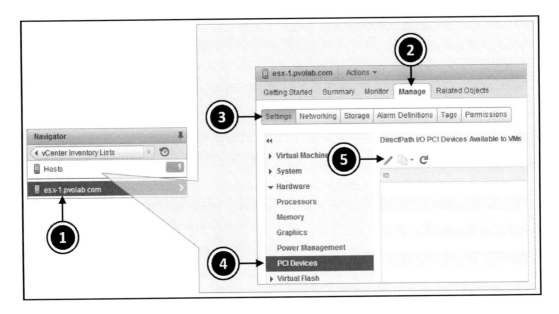

Chapter 5

2. Select the ESXi host server `esx-1.pvolab.com` (1) and then click the **Manage** tab (2). Click the **Settings** button (3) and expand the **Hardware** section. Click on **PCI Devices** (4) and then click the pencil icon (5) to edit the settings. You will now see the **Edit PCI Device Availability** screen, as shown in the following screenshot:

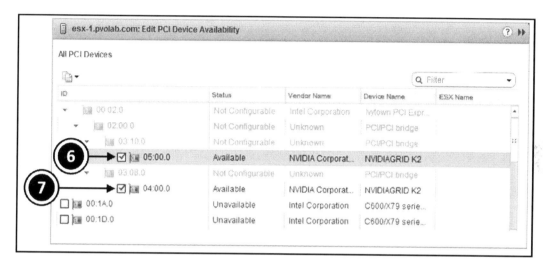

As you can see, this host server has been configured with two NVIDIA GRID K2 graphics cards. Check boxes (6) and (7) to enable the cards on the host server.

You now configured the ESXi host server to use the NVIDIA GRID K2 GPU cards. These will be used when we build the virtual desktop machines in later this book, in `Chapter 7`, *Building and Optimizing the Virtual Desktop OS*.

Summary

In this chapter, we completed the installation of the Horizon View Environment, including the Replica Server, the Security Server, and the Enrollment Server.

We discussed the initial configuration items that you will need to undertake, such as licensing your environment, connecting your vCenter and View Composer Servers, and configuring the View Security Server for external connections. We also looked at the configuration items that are needed to prepare our environment for advanced graphics with NVIDIA GRID.

The final part of this chapter covered how to initialize and configure the Cloud Pod Architecture feature.

Having completed this chapter, you should have built a fully functioning View deployment, which is ready to deliver virtual desktop machines to your end users. The next steps are to start building the virtual desktops, preparing them for delivery before configuring Horizon View to deliver them.

But before we start building our virtual desktop machines, we are going to look at the security considerations in the next chapter, Chapter 6, *Securing Horizon View with SSL Certificates*, where we are going to configure SSL certificates across our environment to ensure it is secure. We will also take a look at configuring the True SSO feature.

Section 2: Building and Delivering the Virtual Desktop Experience

In the chapters of this section, we are going to look at building virtual desktop images, fine-tuning them, and creating desktop pools ready for delivery.

The following chapters are included in this section:

Chapter 6, *Securing Horizon View with SSL Certificates*
Chapter 7, *Building and Optimizing the Virtual Desktop OS*
Chapter 8, *Configuring and Managing Desktop Pools – Part 1*
Chapter 9, *Configuring and Managing Desktop Pools – Part 2*
Chapter 10, *Fine-Tuning the End User Experience*
Chapter 17, *Managing the End User Environment in Horizon* (Online chapter)

6
Securing Horizon View with SSL Certificates

In this chapter, we will discuss the security aspect of VMware Horizon View 7, and in particular, how we deliver secure communication not only with the end user client but also between the different View infrastructure components in the data center. We are going to look at two ways to deliver this secure communication.

We will start with **Secure Sockets Layer** (**SSL**) certificates and get an overview of SSL, before learning how to create/issue a certificate and configure Horizon View to use it. The second option that will be covered in this chapter is **True SSO**. True SSO provides users with a way to authenticate to their virtual desktops that keeps all of their usual domain privileges but doesn't require them to provide their Active Directory credentials. You will more than likely have SSL certificates already set up in your environment, but for this chapter, we're going to set up a test environment using a server in the example lab.

In this chapter, we will cover the following topics:

- Horizon View and SSL certificates
- Installing SSL cerificates for Horizon View
- Horizon View True SSO

Horizon View and SSL certificates

Let's start by defining SSL. SSL is an encryption technology developed by Netscape.

It is used to create an encrypted connection between a web server and the web browser in which you will view web pages. By using SSL, you can securely view the information sent to your browser, knowing that nobody else can access it.

Securing Horizon View with SSL Certificates

SSL works by means of an SSL certificate that is installed on a server and is used to identify you. So the question is, how do you know whether you are using a secure connection to connect to the server? If you have a secure connection, you will see a padlock icon in your browser or the address bar will be colored green.

 To ensure you have a secure connection, you can also access the site using `https://` in your browser rather than the usual `http://`.

SSL certificates are provided by **Certificate Authorities (CAs)**.

What is a CA?

A **CA** is a service that issues digital certificates to organizations or people after validating them. CAs keep detailed records of the certificates that have been issued and any other information that was used when the certificate was issued. These are regularly audited to ensure compliance.

You can obtain a CA from different organizations, or you can create your own from a root CA.

Why do I need SSL certificates for Horizon View?

If you are transmitting sensitive information from a website to an endpoint device, you need to secure the information with encryption; otherwise, data could be compromised.

As Horizon View is essentially like a web service to which end users connect from their endpoint device to the View Connection Server, you need to ensure that this connection is secured. In this case, SSL is used to establish a secured link between the client device and the virtual desktop machine. Although, with Horizon View, no actual data is transmitted, the pixels from your virtual desktop machine are transmitted, and if a third party intercepts this transmission, they could potentially see your screen by redrawing these pixels. SSL is also used for communication between Horizon View components, such as Connection Servers and Replica Servers.

Having an SSL certificate installed is a requirement for Horizon View.

By default, Horizon View comes with self-signed certificates that are fine for a proof of concept or a small-scale pilot, but for a production environment, you will need to have enterprise-class certificates.

The use of certificates became a requirement with View 5.1, where they were used for the Horizon View components to communicate, such as the Connection Server, Replica Server, and View Composer, as well as the underlying infrastructure of the ESXi hosts and Virtual Center Servers. Each of these components needs to have a certificate installed, along with the client device that is connecting to it.

Installing SSL certificates for Horizon View

In the next sections of this chapter, we will briefly cover how to set up certificates by installing a root CA in our example test environment to get you started with Horizon View. However, we strongly recommend that you engage with your security team to deploy the correct type of certificate for your organization and environment.

Installing a root CA

In this section, we are going to walk through the process of setting up a server that will act as our root CA in the example lab. A server has already been built called **HZN7-CERTS**, which we will use for this role.

Securing Horizon View with SSL Certificates

To configure the root CA, follow these steps:

1. Open a console to the **HZN7-CERTS** server, and launch the **Server Manager**.
2. Click on **Add roles and features** (1), as shown in the following screenshot:

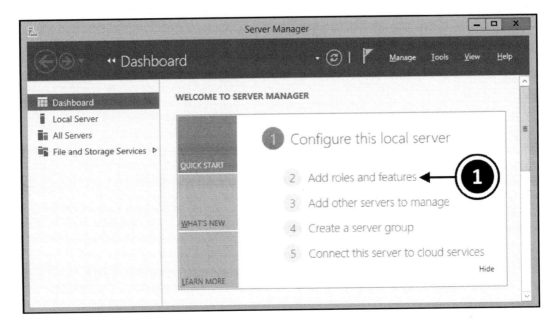

3. You will now see the **Add Roles and Features Wizard** and the **Before You Begin** screen. Click on the **Next >** button to continue.
4. Next, you will see the **Installation Type** screen. Click the radio button for **Role-based or feature-based installation** (2), as shown in the following screenshot:

Chapter 6

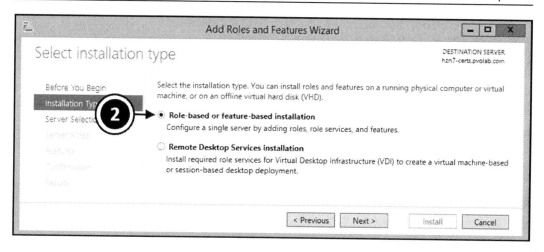

5. Click on the **Next >** button to continue.
6. You will now see the **Server Selection** screen, as shown in the following screenshot:

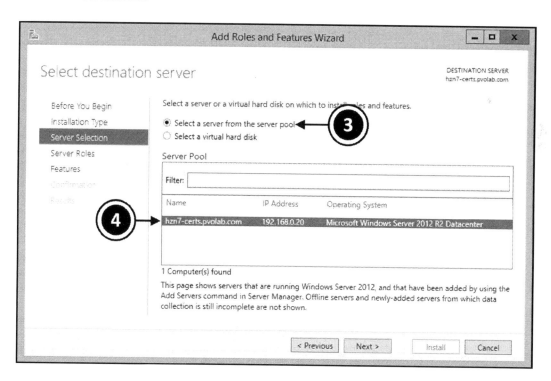

Securing Horizon View with SSL Certificates

7. Click on the radio button for **Select a server from the server pool** (3), and then highlight the `hzn7-certs.pvolab.com` server from the list (4).
8. Click the **Next >** button to continue. You will now see the **Server Roles** screen, as shown in the following screenshot:

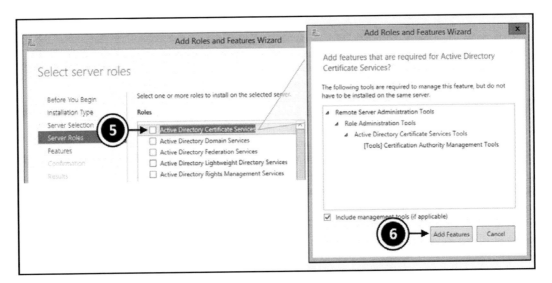

9. Check the box for **Active Directory Certificate Services** (5) and then, in the pop-up box for **Add features that are required for Active Directory Certificate Services**, click on the **Add Features** button (6).
10. You will now return to the **Server Roles** screen, which will show that **Active Directory Certificate Services** is now checked. Click on the **Next >** button to continue.
11. Next, you will see the **Features** configuration screen. Click on the **Next >** button to continue.

Chapter 6

12. The next part of the **Add Roles and Features Wizard** screen is the **Active Directory Certificate Services** screen, as shown in the following screenshot:

13. Click the **Next >** button to continue. You will now see the **Select role services** screen, as shown in the following screenshot:

[273]

14. Under **Role services**, check the box for **Certification Authority** (7), and then click on the **Next >** button to continue.
15. On the **Confirm installation selections** screen, check the box for **Restart the destination server automatically** (8), and then click on the **Install** button.

The certificate services feature has now been installed. There are now some post-deployment configuration to be completed.

Root CA post-deployment configuration tasks

With the core root CA components installed, you can now complete the post-deployment configuration tasks:

1. From the menu bar along the top of the **Server Manager Dashboard**, click the warning yellow triangle warning box, and from the options that pop up, click the **Configure Active Directory Certificate Services** entry (**1**), as shown in the following screenshot:

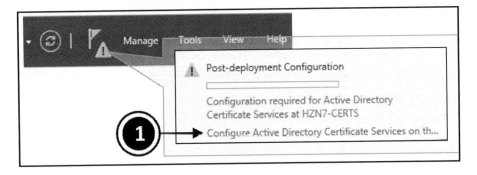

Chapter 6

2. You will now see the **AD CS Configuration** screen and the **Credentials** configuration section:

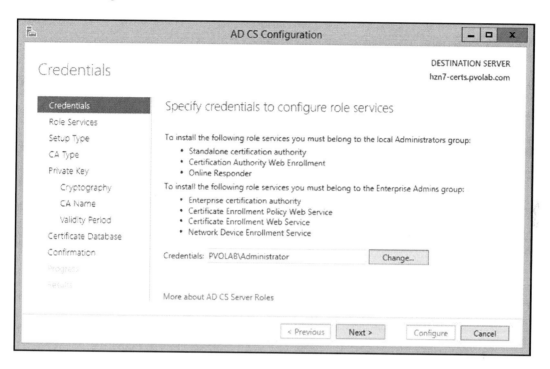

3. Click on the **Next >** button to continue. You will now see the **Role Services** configuration screen, as shown in the following screenshot:

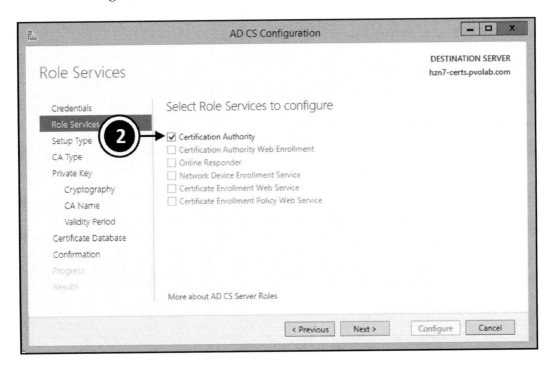

4. Check the **Certification Authority** box (2), and then click on the **Next >** button to continue.

5. You will now see the **Setup Type** configuration screen, as shown in the following screenshot:

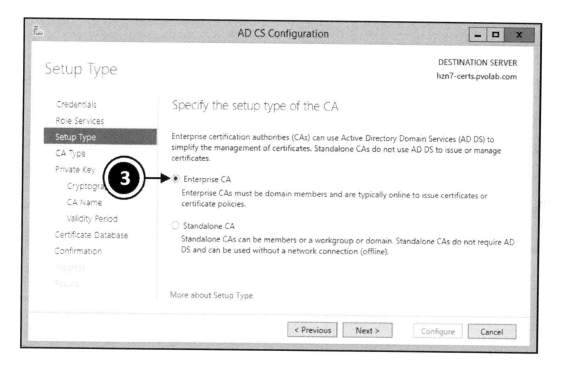

6. Click on the radio button to select the **Enterprise CA** option (3), and then click on the **Next >** button to continue. You will now see the **CA Type** configuration screen:

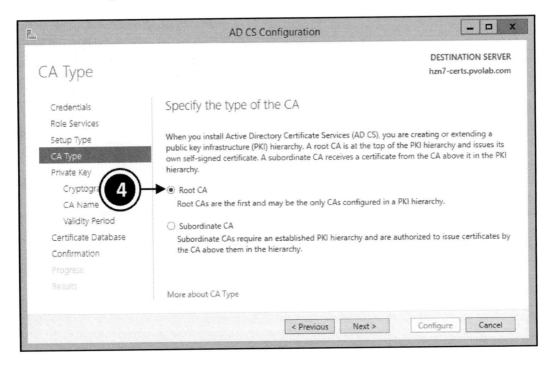

7. Next, click on the radio button to select the **Root CA** option (4), and then click on the **Next >** button to continue.

Chapter 6

8. You will now see the **Private Key** configuration screen, as shown in the following screenshot:

Securing Horizon View with SSL Certificates

9. Click on the radio button to select the **Create a new private key** option (5), and then click on the **Next >** button to continue. You will now see the **Cryptography for CA** configuration screen:

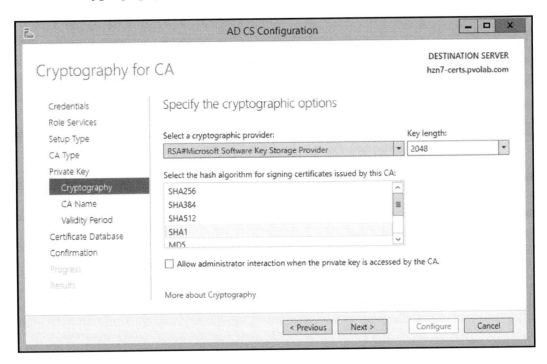

10. Accept the default settings and click the **Next >** button to continue.

11. You will now see the **CA Name** configuration screen, where you can specify the name of the CA, as shown in the following screenshot:

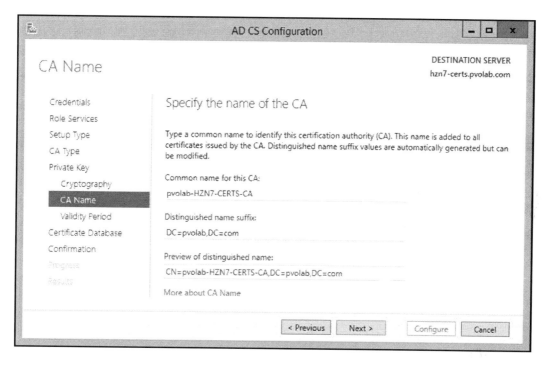

12. Accept the default settings and click on the **Next >** button to continue.

13. You will now see the **Validity Period** configuration screen, as shown in the following screenshot:

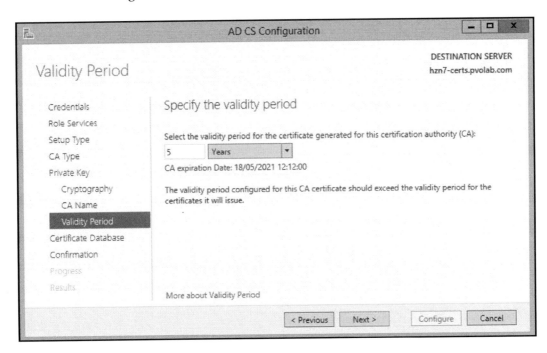

14. Accept the default settings and click on the **Next >** button to continue.

Chapter 6

15. You will now see the **CA Database** configuration screen, as shown in the following screenshot:

Securing Horizon View with SSL Certificates

16. Accept the default settings and click on the **Next >** button to continue. You will now see the **Confirmation** screen, as shown in the following screenshot:

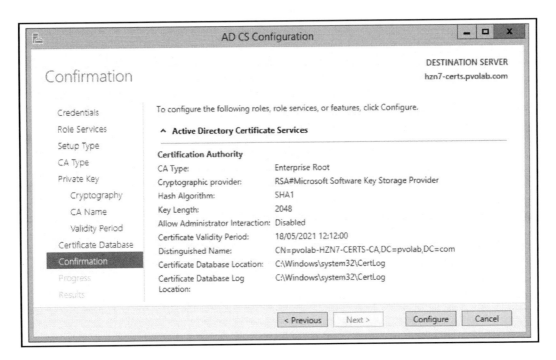

17. Click on the **Configure** button at the bottom of the screen to complete the configuration. Once the configuration has successfully completed, you will see the following message pop up:

18. Click on the **Close** button to close the Server Manager.

Now that we have our certificate server set up and running, we can start configuring the Horizon View software infrastructure components and clients to use it.

We will start by installing the certificate on the Horizon View Connection Server first.

Installing an SSL certificate on the View Connection Server

With the certificate server installed and configured, we are now going to install the newly created certificate on the View Connection Server:

1. Open a remote console session to the View Connection Server named **HZN7-CS1**, and then open a **Run** command box. In the **Run** box, type mmc, and then click on **OK** to launch the **Microsoft Management Console** (**MMC**), as shown in the following screenshot:

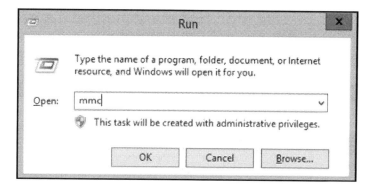

2. You will now see the MMC console screen, as shown in the following screenshot:

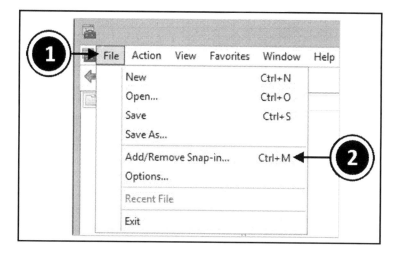

3. On the MMC console screen, click on **File (1)**, and then click on the option for **Add/Remove Snap-in... (2)**.
4. You will now see the **Add or Remove Snap-ins** screen:

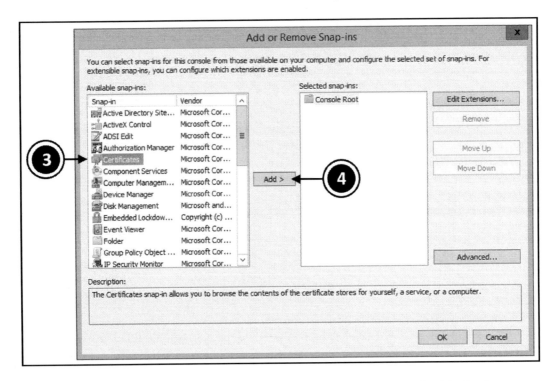

5. From the **Available snap-ins** section on the left, click to highlight the **Certificates** entry (3), and then click, the **Add >** button (4), as shown in the previous screenshot.

6. You will now see the **Certificates snap-in** box appear, as shown in the following screenshot:

7. Click on the radio button for **Computer account** (5), and then click the **Next >** button to continue. You will now see the **Select Computer** configuration box:

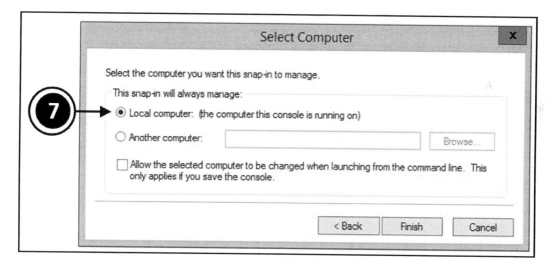

8. Click on the radio button for **Local computer** (6), and then click on the **Finish** button. You will return to the **Add or Remove Snap-ins** screen, which now shows the certificates snap-in as being selected.
9. Click on **OK** to close the **Add or Remove Snap-ins** screen.

You have now successfully added **Certificates** to the management console as an option for configuration, as shown in the following screenshot:

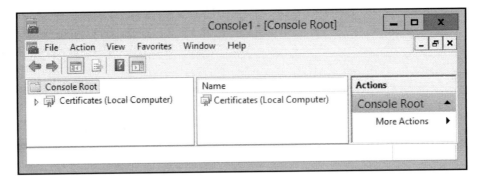

Now you have the certificates available to manage and configure from the management console, the next task is to request a certificate from the root CA:

1. From the `Console Root`, expand the `Certificates (Local Computer)` folder, and then right-click on the `Personal` folder (**1**). From the contextual menu, navigate to **All Tasks** (**2**) and then select **Request New Certificate...** (**3**):

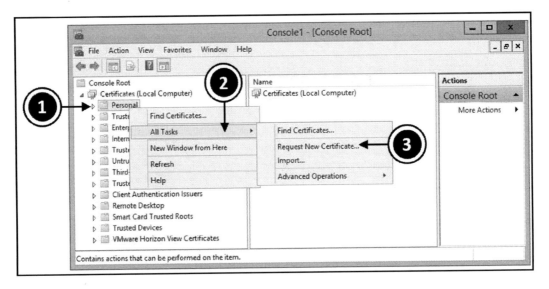

2. You will now see the **Before You Begin** section on **Certificate Enrollment** screen. Click on the **Next** button to continue.

Chapter 6

3. Now the **Select Certificate Enrollment Policy** screen is displayed, as shown in the following screenshot:

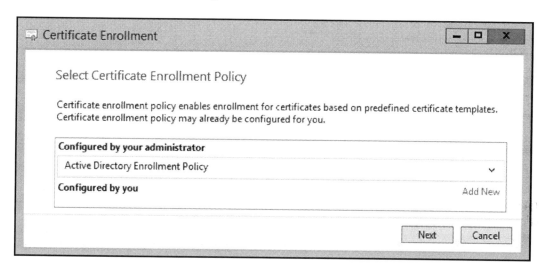

4. Click on the **Next** button to continue. You will now see the **Certificate Enrollment Request Certificates** screen:

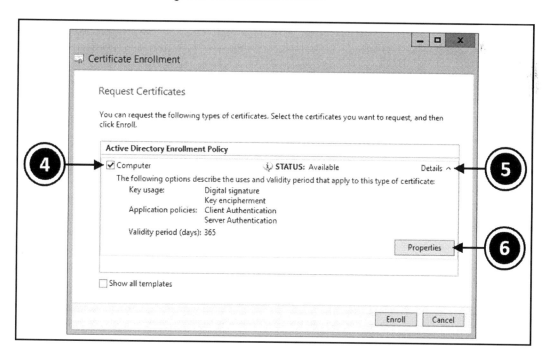

5. In the **Active Directory Enrollment Policy** box, check the box for **Computer** (4). We will use this policy template for our certificate; however, you can create your own template on the root CA server.
6. Now click on the arrow next to **Details** (5), and then click on the **Properties** box (6) so that we can configure the properties of the certificate. You will now see the **Certificate Properties** configuration box, as shown in the following screenshot:

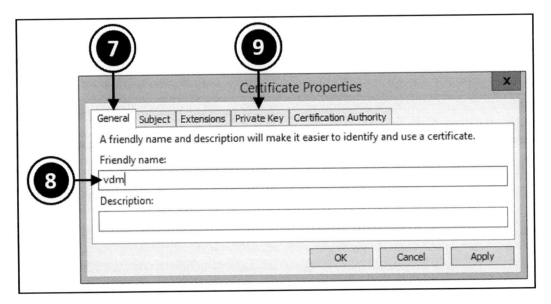

7. Click on the **General** tab (7), and then in the **Friendly name:** box (8), type in a friendly name for this certificate. In the example lab, we will call this vdm. Optionally, you can enter a **Description** as well.

Chapter 6

8. Next, from the **Certificate Properties** box again, click on the **Private Key** tab, as shown in the following screenshot:

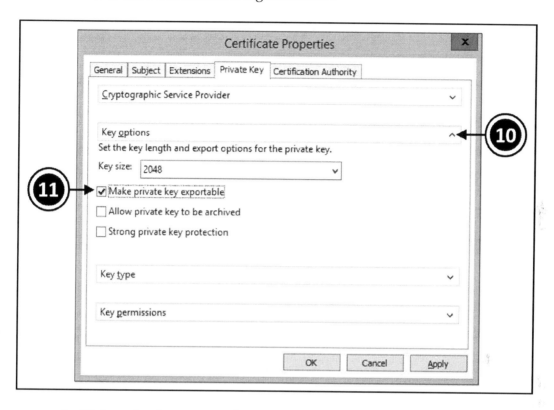

9. Click on the down arrow for **Key options** (10) to expand the configuration options, and check the box for **Make private key exportable** (11).

10. Finally, click on the **Certification Authority** tab (12), as shown in the following screenshot:

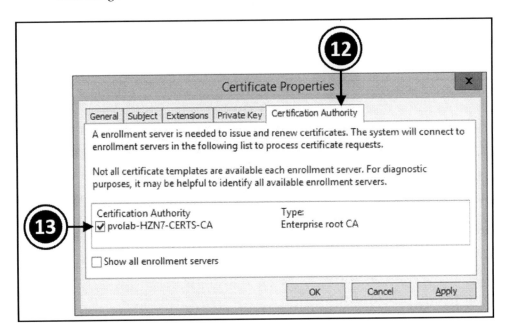

Chapter 6

11. Check the box to select the **pvolab-HZN7-CERTS-CA (13)** enrollment server. Now click on the **OK** button. You will return to the **Request Certificates** screen, as shown in the following screenshot:

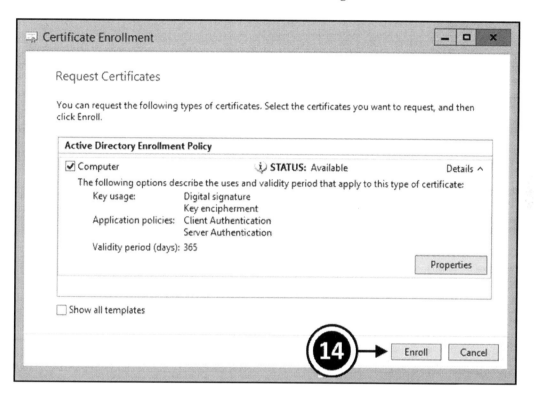

12. Click on the **Enroll** button **(14)** to continue and enroll the Connection Server. If the enrollment is successful, then you will see the following screenshot:

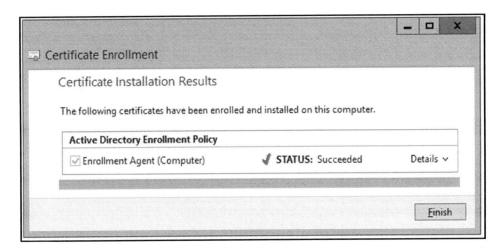

13. Click the **Finish** button to complete the certificate enrollment process.

Don't forget that you need to complete the certificate enrollment process on all of the Horizon View components, so if you have additional servers such as Replica Servers and View Composer Servers then these will all need a certificate to be installed on each and every one of them.

In the next section, we will take a look at what to do now that we have our root CA certificate server and the certificate is installed on our Connection Servers.

Post-certificate enrollment configuration tasks

Even though you have installed a certificate server and installed a valid certificate on the Connection Server, there are still a few things to configure.

If you were to try and connect to the View Administrator using your browser, you will still see an error message saying there is a problem with the website's security certificate. A typical message would look something like the following:

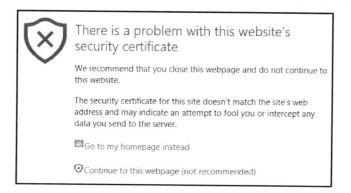

If you remember from the beginning of this chapter, we also discussed accessing web pages using http:// or https:// for secure web pages. If the address bar in your browser is red, as shown in the following screenshot, then the connection is not secure and there are no certificates installed:

You can of course ignore these errors and just click **Continue to this website (not recommended)**, which allows you to continue past the warning and log on to View Administrator.

However, when you log on, you will see that, in the **System Health** section of the View Administrator dashboard, there is also a red warning box. As far as View is concerned, if you don't have a valid certificate installed, the health warning tells you that the connections will be untrusted and therefore that's a bad thing! An example of this is shown in the following screenshot:

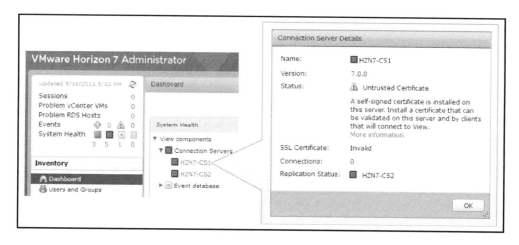

Securing Horizon View with SSL Certificates

If you click on the Horizon 7 Administrator dashboard, and under **System Health** on the **Dashboard** view, select one of the Connection Servers displaying a red warning box. You can see in the server details box that opens that there is a yellow warning sign telling you that there is an untrusted certificate on this particular server. In the example lab environment, we are going to continue using the Horizon View Manager rather than the newer Horizon Console web-based management console. The reason is that at the time of writing, not all of the features we are going to cover can be accessed using the Horizon console.

It's the same thing from the end user perspective. If they try to log on via the Horizon Client, they will see the following:

You can see in the **Server:** box highlighted in the preceding screenshot, that the `https://` address of the Connection Server is colored red, has been crossed out, and a warning symbol is displayed on the padlock, all indicating that there is no trusted certificate installed.

Now that we have created and installed a certificate on the Connection Server, in order for Horizon View to pick up the installed certificate, you need to restart the View Connection Server service in Windows services. To do this, follow these steps:

1. Open a **Run** dialog box, and in the **Run** dialog box, type `services.msc` to open the **Services (Local)** screen. Scroll down to the entry for **VMware Horizon View Connection Server** (1), as shown in the following screenshot:

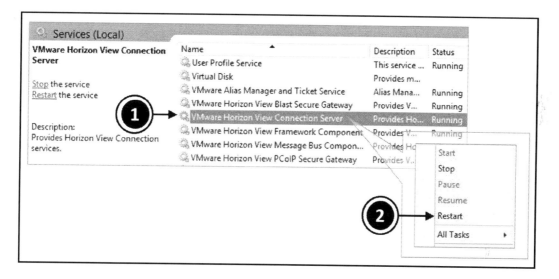

2. Select the option for **VMware Horizon View Connection Server**, right-click, and then from the contextual menu, click on **Restart** (2). Once the VMware Horizon View Connection Server service has restarted, you can log in to the View Administrator again, and check the certificate has been applied.

Securing Horizon View with SSL Certificates

3. To do this, once you have logged in, from the **Dashboard**, and under **System Health**, click on **Connection Servers** to expand this section, and then click on the Connection Server **HZN7-CS1 (3)**, or the server onto which you have just installed the certificate. In the **Connection Server Details** box that pops up, you will now see that the SSL certificate is shown as **Valid (4)** and that the error boxes have now changed from red to green:

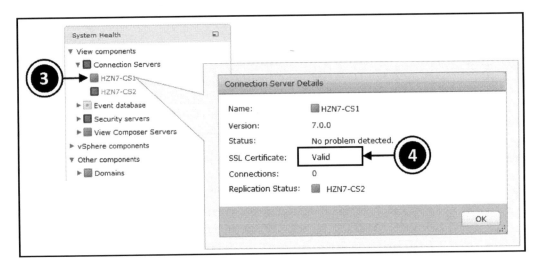

4. Finally, click on **OK** to close the dialog box for the **Connection Server Details** and then log out of the View Administrator.

You have now successfully created and installed a certificate for Horizon View. Don't forget that you need to install a certificate on all of the Horizon View components, such as any Replica Servers or View Composer servers.

Horizon View True SSO

In Chapter 2, *Understanding Horizon 7 Architecture and Components*, we introduced you to the True SSO feature and its architecture. In this section, we are going to look at how to configure True SSO.

To set up True SSO, you first need to configure a CA, which we have already configured earlier on in this chapter in the *Installing a root CA* section. There are then a number of configuration steps to complete in preparation for installing True SSO.

Preparing AD for True SSO

The first step is to create an **Active Directory** (**AD**) group for the Enrollment Server. To do this, follow these steps:

1. Open a console to your Domain Controller. In the example lab, this is the machine called `dc.pvolab.com`. Launch the **Active Directory Users and Computers** configuration screen, as shown in the following screenshot:

2. Click on and select Users **(1)**, and then right-click. From the contextual menu, click on **New (2)**, and then from the expanded options, select **Group (3)**. You will now see the **New Object – Group** dialog box, as shown in the following screenshot:

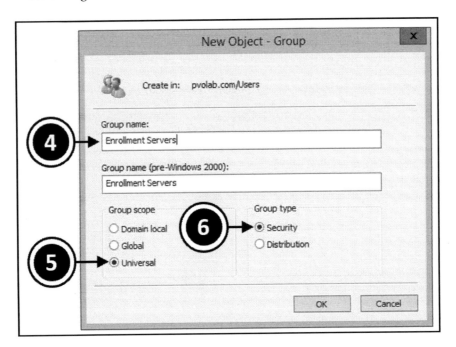

3. In the **Group name** box **(4)**, type in a name for the new group. In the example lab, this is called Enrollment Servers. In the **Group scope** box, click on the radio button for **Universal (5)**, and in the **Group type** box, click on the radio button for **Security (6)**. Once configured, click on the **OK** button. Next, you need to add the Enrollment Server into this newly created group.

Chapter 6

4. In the **Active Directory Users and Computers** configuration screen, click on Computers **(7)**, and then double-click on the Enrollment Server. In the example lab, this is the computer called **HZN7-ENROL**, as shown in the following screenshot:

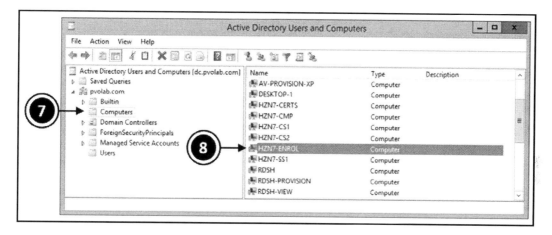

5. You will now see the **HZN7-ENROL Properties** dialog box, as shown in the following screenshot:

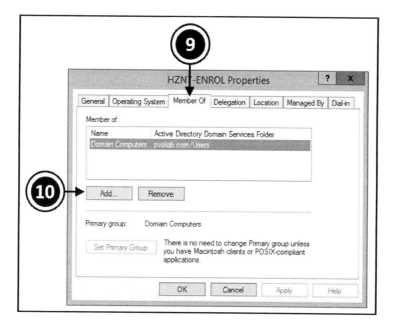

[301]

6. Click on the **Member Of** tab (**9**), and then click on the **Add...** button (**10**). You will now see the **Select Groups** dialog box:

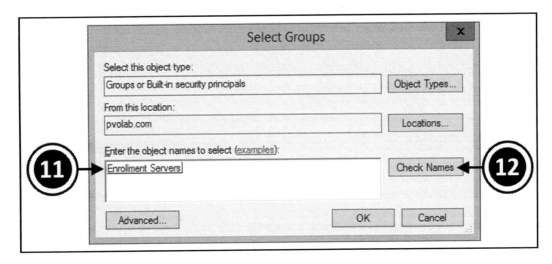

7. In the **Enter the object names to select** box (**11**), type in the name of the group you created for the `Enrollment Servers`. You can just type the first part of the name and then click the **Check Names** button (**12**). This will find any names that match the first part of what you type in. In this example, it will find the **Enrollment Servers** group. With the correct group name selected, click on the **OK** button to continue.

8. You will return to the **HZN7-ENROL Properties** dialog box, which now shows that the Enrollment Server called **HZN7-ENROL** is a member of the **Enrollment Servers** group. This is shown in the following screenshot:

Chapter 6

With the Domain Controller elements now configured, the next step is to create a new certificate template.

Creating a certificate template for TrueSSO

The next step is to create a certificate template. To do this, we are going to work through the following steps:

1. Open a console to the certificate server and launch the **Certificate Management Console**. In the example lab, this is the server called **HZN7-CERTS**. This is shown in the following screenshot:

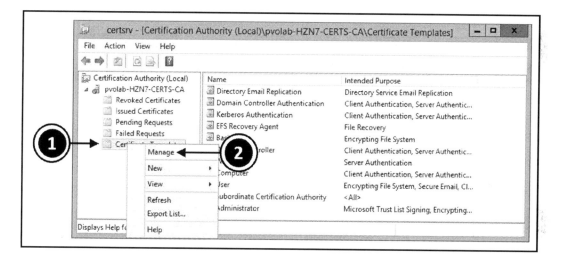

[303]

Securing Horizon View with SSL Certificates

2. Click on the `Certificate Templates` folder **(1)**, and then right-click. From the contextual menu now displayed, click on **Manage (2)**. You will now see the **Certificate Templates Console**, as shown in the following screenshot:

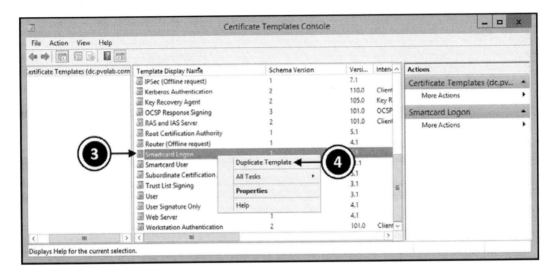

3. Scroll down the **Template Display Name** pane until you find the template for **Smartcard Logon (3)**, and click to highlight it. Now right-click, and then from the contextual menu now displayed, click on **Duplicate Template**. You will now see the **Properties of New Template** configuration box, as shown in the following screenshot:

Chapter 6

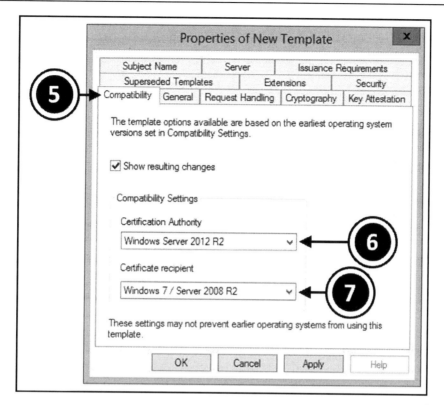

4. Click on the **Compatibility** tab (5). In the **Compatibility Settings** section, from the drop-down menu for **Certification Authority** (6), select the appropriate setting for the server version that is running as the CA. In the example lab, the CA server is running Windows Server 2012 R2.
5. Next, from the drop-down menu for **Certificate recipient** (7), select the appropriate setting for the machines that will be in receipt of this certificate. In the example lab, we will set this to **Windows 7 / Server 2008 R2**.

 When changing these settings, you will see a dialog box appear warning you about compatibility changes, and changes to the template that you are about to make. Click **OK** to accept these messages and to continue.

Securing Horizon View with SSL Certificates

6. Now click on the **General** tab **(8)** box as shown in the following screenshot:

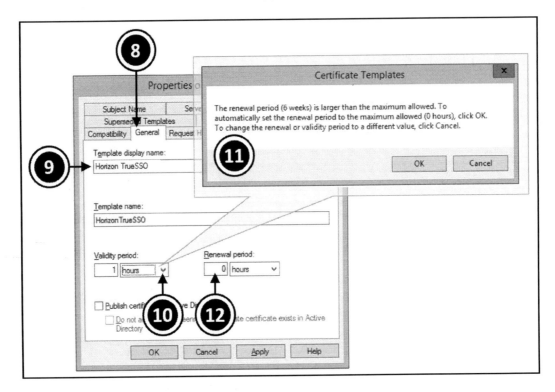

7. In the **Template display name** box **(9)**, type in a name for the new certificate template. In the example lab, this is called `Horizon TrueSSO`.
8. Next, you need to configure a validity time. From the drop-down menu under **Validity period (10)**, select the option for **hours**. You will then see the **Certificate Templates** warning box **(11)**.
9. Click on **OK** to accept. Accepting the warning will automatically set the **Renewal period** to 0 **hours (12)**.

Chapter 6

10. Now click on the **Request Handling** tab (13) box, as shown in the following screenshot:

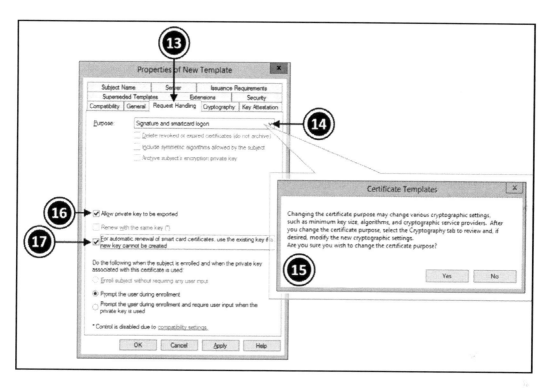

11. In the drop-down box next to **Purpose** (14), select the option for **Signature and smartcard logon**. You will then see the **Certificate Templates** warning box (**15**), which warns you that you are about to change the purpose of the certificate. Click **Yes** to accept the warning message and close the dialog box.

12. Finally, on this screen, check the box for **Allow private key to be exported** (**16**), and check the box for **For automatic renewal of smartcard certificates** (**17**).

13. Next, click the **Cryptography** tab **(18)**, as shown in the following screenshot:

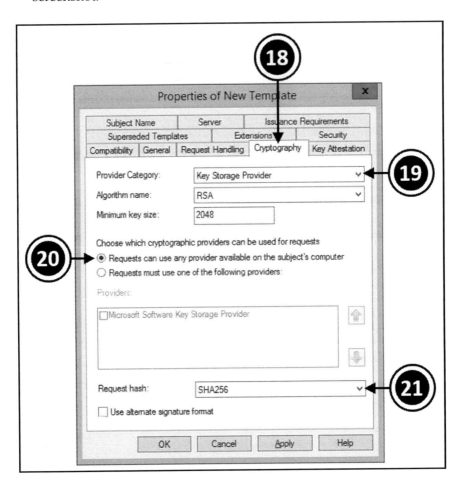

14. In the **Provider Category** box, click on the drop-down arrow **(19)** and select the option for **Key Storage Provider**. Then, click on the radio button for **Requests can use any provider available on the subject's computer** **(20)**, and then in the **Request hash** box, click on the drop-down arrow **(21)** and select the option for **SHA256**.

15. The next tab to configure is the **Subject Name** tab (22), as shown in the following screenshot:

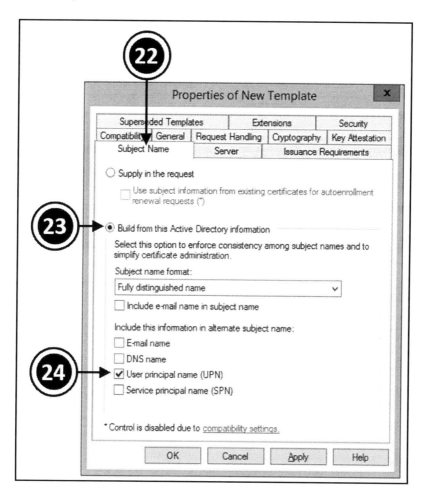

16. Click on the radio button for **Build from this Active Directory information** (23), and then check the box for **User principal name (UPN)** (24).
17. The next tab to configure is the **Server** tab (25), as shown in the following screenshot:

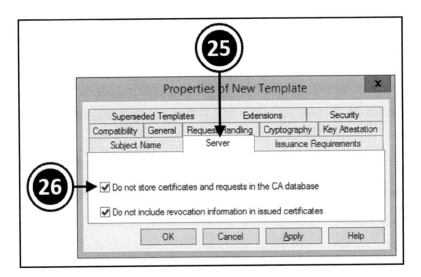

18. Check the **Do not store certificates and requests in the CA database** box (26). Now click on the **Issuance Requirements** tab (27), as shown in the following screenshot:

Chapter 6

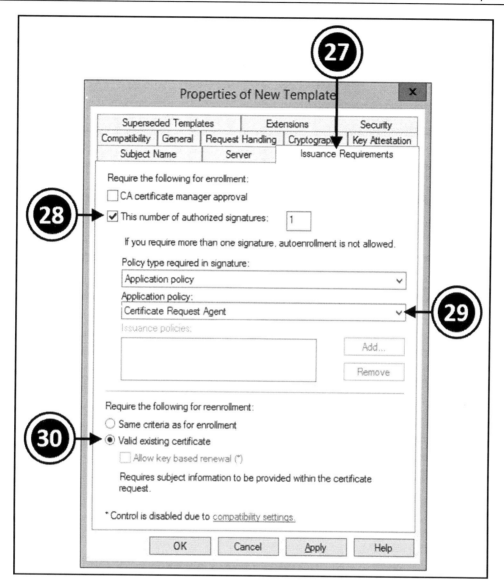

19. Check the box for **This number of authorized signatures** (28), and ensure the value for this option is set to 1.

20. From the **Application policy** box, click on the drop-down arrow **(29)** and select the option for **Certificate Request Agent**. Finally, on this tab, click on the radio button for **Valid existing certificate (30)**.
21. For the final part of the **Properties of New Template** configuration, click on the **Security** tab **(31)** as shown in the following screenshot:

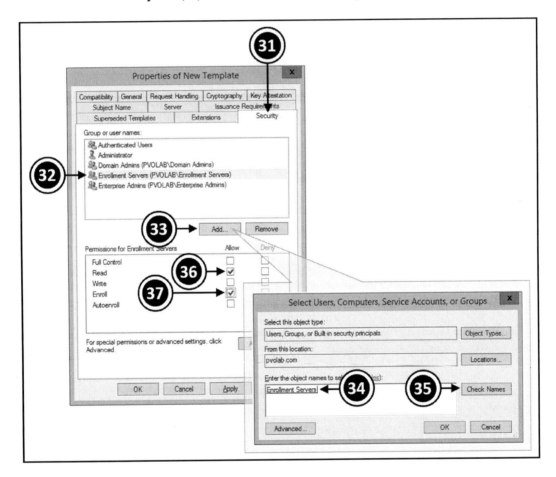

22. Click to select the **Enrollment Servers** group **(32)**, and then click on the **Add...** button **(33)**.

23. You will now see the **Select Users, Computers, Service Accounts or Groups** dialog box pop up. In the **Enter the object names to select** box (34), type in the name of the `Enrollment Servers` group. You can just type the first few letters of the group name and then click on the **Check Names** button (35) to find any matches. You will now see the **Enrollment Servers** group (34).

24. Finally, in the **Permissions for Enrollment Servers** section, check the box under the **Allow** heading for **Read** (36) and **Enroll** (37).

25. This step is now complete so click on the **OK** button to finish the configuration and close the dialog box.

In the next section, we are going to issue the newly created certificate template.

Issuing the TrueSSO certificate template

Now that the certificate template has been created, the next task is to issue it. To do this, follow the steps as described:

1. From the **Certificate Management Console** screen, click on the `Certificate Templates` folder (1), right-click, and then from the contextual menu that is displayed click on **New** (2), and then select the option for **Certificate Template to Issue** (3). This is shown in the following screenshot:

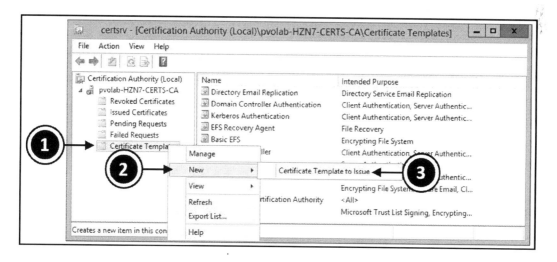

Securing Horizon View with SSL Certificates

2. You will now see the **Enable Certificate Templates** dialog box, as shown in the following screenshot:

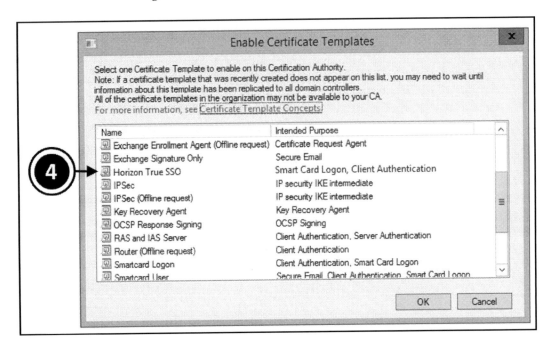

3. Click on **Horizon True SSO (4)**, and then click on the **OK** button.
4. You will now go back to the **Enable Certificate Templates** dialog box, as shown in the following screenshot:

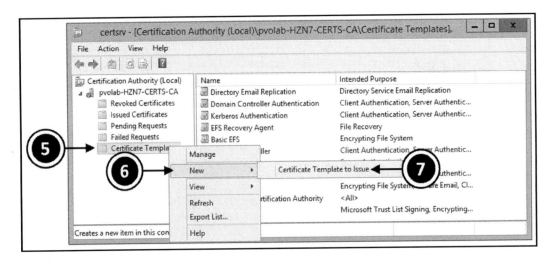

Chapter 6

5. Next, we need to enable the Enrollment Agent. As in the previous step, from the **Certificate Management Console** screen, click on the `Certificate Templates` folder **(5)**, right-click, and then from the contextual menu that is displayed, click on **New (6)**, and then select the option for **Certificate Template to Issue (7)**. You will now see the **Enable Certificate Templates** dialog box, as shown in the following screenshot:

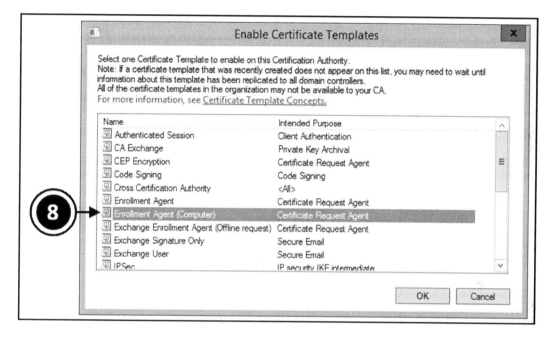

6. Click on and select the option for **Enrollment Agent (Computer) (8)**. Now click on the **OK** button. You will return to the **Enable Certificate Templates** dialog box. You can now exit the **Certificate Management Console**.

You need to check that the **Enrollment Agent (Computer)** template has the same security settings as the template for `TrueSSO` template was configured with. This means it has been added to the Enrollment Servers Security group and has been granted read and enroll permissions.

[315]

Securing Horizon View with SSL Certificates

The final few configuration tasks are command-line-based, so from the desktop of the certificate server, launch a **Run** dialog box. In the **Run** dialog box, type cmd to open a Command Prompt box.

The first thing you need to do is to configure the CA for non-persistent certificate processing. To do this, at Command Prompt, type the following command:

```
certutil -setreg DBFlags +DBFLAGS_ENABLEVOLATILEREQUESTS
```

The output from running this command is shown in the following screenshot:

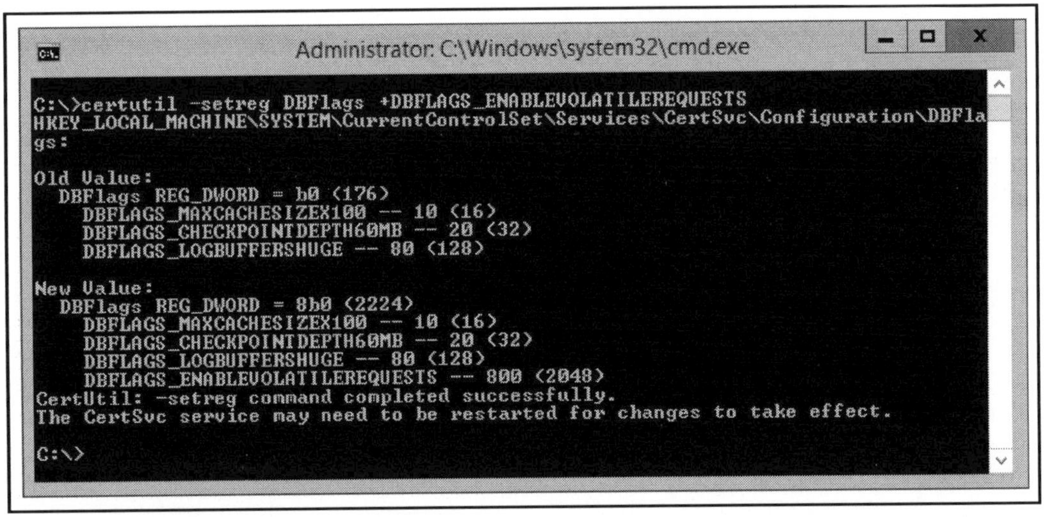

```
C:\>certutil -setreg DBFlags +DBFLAGS_ENABLEVOLATILEREQUESTS
HKEY_LOCAL_MACHINE\SYSTEM\CurrentControlSet\Services\CertSvc\Configuration\DBFla
gs:

Old Value:
  DBFlags REG_DWORD = b0 (176)
    DBFLAGS_MAXCACHESIZEX100 -- 10 (16)
    DBFLAGS_CHECKPOINTDEPTH60MB -- 20 (32)
    DBFLAGS_LOGBUFFERSHUGE -- 80 (128)

New Value:
  DBFlags REG_DWORD = 8b0 (2224)
    DBFLAGS_MAXCACHESIZEX100 -- 10 (16)
    DBFLAGS_CHECKPOINTDEPTH60MB -- 20 (32)
    DBFLAGS_LOGBUFFERSHUGE -- 80 (128)
    DBFLAGS_ENABLEVOLATILEREQUESTS -- 800 (2048)
CertUtil: -setreg command completed successfully.
The CertSvc service may need to be restarted for changes to take effect.

C:\>
```

The second thing you need to do it to configure the CA to ignore offline **Certificate Revocation Lists** (**CRL**) errors. To do this, at Command Prompt, type the following command:

```
certutil -setreg ca\CRLFlags +CRLF_REVCHECK_IGNORE_OFFLINE
```

The following screenshot shows the command successfully executing:

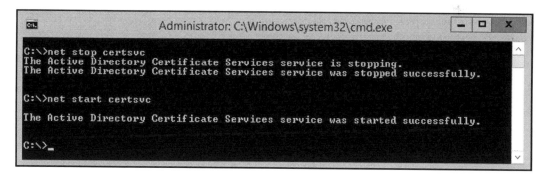

Finally, as it states in Command Prompt, you need to restart the certificate service. To do this at Command Prompt, run the following two commands, one after the other:

```
net stop certsvc
net start certsvc
```

You should see something similar to the following screenshot, which shows that the certification service was successfully stopped and then started again:

Securing Horizon View with SSL Certificates

The next step in the process is to deploy the certificates on the Enrollment Server and the Connection Server.

Certificate deployment

The next task to perform is to deploy the **Enrollment Agent (Computer)** certificate on to the Enrollment Server.

By deploying the Enrollment Agent (Computer) certificate onto this server, you are authorizing this Enrollment Server to act as an Enrollment Agent and generate to be able to generate certificates on behalf of the end users.

If you are following the example lab, then in `Chapter 4`, *Installing and Configuring Horizon 7 - Part 1*, you will already have an Enrollment Server called **HZN7-ENROL**, onto which we will deploy the certificate. The first thing to do is to open a remote console to this server:

1. Launch a **Run** command box and type `mmc` into the **Open** box (**1**) to launch the **Microsoft Management Console**, as shown in the following screenshot:

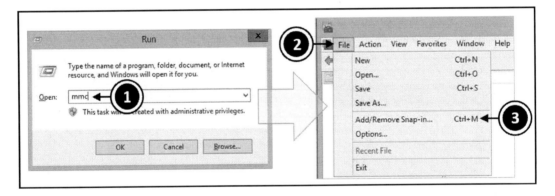

2. On the MMC console screen, click on **File** (**2**) and then **Add/Remove Snap-in…** (**3**).

[318]

Chapter 6

3. You will now see the **Add or Remove Snap-ins** screen, as shown in the following screenshot:

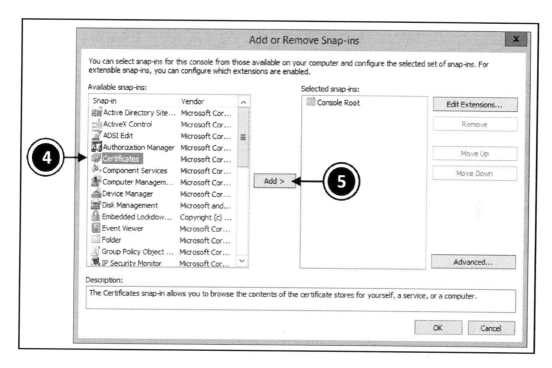

4. From the **Available snap-ins** section on the left, click to highlight and select the **Certificates** entry (4), and then click on the **Add >** button (5). You will now see the **Certificates snap-in** box appear, as shown in the following screenshot:

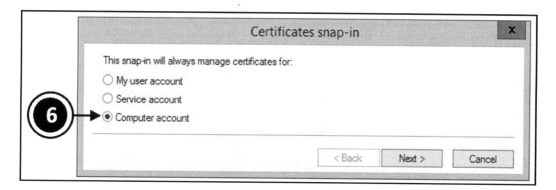

[319]

Securing Horizon View with SSL Certificates

5. Click on the radio button for the **Computer account** (6), and then click on the **Next >** button to continue. You will now see the **Select Computer** configuration box:

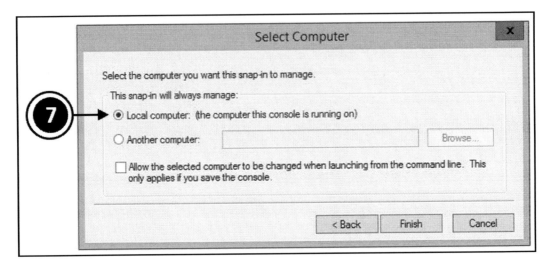

6. Click on the radio button for Local computer (7), and then click on the **Finish** button. You will now return to the **Add or Remove Snap-ins** screen, which now shows the certificates snap-in as being selected.
7. Click on **OK** to close the **Add or Remove Snap-ins** screen.

Now you have the certificates option available in the management console, as shown in the following screenshot:

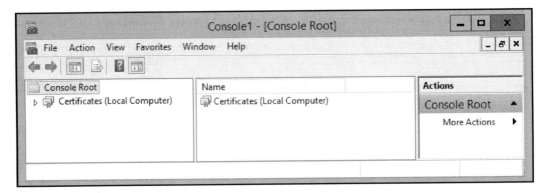

Chapter 6

The next task is to request the Enrollment Agent (Computer) certificate:

1. From the **Console Root**, expand the `Certificates (Local Computer)` folder, and then select and right-click on the `Personal` folder (**1**). From the contextual menu, navigate to **All Tasks** (**2**) and then select **Request New Certificate...** (**3**), as shown in the following screenshot:

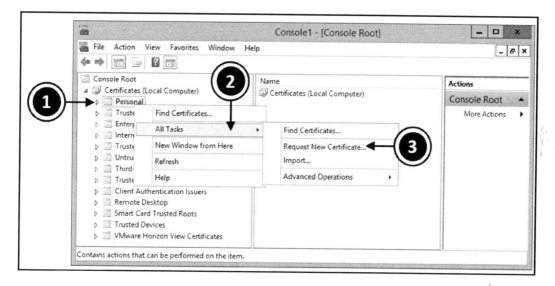

2. You will now see the **Before You Begin** section on Certificate Enrollment screen. Click on the **Next** button to continue.

[321]

3. Next, you will see the **Select Certificate Enrollment Policy** screen. Click on the **Next** button to continue. The next screen you will see is the **Certificate Enrollment Request Certificates** screen, as shown in the following screenshot:

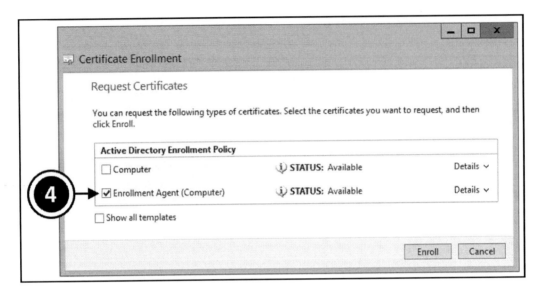

4. Check the box to select the **Enrollment Agent (Computer)** option (4), and then click on the **Enroll** button to request the certificate. You should then see that the certificate has successfully been enrolled:

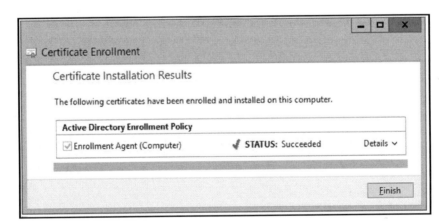

Chapter 6

5. Finally, click on the **Finish** button to complete the configuration, close the **Certificate Enrollment** dialog box, and then close the **Certificate Management** console.

The next task is to import the Enrollment Service Client Certificate, which you need to first export from the Connection Server before importing it onto the Enrollment Server.

Deploying the Enrollment Service Client Certificate from the Connection Server pairs the Connection Server with the Enrollment Server. If you don't do this, then any connection request that is made to the Enrollment Server will be rejected and the result is that no certificate will be generated. The Enrollment Service Client Certificate is automatically generated on the Connection Server when the Connection Server service starts up.

Let's start by exporting the certificate from the Connection Server:

1. Open a console to the Connection Server. In the example lab, this is the server called **HZN7-CS1**. Launch the MMC console and add the Certificates snap-in as we have covered in previous sections, and then launch the Certificates Management Console, as shown in the following screenshot:

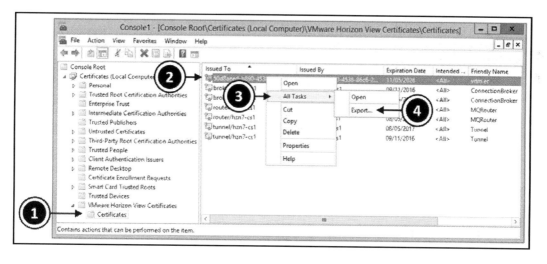

2. From the **Console Root** section in the left-hand pane, navigate to the `VMware Horizon View Certificates` folder, expand it by clicking the arrow, and then click on the `Certificates` folder (**1**).

[323]

3. Click on and select the certificate that contains the friendly name vdm.ec (2), right-click, and then from the contextual menu click on **All Tasks (3)**, and then select the option for **Export… (4)**. You will now see the **Welcome to the Certificate Export Wizard** screen. Click on the **Next** button to continue.
4. You will now see the **Export Private Key** dialog box, as shown in the following screenshot:

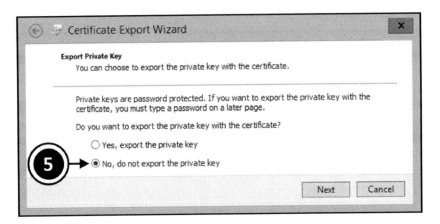

5. Click on the radio button for the **No, do not export the private key (5)**, and then click on the **Next** button.
6. In the **Export File Format** dialog box, accept the default selected format option and then click on the **Next** button to continue.
7. You will now see the **File to Export** dialog box, as shown in the following screenshot:

8. In the **File name** box **(6)**, type in a filename for the certificate. In the example lab, this has been called `cs-cert` and for easy access has been saved in a shared folder called `cert` on the Domain Controller because it needs to be accessible from the Enrollment Server when we come to import it.
9. Click on the **Next** button to continue.
10. You will now see the **Completing the Certificate Export Wizard** dialog box, as shown in the following screenshot:

11. Finally, click on the **Finish** button to complete the certificate export process. You will see a message saying the export was successful.

Securing Horizon View with SSL Certificates

The next task is to import the certificate into the Enrollment Server:

1. Open a remote console to the Enrollment Server. In the example lab, this is the server called **HZN7-ENROL**. Launch the MMC console and add the Certificates snap-in as we covered previously, and then launch the Certificates Management Console, as shown in the following screenshot:

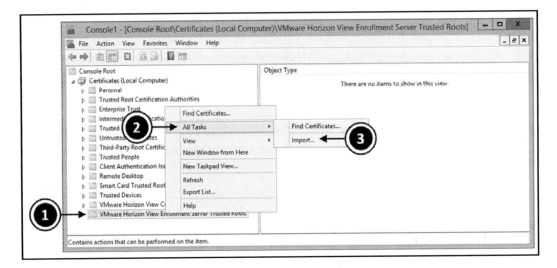

2. From the **Console Root** section in the left-hand pane, navigate to the `VMware Horizon View Enrollment Server Trusted Roots` folder **(1)**, click and select to highlight it and then right-click. From the contextual menu that is now displayed, click on **All Tasks (2)**, and select the option for **Import… (3)**.

3. You will now see the **Welcome to the Certificate Import Wizard** screen. Click on the **Next** button to continue. You will now see the **File to Import** dialog box, as shown in the following screenshot:

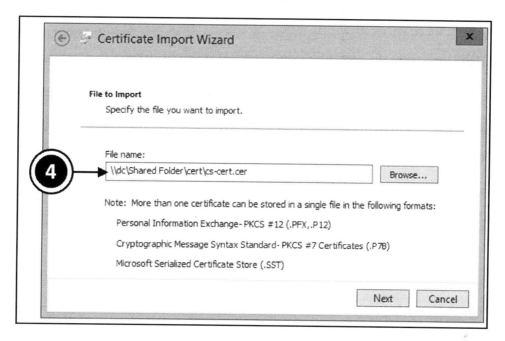

4. Type in the filename for the certificate that you are going to import in the **File name** box (4). In the example lab, this was the file called `cs-cert` that was saved to the shared folder on the domain controller. Click on the **Next** button to continue.

5. In the next screen, **Certificate Store**, you need to select the store in which the certificate will be stored:

6. In the **Certificate Store** dialog box, click on the radio button for **Place all certificates in the following store (5)**, and then ensure that the **Certificate store** is set to `VMware Horizon View Enrollment Server Trusted Roots`.
7. Click on the **Next** button to continue.

8. You will now see the **Completing the Certificate Import Wizard** dialog box, as shown in the following screenshot:

9. Finally, click on the **Finish** button to import the certificate. You should see a message stating that the import was successful.

Once imported, you will see the certificate in the Certificate Management Console, as shown in the following screenshot:

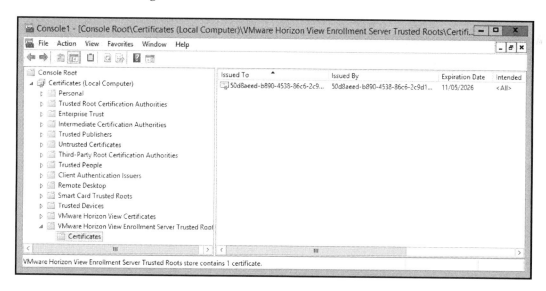

Having successfully imported the certificate, you can now close the Certificate Management Console. In the next step, we are going to configure True SSO on the Connection Server.

Configuring True SSO on the Connection Server

Now that you have all of the necessary certificates in place, the next step is to set up the True SSO feature on the Connection Server.

This setup process is command-line-driven and uses the `vdmUtil` command, so the first step is to open a Command Prompt window on the Connection Server.

The first command you need to run adds the Enrollment Server to the Horizon View environment. This allows you to query the Enrollment Server and gather information about the domain and other useful information such as available templates and CA name:

1. From the Connection Server, open a command-line dialog box and type in the following command:

   ```
   vdmUtil --authAs administrator --authDomain PVOLAB --authPassword password --truesso --environment --add --enrollmentServer hzn7-enrol.pvolab.com
   ```

You will need this information during the configuration process, so make sure you make a note of it.

You will see that the Enrollment Server has now been successfully added to the environment:

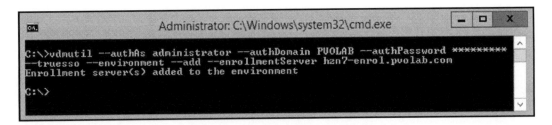

Chapter 6

The next command provides you with detailed information about the various Horizon components in your environment. This will help with the configuration of True SSO.

2. From the command line, type the following command:

   ```
   vdmUtil --authAs administrator --authDomain PVOLAB --
   authPassword password --truesso --environment --list --
   enrollmentServer hzn7-enrol.pvolab.com --domain pvolab.com
   ```

   You will see the following output:

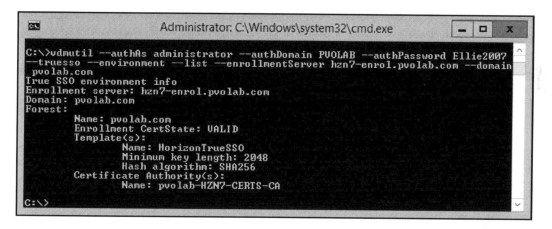

We can now use this information to create a True SSO connector. A True SSO Connector specifies the details of enrollment servers, CAs, and certificate templates to be used. When a Connection Server receives a request to launch a desktop for an end user, it will look up the True SSO Connector for the domain the user belongs to and uses the components that you configure to obtain the Certificate.

3. From the command line, type the following command:

   ```
   vdmUtil --authAs administrator --authDomain PVOLAB --
   authPassword password --truesso --create --connector --
   domain pvolab.com --template HorizonTrueSSO --
   primaryEnrollmentServer hzn7-enrol.pvolab.com --
   certificateServer pvolab-hzn7-certs-ca --mode enabled
   ```

Securing Horizon View with SSL Certificates

You will now see that the connector has been successfully created and enabled, as shown in the following screenshot:

Next, we are going to check that True SSO is installed and is working by following these steps:

1. Log in to the Horizon View Administrator console.
2. From the **Dashboard** screen, under the **System Health** section, click on the arrow to expand the **True SSO** section (**21**), and then click on the link for `pvolab.com` (**22**)
3. You will see the **True SSO Domain Details** box, as shown in the following screenshot:

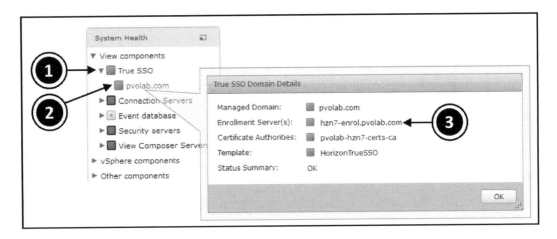

4. Click on the **OK** button to close the box and then log out of the View Administrator.

[332]

You have now successfully configured the View elements for True SSO. The real benefit of the True SSO feature is when used in conjunction with vIDM, allowing a user to single sign-on to their virtual desktop machine or applications from the vIDM portal.

Summary

In this chapter, we discussed some of the security aspects of deploying Horizon View. We started off by describing what an SSL certificate is and why Horizon View uses them, before going on to show this practically by installing and configuring a Root CA server and then configuring the View components in the example lab to use these certificates.

The second part of this chapter explored the True SSO feature of Horizon View. Again, we demonstrated this practically by configuring the certificates server to use this feature and then configuring the Horizon View Enrollment Server and Connection Server so that they "trusted" each other with the user login process.

In the next chapter, we are going to turn our attention to virtual desktops and start to build virtual desktop images.

Building and Optimizing the Virtual Desktop OS

Having built the Horizon View infrastructure and its components in the previous chapters of this book, in this chapter, we will focus our attention on virtual desktops. We are going to look at how to create and configure the virtual hardware elements of virtual desktop machines, install a desktop operating system based on best practices for virtual desktop machines, and then configure that operating system to run at its optimum performance levels.

The steps involved in building the core operating system for a virtual desktop machine are not too dissimilar from the process of building a physical desktop machine. However, there are some additional tasks and software components that we need to install within the operating system to turn it into a true virtual desktop machine that's fit for a Horizon View environment, and more importantly for the end users. This chapter will cover each of these steps in more detail and also build several OS images along the way. We will use the example lab to do so. The build process is shown in the following diagram:

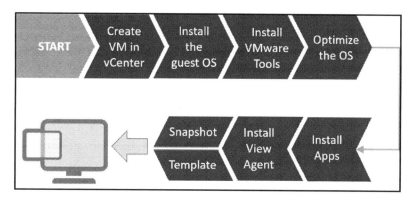

We will build a virtual desktop machine for a Windows 7 desktop. It will be configured with a floating-desktop assignment, built using linked clones, and a second virtual desktop machine running Windows 7, which will be configured with a dedicated assignment and built from a full clone. Finally, we will also look at creating an Instant Clone Windows 10-based desktop, before finishing this chapter with a look at delivering a Linux-based virtual desktop machine.

The following topics will be covered in this chapter:

- Creating a Windows 7 virtual desktop machine
- Creating a Windows 10 virtual desktop machine
- Creating a GPU-enabled virtual desktop machine
- Creating a Linux virtual desktop machine
- Preparing virtual desktops for delivery

Best practices for building virtual desktop images

In this section, we are going to discuss some of the best practices and processes for building your virtual desktop machine images.

In a physical desktop environment, there are a number of ways in which the operating system can be built and deployed. For example, you could use the **Microsoft Deployment Toolkit (MDT)** or maybe the Microsoft **System Center Configuration Manager (SCCM)**. Both of these options can be used along with all the other tools that are available to build desktop images, including VMware's own Mirage product, of course. So, we just talked about a couple of options that you can use to build your desktop images, but let's just highlight the one that you should not use: the **physical-to-virtual tool (P2V)**, which turns your physical image into a virtual one.

A best practice is to build a new virtual desktop image from scratch, so it starts off life as being designed to be a virtual machine from day one. After all, you would potentially build a new image for a new hardware platform, and that's what you are doing in reality. There are a few reasons to not use your physical image to create your virtual desktop image, though. One of the reasons is the size of the image, which more than likely will have become bloated, with numerous patches and updates being applied over the last year or so. You want your VDI image to be lean and fresh, with just the most recent and relevant software installed.

Another reason is that there might be some hardware drivers or other hardware-based software elements within the image, such as a desktop hardware management solution like Intel **Active Management Technology** (**AMT**), which relies on firmware and other components that are built into the chipset of the physical machine. As you are now using a virtual desktop machine, this type of hardware is not present and, therefore, you do not require it to be installed.

The worst-case scenario is having this type of solution installed, because it will affect the performance of your virtual desktop machine.

Technical requirements

Before we get into the build process, we need to look at the specifications of the virtual desktop machine from a virtual hardware perspective and what we need to configure it. The following screenshot lists the virtual desktop machine requirements:

Component	Setting
CPU Requirements	Dual CPU for intensive workloads
	Single CPU for everything else
Memory	2 GB for 32-bit OS (3 GB maximum)
	4 GB for 64-bit OS and high-end graphics
SCSI Controller	LSI Logic SAS
Graphics Card	N/A as it will be overridden by pool settings
Diskette Drive	Set to disabled
Network Card	VMXNET 3
Optical Drive	Set to client device to mount ISO images
Serial and Parallel Port	Set to disabled

You should be able to work out the requirements for your particular environment by using the assessment data that you captured at the start of the project. One thing to bear in mind is that you can quite easily change the configuration should you need to when fine-tuning the performance and the end user experience.

Another important factor when configuring the size of virtual desktop machines is not to fall into the trap of over-sizing. For example, if you only need one CPU, then only give the virtual desktop machine one CPU. Don't be tempted to add unnecessary resources, as you will ultimately end up lowering the number of virtual desktop machines that you can host on your server infrastructure, thus increasing costs and management with the extra hardware. You could also potentially make the virtual desktop performance slower. As we mentioned previously, this is why your assessment data is critical.

The VDI desktop should be configured using the guidelines for the hardware specifications that were outlined in the previous table.

Creating a Windows 7 virtual desktop machine

In this section, we are going to build a virtual desktop machine with Windows 7. This will be as the operating system to use as the master image that we will create virtual desktops from. We will follow the steps that were outlined in the diagram at the very start of this chapter and the first diagram to optimize and prepare the image that's going to be used as a floating-assigned, linked-clone virtual desktop machine.

Chapter 7

Creating the virtual desktop machine container

The first thing we need to do is build and configure the actual virtual desktop machine on our vCenter server. This will define the virtual hardware configuration. To define the configuration, follow these steps:

1. Open a browser and log into the vSphere web client for the vCenter `vcs1.pvolab.com`, as follows:

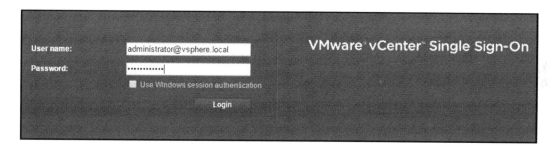

Once logged in, you will see the **vSphere Client** home page, as shown in the following screenshot:

[339]

Building and Optimizing the Virtual Desktop OS

2. From the navigation shortcuts on the left-hand side of the screen, click on **VMs and Templates** (1), as shown in the following screenshot:

3. Expand the vCenter `vcs2.pvolab.com`, and then click to highlight the datacenter name of where you want to create the virtual desktop machine. In the example lab, the data center is called **PVO's Datacenter** (2). Right-click it, and from the contextual menu, click the option for **New Virtual Machine...** (3). You will now see the **New Virtual Machine** configuration box, as shown in the following screenshot:

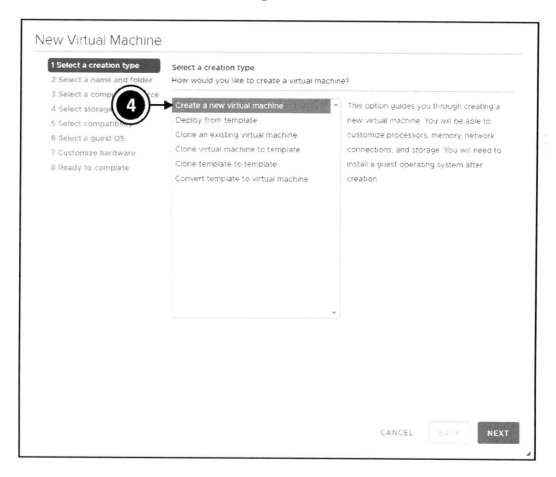

Building and Optimizing the Virtual Desktop OS

4. The first task is to **Select a creation type**. From the list of options, click to highlight **Create a new virtual machine (4)**, and then click the **NEXT** button to continue. You will now see the **Select a name and folder** screen, as shown in the following screenshot:

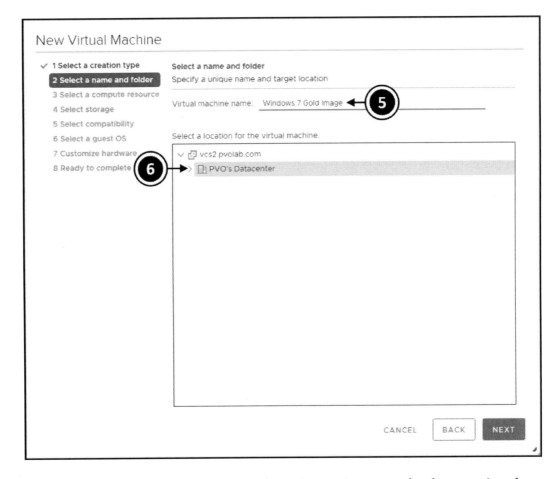

5. In the **Virtual machine name** box (5), type in a name for the new virtual desktop machine. In the example lab, this is called `Windows 7 Gold Image`.
6. Then, in the **Select a location for the virtual machine** section, click to highlight the datacenter where you want this virtual machine to be created. In the example lab, this machine is going to be created in the datacenter called **PVO's Datacenter (6)**.

Chapter 7

7. Click the **NEXT** button to continue. You will now see the **Select a compute resource** screen, as shown in the following screenshot:

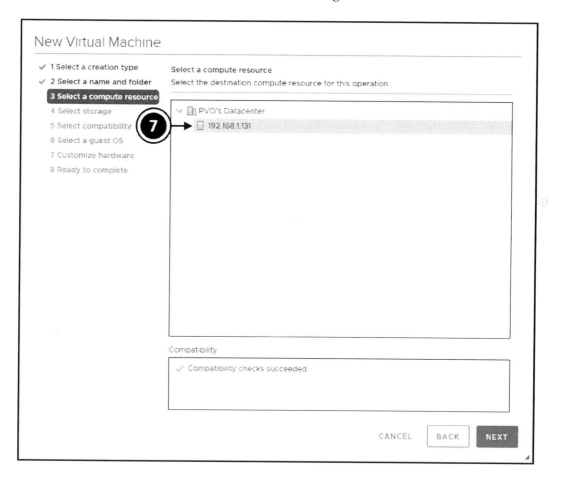

8. Expand the datacenter called **PVO's Datacenter** and then click on the ESX server you want to host this virtual desktop. In the example lab, **192.168.1.131** (7) is the IP address of the host server we are going to use to host this virtual desktop machine.

As this is going to be our gold/master image or parent virtual desktop machine, it's probably not as important in regards to the location compared to the live production virtual desktop machines. So, for the example lab, we will use the management block to host this virtual desktop machine.

Building and Optimizing the Virtual Desktop OS

9. Click the **NEXT** button to continue. You will now see the **Select storage** screen, as shown in the following screenshot:

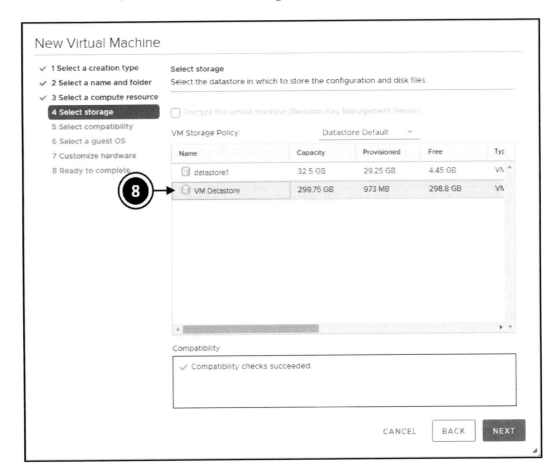

10. Select the datastore where this virtual desktop machine will be stored. In the example lab, the virtual desktop machine is stored on the default datastore called **VM Datastore** (8). Click the **NEXT** button to continue.

[344]

Chapter 7

11. You will now see the **Select compatibility** screen. This is where we will choose the virtual machine version for our virtual desktop machine. As it states, for the best performance, you should use version 13, which means using vSphere 6.5 or later as the hosting platform. If you are using a different hosting platform, then select the one that is relevant to your environment. However, be aware that some features may not be available depending on the version you choose. For example, you will need at least vSphere 6 if you want support for features such as instant clones and vGPU.

12. From the dropdown menu (9), select **ESXi 6.5 and later,** as shown in the following screenshot:

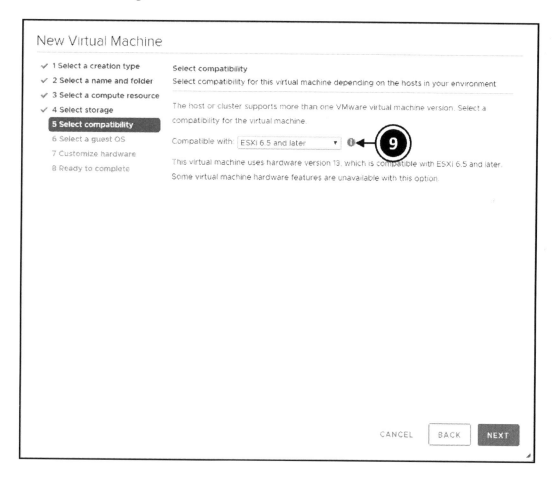

Building and Optimizing the Virtual Desktop OS

13. Click the **NEXT** button to continue. You will now see the **Select a guest OS** screen, as shown in the following screenshot:

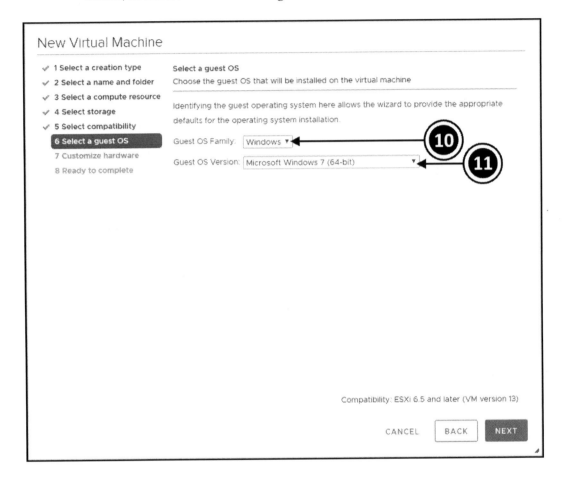

Chapter 7

14. The next step is to choose the operating system for the virtual desktop machine. In our example, this is the first virtual desktop machine that will be used as the gold image template for Windows 7.
15. From the **Guest OS Family** box, click the arrow for the dropdown menu (**10**) and select **Windows**. Then, from the **Guest OS Version** box, click the arrow for the dropdown menu (**11**) and select **Microsoft Windows 7 (64-bit)**. The guest OS selection is important to get right, as it determines which drivers get installed when VMware Tools is installed on the virtual desktop machine.
16. Click the **NEXT** button to continue.
17. You will now see the **Customize Hardware** screen where you can configure the virtual hardware specification for the virtual desktop machine, as shown in the following screenshot:

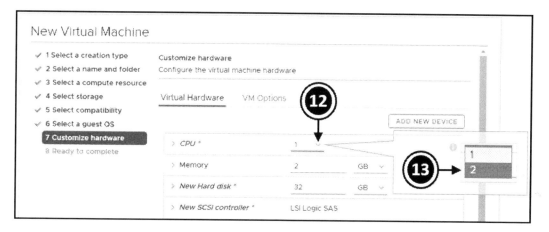

18. There are a couple of things to change on this configuration screen. First, this virtual desktop machine is going to have two vCPUs. In the **CPU** box, click the down arrow (**12**) and select **2** from the dropdown menu (**13**) to configure two vCPUs for this virtual desktop machine.

Building and Optimizing the Virtual Desktop OS

19. Next, expand the **New Network** option by clicking the arrow **(14)**, and then on the **Adapter Type** box, click the down arrow **(15)** and select the option for **VMXNET 3 (16)**, as shown in the following screenshot:

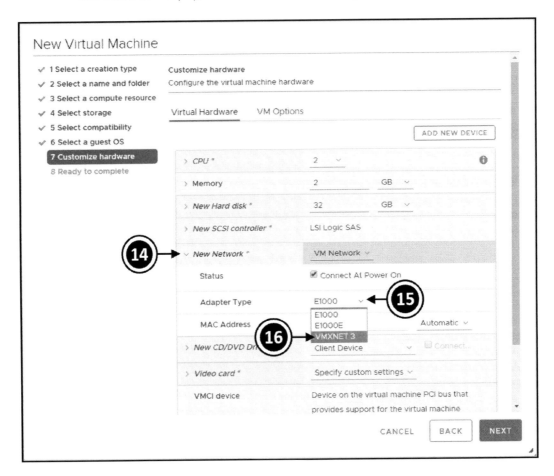

Chapter 7

20. Because we are building a new virtual desktop machine we will need to install the operating system. To do this, we are going to attach the install media to the virtual desktop machine so that it can boot from it and start the install. Scroll down to the **New CD/DVD Drive** option, as shown in the following screenshot:

21. Click on the down arrow (**17**), and from the list of options that are displayed, click on **Datastore ISO File** (**18**). In the example lab, we have already uploaded the ISO images for the installation media to a datastore on the host servers.

[349]

Building and Optimizing the Virtual Desktop OS

22. You will now see the **Select File** screen displayed, as shown in the following screenshot:

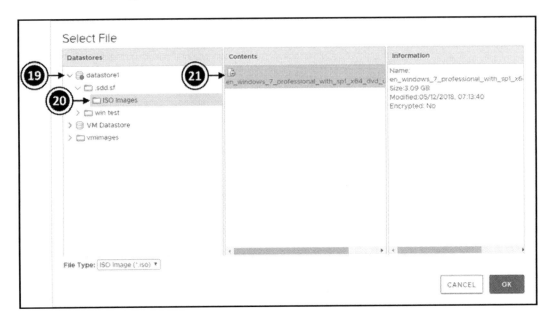

23. Expand the datastore (**19**) and then click on the ISO Images folder (**20**). Then, click to select the OS that is going to be installed on this virtual desktop machine. In this example, we are going to install Windows 7, so click on the **en_windows_7_professional_with_sp1_x64_dvd** option (**21**). You may have your ISO images stored in a different location, so just follow this as a guide using your folder locations.
24. Click the **OK** button to return to the virtual hardware screen.
25. One final thing to ensure on this screen is that the ISO file you have just added is connected as a **New CD/DVD Drive**. To do this, check the **Connected** box (**22**), as shown in the following screenshot:

26. In the last part of the hardware configuration, you need to change one of the boot options so that the next time the virtual desktop machine powers on and boots, it goes straight into the BIOS setup screen. You could, of course, open a console to the virtual desktop machine and press the *F2* key as it boots; however, that screen can flash past so quickly that you might miss it, so the former option is much easier. The reason you need to select this option and go into the BIOS setup screen is that we need to change some of the configuration settings so that this virtual desktop machine behaves as a virtual machine, rather than as a physical desktop PC. We will cover this a bit later when we power on the newly created virtual desktop machine for the first time.

27. To configure the boot options, click the **VM Options** tab (**23**), and then expand the arrow for **Boot Options** (**24**). Check the tick box for **Force BIOS setup** (**25**). This is shown in the following screenshot:

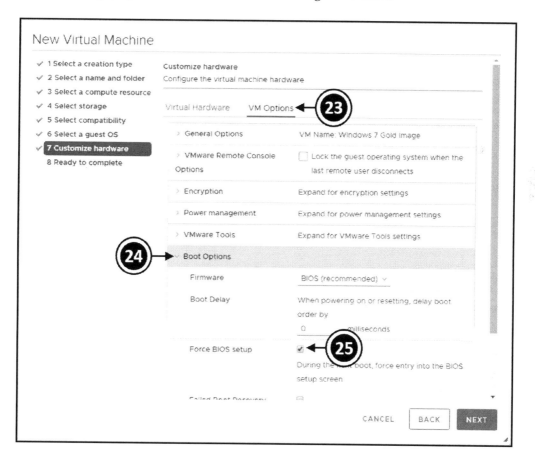

Building and Optimizing the Virtual Desktop OS

28. Once you have completed the configuration, click the **NEXT** button to continue. You will now see the **Ready to complete** screen, as shown in the following screenshot:

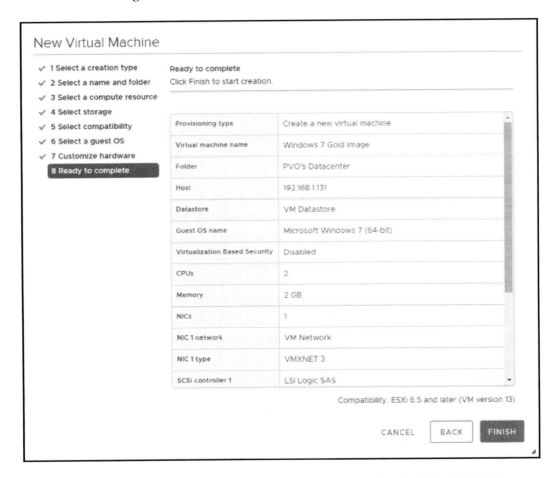

29. Once you are happy with the configuration details, click the **FINISH** button to complete the configuration.

30. If you now check the **Recent Tasks** box, you will see that the virtual desktop machine has been successfully created, as shown in the following screenshot:

31. With the virtual desktop machine now built and configured, it's time to power it on and continue the build process. Navigate to the virtual desktop machine in the inventory. You should see an entry called **Windows 7 Gold Image**.

32. Highlight the virtual desktop machine **Windows 7 Gold Image** (26), right-click it, and from the contextual menu that's shown, click on **Power** (27) and then click on **Power On** (28), as shown in the following screenshot:

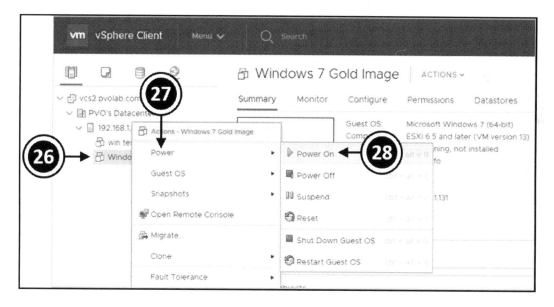

Building and Optimizing the Virtual Desktop OS

33. The virtual desktop machine will now power on and boot into the BIOS setup screen, as that's what we configured to happen on the next boot. Any subsequent bootups will boot as normal into the operating system once it's installed.

In the next section, we will make configuration changes to the virtual desktop machine's BIOS settings.

Updating the virtual desktop machine BIOS

With the virtual desktop machine now powered on and booted into the BIOS setup screen, we are going to launch a remote console screen to it so that you can perform the configuration steps. To do this, perform the following steps:

1. Highlight the **Windows 7 Gold Image** virtual desktop machine in the **Inventory** section, and then under the **Summary** tab, click the **Launch Remote Console** link (1), as shown in the following screenshot:

2. You will now see the **PhoenixBIOS Setup Utility** screen of the virtual desktop machine, as shown in the following screenshot:

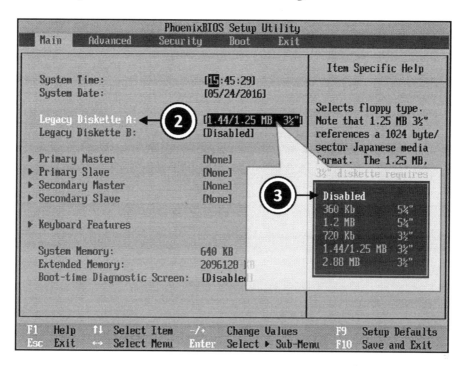

3. The first thing you need to do is disable the floppy drive. On the **Main** section of the BIOS setup screen, use the cursor keys to move down, highlight the option for **Legacy Diskette A:** (2), and then press *Enter*.
4. You will now see a popup box displaying the diskette options. Again, use the cursor keys to highlight the **Disabled** option (3) and then press *Enter*.

Building and Optimizing the Virtual Desktop OS

5. Next, you need to navigate to the **Advanced** section of the BIOS setup screen. To do this, press the right arrow cursor key to move across the tabs along the top until the **Advanced** tab is highlighted (4), as shown in the following screenshot:

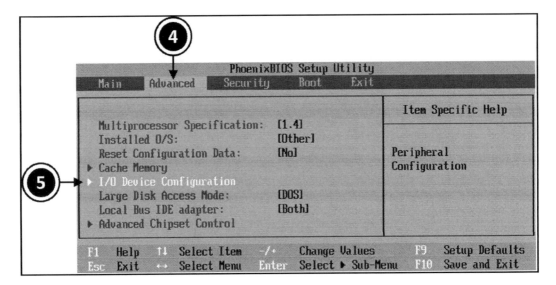

6. Using the down-arrow cursor, move down to the option for **I/O Device Configuration** (5) and press *Enter*. You will now see the **Advanced** configuration screen, as shown in the following screenshot:

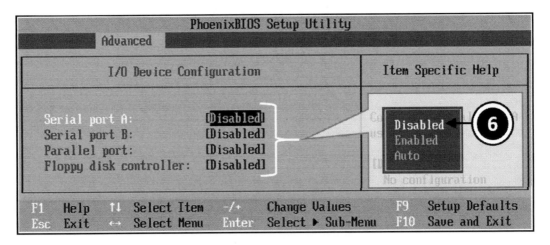

[356]

7. Move the cursor to the entry for **Serial port A:** and press *Enter*. From the popup box, select the option for **Disabled (6)**.
8. Follow the same procedure to disable the options for **Serial port B:**, **Parallel port:**, and the **Floppy disk controller:** until all of the options have been set to **Disabled**. Once you have completed these configuration changes, press the *F10* key to save and exit. You will see the **Setup Confirmation** box, as shown in the following screenshot:

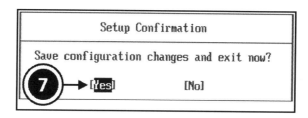

9. Confirm the configuration changes by selecting **Yes (7)**, and then press *Enter*. The BIOS changes are now saved, and the virtual desktop machine will be rebooted automatically.

You have successfully configured the BIOS. The next step is to install the operating system.

Operating system installation options

There are a couple of options you can use to build the operating system for the virtual desktop machines. The first option is to use something such as MDT, SCCM, or VMware's own Mirage product (used for Full Clone desktops), to deploy an image you have already built for VDI, but for the example lab, we will use a different option, which is to build the image manually by using the installation media to show the different tasks you need to perform to optimize the image for VDI.

This build process is no different than how you build any other virtual machine on vSphere, so we will briefly cover some of this as a quick reminder for those who are already familiar with working on the vSphere platform, and in enough detail so that those that are new to the technology can quickly get their first virtual desktop machine image built.

Installing the guest operating system

Since we connected an ISO image as part of the the virtual desktop machine configuration when we built it, as the virtual desktop machine starts up, the ISO image will be mounted, and the Windows 7 installation will automatically start.

We are not going to cover how to install Windows 7, so carry on with a basic install, or how you want to configure the OS for the end users. Once the installation is complete, make sure you apply any Windows updates and patches and then join the virtual desktop machine to the domain.

The reason you need to join the VDI desktop to the domain—even though this machine is effectively the template—is so that all the software components, DLL files, and so on, that are needed on the machine for it to be domain-joined are present. Otherwise, when you create the linked clones from this parent image and try to join them to the domain, the virtual desktop machines will ask for the installation media to be inserted. That's OK for one or two desktops and when testing, but not for thousands in production.

Once you are happy that the operating system for the parent image has been patched and is joined to the domain, you can start installing some of the VMware-specific virtual machine tools and Horizon View components, starting with VMware Tools.

Installing VMware Tools

VMware Tools enhances the usability of the virtual desktop machine. It installs VMware-specific device drivers that allow it to run as a virtual desktop machine, replacing the physical hardware equivalents. The installation of VMware Tools is initiated from the vSphere Client:

1. From the **Windows 7 Gold Image** virtual machine and its **Summary** tab, click on **Install VMware Tools (1)**, as follows:

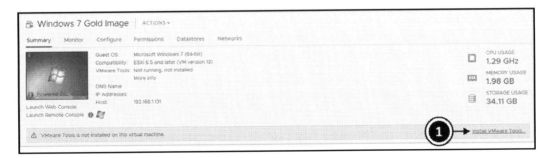

2. Initiating the installation from the vSphere Web Client effectively mounts the VMware Tools installation media as a virtual CD drive on the virtual desktop machine. You will see the following **Install VMware Tools** dialog box pop up, as shown in the following screenshot:

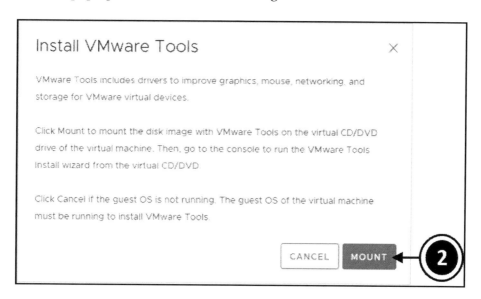

3. Click the **MOUNT** button (2) to mount the VMware Tools installation media, and then switch back to the console of the virtual desktop machine.

4. You will now see the **AutoPlay** dialog box showing that the VMware Tools DVD drive has been mounted and that the installation program is available to launch, as shown in the following screenshot:

5. Click **Run setup64.exe** (3) to launch the VMware Tools installer.
6. If you see the User Account Control box pop up warning you about making changes to the computer, ignore it by clicking on the **Yes** button.
7. You will now see the **Welcome to the installation wizard for VMware Tools** dialog box.

Chapter 7

8. Click the **Next >** button to continue the installation. You will now see the **Choose Setup Type** dialog box, as shown in the following screenshot:

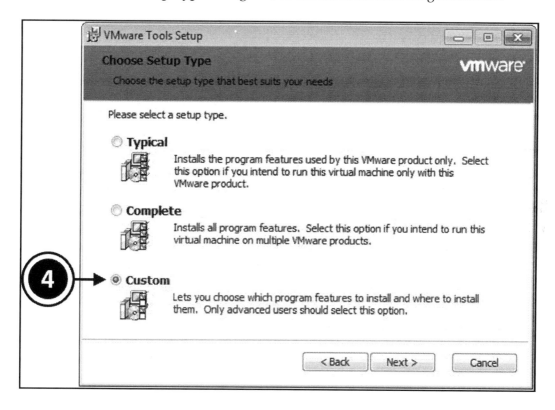

Building and Optimizing the Virtual Desktop OS

9. Click the radio button for **Custom** (4), and then click the **Next >** button to continue. You can also choose the **Typical** option, which installs a standard set of drivers; however, for the purposes of this book, and to describe all the available options, we are going to look at a custom install. You will now see the **Custom** setup dialog box, as shown in the following screenshot:

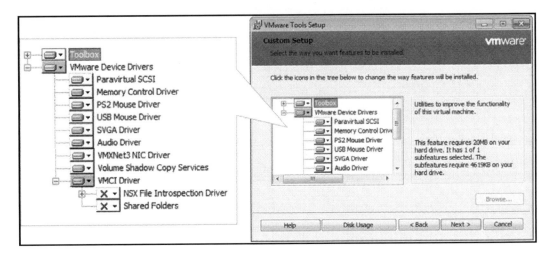

10. VMware Tools will install the following VMware device drivers, depending on whether they are selected. By default, all are selected, excluding the VMCI Drivers. The drivers and their functions are described here:
    - **Paravirtual SCSI**: This is for PVSCSI adapters to enhance the performance of virtualized applications.
    - **Memory Control Driver**: This allows memory management of the virtual desktop machine when running on an ESXi host.
    - **PS2/USB Mouse Driver**: This virtual mouse driver improves the performance of the mouse in a virtual desktop machine.
    - **SVGA Driver**: This enables 32-bit displays, high resolution, and faster graphics performance. It installs a virtual SVGA driver that replaces the standard VGA driver. On Windows Vista and later versions, the VMware SVGA 3D (Microsoft – WDDM) driver is also installed, adding support for Windows Aero.
    - **Audio Driver**: This is required for all 64-bit guest operating systems, since it enables sound capabilities.

[362]

- **VMXNET3 NIC Driver**: This improves network performance and is recommended for virtual desktop machines.
- **Volume Shadow Copy Services**: This allows you to take backup copies or snapshots of the virtual desktop machine.
- **VMCI Driver**: This allows faster communication between virtual machines.
- **NSX File Introspection Driver**: This installs the agent so that you can use antivirus offload scanning.

11. The other options in this dialog box are for **Browse...**, which allows you to change where VMware tools are installed, and **Disk Usage,** to check the disk space requirements so that you can check the amount of disk space that VMware Tools will need to install your chosen options.
12. Click the **Next >** button to continue. You will now see the **Ready to install VMware Tools** dialog box. Click the **Install** button to start the install process.
13. Once completed, you will see the **Completed the VMware Tools Setup Wizard** dialog box. Click on the **Finish** button to complete the installation process.
14. You will now be prompted to restart the virtual desktop machine so that you can start the VMware Tools services. From the dialog box, click the **Yes** button to reboot.
15. Once the virtual desktop machine has restarted, check that the VMware Tools services are up and running by clicking on the taskbar and checking for the VM icon (5), as shown in the following screenshot:

You can also launch the **Services** console from the virtual desktop machine and check that the service is running from there, as shown in the following screenshot:

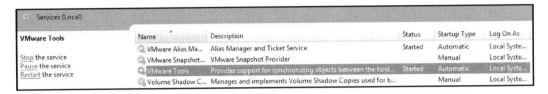

You have successfully installed VMware Tools. The next step is to install any core applications that you want to include as part of the parent image.

Installing applications for the parent image

The next stage is to install any applications that you want to have as part of your parent image. These are typically applications that will be used by every user in your organization. You could also deliver applications using other technologies, such as ThinApp or App Volumes, as, ideally, you would want to try to deliver applications on demand, rather than install them into operating system images, as this would make them harder to manage.

In the example lab, we have installed Adobe Reader in the gold image.

In the next section, we are going to install the Horizon Agent so that the virtual desktop machine is registered with the Horizon environment and the connection server.

Installing the Horizon Agent

The Horizon Agent is installed on each virtual desktop machine and is used for communication between the Horizon View Client and the virtual desktop machine.

Chapter 7

It also adds components for things such as View Persona Management and USB redirection. We will cover these different components in more detail in this section as we install the agent on the virtual desktop machine. To install the Horizon Agent, follow these steps:

1. Open a console to the **Windows 7 Gold Image** virtual desktop machine, and from the desktop, navigate to the installation file for the Horizon Agent. For simplicity, we have created a shared folder on the domain controller so that we can save all the installation media on it.
2. Launch the `VMware-Horizon-Agent-x86_64-7.6.0-9539447` file to start the installation, and if you see the **Open File - Security Warning** message, click the **Run** button to continue. You will now see the **Welcome to the Installation Wizard for VMware Horizon Agent** screen.
3. Click the **Next >** button to continue. You will now see the **License Agreement** page, as shown in the following screenshot:

4. Click on the radio button for **I accept the terms in the license agreement** (**1**).

[365]

Building and Optimizing the Virtual Desktop OS

5. Click the **Next >** button to continue. You will now see the **Network protocol configuration** dialog box, as shown in the following screenshot:

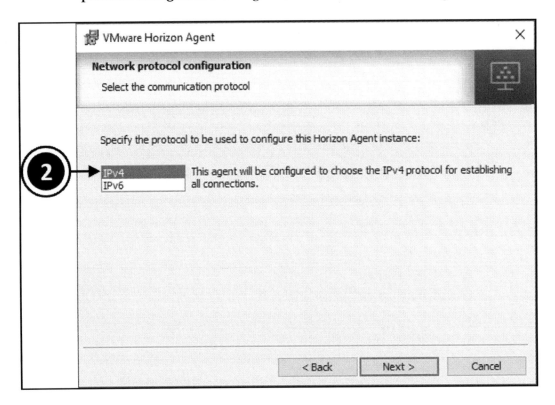

6. As this lab is using IPv4, from the options box, click it to highlight **IPv4 (2)**, and then click the **Next >** button to continue. You will now see the **Custom Setup** page. On the **Custom Setup** page, you can choose the features and functions of the Horizon Agent that you want to install. Not all of these features are installed by default, so on this screen, you might want to review some of them and select/deselect them from the installation process, as you might not want to use some of the features. You can always install them again later if need be. Features that are not installed by default are marked with a red X. These features are shown in the following screenshot:

Chapter 7

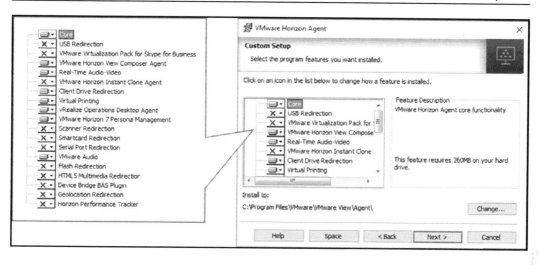

7. You can choose to install the following features. Note that some of the features are OS dependent and therefore may not show as available options:

- **3D RDSH**: This enables hardware-based 3D rendering in RDSH sessions.
- **USB Redirection**: This allows a USB device to be plugged into the endpoint device and then redirects the USB traffic to the virtual desktop machine.
- **VMware Virtualization Pack for Skype for Business**: This allows end users to make optimized audio and video calls with Skype for Business, running inside a virtual desktop machine.
- **VMware Horizon View Composer Agent**: This allows the virtual desktop machine to be run as a linked-clone desktop.
- **Real-Time Audio-Video**: This allows you to redirect locally connected audio and video devices (such as USB webcams) to your virtual desktop machine.
- **VMware Horizon Instant Clone Agent**: This allows the virtual desktop machine to be run as an Instant Clone desktop.
- **Client Drive Redirection**: This allows View Clients to share local drives with remote desktops and applications (IPv4 only).
- **Virtual Printing**: This allows users to print to printers without the need to install print drivers.

Building and Optimizing the Virtual Desktop OS

- **vRealize Operations Manager Agent**: This allows the virtual desktop machine to be monitored by the vRealize Operations Manager for Horizon View.
- **VMware Horizon 7 Persona Management**: This synchronizes a user's profile from the virtual desktop machine to a repository on a central server, meaning that a profile can be delivered to a floating assigned desktop so that you can personalize it for that user so that they can access their profile.
- **Scanner Redirection**: This allows you to redirect a local scanner to the virtual desktop machine.
- **Smartcard Redirection**: This allows users to use a smart card for authentication.
- **Serial Port Redirection**: This allows users to redirect the local serial port to the virtual desktop machine.
- **VMware Audio**: This enables sound on the local device.
- **Flash Redirection**: This offloads the processing of Flash-based content to the local device.
- **HTML5 Multimedia Redirection**: This redirects HTML5 multimedia content in a Chrome or Edge browser to the client, and is used for performance optimization.
- **Device Bridge BAS Plugin**: This enables fingerprint readers that are supported by the BAS system.
- **SDO Sensor Redirection:** This enables the **Simple Device Orientation (SDO)** sensor redirection feature.
- **Geolocation Redirection**: This enables the redirection of the client's geolocation to the remote desktop.
- **Horizon Performance Tracker**: This enables the Horizon performance tracker. This utility runs inside a remote desktop and monitors the performance of the display protocols and the system resource usage.

3D RDSH option is not shown but will be available when installing on an RDSH host server.

8. When you are happy with the features you have chosen to install, click on the **Next >** button to continue.
9. On the next screen you will see the **Remote Desktop Protocol Configuration** dialog box. You need remote desktop support enabled for the View Agent to work. You could always enable this using a Group Policy:

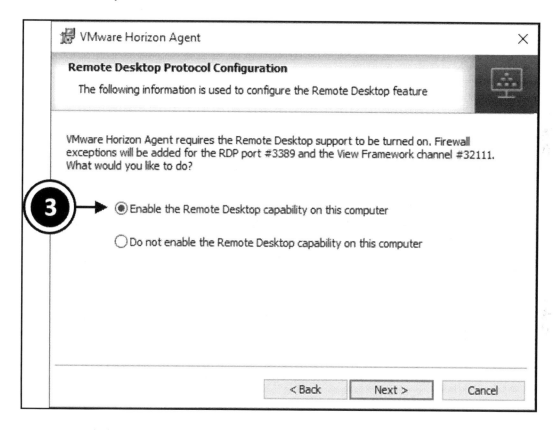

10. Click on the radio button to **Enable the Remote Desktop capability on this computer** (3), as shown in the preceding screenshot.
11. Click on the **Next >** button to continue.

Building and Optimizing the Virtual Desktop OS

12. You will now see the **Register with Horizon 7 Connection Server** dialog box, as shown in the following screenshot:

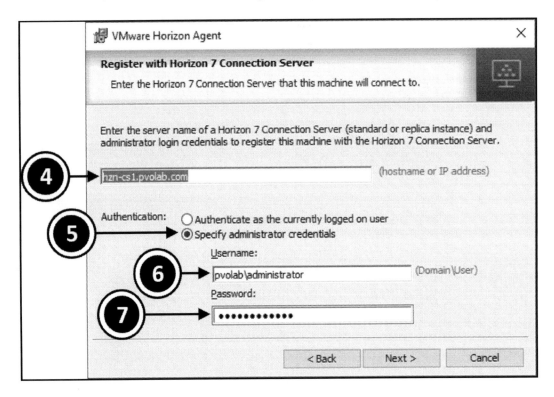

13. In the **(hostname or IP address)** box (4), enter the name of the connection server you want to register this virtual desktop machine with. In the example lab, this is our first connection server, called `hzn7-cs1.pvolab.com`.
14. In the **Authentication** section, click the radio button for **Specify administrator credentials** (5).
15. In the **Username** section (6), enter the administrator username. In the example lab, this is `administrator`. Note that you need to enter the details in the format **Domain\User**, so in our example, you would type `pvolab\administrator`.

[370]

16. Now, enter the administrator password in the **P**assword box.
17. Click **Next >** to continue. You will now see the **Ready to Install the Program** screen.
18. Click the **Install** button to start the installation.
19. Once the installation has finished, you will see the **Installer Completed** screen.
20. Click on the **Finish** button to close the installer.

Finally, you will be prompted to reboot the virtual desktop machine. Click on the **Yes** button to reboot. You will have successfully installed the Horizon Agent.

In the next section, we will start optimizing the parent image to run as a virtual desktop machine.

Optimizing the guest operating system

There are various automated tools and manual processes to optimize the virtual desktop operating systems.

Previously, the optimization process was delivered via a set of scripts that you would manually execute on the virtual desktop machine that was being used to create the gold image. However, in this chapter, we will take a look at the GUI-based **VMware Optimization Tool**, as this is available to download as a **fling**.

 A *fling*, in VMware terms, is a free piece of software for end users to try out and provide feedback to VMware on. Often, these products make it into production as products in their own right, or they form part of a new feature of an already existing product. The only thing to bear in mind, should you choose to use them in your production environment, is that these product flings don't have any official support; however, you will find a number of blogs that may help you with this.

Download the optimization tool and save it in the shared folder. You can download the tool from the following link:

https://labs.vmware.com/flings/vmware-os-optimization-tool.

Building and Optimizing the Virtual Desktop OS

Once downloaded, we are going to run the optimization tool on the newly built Windows 7 Gold Image virtual desktop machine. Follow these steps to do so:

1. From the **Windows 7 Gold Image** virtual desktop machine being used to create the parent image, navigate to the shared software folder and locate the VMware OS Optimization Tool application, as shown in the following screenshot:

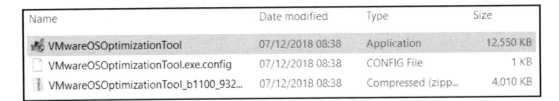

2. Launch the `VMwareOSOptimizationTool` file to launch the optimization tool. if you see the **Open File - Security Warning** message, click the **Run** button to continue. You will now see the tool launch, as shown in the following screenshot:

3. At the top of the screen (1), you can see the details of the virtual desktop machine's operating system and hardware configuration.
4. The next section is **Template** (2), and this is where you choose the template you want to use for the optimization. From the dropdown menu, select the relevant operating system template that you want to apply to this image. You have the ability to create new templates using this tool by clicking on the **Template** tab from the list of tabs across the top of the screen.
5. To start this process, the tool analyzes the differences between the current virtual machine state and the optimizations contained within the chosen template. Click on the **Analyze** button (3) to start the process.
6. The tool will run the analysis and then come back with a report showing the components that need to be optimized (4). At this stage, you can select or deselect options before you actually run the optimization. Scroll through the analysis results to understand what is going to be changed.
7. When you are happy with the options, click the **Optimize** button (5) to start the optimization process. The image will now be optimized as per the settings and configuration details contained within the template that you chose. The progress of the optimization is shown in the following screenshot:

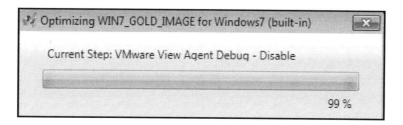

Building and Optimizing the Virtual Desktop OS

8. Once the optimization process has completed, you will automatically see the Optimize tab and the results of the optimization, as shown in the following screenshot:

For more detailed information on how to optimize the desktop operating system for running in a virtual environment, have a look at the following link, which will take you to the VMware Windows Operating System Optimization Tool Guide:

https://www.vmware.com/content/dam/digitalmarketing/vmware/en/pdf/techpaper/vmware-view-virtual-desktops-windows-optimization.pdf.

Once you have completed the optimization process, exit the tool. In the next section, we will look at what's next for the example lab-based virtual desktop machine.

Post-optimization tasks

One of the final things to do is to release the IP address if you have been using DHCP so that when the new virtual desktop machines are created from this parent image, they don't have a duplicate IP address and, therefore, will obtain a new IP address:

1. Open a command prompt window by pressing the Windows key and *R*, and then in the **Run** dialog box, type `cmd`.
2. In the command prompt window that opens, type in the following command:

    `ipconfig /release`

Before shutting down the virtual desktop and completing the image build, there are just a few other housekeeping tasks to perform.

The key one is not to forget to tidy up after yourself. For example, empty the recycle bin and delete any browser history or temporary files. Basically, delete everything that is not part of that parent image. Once you are happy that the image is optimized to your specific requirements, you can shut down the virtual desktop machine.

With the image build for Windows 7 now complete, we will finalize the preparation of this image so that it's ready for delivery.

Creating a Windows 10 virtual desktop machine

For the example lab, we will repeat the build and optimization process to build a second parent image but, this time, we are going to build a Windows 10 virtual desktop machine.

Once built, this Windows 10 parent image will then be used to create an Instant Clone virtual desktop machine pool.

Rather than go through every step again screen by screen, we will list the steps we followed when creating the Windows 7 parent image and then just show some screenshots to highlight the differences. You can refer to the previous section to get more details.

Creating the virtual desktop machine container

Like with creating the previous virtual desktop machine, the first thing we need to do is build and configure the actual virtual desktop machine on the vCenter server. This will define the virtual hardware configuration. As we mentioned previously, the process is identical to the one we followed for Windows 7, and so we are going to cover the tasks and just highlight specific screenshots that are different:

1. Follow the steps we described previously for the Windows 7 build up to the point where you get to **Select a name and folder,** as shown in the following screenshot:

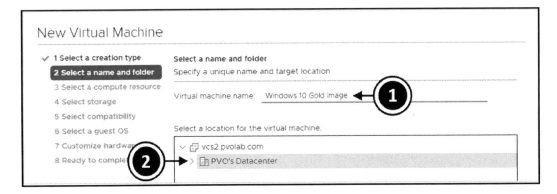

2. In the **Virtual machine name** box (**1**), type in a name for the new virtual desktop machine. In the example lab, this is called `Windows 10 Gold Image`.
3. Then, in the **Select a location for the virtual machine** section, click to highlight the datacenter where you want this virtual machine to be created. In the example lab, this machine is going to be created in the datacenter called **PVO's Datacenter** (**2**).
4. Click the **NEXT** button to continue. Continue with the steps that were described in the Windows 7 build until you get to the **Select a guest OS** screen, as shown in the following screenshot:

Chapter 7

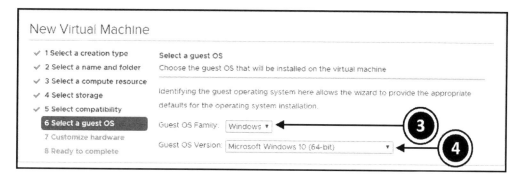

5. The next step is to choose the operating system for the virtual desktop machine. In the example, this is the second virtual desktop machine that will be used as the gold image template for Windows 10.
6. From the **Guest OS Family** box, click the arrow for the dropdown menu (**10**), and select **Windows**. Then, from the **Guest OS Version** box, click the arrow for the dropdown menu (**11**) and select **Microsoft Windows 10 (64-bit)**. The guest OS selection is important to get right, as it determines which drivers get installed when VMware Tools is installed on the virtual desktop machine.
7. Click the **NEXT** button to continue with the steps that were described in the Windows 7 build process until you get to the **Select File** screen being displayed, as shown in the following screenshot:

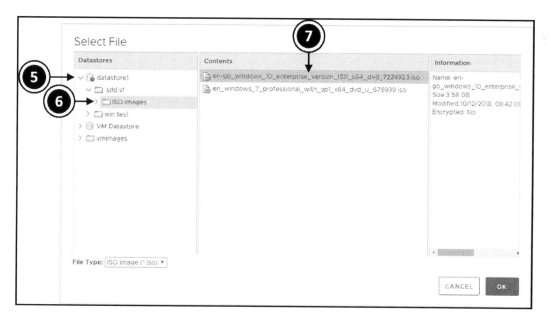

[377]

Building and Optimizing the Virtual Desktop OS

8. Expand the datastore **(5)** and then click on the `ISO Images` folder **(6)**. Then, click to select the OS that is going to be installed on this virtual desktop machine. In this example, we are going to install Windows 10, so click on the **engb_windows_10_enterprise_version_1511_x64_DVD_7224923.iso** option **(7)**. You may have your ISO images stored in a different location, so just follow this as a guide by using your folder locations.
9. Click the **OK** button to return to the virtual hardware screen, and then continue with the steps that were described in the Windows 7 build process.
10. With the virtual desktop machine now built and configured, it's time to power it on and continue the build process. Navigate to the virtual desktop machine in the inventory. You should see an entry called **Windows 10 Gold Image**.
11. Highlight the virtual desktop machine **Windows 10 Gold Image**, right-click it, and from the contextual menu now shown, click on **Power** and then click on **Power On**.
12. The virtual desktop machine will now power on and boot into the BIOS setup screen, as that's what we configured to happen on the next boot. Any subsequent bootups will boot as normal into the operating system once it's installed.

In the next section, we will make the configuration changes to the virtual desktop machine.

Completing the Windows 10 build

Like with the Windows 7 virtual desktop machine, you need to power on the newly created Windows 10 virtual desktop machine and finish the configuration. This consists of the following tasks that need to be completed:

- Updating the virtual desktop machine BIOS
- Installing the guest operating system (Windows 10)
- Installing VMware Tools
- Installing applications for the parent image
- Installing the Horizon Agent
- Optimizing the guest operating system
- Completing post-optimization tasks

Now that we have completed all the build tasks, all that remains is releasing the IP address and then clearing up any temporary files, browser history, and so on. Once we have finished doing this, power off the virtual desktop machine, which is ready for us to prepare the image as our virtual desktop machine template.

Creating a GPU-enabled virtual desktop machine

In this section, we are going to build a second Windows 10 virtual desktop machine, but this time for using with a dedicated hardware-based NVIDIA GPU card. As we discussed previously, there are three models for delivering high-end graphics. In the next example, we will set up a virtual desktop machine to use NVIDIA GRID vGPU.

Creating the virtual desktop machine container

The first step, as with the build process we covered previously for Windows 10, is to build the virtual machine itself. We will follow the steps that were previously described in this chapter to build a Windows 10 virtual desktop machine, up to the point where we configure the virtual hardware differently, as we need to add in the NVIDIA GRID vGPU at this point.

At the time of writing this book, and since we are using vSphere 6.5 as the hosting platform, you will also need to use the older Flash-based vSphere client for configuring the vGPU settings.

Building and Optimizing the Virtual Desktop OS

1. Follow the steps to build a Windows 10 machine as described in the previous section, *Creating a Windows 10 Virtual Desktop Machine*, until you get to the **Customize Hardware** section, as shown in the following screenshot:

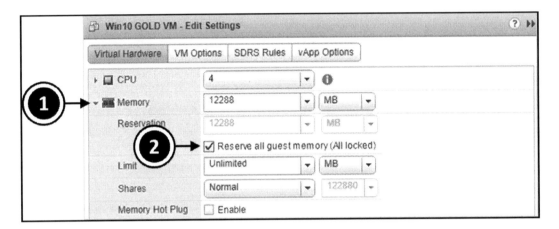

2. Under the **Virtual Hardware** tab, click on the dropdown arrow for **Memory** (1), and check the box for **Reserve all guest memory (All locked)** (2).

If you do not configure memory reservation, then the virtual desktop machine will fail to power on, as it can't guarantee that the memory will be available.

3. Next, at the bottom of the box, in the **New device** section, click the dropdown arrow (3), and from the list of options, click on **Shared PCI Device** (4), as shown in the following screenshot:

Chapter 7

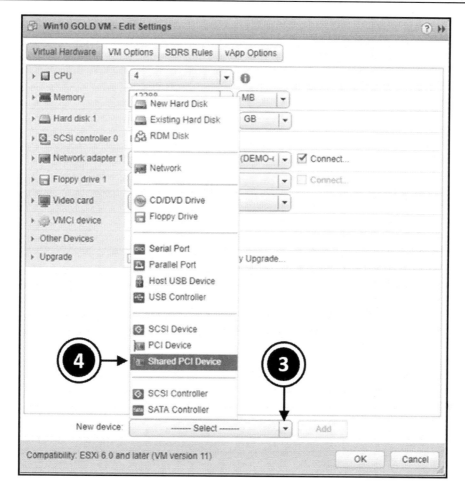

4. Now, click the **Add** button (5) to add the new PCI device, as shown in the following screenshot:

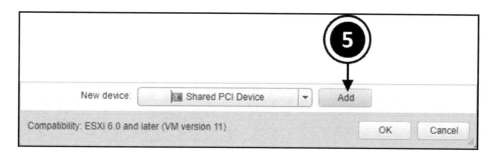

Building and Optimizing the Virtual Desktop OS

5. You will now see that the **NVIDIA GRID vGPU** has been added as a device (**6**). This device was configured for PCI pass-through when the ESXi host server was configured in `Chapter 4`, *Installing and Configuring Horizon 7 – Part 1*. This is shown in the following screenshot:

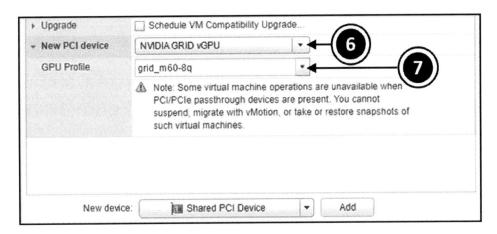

6. If you click the down arrow on the **GPU Profile** box (7), you will see a list of the supported GRID profiles you can apply to this desktop. You can select the required profile from the list, based on the graphics requirements of the virtual desktop machines, and the users that will use it:

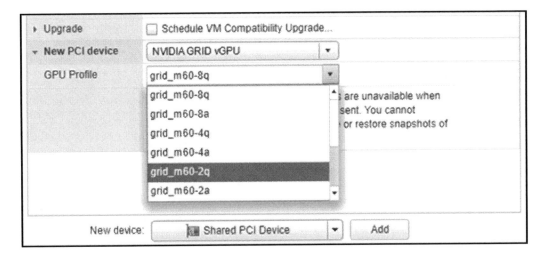

With these steps complete, you can now complete the build steps to update the BIOS settings before we move on to installing the guest operating system and optimizing it.

Installing the operating system for GPU-enabled desktops

In the example lab, we are going to build a Windows 10 virtual desktop machine to deliver high-end graphics. To install the operating system, follow the steps described in the *Installing the guest operating system* section under the *Creating a Windows 10 Virtual Desktop Machine* section of this chapter, but with one difference.

After you have installed the Horizon Agent, you need to install the NVIDIA drivers on the virtual desktop machine. The drivers can be downloaded from the following link: https://www.nvidia.com/Download/index.aspx?lang=en-us.

From here, you can select the correct graphics card for your needs, as shown in the following screenshot:

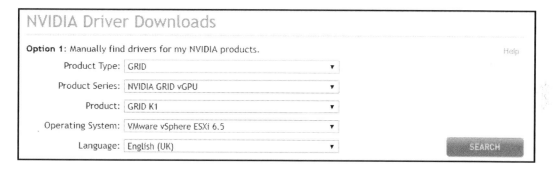

One thing to note is that when you install the NVIDIA driver software, make sure that you select all the components to be installed and don't use the express option. Express will miss out some of the key components that need to be run in a virtual desktop machine.

Building and Optimizing the Virtual Desktop OS

Once you have the drivers installed, completed the operating system setup by installing any additional applications, and then performed the optimization steps, it's probably worth checking that the graphics card has been installed correctly. Do this by checking the device manager of the virtual desktop machine, as shown in the following screenshot:

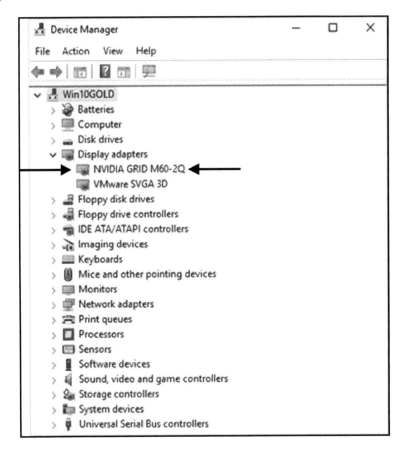

You should now have a GPU-enabled virtual desktop image ready to be prepared for delivery to end users.

Completing the GPU-enabled desktop build

With the operating system now built and the NVIDIA components installed, you can follow the remaining tasks to complete the build. These are all covered in the previous section and are listed as follows:

- Installing VMware Tools
- Installing applications for the parent image
- Installing the Horizon View Agent
- Optimizing the guest operating system
- Post-optimization tasks

Once these tasks are complete, you will now have three virtual desktop machines built to use as the parent image, ready to create new virtual desktop machines to deliver to your end users.

Before we look at the final preparation steps, we are going to create one final virtual desktop machine, this time using a Linux-based operating system.

Creating a Linux virtual desktop machine

The final virtual desktop that we are going to build is for a Linux operating system, and for this example, CentOS is going to be the Linux distribution that is used.

The process is almost the same as for installing a Windows-based operating system; however, there are some differences when it comes to installing the Horizon Agent. The process starts with creating the virtual desktop machine itself.

Like with creating the previous virtual desktop machine, the first thing we need to do is build and configure the actual virtual desktop machine on the vCenter server. This will define the virtual hardware configuration.

Building and Optimizing the Virtual Desktop OS

As we mentioned previously, the process is identical to the one we followed for Windows 7 and Windows 10, and so we are going to cover the tasks and just highlight specific screenshots that are different:

1. Follow the steps we described previously for the Windows 7 build, up to the point where you get to **Select a name and folder,** as shown in the following screenshot:

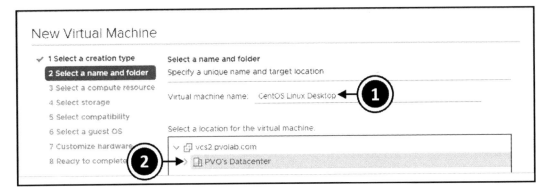

2. In the **Virtual machine name** box **(1)**, type in a name for the new virtual desktop machine. In the example lab, this is called `CentOS Linux Desktop`.
3. Then, in the **Select a location for the virtual machine** section, click to highlight the datacenter where you want this virtual machine to be created. In the example lab, this machine is going to be created in the datacenter called **PVO's Datacenter (2)**.
4. Click the **NEXT** button to continue with the build process, as described in the Windows 7 build, until you get to the **Select a guest OS** screen, as shown in the following screenshot:

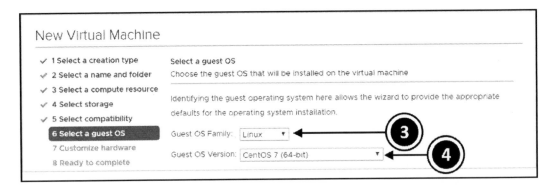

Chapter 7

5. The next step is to choose the operating system for the virtual desktop machine. In the example, this is the second virtual desktop machine that will be used as the gold image template for Windows 10.
6. From the **Guest OS Family** box, click the arrow for the dropdown menu (**10**) and select **Linux**. Then, from the **Guest OS Version** box, click the arrow for the dropdown menu (**11**) and select **CentOS 7 (64-bit)**. The guest OS selection is important to get right as it determines which drivers get installed when VMware Tools is installed on the virtual desktop.
7. Click the **NEXT** button to continue with the build, process as described in the Windows 7 build, until you get to the **Select File** screen, as shown in the following screenshot:

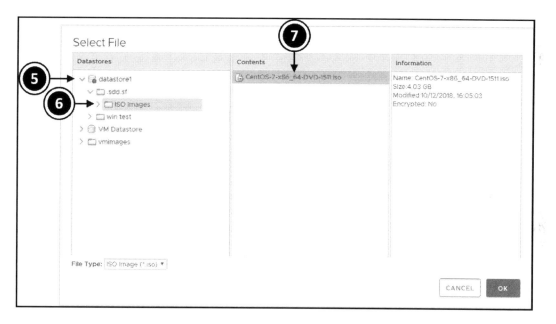

8. Expand the **datastore1** (**5**), and then click on the `ISO Images` folder (**6**). Then, click to select the OS that is going to be installed on this virtual desktop machine. In this example, we are going to install Windows 10, so click on the **CentOS-7-x86_64-DVD-1511.iso** option (**7**). You may have your ISO images stored in a different location, so just follow this as a guide while using your folder locations.

[387]

9. Click the **OK** button to return to the virtual hardware screen and continue with the build process, as we described previously. With the virtual desktop machine now built and configured, it's time to power it on and continue the build process. Navigate to the virtual desktop machine in the inventory. You should see an entry called **CentOS Linux Desktop**.
10. Highlight the virtual desktop machine called **CentOS Linux Desktop**, right-click it, and from the contextual menu that's now shown, click on **Power** and then click on **Power On**.
11. The virtual desktop machine will now power on and boot into the BIOS setup screen, as that's what we configured to happen on the next boot. Any subsequent bootups will boot as normal into the operating system once it's installed.

In the next section, we will make the configuration changes to the virtual desktop machines.

Completing the Linux virtual desktop build

Like with the Windows 7 and Windows 10 virtual desktop machine, you need to power on the newly created Linux virtual desktop machine and finish the configuration. This consists of the following tasks:

- Updating the virtual desktop machine BIOS
- Installing the guest operating system (Windows 10)
- Installing VMware Tools
- Installing applications for the parent image
- Installing the Horizon Agent (see the following)
- Optimizing the guest operating system
- Completing post-optimization tasks

Now that we have completed all the build tasks, all that remains is releasing the IP address and then clearing up any temporary files, browser history, and so on. Once we have finished these, power off the virtual desktop machine, which is ready so that we can prepare the image as our virtual desktop machine template.

Installing the Horizon Agent

Now, we can install the Horizon View Agent. The installation process is a little different than previous installations, as this is a Linux-based operating system:

1. You can either download the Horizon Agent for the Linux installer from the VMware download website by using the Linux desktop or from the example lab since the installer was copied onto the Linux desktop using WinSCP.

2. The .tar file called VMware-horizonagent-linux-x86_64-7.0.0-3617131.tar.gz (**1**) is copied and then extracted to get the installer, as shown in the following screenshot:

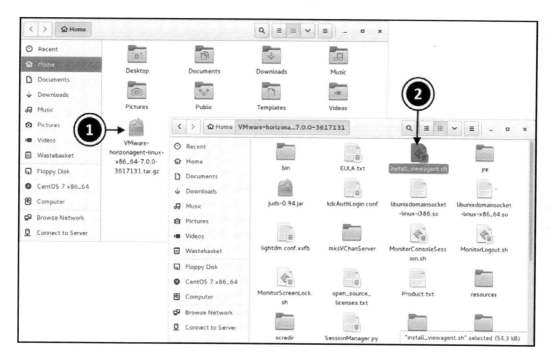

3. With the software extracted, the next task is to run the installer script.

Building and Optimizing the Virtual Desktop OS

4. From the desktop of the Linux virtual desktop, open a Terminal session by clicking **Applications** (3), **Favourites** (4), and then **Terminal** (5), as shown in the following screenshot:

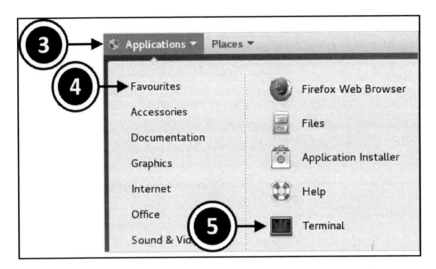

5. Once you have an open terminal session, change to the directory of where the VMware Agent software was extracted to, as shown in the following screenshot:

```
Desktop    Pictures   VMware-horizonagent-linux-x86_64-7.0.0-3617131
Documents  Public     VMware-horizonagent-linux-x86_64-7.0.0-3617131.tar.gz
Downloads  Templates
Music      Videos
[root@linux-desktop pvo]# cd VMware-horizonagent-linux-x86_64-7.0.0-3617131/
```

6. Next, launch the installer script using the following syntax and options:

    ./install_viewagent.sh -b hzn7-cs1.pvolab.com -d pvolab.com -u administrator -p xxxxxxxx

7. The switch options are as follows:
    - -b: The fully qualified name of the connection server for the agent to register with
    - -d: The name of your domain
    - -u: The username of the account that has privileges to register with the connection server
    - -p: The password for the account

8. When the installer script launches, you will first see the EULA message. At the bottom of the screen, you will see the `Are you sure you want to install linux agent y/n?` prompt, as shown in the following screenshot:

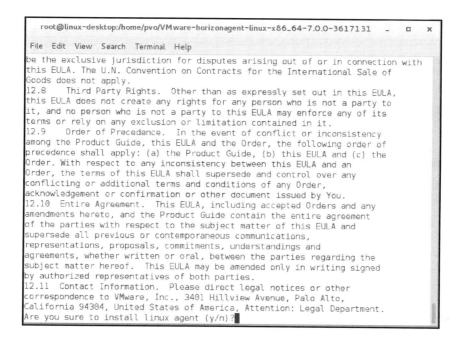

9. Type *Y* and then press *Enter*. Once completed, you will see the following screenshot:

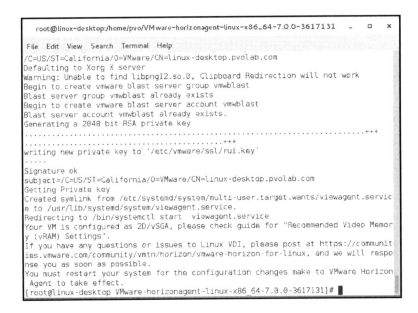

The Horizon Agent for Linux has now been successfully installed. Restart the virtual desktop machine to complete the installation.

Optimizing the guest operating system

Unlike Windows-based operating systems, there is no automated optimization tool available; however, you should still look at optimizing the image by switching off any tasks or applications that take up unnecessary resources, such as disk I/O or CPU cycles. You also need to ensure that you configure the operating system to work with the Active Directory authentication.

With the desktop images now built, we can now prepare them so that we can deliver them to the end users.

Preparing virtual desktops for delivery

Now that we have our fully optimized virtual desktop machine parent images that can be used by Horizon View, the next stage of the process is to prepare them for delivery to the end users.

There are two different ways in which a desktop needs to be prepared, depending on whether you are using a Full Clone desktop or a Linked/Instant Clone desktop. Full Clones will use a VM template to create virtual desktop machines, while Linked/Instant Clones will use a snapshot to create virtual desktop machines.

Pool design – a quick overview

We will cover creating desktop pools in more detail in `Chapter 8`, *Configuring and Managing Desktop Pools – Part 1*, but, for now, let's just have a quick overview of the basics around pool design and where the images that we created in this chapter are going to be used.

You will typically have a desktop pool for each type of virtual desktop machine you want to deliver, probably categorized by use case or department. In this chapter, we have built several different types of virtual desktop machines that will be used in the following desktop pools:

- **Windows 7**: This is to be used as a non-persistent, linked clone-built desktop
- **Windows 10**: This is to be used as a dedicated full clone with a hardware-enabled GPU
- **Windows 10**: This is to be used as a non-persistent instant clone-built desktop
- **CentOS 7**: This is to be used as a persistent Linux desktop

Building and Optimizing the Virtual Desktop OS

As we have Linked Clone, Full Clone, and Instant Clone desktops, the preparation method for each is different. We will cover this in the following sections.

Creating a snapshot for linked clones

The first virtual desktop machine we are going to prepare for delivery is for the Windows 7 non-persistent, linked clone virtual desktop machine. To prepare this image for delivery, we will need to take a snapshot of the virtual desktop machine using vCenter and the vSphere web client. Once you have taken the snapshot, it can then be used by the **View Administrator** to create a new desktop pool for virtual desktop machines, which is built using Linked Clones. It will be used to create the replica in View Composer:

1. To create the snapshot, log into the vSphere Web Client and navigate to the **Windows 7 Gold Image** virtual desktop machine (**1**), ensuring that it's powered off before you do this.
2. Click on the virtual desktop machine to highlight it, right-click it, and from the menu that pops up, click on **Snapshots** (**2**), and then select the option for **Take Snapshot...** (**3**), as shown in the following screenshot:

3. You will now see the **Take VM Snapshot for Windows 7 Gold Image** dialog box, as shown in the following screenshot:

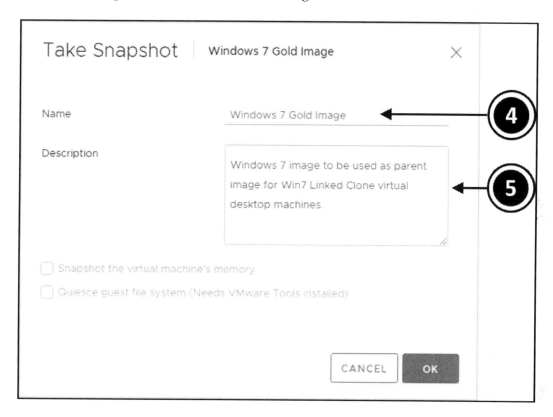

4. Type in a name for this snapshot in the **Name** box (**4**). In the example lab, we have called this **Windows 7 Gold Image**. It's a best practice to call it something that you easily recognize, as you will search for this snapshot in the View administrator when configuring desktop pools. In the **Description** box (**5**), type in a description to describe the purpose of the snapshot in more detail.

Building and Optimizing the Virtual Desktop OS

5. Click the **OK** button when you are ready to create the snapshot.
6. To check that the snapshot has been taken, navigate to the snapshot manager.
7. To do this, from the vSphere Web Client, highlight the **Windows 7 Gold Image** virtual desktop machine (**6**). Right-click it, and from the menu that pops ups, click on **Snapshots** (**7**), and then select the option for **Manage Snapshots** (**8**), as shown in the following screenshot:

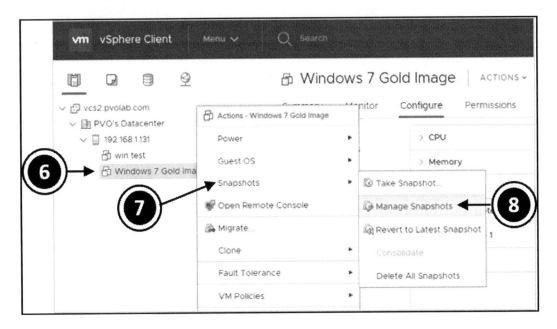

8. You will now see the **Manage Snapshots** for the **Windows 7 Gold Image** dialog box, where you will be able to see the snapshot that was just taken, as shown in the following screenshot:

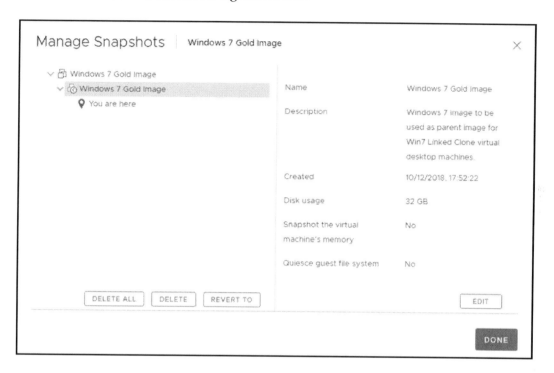

9. You will also be able to see how many snapshots have been taken and also when they were created. This will help with version control of your parent images.
10. Click on **DONE** to close the **Manage Snapshots** screen.

You have now successfully taken a snapshot that can be used as the base image for all virtual desktop machines that are created from it. We will see how this snapshot is used to deliver the linked clone virtual desktop machines in Chapter 8, *Configuring and Managing Desktop Pools – Part 1*.

Building and Optimizing the Virtual Desktop OS

Creating a snapshot for instant clones

The next image to prepare for delivery is the Windows 10 image. As this is going to be used with an Instant Clone desktop pool, then the base image again starts off life as a snapshot of the parent image.

To create the snapshot, follow the process as we described in the previous section to create a new snapshot, but this time use the Windows 10 Gold Image virtual desktop machine to create the snapshot.

Creating a template for full clones

For the second Windows 10 virtual desktop machine (with GPU-enabled), and the CentOS Linux virtual desktop machines, we are going to create persistent full clone virtual desktop machines. To do this, we are going to follow the tasks that were described in this section.

To use these virtual desktop machines as parent virtual desktop machines for full clone virtual desktops, you will first need to convert them into a virtual machine template or use the clone-to- template feature using vCenter and the vSphere Client.

Once that's completed, you can then use View Administrator to create new desktop pools (one for Linux and one for Windows 7 GPU), based on the virtual desktop machines, using these templates for each desktop pool.

In the example lab, we will use the Windows 7 image. The process for creating the Linux virtual desktop machine is exactly the same, so repeat these instructions to create the template for that particular operating system. However, the pool configuration will be different for each one, as we will see in `Chapter 8`, *Configuring and Managing Desktop Pools - Part 1*:

> 1. To create the snapshot, log into the vSphere Web Client and navigate to the **Windows 10 Gold Image** virtual desktop machine (**1**), ensuring that it's powered off.

Chapter 7

2. Click on the virtual desktop machine to highlight it, right-click it, and from the menu that pops ups, click on **Clone** (2), and then select the option for **Clone to Template...** (3), as shown in the following screenshot:

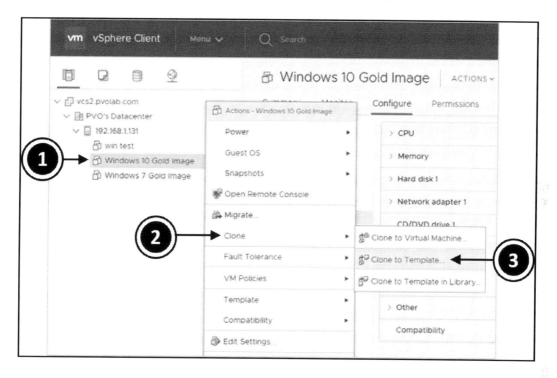

3. You will now see the **Windows 10 Gold Image – Clone Virtual Machine to Template** configuration dialog box.
4. In the **VM template name** box (4), type in a name for the template. In the example lab, this is called **Windows 10 Gold Image Template**.

5. Then, in the **Select a location for the template** section, click to highlight the datacenter where you want this virtual machine to be created (**6**). In the example lab, this machine is going to be created in the datacenter called **PVO's Datacenter,** as shown in the following screenshot:

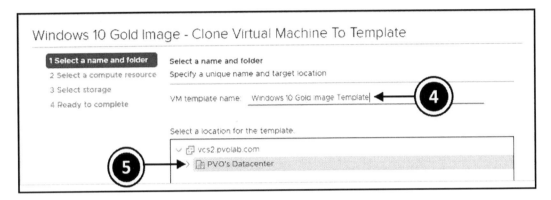

6. Click the **NEXT** button to continue.
7. You will now see the **Select a compute resource** screen. Expand the datacenter called **PVO's Datacenter** and then click on the ESXi host server you want to host this template on. In the example lab, `esx-1.pvolab.com` is going to be the host server.
8. Click the **NEXT** button to continue.
9. You will now see the **Select storage** screen. Select the datastore where this template will be stored. In the example lab, the template is stored on **VM Datastore.**
10. Click the **NEXT** button to continue. You will now see the **Ready to complete** screen.
11. Click the **FINISH** button to complete the configuration and create the virtual desktop machine template for Windows 10.

You have successfully created a template that can be used as the parent image to create a new virtual desktop machine. Repeat the same process and create a template for the Linux desktop virtual machine, and call the template **CentOS Linux Desktop Template.** Once completed, if you navigate to the VMs and templates view in vCenter, you will see the following:

We will use these templates in Chapter 8, *Configuring and Managing Desktop Pools – Part 1*, when we create the desktop pools.

Summary

In this chapter, we have built several virtual desktop machine images that will act as the parent images from which all the virtual desktop machines in the environment will be created from.

To build and configure the virtual desktop machines, we outlined and followed a process. This process is started by creating the virtual hardware containers, installing the guest operating systems, installing the Horizon-specific components, optimizing them to run as Horizon virtual desktop machines, and then finally preparing them by creating either templates or snapshots that are ready to be used to create virtual desktop machines that are going to be delivered to the end users.

In the next chapter, we are going to start looking at how to configure and manage desktop pools.

8
Configuring and Managing Desktop Pools - Part 1

Now that you have prepared a number of desktop images in the previous chapter, the next step is to configure desktop pools that will deliver these desktops to the end users, and so, in this chapter, we will look at how to create and manage desktop pools within Horizon View.

To recap, desktop pools are collections of one or more virtual desktop machines that have similar attributes. By this, we mean that they have the same operating system versions, applications, memory, CPU, or other configuration.

In this chapter, we will cover the following topics:

- Automated desktop pools
- Creating a manual desktop pool
- Managing Linked Clone desktop pools
- Reviewing the infrastructure post-deployment

Types of desktop pools

Different desktop pools can also be built and assigned differently. For example, one pool may be built using Linked Clones, and another could have a dedicated user assignment. The types of desktop pools available are as follows:

- Automated desktop pool
- Manual desktop pool
- RDS desktop pool

So, let's take a minute to describe what each of these types of desktop pools is used for.

An **automated desktop pool** is a collection of desktops that are automatically created from a snapshot or a virtual machine template by Horizon View. Desktops within an automated pool may be created on demand or built in advance. They can also be deleted or refreshed on logoff. Automated pools are generally the most widely used pools within Horizon View deployments, as they allow great flexibility for administration.

A **manual desktop pool** provides access to an existing desktop, whether it is virtual or physical, just so long as it has the View Agent installed on it. A manual pool is used for niche use cases due to the administrative overhead. Also, you would generally use an image management tool, such as VMware Mirage or SCCM, with these machines to simplify the management as far as possible.

Finally, an **RDS desktop pool** is a great way of offering high levels of consolidation for task workers within your Horizon View environment. An example of where an RDS desktop might be suitable would be for call center users, where the user is using one or two simple applications and doesn't require a full-blown desktop. We will cover RDS desktops in `Chapter 18`, *Delivering Published Desktops with Horizon 7*.

In the next sections, we are going to configure the different pool options using the example lab and the parent desktop images created in the previous chapter. We are going to build the following desktop pools:

- Automated desktop pools for the following:
    - Windows 7 dedicated, Linked Clone desktop pool
    - Windows 7 dedicated, Full Clone desktop pool
    - Windows 7 floating, Linked Clone desktop pool
    - Windows 7 floating, Full Clone desktop pool
    - Windows 10 floating, Instant Clone desktop pool
- Manual desktop pool

We are also going to show you how to build the desktop pools using the Horizon View administrator classic console, as well as the new web-client style Horizon Console.

Automated desktop pools

Automated desktop pools will be the largest use case within our Horizon View environment, and so we will start by looking at how to create and manage those first.

As you start running through the configuration wizards to create the automated desktop pools, you will be asked a number of questions that will further define how the users will use the desktop pool. The first of these questions is how is the desktop going to be assigned to the end users?

The first option is for creating dedicated desktop assignments. Along with this option, you will get the choice of having an automatic assignment. Dedicated desktops are generally used due to something being stored or configured within the user's desktop that is important for that user, or due to application-specific nuances (for example, a licensing restriction that requires a specific MAC address to be used). This means that every time the user wants to connect to a desktop, they will always be given the same desktop.

Dedicated desktops can be built using either Full Clones, Linked Clones, or Instant Clones.

With a dedicated virtual desktop machine that is built using Linked Clones, you can also add a persistent disk to the virtual desktop to save all the changes that happen to the desktop while the user is using it. If you then need to refresh or recompose the desktop operating system, then the user won't lose the customizations or their personal data stored on their desktop as they are stored on a separate disk. However, you need to keep in mind that there is no easy way to back up the persistent disks and, as such, you might decide to use another tool to protect and update these desktops.

Creating dedicated, Linked Clone desktop pools

In this section, we will work through the configuration wizard to create the first desktop pool to build a dedicated Windows 7 desktop, built using Linked Clones and taking the Windows 7 Gold Image snapshot created in the previous chapter as the parent image from which to create the virtual desktop.

To create the desktop pool, we are going to work through the following steps using the Horizon View Administrator console first, and then the new Horizon Console.

Using the Horizon View Administrator Console

To set up the desktop pool using the Horizon View Administrator, perform the following steps:

1. From a workstation, open a browser and enter the address details of the View Connection Server. In the example lab, the address of the Connection Server is `https://hzn7-cs1.pvolab.com/admin`. Don't forget the `/admin` at the end; otherwise, you will end up on the Horizon Client page.
2. You will now see the View Administrator login screen, as shown in the following screenshot:

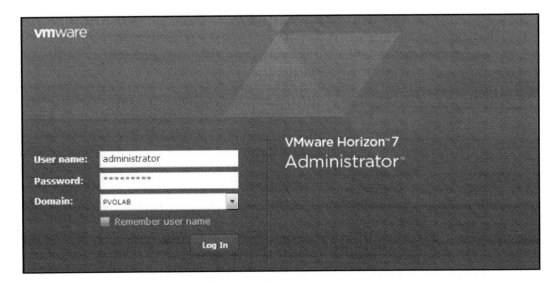

3. Log in using the administrator account that was set up for the View Administrator. You will now see the Horizon View Administrator **Dashboard** screen, as shown in the following screenshot:

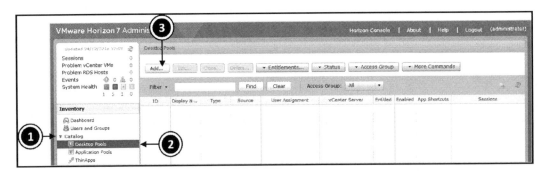

4. From the Horizon View Administrator, click to expand the **Catalog** option (**1**), and then click on **Desktop Pools** (**2**). Then from the **Desktop Pools** pane that is now displayed, click the **Add...** button (**3**).
5. You will now see the **Add Desktop Pool** screen, starting with the **Type** section where we select the type of desktop pool you want to create:

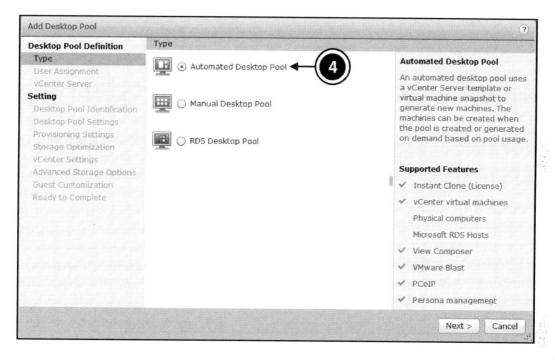

6. Click the radio button for **Automated Desktop Pool** (**4**). When selecting the various types of desktop pools that are available, the description on the right-hand side will change, reminding you of the differences between the pool types, as well as the features that are supported within each desktop pool.
7. Now click the **Next >** button to continue.

8. You will now see the **User Assignment** screen, as shown in the following screenshot:

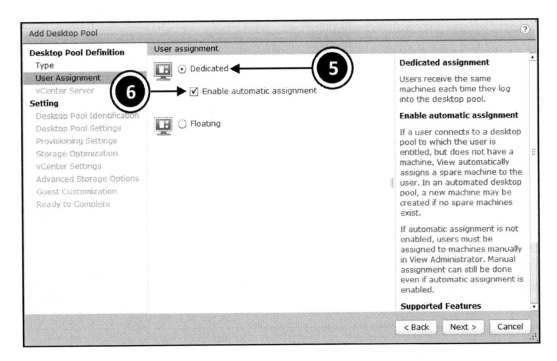

9. Click the radio button for **Dedicated** (5). The **Enable automatic assignment** option (6) will already be selected by default. This means the desktops will be assigned to the users on a first come, first served, as they log in. If, for some reason, you need to ensure a user is assigned a specific desktop, then you will need to uncheck this box, and manually assign them a virtual desktop machine.

10. Click the **Next>** button to continue the configuration. You will now configure how the virtual desktop machines will be built, using the vCenter Server linked with this Connection Server, as shown in the following screenshot:

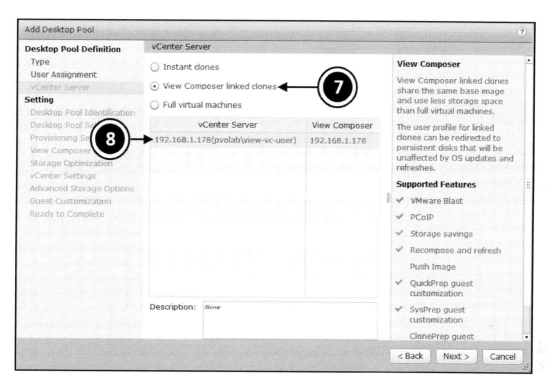

On this configuration screen, you have the option to build either **Instant clones**, **View Composer linked clones**, or **Full virtual machines**.

11. For this first desktop pool, we are going to use Linked Clones, so click the radio button for **View Composer linked clones** (7).
12. Next, you need to select the relevant vCenter Server from the list. In the example lab, the vCenter `192.168.1.178` is shown, along with the vCenter user account we set up for the View (8).

Configuring and Managing Desktop Pools - Part 1

13. Click the **Next>** button to continue the configuration. The next configuration screen is for the **Desktop Pool Identification,** as shown in the following screenshot:

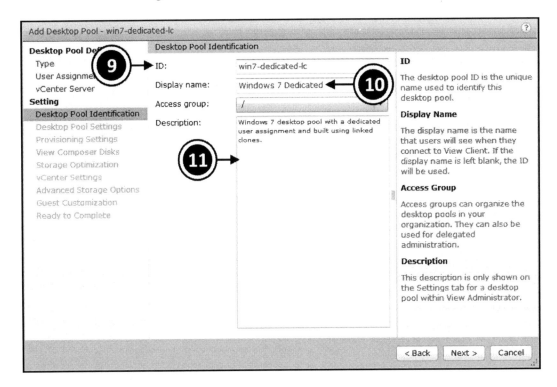

14. In the **ID** box (**9**), type in an ID for this desktop pool. In the example lab, we have entered the ID of `Win7-dedicated-lc`.

You can only use the characters *a-z, A-Z, 0-9, -,* and _ in the pool ID.

15. In the **Display name** box (**10**), type in a name for this pool. Bear in mind that the display name is what is displayed to the end users, so make sure you give it a non-technical name that the users will understand.
16. Finally, in the **Description** box (**13**), type in a detailed description that describes the desktop pool and what it is used for.

Chapter 8

17. Click the **Next>** button to continue the configuration. You will now see the **Desktop Pool Settings** configuration screen, as shown in the following screenshot:

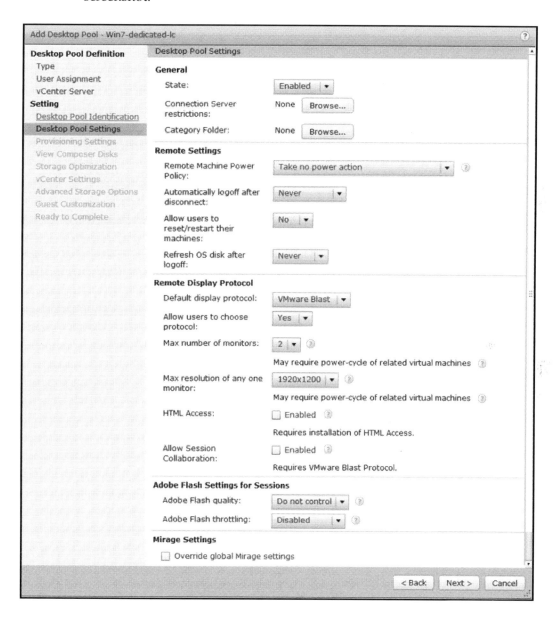

Configuring and Managing Desktop Pools - Part 1

This configuration page is where we start to configure the settings that will define the way the virtual desktop machines behave within the desktop pool. It provides configuration options for before users connect, while they are using their virtual desktop machine, and finally, once they disconnect from it.

There a number of options to configure on this screen so we are going to break them down into individual sections.

General settings

We are going to start by configuring the **General** settings first, by performing the following steps:

1. First, in the **General** section, you can configure the **State** of the desktop pool. From the drop-down menu, select the **Enabled** option (12) to enable this pool, meaning that it will be available to users who are entitled to use it and, therefore, any virtual desktop machines will be provisioned within the pool and made available for end users to use. If you set the **State** to **Disabled**, virtual desktop machines will not be provisioned and will not be made available to end users. You might want to set the **State** to **Disabled** if you are pre-configuring a new pool for users and then go back and enable it once you are happy it is configured correctly:

Chapter 8

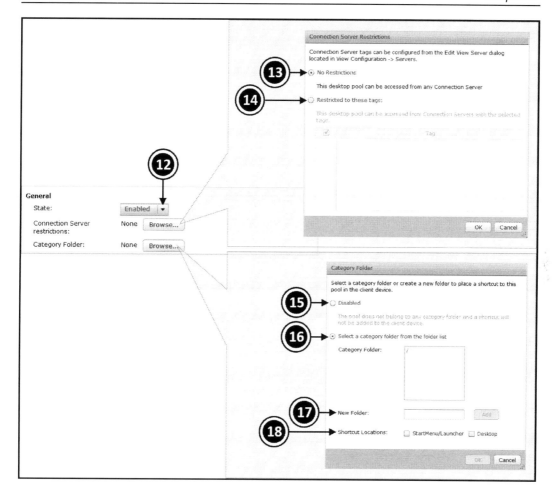

2. The second option under the **General** section is for **Connection Server restrictions**, where you are able to select tags associated with the Connection Server to restrict where the users can connect from. Click the **Browse...** button to configure the restrictions. If you want to allow this desktop pool to be accessed from any Connection Server, then you would click the radio button for **No Restrictions** (13). If you click the radio button for **Restricted to these tags** (14) then you would see a list of the configured tags. Simply highlight the tag from the list and then click **OK**.

Configuring and Managing Desktop Pools - Part 1

3. The final setting under the **General** section is for **Category Folder**. This setting allows you to create a shortcut directly onto the client device, with the details of this desktop pool so the end users can easily access their resources. To configure this option, click the **Browse...** button. The first radio button option is for **Disabled** (15) to turn this feature off. To enable the feature, click the radio button for **Select a category folder from the folder list** (16). You then have the option to select the **Category Folder** from the list, or you can create a new one by starting to type in the name of the folder you want to create in the **New Folder** box (17). Once you have typed in the name, you can click the **Add** button. Finally, you can select the **Shortcut Locations** (18). You can choose from the **Start Menu/Launcher** or the **Desktop** of the client device onto which to place the shortcut.
4. Click the **OK** button once you have completed configuring your options.

The next section to configure is for the **Remote Settings**.

Remote Settings

These settings define the power state of the virtual desktop machines and what happens when end users connect and disconnect. The settings options are shown in the following screenshot:

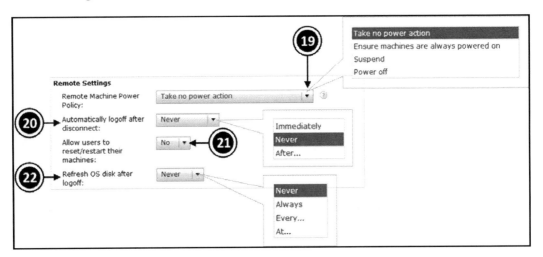

[414]

You then have the following options for configuring the **Remote Settings**:

1. The first option is for the **Remote Machine Power Policy** option, which defines the power state of the virtual desktop machine when users connect and disconnect. Click on the drop-down menu (**19**) and you will see the following options:
    - **Take no power action**: The virtual desktop machine will remain in the last state it was left in. For example, if the desktop was left powered on, then it will remain powered on.
    - **Ensure machines are always powered on**: The virtual desktop machines will always be restored to a powered on status after being shut down by an end user or an administrative task.
    - **Suspend**: Virtual desktop machines will be suspended when a user logs off. Note, **Suspend** is not available when using NVIDIA GRID vGPU desktops.
    - **Power Off**: Virtual desktop machines will be powered off when a user logs off.

    When configuring power policies, the most important thing to do is to understand your use case and choose the correct options as appropriate. For example, if you have 200 users, all planning on logging in within a 10-minute window at 9:00 A.M., and the desktops are powered off or suspended, then this could cause some delay and a large performance spike while the desktops are resumed or powered on. Alternatively, if you are using a dedicated desktop model with a shift-based work pattern and choose to leave the desktops always powered on, this could cause your environment to be over-allocated in terms of desktop resources, as well as you potentially having more OS and software application licenses than you actually need or use.

2. The next setting is for **Automatically logoff after disconnect** (**20**). This option allows you to define what happens when a user simply disconnects from their desktop and doesn't choose to log off. Click the drop-down menu to see the following available options:
    - **Immediately**: When the user disconnects from the virtual desktop machine, it is immediately logged off.
    - **Never**: When the user disconnects from the virtual desktop machine, it is never logged off.
    - **After...**: When the user disconnects from the virtual desktop machine, it is logged off after a set period of time. You can choose how many minutes before the desktop will be logged off.

Again, how you configure this setting will very much depend on how your users will use the desktop. Very rarely would you choose to log off the desktop immediately in case the user has only temporarily disconnected from their desktop or has been disconnected due to a network connection glitch. You should give them at least a 5- to 10-minute window to allow them to reconnect rather than just logging them out straight away.

3. The next setting to configure is the **Allow users to reset/restart their machines (21)** option. If this option is set to **Yes**, it means that the users are able to effectively use a reset button to hard reset their virtual desktop machine. This can be a useful feature to allow end users to perform troubleshooting steps without the assistance of IT. However, it can also cause some confusion when the end user believes they are simply resetting the endpoint device but instead they are resetting their virtual desktop machine. If this is a Linked Clone desktop, then they could end up with a completely new virtual desktop machine being provisioned resulting in them potentially losing any current work.

4. The final setting in this section is for **Refresh OS disk after logoff (22)**. As this pool is going to be created using Linked Clone images, this option defines how the operating system disk of the Linked Clone behaves when a user logs off.

5. To configure this option, click the drop-down menu for the following available options:

    - **Never**: The operating system disk will never be refreshed automatically; this will result in the Linked Clone growing over time, especially if a persistent disk and/or a disposable disk isn't configured in the later stages of this wizard. By refreshing the OS disk, the disk is refreshed to a snapshot that is taken when the desktop is originally created. Without a persistent disk, redirected profiles, and so on, all user settings/data will be lost.
    - **Always**: The desktop will be refreshed every time the user logs off.
    - **Every...**: Allows you to define the number of days after which the desktop will be refreshed.
    - **At...**: Allows you to set at what percentage of OS disk utilization should the desktop be refreshed.

Chapter 8

Again, as with the other configuration settings, how you configure these settings will depend greatly on your use cases and how your users work.

The next section in this configuration screen is to configure the **Remote Desktop Protocol**.

Remote Desktop Protocol settings

These settings define the behavior of the delivery protocol for the virtual desktop machines and any user configurable options. The settings options are shown in the following screenshot:

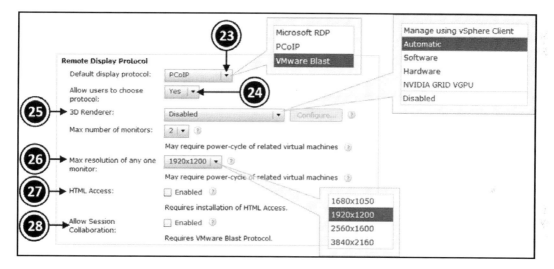

You then have the following options for configuring the **Remote Display Protocol**:

1. The first option in the **Remote Display Protocol** section is to select the **Default display protocol**. From the drop-down menu (**23**), you have the options of **Microsoft RDP**, **PCoIP**, or **VMware Blast**. Note that some of the display-based features are dependent on which protocol you choose. For example, session collaboration is only available when you use the Blast protocol.

2. Next, you have the option to **Allow users to choose protocol** (24). If you set this to **Yes**, then the end user can choose the protocol. Typically, you would use PCoIP or VMware Blast as the default protocol, and not let the end user change this unless there is a specific use case that determines where another protocol is required. For example, if more than four screens are required, then you would use RDP, as this is the protocol that supports this, or maybe the end user could be connected behind a very strict outbound firewall that blocked the PCoIP port, `4172`, and therefore would not be able to see their virtual desktop machine. In these use cases, allowing the end user to change the default protocol means that they can continue to work.

3. You can then choose the **3D Renderer** model you want the desktop pool to use **(25)**. Click the drop-down arrow to select the required 3D renderer. You have the following options:
   - **Manage using vSphere Client**: The **Configure VRAM for 3D Guests**, **Max number of monitors**, and **Max resolution of any one monitor** configuration settings are not available in the Horizon Administrator when you select this setting. Settings are instead managed using the vSphere Web Client.
   - **Automatic**: 3D rendering is enabled and is managed by the host server, which automatically selects the best model to use is. For example, the host server will reserve GPU resources on a, first served basis as a virtual desktop machine is powered on. If there are no GPU resources available when a virtual desktop machine is powered on, then the host server will revert to using software-based rendering. This setting comes in useful in a DR scenario where the host server at the DR site has not been configured with any hardware-based GPU resources. This allows users to revert to software rendering, meaning they can continue to work.
   - **Software**: The host server will always use software 3D graphics rendering.
   - **Hardware**: The host server will reserve GPU hardware resources on a first come, first served basis as virtual desktop machines are powered on. In the scenario where there are hardware resources available from the host server, then the virtual desktop machine will not power on.

- **NVIDIA GRID VGPU**: The host server will again reserve GPU hardware resources on a first come, first served basis as virtual desktop machines are powered on. If a user logs on and connects to a virtual desktop machine, and GPU hardware resources are already allocated to another virtual desktop machine on the same host server, then the Connection Server will attempt to move the virtual desktop machine to a different host server in the same cluster and then power it on once it has the resources. By selecting the **NVIDIA GRID VGPU** option, you will lose the Configure **VRAM for 3D Guests**, **Max number of monitors**, and **Max resolution of any one monitor** settings. You will also need to ensure that you configure the parent virtual desktop machine or virtual desktop machine template to reserve all the memory.
- **Disabled**: 3D rendering is switched off.

4. When you choose one of the valid 3D Renderer options (does not work with **NVIDIA GRID VGPU** or **Manage using vSphere Client**), you will also now see that the **Configure...** button next to the chosen model is now active. If you click on this, then you will see the **Configure VRAM for 3D guests** box, which allows you to specify an amount of video memory to use, up to a maximum of **512 MB,** as shown in the following screenshot:

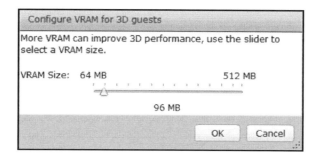

5. The next option is to select the **Max number of monitors**. If you click the drop-down arrow, you can choose from **1**, **2**, or **4** monitors. Note that this setting only applies to the PCoIP and Blast protocols. When 3D is disabled, the **Max number of monitors** and **Max resolution of any one monitor** settings determine the amount of VRAM assigned to the virtual desktop machines in the desktop pool. The greater these values are, the more memory will be consumed on the associated ESXi host servers.

If 3D is disabled, up to three monitors are supported running at a resolution of 3,840 x 2,160 on a Windows 7 guest operating system, with Aero disabled. For other operating systems, or for Windows 7 with Aero enabled, only one monitor is supported at this resolution. When 3D is enabled, one monitor is supported at 3,840 x 2,160 resolution. Multiple monitors are best supported at a lower resolution.

6. The next option is for **Max resolution of any one monitor** (26). Click the drop-down arrow to select the required resolution, noting the previous discussion in point 3.
7. Next, you have the option to enable **HTML Access** (27). To enable HTML, check the box. Note that the Connection Server will need to have HTML Access installed on it for this to work.
8. Finally, you have the option to **Allow Session Collaboration** (28). To enable this feature, check the box. Session collaboration allows users of this desktop pool to invite other users to join their session. Note that this feature only works with the VMware Blast protocol.

The next section in this configuration screen is to configure the **Adobe Flash Settings for Sessions**.

Adobe Flash Settings

These settings define the behavior of Adobe Flash within the virtual desktop machine sessions. The settings options are shown in the following screenshot:

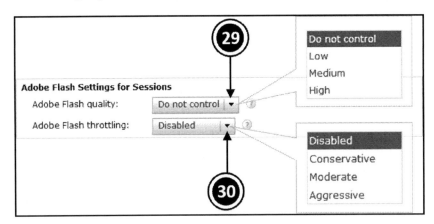

The configuration options for **Adobe Flash Settings for Sessions** are detailed here:

1. On the option for **Adobe Flash Quality**, click the drop-down menu **(29)** for the available options:
   - **Do not control**: This allows the web page to determine the best setting
   - **Low (default)**: Low quality means less bandwidth consumption
   - **Medium**: Medium quality means average bandwidth consumption
   - **High**: High quality means more bandwidth consumption

2. The other configurable setting is for **Adobe Flash throttling**. Adobe Flash updates the screen by default, using a timer service to determine the update interval. By changing this time interval setting, you can control the frame rate of the screen updates and therefore reduce the bandwidth requirements. Click the drop-down menu **(30)** for the available options:
   - **Disabled**: Throttling is turned off
   - **Conservative**: The update interval is set to 100 ms
   - **Moderate**: The update interval is set to 500 ms
   - **Aggressive**: The update interval is set to 2,500 ms

The final section in this configuration screen is to configure the **Mirage Settings**. These settings define how VMware Mirage interacts with the virtual desktop machine images. The settings options are shown in the following screenshot:

The Mirage Settings are described here:

1. The only option here is to **Override global Mirage settings (31)**. To enable the override, check the box.
2. Then, in the **Mirage Server configuration** box **(32)**, enter the address of the Mirage server you want to use. To find out more about the VMware Mirage solution, you can read the book titled *Learning VMware Mirage*, by Packt Publishing.

Configuring and Managing Desktop Pools - Part 1

 This setting only applies to those who have a current Mirage deployment, as Mirage is now end of life.

Once you have completed the configuration settings on this screen, then click on **Next >** button to continue to the next configuration screen. This next screen is where you configure **Provisioning Settings,** as shown in the following screenshot:

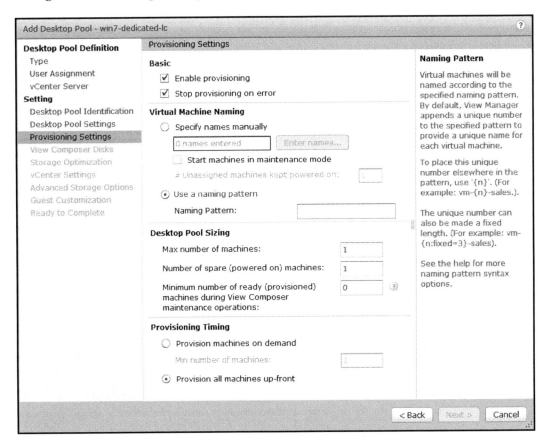

As done previously, we are going to break this screen down into its different configuration sections, starting with the **Basic** section, as shown in the following screenshot:

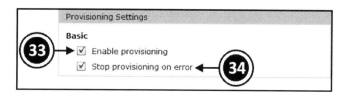

The **Provisioning Settings** are described here:

1. The first setting in the **Basic** section is to **Enable provisioning**. Tick the **Enable provisioning** box **(33)** to basically switch provisioning on. This setting means that virtual desktop machines can be provisioned as per the configuration settings.
2. The next setting is for **Stop provisioning on error** **(34)**. By checking this box, it means that provisioning will stop if there is an error during the provisioning process. This is quite important, as rather than going ahead to continue provisioning hundreds of virtual desktop machines that have errors, you would want to stop provisioning so that you can go back in and fix the issues first.

The next section to configure is for the **Virtual Machine Naming,** as shown in the following screenshot:

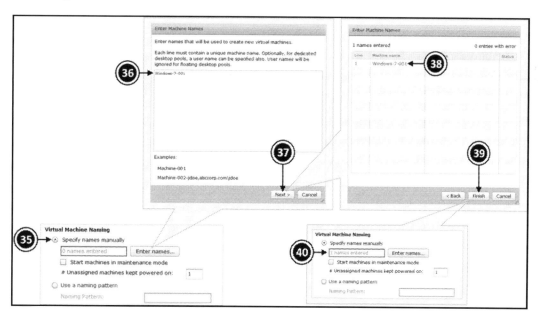

Configuring and Managing Desktop Pools - Part 1

In this section, there are two options for configuring how newly built virtual desktop machines are named, either manually, or automatically. The name we are referring to here is the machine name that will also appear as the computer account in Active Directory. With this in mind, it's worthwhile picking a suitable naming convention.

In the first example, we are going to take a look at the manual option, before configuring the naming pattern method, as this method is the recommended way to name your virtual desktop machines unless there is some reason your desktops need unique non-contiguous names. To do this, perform the following steps:

1. Click the radio button for **Specify names manually** (35).
2. You will now see the **Enter Machine Names** box. In the empty box (36), type in a name for the first virtual desktop machine. In this example, we have called this machine `Windows-7-001`. You could also add a username to this machine if it is going to be a dedicated assignment. So in the example lab, we could enter this machine name as `Windows-7-001,pvolab.com\peter`.
3. Continue entering machines as required and then click **Next >** (37) when you have entered all the machine names you want to add.
4. Now you will see a list of the entered names (38). You can now either go back and enter more names or, if you have completed entering names, click the **Finish** button (39).
5. Finally, you will return to the **Virtual Machine Naming** screen where you will see that it now says **1 names entered** (40) to show how many machine names have been manually entered.
6. You also have a couple of other options under the manual section. You can **Start machines in maintenance mode**, which allows virtual desktop machines to be customized manually before users can log in. This mode must be exited manually. You also have the option to configure # **Unassigned machine kept powered on**. This allows you to keep virtual desktop machines powered on ready, even if they have not been assigned to an end user yet. This option would allow you to quickly assign a machine that had already been built and customized, thereby speeding up the process.

Chapter 8

Now we have looked at how to enter a machine name manually, we are going to look at the option to use a naming pattern, as shown in the following screenshot:

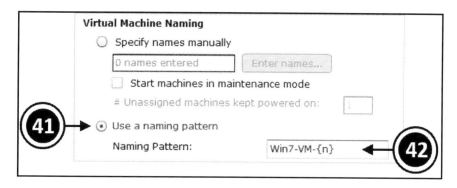

Configure the **Virtual Machine Naming** using the following settings:

1. Click the radio button for **Use a naming pattern** (41).
2. In the **Naming Pattern** box (42), type in a name for the virtual desktop machines. In the example lab, and for this pool, we are going to enter Win7-VM-{n}. This will result in the virtual desktop machines being named Win7-VM-1, Win7-VM-2, and so on, up to the number of machines you specify that you want to build. By using {n} somewhere in the machine name, Horizon View will add a single digit to the name in the required location. By adding {n:fixed=2}, you can allow for for two digits, and {n:fixed=3} for three, and so on. This will ensure the desktops appear in numerical order.

The next section is the **Desktop Pool Sizing** section.

Desktop Pool Sizing

In this section, you can specify the number of virtual desktop machines that are created and provisioned, as shown in the following screenshot:

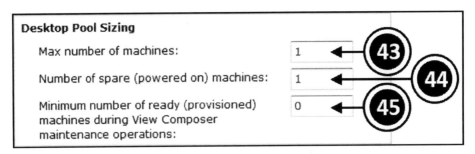

Configure the **Desktop Pool Sizing** using the following settings:

1. In the **Max number of machines** box (**43**), enter the maximum number of machines that can be provisioned in this desktop pool. This sets the limit of the number of virtual desktop machines in this desktop pool.
2. Next is the setting for the **Number of spare (powered on) machines**. In the box (**44**), enter the number of machines that should be powered on and waiting for users to connect to them.
3. Finally, in this section, is the **Minimum number of ready (provisioned) machines during View Composer maintenance operations** option. Here you can enter the number of virtual desktop machines (**45**) that you want to have still available during maintenance operations. So, for example, if you initiated a recompose operation, Horizon View could ensure that there was a minimum number of virtual desktop machines still available for end users to log in to.

How you configure these options is going to be critical to the success of the pool within your View Solution. You need to ensure that there are enough virtual desktop machines provisioned and available for the users as and when they are required. This also means ensuring that you are able to meet user demand even during maintenance operations.

The final section to configure is for **Provisioning Timing**. You have the option of provisioning machines on demand, as users log in and request them, or pre-provision them in advance, as shown in the following screenshot:

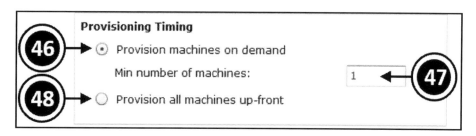

Let's start with the configuration:

1. To provision on demand, click the radio button for **Provision all machines on demand** (46). This means that the virtual desktop machines will be created and provisioned in advance ready for users to connect and log in to. You can select a number of machines to have as a minimum in the **Min number of machines** box (47). If you choose to provision on demand, then you need to ensure there are enough desktops already provisioned in order to meet user demand without causing long delays. This is where making sure you have enough provisioned up-front versus the number of spares as per what you would have configured in the desktop pool sizing section previously.

2. In the example lab, we are going to provision up-front, so click on the radio button for **Provision all machines up-front** (48). If you are going to provision all the virtual desktop machines up-front, you need to ensure that you do this at a time when the increase in performance that will result on a large number of virtual desktop machines being built, is not going to have a knock-on effect on your end users.

Configuring and Managing Desktop Pools - Part 1

Once you have completed the configuration settings on this screen, then click the **Next >** button to continue to the next configuration screen. As this desktop pool is going to use virtual desktop machines built from Linked Clones, then the next configuration screen is the **View Composer Disks** configuration screen, as shown in the following screenshot:

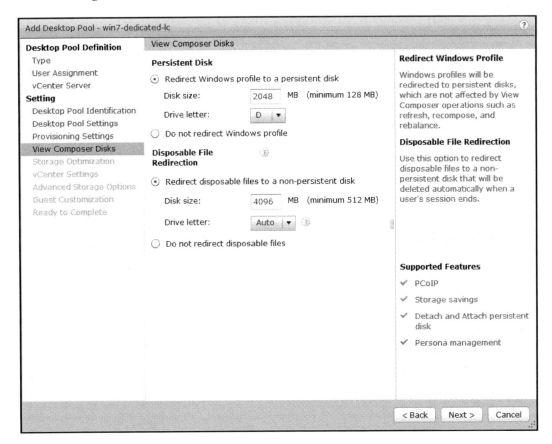

On this configuration screen, there are two options. One OS to configure the persistent disk, and the disposable file redirection. Careful consideration needs to be given as to whether or not you need to utilize these settings within your desktop pool architecture or not, and also depending on whether you are planning on using any additional VMware or third-party solutions to deliver the same functionality.

The first section to configure is for **Persistent Disk,** as shown in the following screenshot:

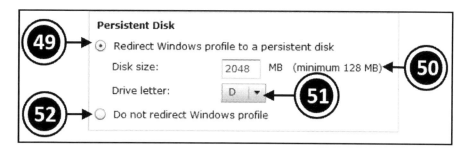

With a persistent disk, the Windows profile will be redirected to a dedicated disk that will be kept even if the OS disk is refreshed during a View Composer operation. This can be a great way to protect user configuration. However, you might also wish to investigate other solutions for this, such as VMware View Persona Management, VMware UEM, or Liquidware ProfileUnity that can offer you similar, if not better, functionality:

1. To configure this setting, click the radio button for **Redirect Windows profile to a persistent disk (49).**
2. In the **Disk size** box (**50**), enter a size for the persistent disk.
3. Lastly, in the **Drive letter** drop-down box (**51**), you can select a drive letter for this persistent disk.
4. To disable the profile redirection, or if you are using another profile management tool, then click the radio button for **Do not redirect Windows profile (52).**

Configuring and Managing Desktop Pools - Part 1

The next section to configure is for **Disposable File Redirection**. The disposable disk contains all page and temporary files and is refreshed after every desktop reboot. This can be a great way to reduce the size of the Linked Clone between desktop refreshes. The **Disposable File Redirection** settings are shown in the following screenshot:

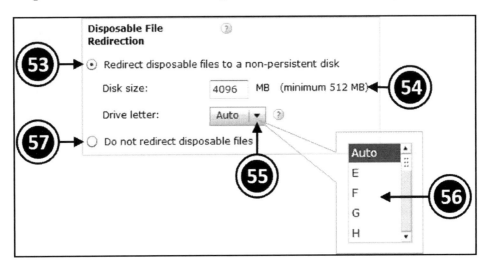

To configure the **Disposable File Redirection** setting, perform the following this steps:

1. Click the radio button for **Redirect Windows profile to a persistent disk** (**53**).
2. In the **Disk size** box (**54**), enter a size for the persistent disk.
3. Lastly, in the **Drive letter** drop-down box, you can select a drive letter for this persistent disk. If you click the arrow (**55**), you will see the drive letter options (**56**). The letter assigned to a disposable disk drive is not necessarily visible to the end user.
4. To disable the **Disposable File Redirection** feature, click the radio button for **Do not redirect disposable files** (**57**).

When configuring either of these, ensure you set the sizes appropriate for your use cases. This is where the POC or desktop assessment will help you understand how large these need to be. Items such as whether an Outlook local cache is being used can affect the size of the persistent disk dramatically.

5. Once you have completed the configuration settings on this screen, then click the **Next >** button to continue to the next configuration screen.

The next configuration screen is for **Storage Optimization**. On this screen, you are able to configure advanced options with regard to storage management and the placement of the OS, persistent, and replica disks. You have the option to select the location of the various different disks that get created for the virtual desktops in this desktop pool. Horizon View effectively allows you to tier your storage and so, depending on your storage design, you might want to place the replica images on faster, local SSD-based storage, and the OS disks on a different tier of storage, such as spinning hard drives.

These configuration options are shown in the following screenshot:

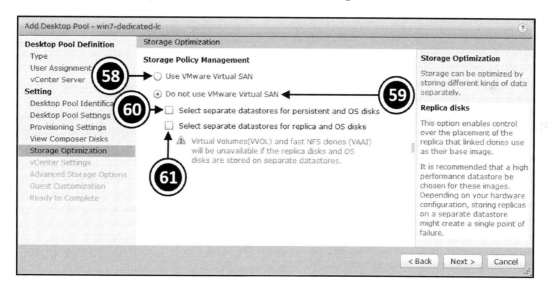

Configuring and Managing Desktop Pools - Part 1

To configure the **Storage Policy Management** setting, perform the following steps:

1. The only option on this screen is to configure the **Storage Policy Management**, starting with VMware Virtual SAN. To enable VSAN, click the radio button for **Use VMware Virtual SAN (58)**. As we don't have this configured in the example lab, then we will click the radio button for **Do not use VMware Virtual SAN (59)**.
2. You can then configure the locations for where the different disk types are stored. Here you have two options. The first is for **Select separate datastores for persistent and OS disks (60)**. This allows the persistent disks and OS disks to be stored on different datastores. The second option is for **Select separate datastores for replica and OS disks (61)**. It is recommended that a high-performance datastore be chosen for these images, such as a flash-based array. Depending on your hardware configuration, storing replica disks on a separate datastore might create a single point of failure.
3. Check the relevant box to configure where you want to store the different disks or leave the boxes unchecked to use a single datastore for all disks. As the example lab only has a single datastore, we will leave them unchecked.

The next configuration screen is the **vCenter Settings** configuration screen.

vCenter Settings

On the **vCenter Settings** screen, we are going to select the parent VM from which to build the virtual desktop machines, and then the location and resources that are going to run them. As such, the configuration options fall into three categories. **Default Image**, **Virtual Machine Location**, and **Resource Settings,** as shown in the following screenshot:

Chapter 8

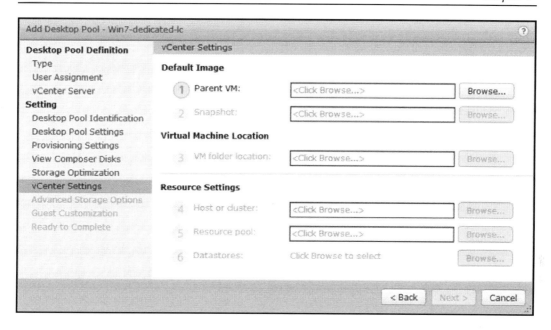

The first thing to configure is the details of the **Default Image** to be used as the parent image from which to create the virtual desktop machines for this desktop pool. This section is shown in the following screenshot:

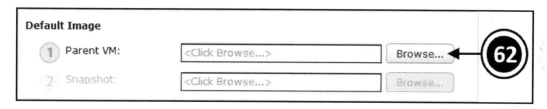

Configuring and Managing Desktop Pools - Part 1

So, let's start with the configuration:

1. On the first box, **Parent VM**, click the **Browse...** button **(62)**. You will now see the **Select Parent VM** box, as shown in the following screenshot:

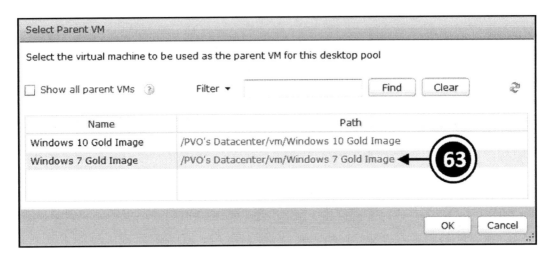

2. You will now see a list of the available **valid** parent VMs. By valid, this means that these will be VMs that contain snapshots and have the Horizon View Agent installed within them. The VMs that will be filtered by default are virtual machines running on ESX/ESXi hosts older than 4.0, VMs that don't have a snapshot, VMs with an unsupported guest OS, VMs already used by another desktop pool, and View Composer Replicas. It is possible to add these VMs to the configuration by clicking on the **Show all parent VMs** button. However, if they are not compatible, you will not be able to select them.
3. The images displayed using the example lab are the gold images that we created previously. As we are building the Windows 7 desktop pool, we are going to use the Windows 7 parent machine, so select the entry for **Windows 7 Gold Image (63)**.
4. Once you have selected the parent VM you want to use, click **OK** to continue.
5. You will now return to the **vCenter Settings** screen, where we can configure the second of the options on the **Default Image** section. You will also see that the **Parent VM** box **(64)** has now been populated with the details of the Windows 7 gold image, as shown in the following screenshot:

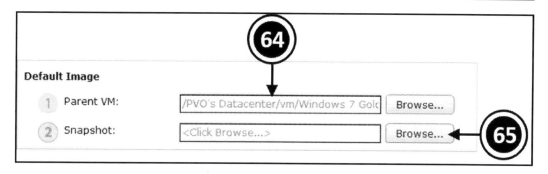

6. As this is a Linked Clone virtual desktop machine, the next configuration task is to configure the details of the snapshot that was created from the parent image.
7. On the **Snapshot** box, click the **Browse...** button (**65**). You will now see the **Select default image**, box as shown in the following screenshot:

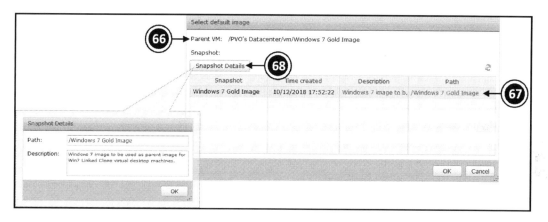

8. The first thing you can see is the details of the parent image (**66**).
9. Below that, you will see the list of snapshots created from this parent VM. In this case, we have just one, the snapshot for **Windows 7 Gold Image**, which we will click to select (**67**). If you had more than one snapshot for this image, then they will all be listed, allowing you to select the correct one.
10. When you click the snapshot, you will see the **Snapshot Details** button (**68**) is now available to click. If you click this, then you will see the full details of the snapshot, as shown. Click **OK** to close the **Snapshot Details** box.

11. Click **OK** on the **Select default image** box to complete the configuration.
12. You will now see that the snapshot has been added, as shown in the following screenshot:

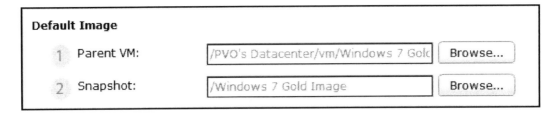

The next part of the **vCenter Settings** is the **Virtual Machine Location** setting, as shown in the following screenshot:

To proceed further, perform the following steps:

1. On the **VM folder location** box, click the **Browse...** button (**69**).
2. You will now see the **Select the folder to store the VM** box, as shown in the following screenshot:

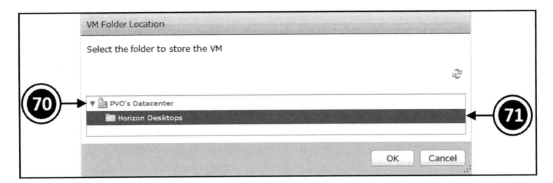

3. Expand **PVO's Datacenter** by clicking the arrow (**70**) and then select the folder in which you want to create the virtual desktop machine. In the example lab, this folder has been called **Horizon Desktops** (**71**).

[436]

Chapter 8

 You might want to consider a folder structure for the virtual machines to help with management; otherwise, you could end up creating hundreds of different virtual desktop machines that reside in different pools, all in the same folder.

4. Click **OK** to continue.
5. You will return to the **vCenter Settings** screen where you will see that the **VM folder location** has now been added, as you can see in the following screenshot:

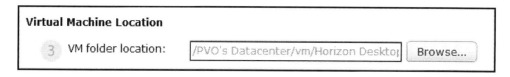

The next configuration section is for the resources that are going to host and run the virtual desktop machines in the pool:

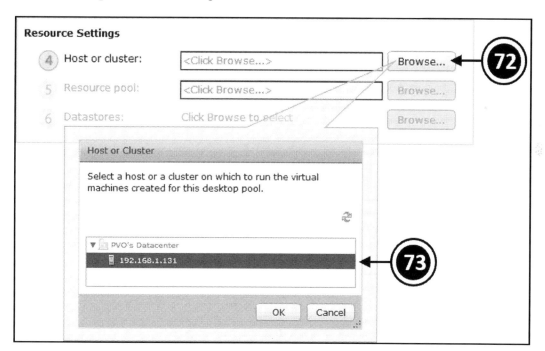

The options shown are as follows:

1. First, in the **Host or cluster** box, click the **Browse...** button (72).
2. You will then see the **Host or Cluster** box appear, listing the available host resources. The host resources are the ESXi servers available. In this example, we can see the IP address of the example lab ESXi server.

 In a production environment, the hosting infrastructure used in this part of the configuration would be part of the desktop block hosting infrastructure.

3. Click on the IP address `192.168.1.131` (73).
4. Click **OK** to continue.
5. You will now return to the **vCenter Settings** screen, where you will see that the **Host or cluster** has now been added, as you can see in the following screenshot:

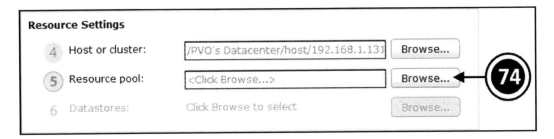

6. Next, we are going to configure the resource pool for this desktop pool to use.

[438]

7. In the **Resource pool** box, click the **Browse...** button (**74**). You will now see the **Select a resource pool to use for this desktop pool** box, from where you can select the resource pool, as shown in the following screenshot:

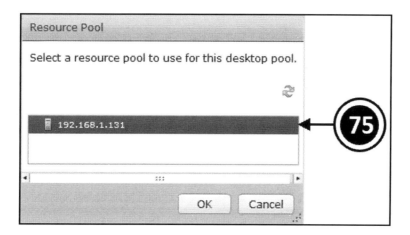

8. The resource pool for the example lab is the ESXi host server again, so click the IP address `192.168.1.131` to select this from the list (**75**).
9. Click **OK** to continue.
10. You will now return to the **vCenter Settings** screen, where you will see that the **Resource pool** has now been added, as you can see in the following screenshot:

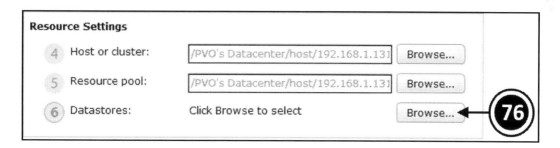

Configuring and Managing Desktop Pools - Part 1

The final configuration option in this section is for **Datastores**. In the example lab, we are using a single datastore, which was selected from the **Storage Optimization** settings screen. If you had opted to place the different disks on different datastores, then you would now see options to configure the location for the OS disk datastore, persistent disk datastore, and replica disk datastore:

1. In the **Datastores** box, click the **Browse...** button (76).
2. You will now see the **Select Linked Clone Datastores** configuration screen, which shows all available datastores, as shown in the following screenshot:

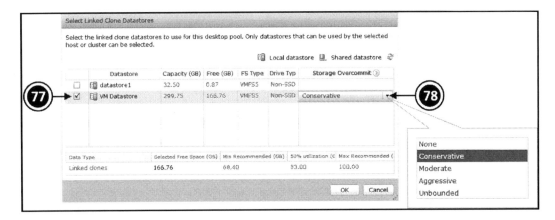

3. Check the box for **VM Datastore** (77). You then have the option to configure **Storage Overcommit**. The overcommit level represents the multiplier that, when applied to the capacity of the full desktop, gives you the amount you wish to allow in the datastore.
4. To configure an overcommit, click the drop-down menu (78), from where you can select from the following options:
   - **None**: No overcommit allowed
   - **Conservative**: Allows four-time overcommit
   - **Moderate**: Allows seven-time overcommit
   - **Aggressive**: Allows 14-time overcommit
   - **Unbounded**: Has no restriction

5. For example, if the size of your full desktop was 10 GB and you had a 100 GB datastore, then selecting **None** would allow you to provision 10 desktops, **Conservative** would allow you 40 desktops, **Moderate** would allow 70 desktops, **Aggressive** would allow 150 desktops, and **Unbounded** would have no restriction.

> You need to be careful with choosing how you are going to configure the overcommit setting, and the only real way to judge this is to monitor Linked Clone growth during the POC.

6. Once configured, click the **OK** button. You will return to the **vCenter Settings** configuration screen, where you will see that the details of the Linked Clone datastores have now been entered by displaying the text **1 selected (79)**, as shown in the following screenshot:

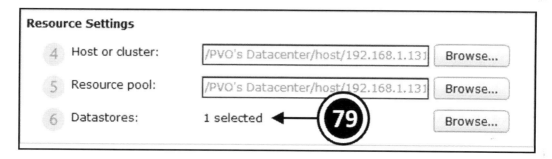

7. With the **vCenter Settings** configuration now complete, click the **Next >** button to continue to the next configuration screen.

The next configuration screen is for **Advanced Storage Options**.

Advanced Storage Options

In the next screen, we are going to configure the **Advanced Storage Options**, as shown in the following screenshot:

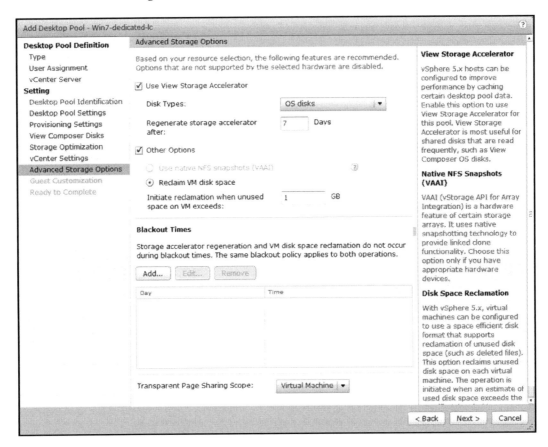

In the first section of this configuration screen, you can configure the **View Storage Accelerator** and how to manage disk space. **View Storage Accelerator** allows you to configure desktop pools to enable ESXi hosts (vSphere 5.x or later) to cache virtual machine disk data. This feature uses the **Content Based Read Cache** (**CBRC**) feature of the ESXi host server. The View Storage Accelerator, or VSA, reduces the disk IOPS and therefore improves the performance during boot storms.

Chapter 8

A boot storm occurs when a large number of virtual desktop machines all start up and boot at the same time, and they all run an anti-virus scan at the same time. The feature is also beneficial when administrators or users load applications or data frequently:

1. To enable the **View Storage Accelerator**, check the box for **Use View Storage Accelerator** (80), as shown in the following screenshot:

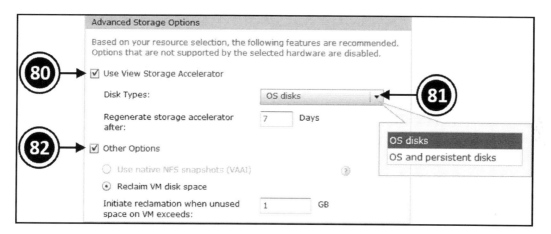

2. In the **Disk Types** section, you then have the option of which particular disks you want the **View Storage Accelerator** to apply to. From the drop-down menu (81), you can choose from **OS disks** or **OS and persistent disks**. In the example lab, we are going to choose the **OS disks** option.
3. The **Regenerate storage accelerator after** option, then allows you to specify a time limit on when you want to regenerate the data that has been cached. This basically clears the cache and rebuilds it. By default, this is set to 7 days.
4. If you check the **Other Options** box (82), you have two options here. The first, which is grayed out in the example lab, is for **Use native NFS snapshots (VAAI)**. VAAI, or vStorage API for Array Integration, is a hardware feature integrated into specific hardware-based arrays. It uses native snapshotting technology to provide Linked Clone functionality. You would only choose this option if you have appropriate hardware devices that support VAAI. This is grayed out in the example lab, as we don't have any supported devices.

Configuring and Managing Desktop Pools - Part 1

5. The next option in this section is for **Reclaim VM disk space**. Virtual desktop machines hosted on vSphere 5.x and later can be configured to use a space-efficient disk format that supports reclamation of unused disk space (such as deleted files). Enabling this option, by clicking the radio button, reclaims unused disk space on each virtual machine and is initiated when an estimate of used disk space exceeds the disk size specified in this setting. By default, this threshold is set to 1 GB.

6. The next setting under **Advanced Storage Options** is to configure blackout times for cache regeneration and space reclamation. This should be set to ensure that these operations won't be scheduled during working hours and ensure users are not affected. The **Blackout Times** configuration box is shown in the following screenshot:

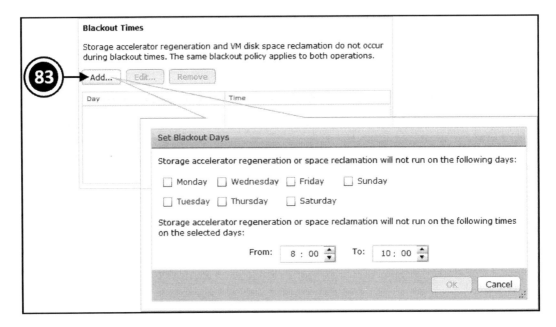

7. Click the **Add...** button (83) to add a blackout time.
8. You will then see the **Set Blackout Days** configuration box. Here, you can select the days by checking the box to configure the days you **DO NOT** want to run regeneration or space reclamation tasks. You can also select specific times not to run the tasks.
9. Click **OK** once you have configured your blackout days and times. You will return to the **Blackout Times** configuration box, which will detail your configured times, as shown in the following screenshot:

Day	Time
Mon, Tue, Wed, Thu, Fri	08:00-19:00

10. In this example, we have configured the blackout for weekdays between `08:00` and `19:00`. You can add additional blackout times as well as delete or edit existing configurations.

The final setting under **Advanced Storage Options** is to configure a **Transparent Page Sharing Scope,** as shown in the following screenshot:

What is transparent page sharing, or TPS? TPS is a memory management technology that is used in virtualization solutions. In desktop virtualization, you are running potentially thousands of copies of exactly the same operating system, all consuming memory, and using exactly the same memory pages. TPS reduces the number of redundant memory pages on a host server down to a single page. The ESXi hypervisor looks for these duplicate pages and if it identifies identical memory pages on multiple virtual machines (VMs) on the same host server, then it shares the single page across the virtual desktop machines, putting in place memory pointers to refer back to the page. This is a much more efficient use of memory, and frees up space to allow more virtual desktops to run.

Configuring and Managing Desktop Pools - Part 1

11. From the drop-down menu **(84)**, select the scope for TPS. You have the option of sharing memory across a **Virtual Machine**, the virtual desktop machines in a **Desktop Pool**, the virtual desktop machines in a **Pod**, or at a **Global** level.
12. Click the **Next >** button once you have completed configuring the **Advanced Storage Options**.

The next configuration screen is for **Guest Customization**, as shown in the following screenshot:

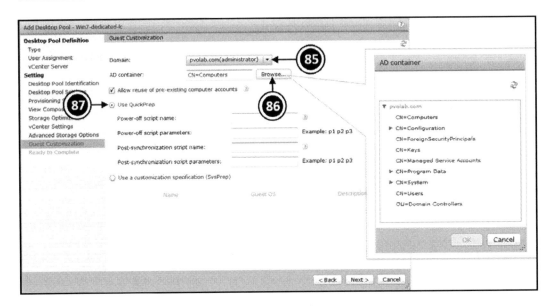

On this configuration screen, you can configure where in Active Directory virtual desktop machines reside, as well as how to customize the guest OS:

1. In the **Domain** section, on the drop-down menu **(85)**, select the domain where you want the machine accounts to reside. In the example lab, this is our `pvolab.com` domain.
2. Next, you can choose the **AD container** where you want the machine accounts to reside. The default setting for this is the computers container, so you will see `CN=Computers`. To change this, click the **Browse...** button **(86)**.

3. You will now see the AD container box. If you expand out the domain, you will see all your containers, so select the appropriate container where you want to store the virtual desktops created with this desktop pool. For example, this desktop pool could be for the technical department, and so you may have a container in AD that reflects this. It's worth creating a folder/container structure that reflects your organization and makes it easier to manage your virtual desktop machines rather than have them all in the standard computers container.
4. Click to highlight the container you want to use and then click **OK**.
5. You will now return to the **Guest Customization** screen.
6. Check the box for **Allow reuse of pre-existing computer accounts**. This allows you to reuse existing AD computer accounts if the virtual desktop machine names of newly created Linked Clones match the existing computer account names. This is particularly useful when creating non-persistent desktops.
7. Next, click the radio button for **Use QuickPrep (87)**. QuickPrep will allow you to prepare your desktops in a quicker fashion than Sysprep. However, no unique SID will be created. Sysprep will create a new SID but will take longer for each desktop to prepare. Which one you choose to use will depend on your use cases. It is recommended that you test your configuration during the POC. As part of QuickPrep, you can also specify additional scripts along with any parameters you want to use for those scripts.
8. The final option is to use SysPrep instead of QuickPrep. To use this feature, click the radio button for **Use a customization specification (SysPrep)**. This will utilize an existing script from the vCenter Server. In the following example, we have used a pre-built script called **Virtual Desktop Customization:**

Name	Guest OS	Description
Virtual Desktop Customization	Windows	Windows 7 VM customization

(●) Use a customization specification (SysPrep)

Configuring and Managing Desktop Pools - Part 1

9. To use this script, click to highlight it. In the example lab, we are going to use QuickPrep, so ensure this option is selected.
10. Click the **Next >** button when you have completed the configuration.
11. You will now see the final screen, the **Ready to Complete** screen, as shown in the following screenshot:

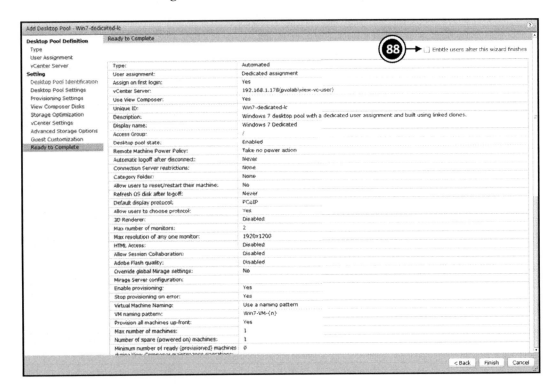

Review your configuration settings, and then click the **Finish** button to create the desktop pool.

You also have the option of ticking the **Entitle users after this wizard finishes** box (88) at the top of the screen, which will automatically launch the entitlement configuration screen so you can give end users access to the virtual desktop machines in this pool. However, in the example lab, we will do this later, after we have created some additional desktop pools.

You will now see that the pool has been created, as shown in the following screenshot:

You will also see on the vCenter Server, that the folder structure for Linked Clones has been set up. You will see, under the `Horizon Desktops` folder, a new folder called `Win7-dedicated-lc`, the name reflecting the ID you entered for the pool. The virtual desktop machines to be built will reside in this folder. This is shown in the following screenshot:

In the next section, we are going to show you how to create another desktop pool, but this time we will use the Horizon Console instead of the View Administrator.

Horizon Console method

As well as the current Horizon View Administrator management console, there is a new web-based console. This is called the **Horizon Console**. However, at the time of writing this book, there are several features that are **not** supported by the Horizon Console, including the following:

- Automated, floating-assignment pools of full virtual machines
- Automated Linked Clone desktop pools
- Automated Linked Clone farms
- Cloning an automated desktop pool
- Cloud pod architecture configuration
- Manual desktop pools
- ThinApp applications

In this section, we are going to create the same desktop pool that we created previously, but this time using the Horizon Console. We will run through the screenshots and configuration options, but for more details on each configuration option, please refer back to the previous section.

The first thing to do is to launch the Horizon Console. There are two ways of doing this. The first way is to log in to the classic View Administrator and click on the link for **Horizon Console (1)**, as shown in the following screenshot:

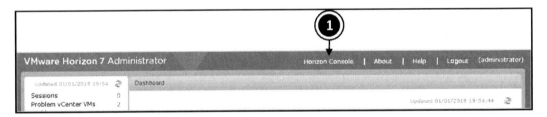

The other way is to use your browser to navigate directly to the URL of the Connection Server, but this time add `/newadmin` to the end of the URL. So, for the example lab, you would type `https://hzn7-cs1/newadmin`. You will then see the login screen, as shown in the following screenshot:

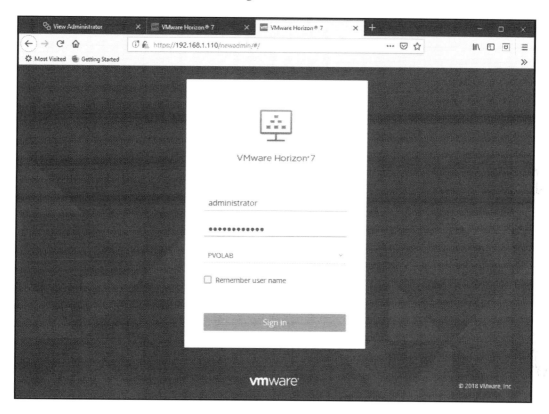

Enter the username and password, ensuring you select the correct domain from the drop-down menu, and then click on the green **Sign in** button. Now you are logged in, you will now see the **Horizon Console** main screen, as shown in the following screenshot:

We are now going to configure a desktop pool by performing the following steps:

1. Unlike with the classic View Administrator console, desktop pools in the Horizon Console come under the general heading of desktops, so, from the menu options on the left-hand side, expand **Inventory** and then click on **Desktops (2)**. You will now see the **Desktop Pools** configuration screen, as shown in the following screenshot:

Chapter 8

2. Click the **Add** button (3). You will now see the **Add Pool** screen with the first section highlighted for **Type,** as shown in the following screenshot:

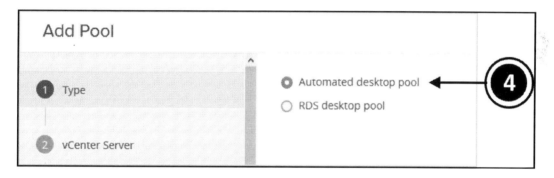

3. Click on **Automated desktop pool** (4). Remember, currently, there is no option to configure a manual desktop pool.
4. Click the **Next** button to continue.

Configuring and Managing Desktop Pools - Part 1

5. You will now move onto the next item on the list, **vCenter Server,** as shown in the following screenshot:

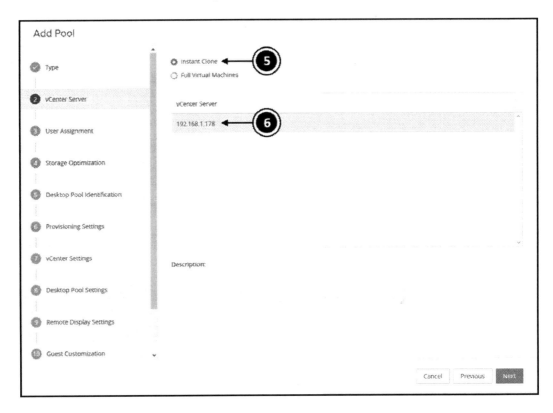

6. Click the radio button for **Instant Clone** (5). Remember, the version of the Horizon Console used in the example lab currently does not support Linked Clone configuration.
7. Next, from the list, select the vCenter Server you want to use for creating the Instant Clones from. In the example lab, the vCenter Server is listed by its IP address, so click on `192.168.1.178` **(6)** and then click **Next** to continue. You will now see the **User Assignment** configuration, as shown in the following screenshot:

Chapter 8

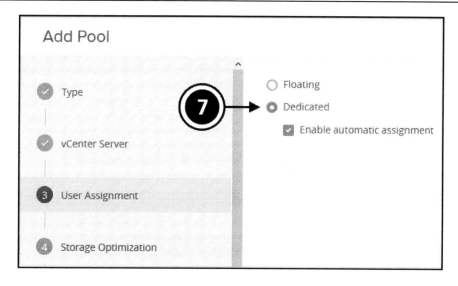

8. Click the radio button for **Dedicated** (7) and also ensure that you check the box for **Enable automatic assignment**.
9. Click **Next** to continue. You will now see the **Storage Optimization** option, as shown in the following screenshot:

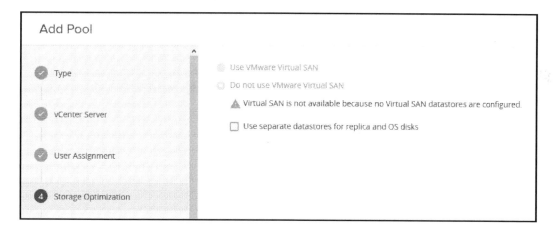

[455]

Configuring and Managing Desktop Pools - Part 1

10. Click the radio button to select whether you want to use VMware Virtual SAN or not. In the example lab, this has not been configured. Also on this configuration screen, you can choose whether or not to use separate datastores for replica and OS disks.
11. Click **Next** to continue.
12. You will now see the **Desktop Pool Identification,** screen as shown in the following screenshot:

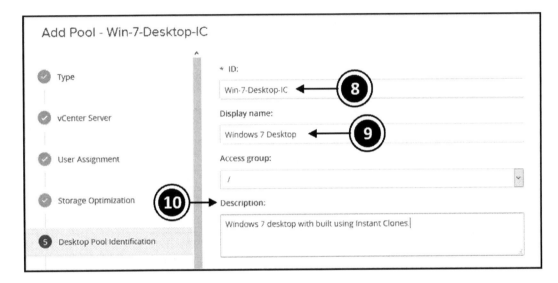

13. In the **ID** box **(8)**, enter a name to use to identify this desktop pool. In this example, we have called it `Win-7-Desktop-IC`.
14. Next, in the **Display name** box **(9)**, enter a name that end users will see to identify this particular desktop pool. In this example, we have called it `Windows 7 Desktop`.
15. If you have configured an **Access group,** then select it from here by clicking on the drop-down menu.
16. Finally, in the **Description** box **(10)**, enter a description to describe this desktop pool.
17. Click **Next** to continue.

18. You will now see the **Provisioning Settings** screen, as shown in the following screenshot:

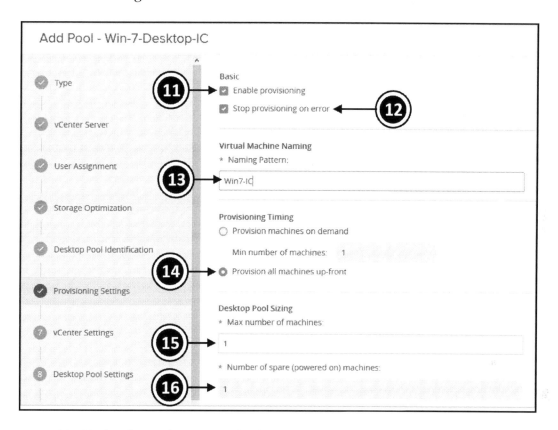

19. Under the **Basic** section, check the box for **Enable provisioning (11)** and the box for **Stop provisioning on error (12)**.
20. Then, in the **Virtual Machine Naming** box (13), type in a name that you want to call the virtual desktop machines that get built. In the example lab, we have entered the name `Win7-IC`.
21. In the **Provisioning Timing** section, click the radio button for **Provision all machines up-front (14)**.
22. And finally, in the **Desktop Pool Sizing** section, in the **Max number of machines** box (15), type in the number of machines you want as a maximum in this desktop pool, and then type in the number of spare virtual desktop machines you want in the **Number of spare (powered on) machines box (16)**.

Configuring and Managing Desktop Pools - Part 1

23. Click **Next** to continue.
24. You will now see the **vCenter Settings** screen, as shown in the following screenshot:

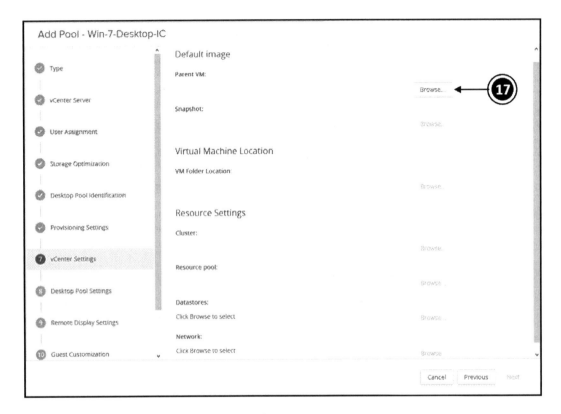

25. The first task is to select the **Default image** from the gold images we have already created. To do this, click the **Browse...** button **(17)** next to the **Parent VM** box. You will now see the **Select a Parent VM** screen, as shown in the following screenshot:

Chapter 8

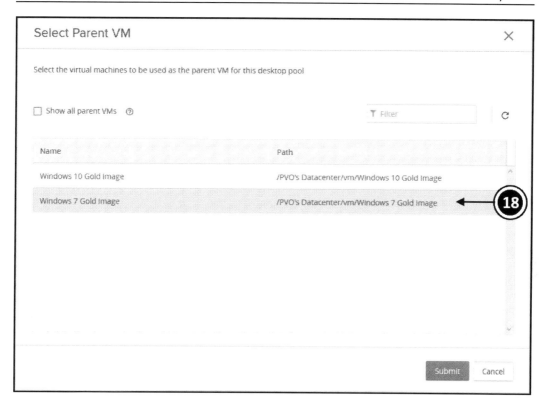

26. In this example, we are going to create a desktop pool using Windows 7 as the operating system, so click to select the option for **Windows 7 Gold Image** from the list of available images, and then click the **Submit** button.
27. You will now return to the **vCenter Settings** screen, where we can configure the next option for **Snapshot**. You will also see that the **Parent VM** box (**19**) has now been populated, as shown in the following screenshot:

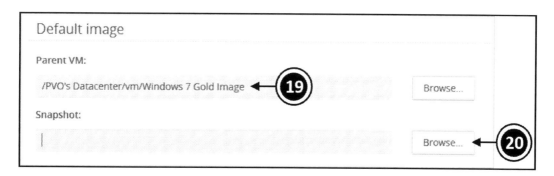

[459]

28. The next **Default image** setting is to configure which snapshot to use. Click the **Browse...** button next to the **Snapshot** box **(20)**. You will now see the **Parent VM in vCenter** screen, as shown in the following screenshot:

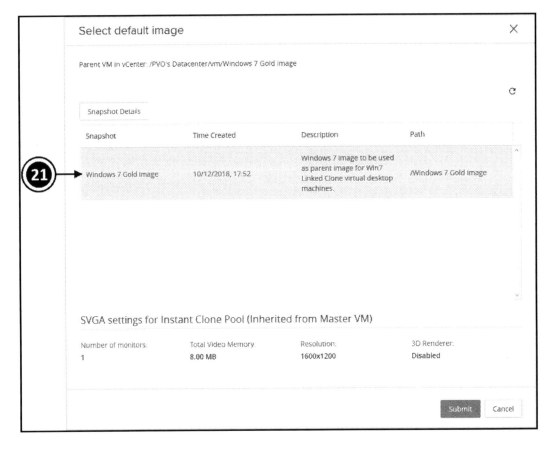

29. From the list of snapshots for this image, select the one you want to use. In the example lab, we only have the one snapshot that we have created, so click the **Windows 7 Gold Image** option from the list **(21)**.
30. Click the **Submit** button to continue. You will now return to the **vCenter Settings** screen, where you will see that the snapshot has been added to the configuration **(22)**, as shown in the following screenshot:

Chapter 8

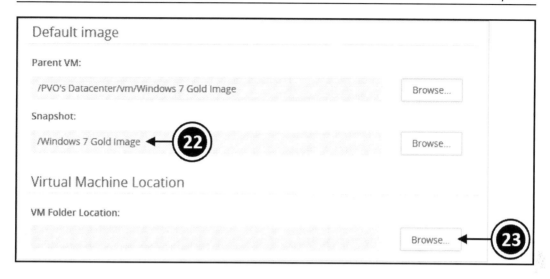

31. Next, we are going to configure the next set of options for **Virtual Machine Location**. Click the **Browse...** button next to the **VM Folder Location** box (**23**). You will now see the **Select the folder to store the VM** screen, as shown in the following screenshot:

32. Select the folder where you want to store the virtual desktop machines that will be created as part of this desktop pool. In the example lab, expand out the entry for **PVO's Datacenter** and then click on the **Horizon Desktops** folder (**24**).

33. Click the **Submit** button to continue. You will now return to the **vCenter Settings** screen, where you will see that the VM folder location has been added to the configuration, as shown in the following screenshot:

34. The next set of configuration options are for **Resource Settings,** as shown in the following screenshot:

35. First, we are going to configure which cluster is going to host the virtual desktop machines in this desktop pool. Click the **Browse...** button next to the **Cluster** box **(25)**. You will now see the **Select Cluster** screen, as shown in the following screenshot:

Chapter 8

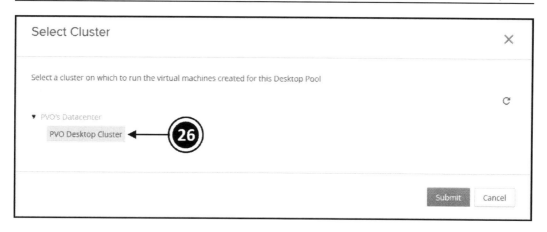

36. In the example lab, expand out the entry for **PVO's Datacenter** and then click on the **PVO Desktop Cluster** option (**26**). Now click the **Submit** button. You will now return to the **vCenter Settings** screen, where you will see that the details of the **Cluster** (**27**) have been added to the configuration, as shown in the following screenshot:

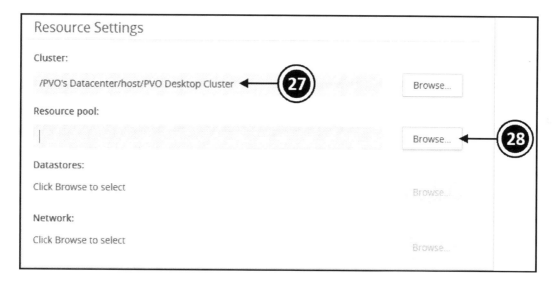

[463]

37. Next, we are going to select the **Resource Pool**. Click the **Browse...** button next to the **Resource Pool** box (28). You will now see the **Select a resource pool to use for this Desktop Pool** screen, as shown in the following screenshot:

38. From the list, click on the resource pool you want to use. In the example lab, click on the entry for **PVO Desktop Cluster** (29).
39. Click the **Submit** button to continue. You will now return to the **vCenter Settings** screen, where you will see that the **Resource pool** details have been added to the configuration (30), as shown in the following screenshot:

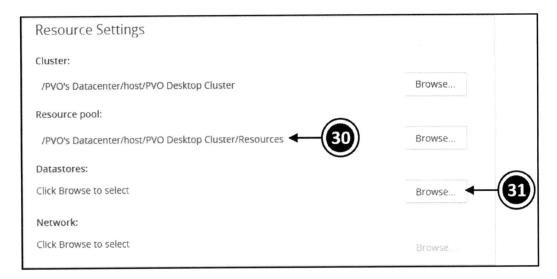

Chapter 8

40. Next to configure is the datastore where the virtual desktop machines in this desktop pool are going to be stored. Click the **Browse...** button next to the **Datastores** box (31). You will now see the **Select Datastores** screen, as shown in the following screenshot:

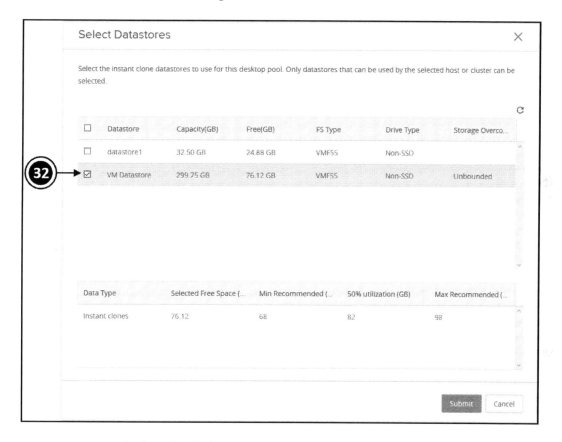

41. From the list, check the box for the datastore that you want to use. In the example lab, this is the **VM Datastore** (32).
42. Click the **Submit** button.

[465]

Configuring and Managing Desktop Pools - Part 1

43. In the example lab, as we are using a local datastore, you will see the following warning message:

 Warning

You have selected a local datastore for your instant clone pool. Please note the following:

1) If you are deploying instant clones on a single ESXi host with local datastore, you must configure a cluster containing that single ESXi host. If you have a cluster of two or more ESXi hosts with local datastores, select the local datastore from each of the hosts in the cluster. Instant clone creation fails otherwise.

2) VMotion, VMWare High Availability, and vSphere Distributed Resource Scheduler (DRS) are not supported.

3) We recommend that you use direct Solid-State Disks (SSDs). Local spinning-disk dirves may not have the throughput required by instant clones.

OK

44. Click **OK** to acknowledge the warning message and to close the box.

45. You will now return to the **vCenter Settings** screen, where you will see that the **Datastore** section now shows that a datastore has been selected **(33)**, as shown in the following screenshot:

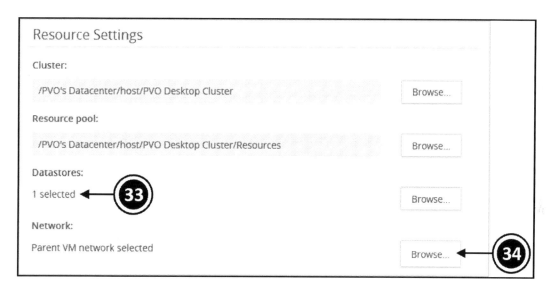

46. The final thing to configure is the **Network** section, which allows you to configure which virtual network the virtual desktop machines in this desktop pool are going to connect to.
47. By default, this is configured as the same virtual network that the parent VM was set to. To change the network configuration, click the **Browse...** button **(34)** and then select the relevant network. In the example lab, we are going to leave this as the default configuration setting.

Configuring and Managing Desktop Pools - Part 1

48. Click **Next** to continue to the next configuration option. You will now see the **Desktop Pools** configuration screen, as shown in the following screenshot:

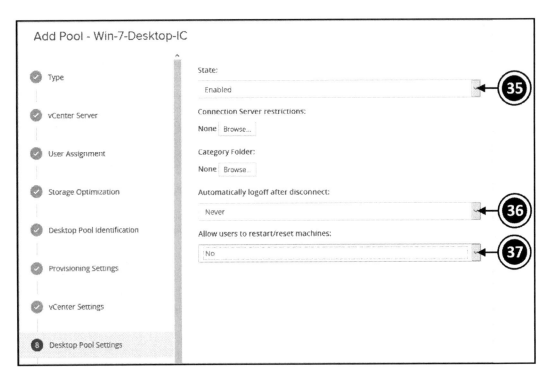

49. The first thing to configure is to enable the desktop pool so that users can access the virtual desktop machines within the desktop pool. In the **State** box (**35**), from the drop-down menu, ensure that **Enabled** is selected.
50. You can then configure the **Connection Server restrictions** and the **Category Folder**.
51. Next, in the **Automatically logoff after disconnect** box (**36**), from the drop-down menu, choose the appropriate action to take. In this example, we have chosen **Never** so that the user never logs off when they disconnect from their virtual desktop machine.
52. Then, in the **Allow users to restart/reset machines** box (**37**), from the drop-down menu, choose the appropriate action to take. In this example, we have chosen **No**, so users cannot restart or reset their virtual desktop machines.

53. Click **Next** to continue. You will now see the **Remote Display Settings** configuration screen, as shown in the following screenshot:

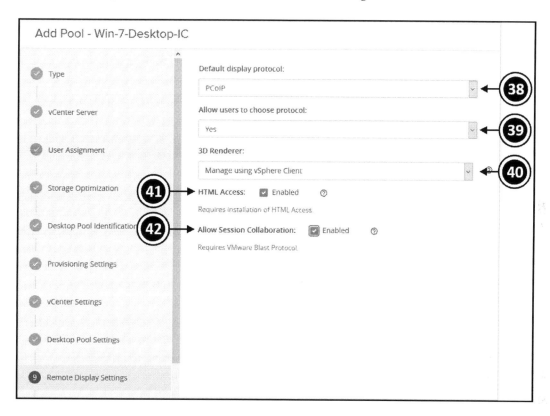

54. First, on the **Default display protocol** box (**38**), from the drop-down menu, choose the display protocol that you want this desktop pool to use. In the example lab, we have chosen **PCoIP**.
55. Next, on the **Allow users to choose protocol** box (**39**), from the drop-down menu, choose the whether you want to allow users to change from the default protocol. In the example lab, we have chosen **Yes**.
56. On the **3D Renderer** box (**40**), choose the relevant 3D rendering model for this desktop pool.
57. Finally, check the **Enabled** boxes for **HTML Access** (**41**) and also **Allow Session Collaboration** (**42**). Note that session collaboration requires the VMware Blast protocol.

Configuring and Managing Desktop Pools - Part 1

58. Click **Next** to continue to the next configuration option. You will now see the **Guest Customization** screen, as shown in the following screenshot:

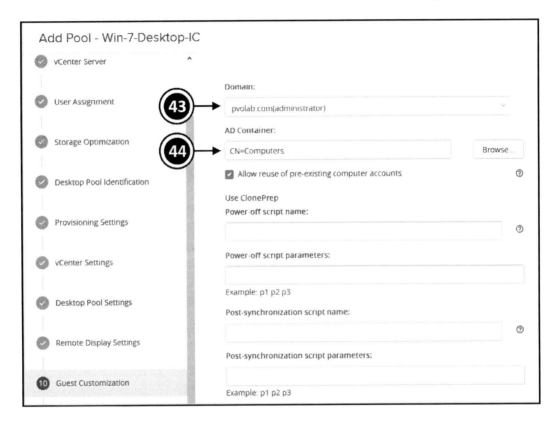

59. On this configuration screen, you can select where the virtual desktop machines are going to reside in Active Directory. In the **Domain** box (43), from the drop-down menu, select the domain name of where they will live. In the example lab, this is the domain called `pvolab.com`.

60. Next, in the **AD Container** box, click the **Browse...** button and then choose the relevant container into which the virtual desktop machines in the desktop pool are going to reside. In the example lab, this is the default setting of `CN=Computers`.

Chapter 8

59. Click **Next** to continue to the **Ready to Complete** screen, as shown in the following screenshot:

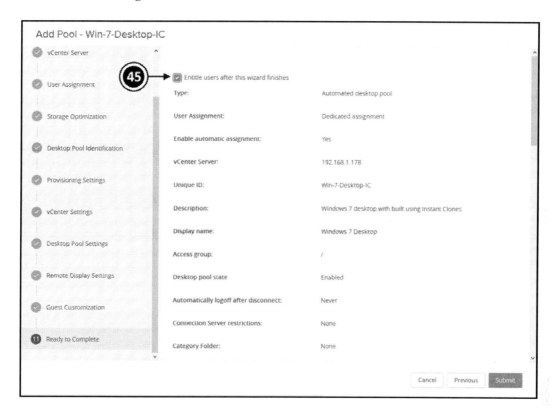

62. The only option on this screen is to check the box **(45)** to choose whether or not you **Entitle users after this wizard finishes**. We will cover the configuring of entitlements later in this chapter, using both the classic View Administrator console and the new Horizon Console.

You have now successfully configured a desktop pool using the Horizon Console. In the next section, we are going to create additional desktop pools to reflect the different types of pools.

Creating dedicated, Full Clone desktop pools

The process for creating a dedicated, Full Clone desktop pool is pretty much the same as we covered in the previous section, where we configured a dedicate Linked Clone desktop pool. There are a few changes, however, as we configuring a Full Clone virtual machine, which will use a template to create the virtual machines from, rather than a snapshot. As we work through this section, we will just highlight the different configuration options in more detail using screenshots, and for the tasks that we have covered previously, we will just describe these using text. You can refer back to the previous section for the screenshots.

To set up the desktop pool using the Horizon View Administrator, perform the following steps:

1. From a workstation, open a browser and enter the address details of the View Connection Server. In the example lab, the address of the Connection Server is `https://hzn7-cs1.pvolab.com/admin`. Don't forget the `/admin` at the end; otherwise, you will end up on the Horizon Client page.
2. You will now see the View Administrator login screen. Log in using the administrator account.
3. You will now see the Horizon View Administrator dashboard screen.
4. From the Horizon View Administrator, click to expand the **Catalog** option, and then click on **Desktop Pools**. Then from the **Desktop Pools** pane that is now displayed, click the **Add...** button.
5. You will now see the **Add Desktop Pool** screen, starting with the **Type** section where we select which type of desktop pool you want to create.
6. Click the radio button for **Automated Desktop Pool**. When selecting the various types of desktop pools that are available, the description on the right-hand side will change, reminding you of the differences between types.
7. Now click the **Next >** button to continue.
8. You will now see the **User Assignment** screen.
9. Click the radio button for **Dedicated**. The **Enable automatic assignment** option will already be selected by default. This means the desktops will be assigned to the users on a first come, first served basis, as they log in. If, for some reason, you need to ensure a user is assigned a specific desktop, then you will need to uncheck this box, and manually assign them a virtual desktop machine.

Chapter 8

10. Click the **Next>** button to continue the configuration. On the **vCenter Server** screen, you will now configure how the virtual desktops machines will be built, using the vCenter Server linked with this Connection Server, as shown in the following screenshot:

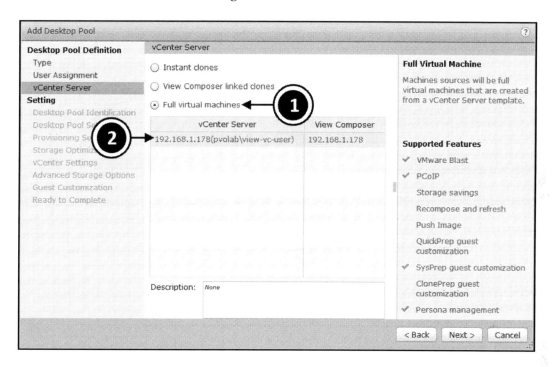

On this configuration screen, you again have the option to build either Instant Clones, View Composer Linked Clone virtual desktop machines, or Full Clone virtual desktop machines.

11. For this second pool, we are going to use full virtual machines, so click the radio button for **Full virtual machines** (1).
12. Next, you need to select the relevant vCenter Server from the list. In the example lab, the vCenter 192.168.1.178 is shown, along with the vCenter user account we set up for the View. Click to highlight and select this vCenter Server (2).

13. Click the **Next>** button to continue the configuration. The next configuration screen is for the **Desktop Pool Identification,** as shown in the following screenshot:

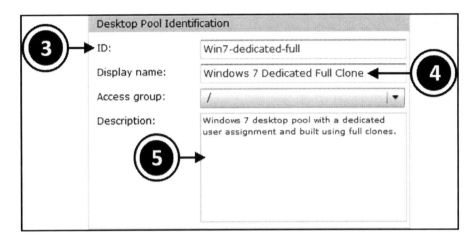

14. In the **ID** box (3), type in an ID for this desktop pool. In the example lab, we have entered the ID of `Win7-dedicated-full`.

 Remember, you can only use the characters *a-z, A-Z, 0-9, -,* and _ in the pool ID.

15. In the **Display name** box (4), type in a name for this pool. Bear in mind that the display name is what is displayed to the end users, so make sure you give it a non-technical name that the users will understand.
16. Finally, in the **Description** box (5), type in a more detailed description which describes the desktop pool.
17. Click the **Next>** button to continue the configuration. You will now see the **Desktop Pool Settings** configuration screen.
18. This configuration page is where we start to configure the settings that will define the way the desktop behaves within the desktop pool for the end users. Configure the setting you want to apply to this pool and then click the **Next >** button to continue.
19. You will now see the **Provisioning Settings** screen.

20. The first setting in the **Basic** section is to **Enable provisioning**. Tick the **Enable provisioning** box to switch provisioning on. This setting means that virtual desktop machines can be provisioned as per the configuration settings.
21. The next setting is for **Stop provisioning on error**. By checking this box, it means that provisioning will stop if there is an error during the provisioning process.
22. The next section to configure is for the **Virtual Machine Naming**, as shown in the following screenshot:

23. Click the radio button for **Use a naming pattern** and then, in the **Naming Pattern** box (6), enter the name pattern you want to use. In the example lab, we have called this `Win7-VM-Full-{n}`. This will result in the virtual desktop machines being named `Win7-VM-Full-1`, `Win7-VM-Full-2`, and so on, up to the number of machines you specify that you want to build.
24. Next, in the **Max number of machines** box, enter the maximum number of machines that can be provisioned in this desktop pool. This sets the limit of the number of virtual desktop machines in this desktop pool.
25. Next is the setting for the **Number of spare (powered on) machines**. In the box, enter the number of machines that should be powered on and waiting for users to connect to them.
26. **Provisioning Timing** is the next option to configure. Either click the radio button for **Provision machines on demand** and then enter the minimum number of machines or click the radio button for **Provision all machines up-front**.

Configuring and Managing Desktop Pools - Part 1

27. The next option, as we are configuring Full Clone virtual desktop machines, is for a **Virtual Device**. The option in question is for **Add a Trusted Platform Module (vTPM) device to the VMs,** as shown in the following screenshot:

```
Virtual Device
    ☐ Add a Trusted Platform Module (vTPM) device to the VMs      ?
```

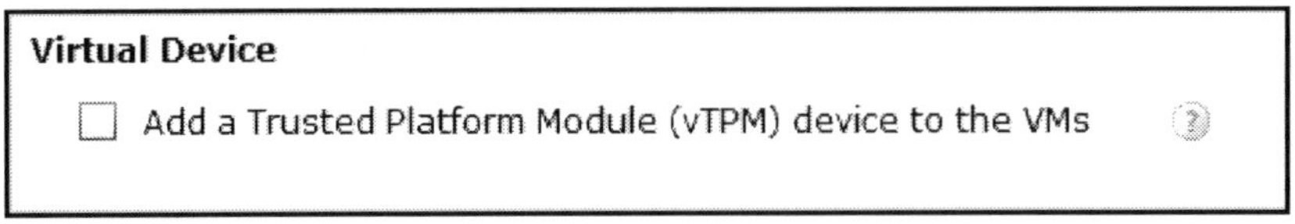

28. TPM is recognized for securing cryptoprocessors. It is basically designed for securing hardware with the help of integrated cryptographic keys. It is located on the motherboard of a physical machine in the form of dedicated microcontroller or microchip. A virtual TPM relies on the hypervisor (available with vCenter version 6.7) to provide virtual desktop machines with an isolated execution environment hidden from the software that is running within the virtual desktop machines. This feature secures their code from the software in the virtual desktop machines, providing a security level that is comparable to a firmware-based TPM.
29. Click the **Next >** button to continue to the next configuration screen.

The next configuration screen is for **Storage Optimization**:

1. The only option on this screen is to configure the **Storage Policy Management**, starting with VMware Virtual SAN. To enable VSAN, click the radio button for **Use VMware Virtual SAN**. As we don't have this configured in the example lab, we will click the radio button for **Do not use VMware Virtual SAN**.
2. Click the **Next >** button to continue to the next configuration screen.

The next configuration screen is the **vCenter Settings** configuration screen. On this screen, we are going to select the parent VM from which to build the virtual desktop machines, and then the location and resources that are going to run them. As such, the configuration options fall into three categories. **Virtual Machine Template**, **Virtual Machine Location**, and **Resource Settings,** as shown in the following screenshot:

Chapter 8

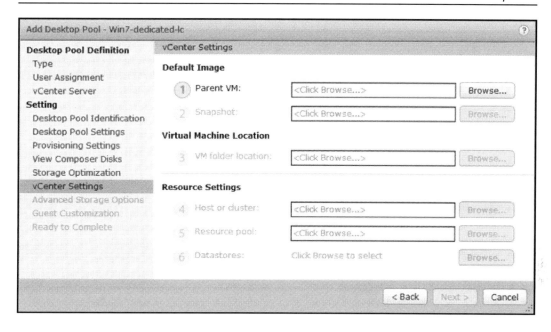

Let's look at all the configuration options:

1. The first thing to configure are the details of the **Virtual Machine Template** to be used as the parent image from which to create the virtual desktop machines for this desktop pool. This section is shown in the following screenshot:

2. On the **Template** box, click the **Browse...** button (7).

Configuring and Managing Desktop Pools - Part 1

3. You will now see the **Select template** screen, as shown in the following screenshot:

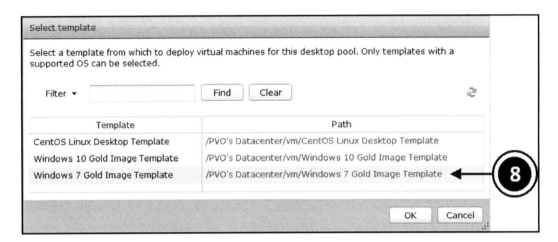

4. On this screen, you will see a list of all the templates that have been created in vCenter. As we are going to build a Windows 7 virtual desktop machine for this pool, select the option for **Windows 7 Gold Image Template** (8) by clicking and highlighting it.
5. Click **OK** to accept and close the **Select template** screen.
6. You will now return to the **vCenter Settings** screen, where we can now configure the second of the options. This is for **Virtual Machine Location**. You will also see that the **Template** box (9) has now been populated with the details of the **Windows 7 Gold Image Template**, as shown in the following screenshot:

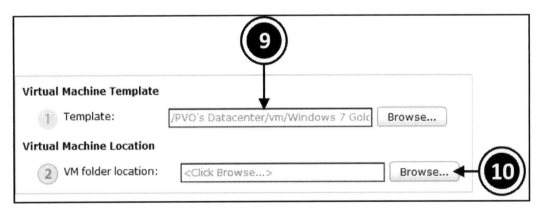

7. Under the **Virtual Machine Location** section, on the VM folder location box, click the **Browse...** button (**10**).
8. You will now see the **Select the folder to store the VM** screen, as shown in the following screenshot:

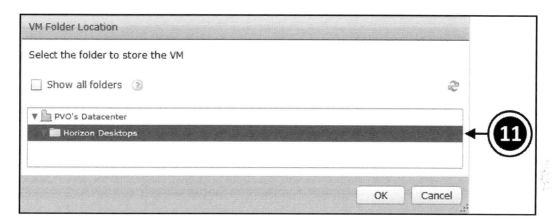

9. Expand **PVO's Datacenter** by clicking the down arrow and then select the folder in which you want to create the virtual desktop machines. In the example lab, this folder has been called `Horizon Desktops` (**11**).

 Don't forget to consider a folder structure for the virtual machines to help with management; otherwise, you could end up creating hundreds of different virtual desktop machines that reside in different pools, all in the same folder.

10. Click **OK** to continue.
11. You will return to the **vCenter Settings** screen, where you will see that the **VM Folder Location** has now been added:

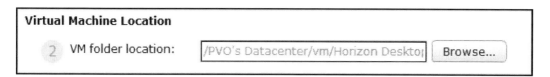

Configuring and Managing Desktop Pools - Part 1

The next configuration section is for the resources that are going to host and run the virtual desktop machines in the pool:

1. First, in the **Host or cluster** box, click the **Browse...** button.
2. You will then see the **Host or Cluster** box appear, listing the available host resources. The host resources are the ESXi servers available. In this example, we can see the IP address of the example lab ESXi server. Click on the IP address `192.168.1.131`.
3. Click **OK** to continue.
4. You will now return to the **vCenter Settings** screen, where you will see that the **Host or cluster** has now been added.
5. Next, we are going to configure the resource pool for this desktop pool to use.
6. In the **Resource pool** box, click the **Browse...** button. You will now see the **Select a resource pool to use for this desktop pool** box, from where you can select the resource pool. The resource pool for the example lab is the ESXi host server again, so click the IP address `192.168.1.131` to select this from the list.
7. Click **OK** to continue.
8. You will now return to the **vCenter Settings** screen, where you will see that the **Resource pool** has now been added.

The final configuration option in this section is for **Datastores**. In the example lab, we are using a single datastore, which was selected from the **Storage Optimization** settings screen:

1. In the **Datastores** box, click the **Browse...** button.
2. You will now see the **Select Datastores** configuration screen, which shows all available datastores, as shown in the following screenshot:

Chapter 8

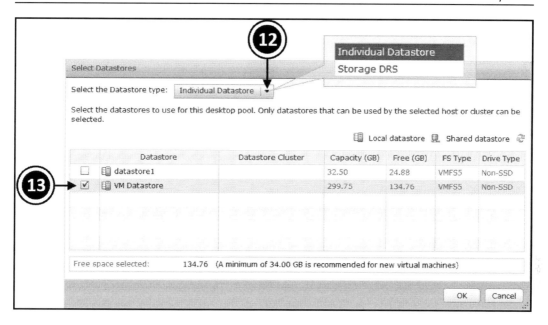

3. The first option on this configuration screen is for **Select the Datastore type** (**12**). Here, you can choose between an **Individual Datastore** or **Storage DRS**. DRS (Distributed Resource Scheduler) load balances storage resources and moves storage workloads to other available datastores rather than using the same one. In the example lab, select the option for **Individual Datastore**.
4. Check the box for **VM Datastore** (**13**), as this is the datastore we are going to use to store virtual desktop machines from this desktop pool.
5. Once configured, click the **OK** button. You will return to the **vCenter Settings** configuration screen, where you will see that the details of the Linked Clone datastores have now been entered by displaying the text 1 selected.
6. With the **vCenter Settings** configuration complete, click the **Next >** button to continue to the next configuration screen.

The next configuration screen is for **Advanced Storage Options**:

1. To enable the **View Storage Accelerator**, check the box for **Use View Storage Accelerator**.
2. Leave the **Regenerate storage accelerator after** option set to the default option of 7 days.

3. If you want to configure a blackout time, then under **Blackout Times**, Click the **Add...** button.
4. The final setting under **Advanced Storage Options** is to configure a **Transparent Page Sharing Scope**. Leave this as the default setting of **Virtual Machine**.
5. Click the **Next >** button once you have completed configuring the **Advanced Storage Options**.

The next configuration screen is for **Guest Customization**, as shown in the following screenshot:

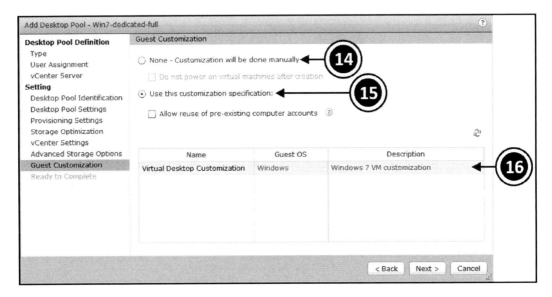

The screen shows following the options:

1. The first configuration option on this screen is for **None - Customization will be done manually (14)**. Click the radio button to select this option if you want to manually configure each virtual desktop machine.
2. Under the previous option, you have the option for **Do not power on virtual machines after creation**. Check this box to prevent the virtual desktop machines from powering on when they have been created. If you are going to manually configure the machines, then it's worth selecting this option, as there is no point powering on machines that have not been configured.

Chapter 8

3. Next, you have the option for **Use this customization specification (15)**. This option allows you to select a pre-built SysPrep script from vCenter. In the example lab, we have a script created called **Virtual Desktop Customization (16)**. Click this option to highlight and select it. Under this option, you can also configure the ability to use pre-existing computer accounts. To enable this option, simply check the box for **Allow reuse of pre-existing computer accounts**.
4. Click the **Next >** button once you have completed configuring the **Guest Customization**.
5. You will now see the final screen, the **Ready to Complete** screen, as shown in the following screenshot:

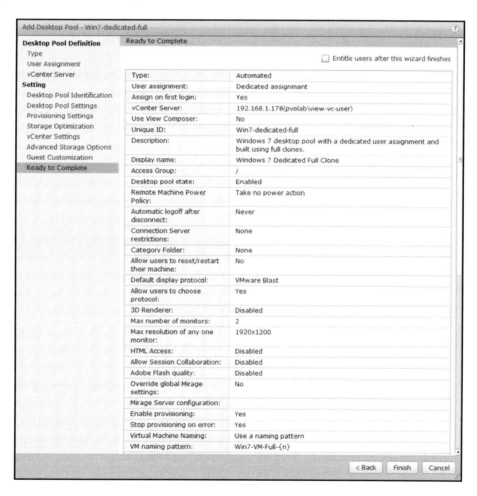

Configuring and Managing Desktop Pools - Part 1

Review your configuration settings, and then click the **Finish** button to create the desktop pool.

You also have the option of ticking the **Entitle users after this wizard finishes** box at the top of the screen, which will automatically launch the entitlement configuration screen, so you can give end users access to the virtual desktop machines in this pool. However, in the example lab, we will do this later, after we have created some additional desktop pools.

You will now see that the pool has been created, as shown in the following screenshot:

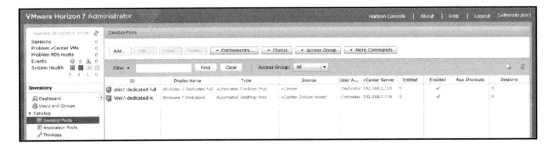

You will also see on the vCenter Server, that the various folder structure for the desktop pool has been set up, and that the first virtual desktop machine, `Win7-VM-Full-1`, has been created and is powered on ready, for end users to log in to, as shown in the following screenshot:

You have now successfully created a dedicated, Full Clone desktop pool.

Summary

In this chapter, we have configured the Horizon View Administrator to deliver our virtual desktop machines by means of creating desktop pools. We have built and configured a dedicated Full Clone desktop pool and a dedicated Linked Clone desktop pool. As part of the configuration of the desktop pools, we looked at how to create these using the classic Horizon View Administrator console, as well as the new web-client style Horizon Console.

In the next chapter, we will look at how to build a number of floating desktop pools, using Linked Clones and Instant Clones. We will also configure a manual desktop pool before going on to look at some of the key management tasks you will need to perform when using Linked Clone desktop pools, and then entitling end users to the newly created desktop pools.

9
Configuring and Managing Desktop Pools - Part 2

Following on from `Chapter 8`, *Configuring and Managing Desktop Pools - Part 1*, where we configured dedicated desktop pools, in this chapter, we are going to create a number of floating desktop pools using Linked Clones, Instant Clones, and also a manual desktop pool. Then, we will entitle end users to these desktop pools and therefore allow them to connect to a virtual desktop machine.

We will also look at some of the management tasks that you will need to undertake when deploying Linked Clone desktop pools, before finally looking at how to review the deployment.

In this chapter, we will cover following topics:

- Creating floating, Linked Clone desktop pools
- Creating floating, Full Clone desktop pools
- Creating floating, Instant Clone desktop pools
- Creating a manual desktop pool
- Adding end user entitlements
- Managing Linked Clone desktop pools
- Reviewing the infrastructure post-deployment

Creating floating, Linked Clone desktop pools

As with the other pools we have created, the process for creating a floating, Linked Clone desktop pool is pretty much the same as we covered in the previous section, with a few changes to reflect this pool having a floating assignment. As such, in this section, we will just highlight the different configuration options:

1. From a workstation, open a browser and enter the address details of the View Connection server. In the example lab, the address of the connection server is `https://hzn7-cs1.pvolab.com/admin`. Don't forget the `/admin` at the end; otherwise, you will end up on the Horizon Client page.
2. You will now see the **View Administrator** login screen.
3. From Horizon View Administrator, click to expand the **Catalog** option, and then click on **Desktop Pools**. Then from the **Desktop Pools** pane that is now displayed, click the **Add...** button.
4. You will now see the **Add Desktop Pool** screen, starting with the **Type** section where we select which type of desktop pool you want to create. In this example, we are creating an automated pool.
5. Click the radio button for **Automated Desktop Pool**.
6. Now click the **Next >** button to continue.
7. You will now see the **User Assignment** screen.
8. For this pool, we are going to click the radio button for **Floating (1)** as shown in the following screenshot:

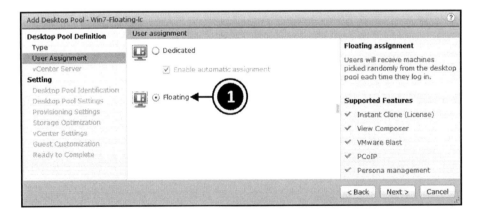

9. Click the **Next >** button to continue.
10. For this pool, we are going to use Linked Clone virtual machines, so click the radio button for **View Composer linked clones**, and select the relevant vCenter server from the list. In the example lab, the `vCenter 192.168.1.178` is shown, along with the vCenter user account we set up for View. Click to highlight and select this vCenter server.
11. Click the **Next >** button to continue the configuration. The next configuration screen is for the **Desktop Pool Identification** as shown in the following screenshot:

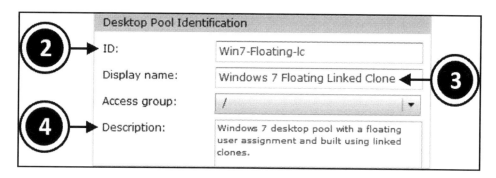

12. In the **ID** box (2), enter a name for this desktop pool. In the example lab, for this pool, we are going to call it `Win7-Floating-lc`.
13. In the **Display name** box (3), enter a name for this desktop pool that the end users will see. In the example lab, we have called this `Windows 7 Floating Linked Clone`.
14. Finally, in the **Description** box (4), enter a description to describe the function of this desktop pool.
15. Click the **Next >** button to continue.
16. You will now see the **Desktop Pool Settings** screen.
17. Configure the setting you want to apply to this desktop pool and then click the **Next >** button to continue.
18. You will now see the **Provisioning Settings** screen.

19. The first setting in the **Basic** section is to **Enable provisioning**. Tick the **Enable provisioning** box to switch provisioning on. This setting means that virtual desktop machines can be provisioned as per the configuration settings.
20. The next setting is for **Stop provisioning on error**. By checking this box, it means that provisioning will stop if there is an error during the provisioning process.
21. The next section to configure is for the **Virtual Machine Naming.**
22. Click the radio button for **Use a naming pattern** and then in the **Naming Pattern** box (6), enter the name pattern you want to use. In the example lab, we have called this `W7-Float-lc-{n}`. This will result in the virtual desktop machines being named `W7-Float-lc-1`, `W7-Float-lc-2`, and so on, up to the number of machines you specify that you want to build, as shown in the following screenshot:

23. Next, in the **Max number of machines** box, enter the maximum number of machines that can be provisioned in this desktop pool. This sets the limit of the number of virtual desktop machines in this desktop pool.
24. Next is the setting for **Number of spare (powered on) machines**. In the box, enter the number of machines that should be powered on and waiting for users to connect to them.
25. **Provisioning Timing** is the next option to configure. Either click the radio button for **Provision machines on demand** and then enter the minimum number of machines, or click the radio button for **Provision all machines up-front**.
26. Click the **Next >** button to continue.
27. You will now see the **View Composer Disks** screen and the **Disposable File Redirection** configuration setting.
28. To configure this setting, click the radio button for **Redirect disposable files to a non-persistent disk** (7), as shown in the following screenshot:

Chapter 9

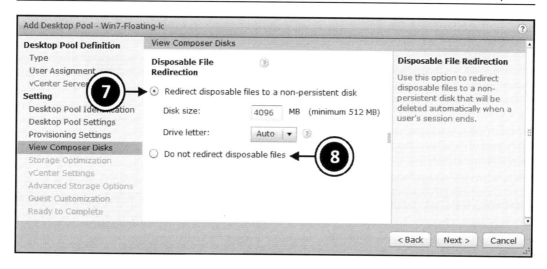

29. In the **Disk size** box, enter a size for the persistent disk, and in the **Drive letter** drop-down box, select a drive letter for this persistent disk.
30. To disable the **Disposable File Redirection** feature, then click the radio button for **Do not redirect disposable files** (8).
31. Click the **Next >** button to continue. The next configuration screen is for **Storage Optimization**.
32. The only option on this screen is to configure the **Storage Policy Management**, starting with VMware Virtual SAN. To enable VSAN, then click the radio button for **Use VMware Virtual SAN**. As we don't have this configured in the example lab, then we will click the radio button for **Do not use VMware Virtual SAN**. You can then choose if you want to use separate datastores for replica and OS disks. To enable this, check the box for **Select separate datastores for replica and OS disks**.
33. Click the **Next >** button to continue to the next configuration screen.
34. You will now see the **vCenter Settings**.
35. First, select the **Parent VM**, in this example our **Windows 7 Gold Image**, and then from the **Snapshot** box, choose which snapshot of the Windows 7 Gold Image virtual desktop machine you want to use.
36. In the **Virtual Machine Location** section, under **VM Folder Location**, select the folder where you want to store these new virtual desktop machines. In the example lab, we are going to use the `Horizon Desktops` folder.
37. Finally, under the **Resource Settings** section, select the **Host or cluster** to run the virtual desktops machines, the **Resource pool**, and then the **Datastore**.

[491]

38. Click the **Next >** button to continue to the next configuration screen.
39. You will now see the **Advanced Storage Options** configuration screen. Leave the default settings and click the **Next >** button to continue.
40. You will see the **Guest Customization** configuration screen. Leave the default settings and click the **Next >** button.
41. You will now see the **Ready to Complete** screen. Review your configuration settings, and then click the **Finish** button to create the desktop pool.
42. You will now see that the pool has been created as shown in the following screenshot:

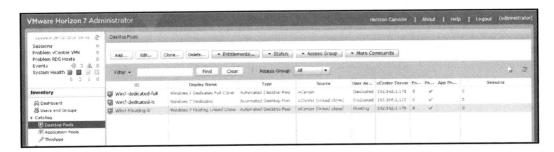

In the next section, we are going to create another automated desktop pool, but this time, we will create a pool with a floating assignment, and built using Full Clone virtual desktop machines.

Creating floating, Full Clone desktop pools

As with the previous pools we have created, the process for creating a floating, full-clone desktop pool is pretty much the same as we covered previously, with a few changes to reflect this pool having a floating assignment. As such, in this section, we will just highlight the key differences in the configuration options:

1. From a workstation, open a browser and enter the address details of the View Connection server. In the example lab, the address of the connection server is https://hzn7-cs1.pvolab.com/admin. Don't forget the /admin at the end; otherwise, you will end up on the Horizon Client page.
2. You will now see the View Administrator login screen.

3. From Horizon View Administrator, click to expand the **Catalog** option, and then click on **Desktop Pools**. Then from the **Desktop Pools** pane that is now displayed, click the **Add...** button.
4. You will now see the **Add Desktop Pool** screen, starting with the **Type** section where we select which type of desktop pool you want to create. In this example, we are creating an automated pool.
5. Click the radio button for **Automated Desktop Pool**.
6. Now click the **Next >** button to continue.
7. You will now see the **User Assignment** screen.
8. For this pool, we are going to click the radio button for **Floating**.
9. Click the **Next >** button to continue. You will now see the **vCenter Server** screen.
10. For this pool, we are going to use full-clone virtual machines, so click the radio button for **Full virtual machines**, and then select the relevant vCenter server from the list. In the example lab, the `vCenter 192.168.1.178` is shown, along with the vCenter user account we set up for View. Click to highlight and select this vCenter server.
11. Click the **Next >** button to continue the configuration. The next configuration screen is for the **Desktop Pool Identification** as shown in the following screenshot:

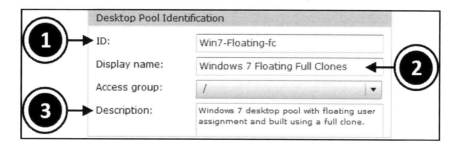

12. In the **ID** box (**1**), enter a name for this desktop pool. In the example lab, for this pool, we are going to call it `Win7-Floating-fc`.
13. In the **Display name** box (**2**), enter a name for this desktop pool that the end users will see. In the example lab, we have called this `Windows 7 Floating Full Clones`.
14. Finally, in the **Description** box (**3**), enter a description to describe the function of this desktop pool.
15. Click the **Next >** button to continue.

Configuring and Managing Desktop Pools - Part 2

16. You will now see the **Desktop Pool Settings** screen. In the **Remote Settings** section, there are a couple of new configurations options as shown in the following screenshot:

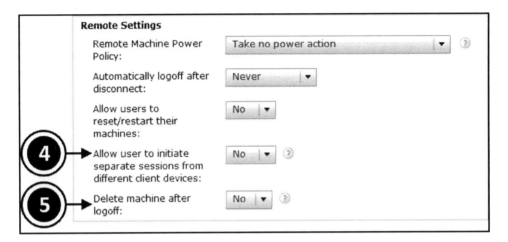

17. The first three configuration options have been described previously, but we now have the **Allow user to initiate separate sessions from different client devices** option (**4**). If this option is set to **Yes**, from the drop-down menu, then if a user connects to the same desktop pool but from a different client device, then they will get a different/new desktop session. The user can only reconnect to an existing session by using the same client device from where the session was originally initiated. When this option is set to **No**, the user will be reconnected to their existing session regardless of the client device used.

18. The final configuration setting is to **Delete machine after logoff** (**5**). If this option is set to **Yes**, from the drop-down menu, then when the user logs off, the virtual desktop machine is deleted. When this option is set to **No**, then the virtual desktop machine is not deleted when they log off. This feature is only supported for desktop pools that use manual naming, as dynamic creation and deletion of virtual desktop machines is not supported.

19. Configure the remaining desktop pool settings so that they are appropriate to your environment; in the example lab, we will leave them as the defaults.

20. Click the **Next >** button to continue.

21. You will now see the **Provisioning Settings** screen.

22. The first setting in the **Basic** section is to **Enable provisioning**. Tick the **Enable provisioning** box to switch provisioning on.

23. Next, check the box for **Stop provisioning on error**.
24. The next section to configure is **Virtual Machine Naming**.
25. Click the radio button for **Use a naming pattern** and then in the **Naming Pattern** box (**6**), enter the name pattern you want to use. In the example lab, we have called this `W7-Float-fc-{n}`. This will result in the virtual desktop machines being named `W7-Float-fc-1`, `W7-Float-fc-2`, and so on, up to the number of machines you specify that you want to build, as shown in the following screenshot:

26. Complete the remaining settings so that they are appropriate to your environment, or in the example lab, we will leave them as the defaults.
27. Click the **Next >** button to continue.
28. You will now see the **Storage Optimization** configuration screen. Leave the default settings and click **Next >**.
29. You will now see the **vCenter Settings**.
30. First, from the **Virtual Machine Template** section, select the template you want to use. In this example, we are going to use the Windows 7 Gold Image template.
31. In the **Virtual Machine Location** section, under **VM Folder Location**, select the folder where you want to store these new virtual desktop machines. In the example lab, we are going to use the `Horizon Desktops` folder.
32. Finally, under the **Resource Settings** section, select the **Host or cluster** to run the virtual desktops machines, the **Resource pool**, and then the **Datastore**.
33. Click the **Next >** button to continue to the next configuration screen. You will now see the **Advanced Storage Options** configuration screen. Leave the default settings and then click the **Next >** button to continue.
34. You will now see the **Guest Customization** configuration screen. Leave the default settings and click the **Next >** button.
35. Finally, you will now see the **Ready to Complete** screen. Review your configuration settings, and then click the **Finish** button to create the desktop pool.

36. You will now see that the pool has been created as shown in the following screenshot:

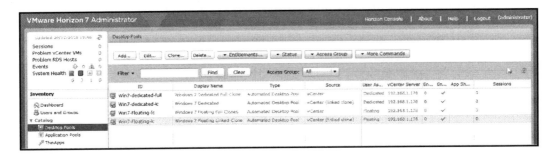

In the final section of *Creating Automated Desktop Pools*, we are going to create another automated desktop pool, but, this time, we will create a pool with a floating assignment, now built using Instant Clone virtual desktop machines.

Creating floating, Instant Clone desktop pools

In this section, we are going to create an automated desktop pool that has a floating assignment and is built using Instant Clones. There are two steps to this configuration. First, we need to configure a domain administrator before we then configure the actual pool itself.

Configuring the Instant Clone domain administrator

Before you can configure a desktop pool using Instant Clones, you first have to add an Instant Clone domain administrator. This account is used to perform the Active Directory tasks required to create new virtual desktop machines. It's similar to the service account used in View Composer, but as Instant Clones don't use Composer, you need to add the account within the View Administrator. The account needs the following permissions:

- **Create Computer Objects**
- **Delete Computer Objects**
- **Write All Properties**

To configure the Instant Clone domain admin, complete the following tasks:

1. From a workstation, open a browser and enter the address details of the View Connection server. In the example lab, the address of the connection server is `https://hzn7-cs1.pvolab.com/admin`. Don't forget the `/admin` at the end; otherwise, you will end up on the Horizon Client page.
2. You will now see the **View Administrator** login screen.
3. To add the account, from the **View Administrator** dashboard, expand the option for **View Configuration** from the **Inventory** menu in the left-hand pane, and then click on the option for **Instant Clone Domain Admins** (1).
4. Then click on the **Add...** button (2), as shown in the following screenshot:

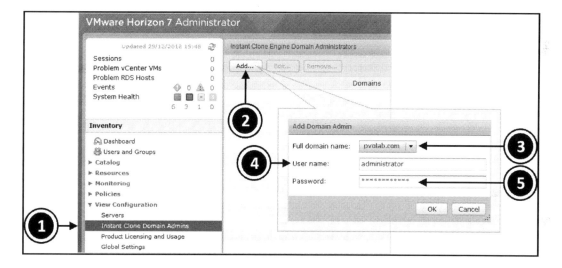

5. You will then see the **Add Domain Admin** box.
6. In the **Full domain** name section, click the drop-down arrow (3) and select the domain. In the example lab, this is our `pvolab.com` domain.
7. In the **User name** box (4), enter a username that has the permissions as outlined at the beginning of this section.
8. Finally, in the **Password** box (5), enter the password for the username account you just entered.
9. Click **OK** when you have completed the details.

10. You will now see that the domain administrator account has now been added as shown in the following screenshot:

You have now successfully configured the domain admin account for Instant Clones. We can now continue with the process of creating an Instant Clone desktop pool.

Creating the Instant Clone desktop pool

As with the other pools we have created, the process for creating a floating, Instant Clone desktop pool is pretty much the same as we covered in the previous section, with a few changes to reflect this pool being built using Instant Clones. As such, in this section, we will just highlight the main differences in the configuration options:

1. From a workstation, open a browser and enter the address details of the View Connection server. In the example lab, the address of the connection server is `https://hzn7-cs1.pvolab.com/admin`. Don't forget the `/admin` at the end; otherwise, you will end up on the **Horizon Client** page.
2. You will now see the **View Administrator** login screen.
3. From the Horizon View administrator, click to expand the **Catalog** option, and then click on **Desktop Pools**. Then, from the **Desktop Pools** pane that is now displayed, click the **Add...** button.
4. You will now see the **Add Desktop Pool** screen, starting with the **Type** section where we select which type of desktop pool you want to create. In this example, we are creating an automated pool.
5. Click the radio button for **Automated Desktop Pool**.
6. Now click the **Next >** button to continue.
7. You will now see the **User Assignment** screen.
8. For this pool, we are going to click the radio button for **Floating**.
9. Click the **Next >** button to continue. You will now see the **vCenter Server** screen where you will configure how the virtual desktops machine will be built, In this example, click the radio button for **Instant Clones** (1) as shown in the following screenshot:

Chapter 9

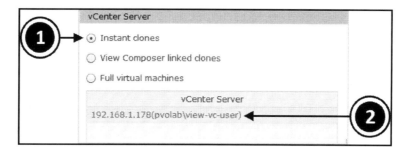

10. Click and select the vCenter Server (**2**), and then click the **Next >** button to continue.
11. The next configuration screen is for the **Desktop Pool Identification** as shown in the following screenshot:

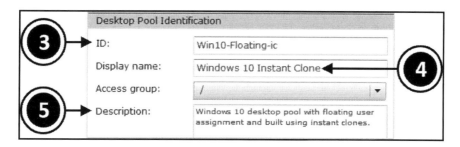

12. In the **ID** box (**3**), enter a name for this desktop pool. In the example lab, for this pool, we are going to call it `Win10-Floating-ic`.
13. In the **Display name** box (**4**), enter a name for this desktop pool that the end users will see. In the example lab, we have called this `Windows 10 Instant Clone`.
14. Finally, in the **Description** box (**5**), enter a description to describe the function of this desktop pool.
15. Click the **Next >** button to continue.
16. You will now see the **Desktop Pool Settings** screen. Complete the configuration details as per your required settings and then click the **Next >** button to continue.
17. The next section to configure is for **Virtual Machine Naming.**
18. Click the radio button for **Provisioning Settings**. Ensure that you check the box for **Enable provisioning** and the box for **Stop provisioning on error**.

[499]

19. In the **Naming Pattern** box (6), enter the name pattern you want to use. In the example lab, we have called this `W10-Float-ic-{n}`. This will result in the virtual desktop machines being named `W10-Float-ic-1`, `W10-Float-ic-2`, and so on, up to the number of machines you specify that you want to build, as shown in the following screenshot:

20. Complete the remaining settings so that they are appropriate to your environment, or in the example lab, we will leave them as the defaults.
21. Click the **Next >** button to continue.
22. You will now see the **Storage Optimization** configuration screen. Leave the default settings and click the **Next >** button to continue. You will now see the **vCenter Settings**.
23. The next configuration screen is the **vCenter Settings** configuration screen. On this screen, we are going to select the parent VM from which to build the virtual desktop machines, and then the location and resources that are going to run them as shown in the following screenshot:

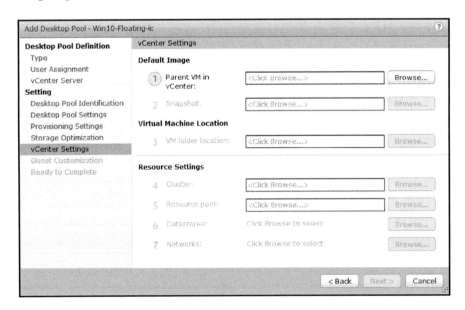

Chapter 9

24. The first thing to configure is the details of the **Default Image** to be used as the parent image from which to create the virtual desktop machines for this desktop pool. This section is shown in the following screenshot:

25. On the first box, **Parent VM in vCenter**, click the **Browse...** button (7). You will now see the **Select Parent VM** box as shown in the following screenshot:

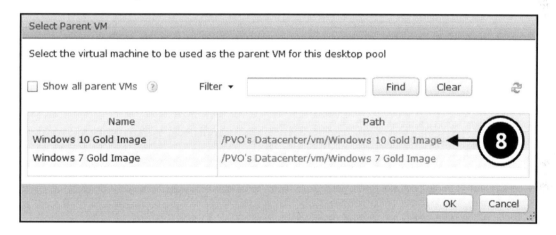

26. For this desktop pool, we are going to use Windows 10 as the virtual desktop machine operating system, so select the entry for **Windows 10 Gold Image** (8).
27. Once you have selected the parent VM you want to use, click **OK** to continue.

[501]

Configuring and Managing Desktop Pools - Part 2

28. You will now return to the **vCenter Settings** screen, where we can now configure the second of the options on the **Default Image** section for **Snapshot**. You will also see that the **Parent VM** box (**9**) has now been populated with the details of the Windows 10 Gold Image as shown in the following screenshot:

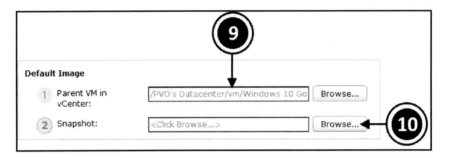

29. As this is an Instant Clone virtual desktop machine, the next configuration task is to configure the details of the snapshot that was created from the parent image.
30. On the **Snapshot** box, click the **Browse...** button (**10**). You will now see the **Select default image** box as shown in the following screenshot:

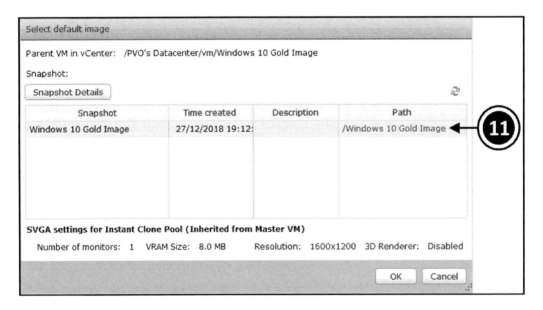

31. Click to highlight the snapshot you want to use (11) and then Click **OK**. You will now see that the snapshot has been added as shown in the following screenshot:

The next part of the vCenter Settings is the **Virtual Machine Location** setting as shown in the following screenshot:

32. On the **VM folder location** box, click the **Browse...** button (12).
33. You will now see the **Select the folder to store the VM** box. Expand **PVO's Datacenter** by clicking the arrow and then select the folder in which you want to create the virtual desktop machines into. In the example lab, this folder has been called `Horizon Desktops`.
34. Click **OK** to continue.
35. You will return to the **vCenter Settings** screen where you will see that the **VM Folder Location** has now been added as you can see in the following screenshot:

Configuring and Managing Desktop Pools - Part 2

The next configuration section is for the resources that are going to host and run the virtual desktop machines in the pool:

1. First, in the **Cluster** box, click the **Browse...** button (**13**), as shown in the following screenshot:

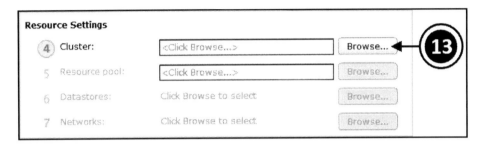

2. You will now see the **Cluster** box appear, listing the available cluster resources as shown in the following screenshot:

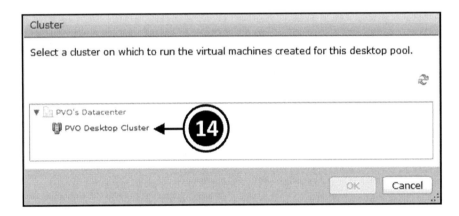

3. Click and highlight on the cluster you want to run this Instant Clone desktop pool on. In the example lab, the cluster is called **PVO Desktop Cluster** (**14**).

> When it comes to configuring the Resource Settings section of this configuration, it's worth noting that you need to have a host cluster and resource pool configured. You cannot use standalone hosts for Instant Clone desktop pools.

4. Click **OK** to continue.

[504]

Chapter 9

5. You will now return to the **vCenter Settings** screen where you will see that the **Cluster** has now been added.
6. Next, we are going to configure the resource pool for this desktop pool to use.
7. In the **Resource pool** box, click the **Browse...** button. You will now see the **Select a resource pool to use for this desktop pool** box from where you can select the resource pool to run the desktop pool. The resource pool for the example lab is the cluster again, so click and highlight **PVO Desktop Cluster** from the list.
8. Click **OK** to continue.
9. You will now return to the **vCenter Settings** screen where you will see that the **Resource pool** has now been added.
10. The next configuration option in this section is for **Datastores**. In the **Datastores** box, click the **Browse...** button.
11. You will now see the **Select Instant Clone Datastores** configuration screen, which shows all available datastores.
12. Check the box for **VM Datastore** and click the **OK** button. You will return to the **vCenter Settings** configuration screen, where you will see that the details of the Instant Clone datastores have now been entered by displaying the text **1 selected**.
13. Finally, on the Instant Clone configuration of the **vCenter Settings** screen, you can configure **Networks** as shown in the following screenshot:

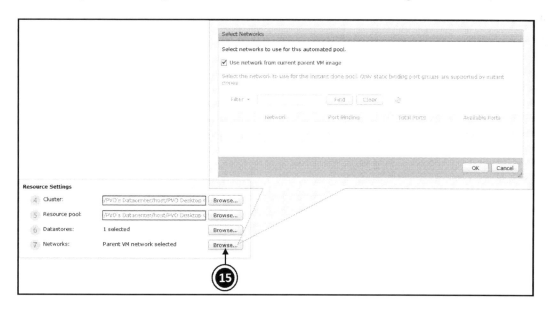

[505]

Configuring and Managing Desktop Pools - Part 2

14. In the **Networks** box, click the **Browse ...** button **(15)**. You will then see the **Select Networks** box. Here, you can use the network that is currently configured within the virtual desktop machine image, or you can select another network from the list. Click **OK** to continue and to return to the **vCenter Settings** screen.
15. Now click the **Next >** button to continue to the next configuration screen.
16. You will now see the **Guest Customization** configuration screen. Leave the default settings and click the **Next >** button to continue.
17. Finally, you will now see the **Ready to Complete** screen. Review your configuration settings, and then click the **Finish** button to create the desktop pool.
18. You will now see that the pool has been created as shown in the following screenshot:

You can also see from within the folder view of the vCenter Server, that the Instant Clone folder structure has been created, as shown in the following screenshot, by the folder names starting with **ClonePrep**:

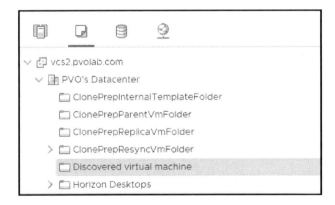

[506]

Chapter 9

You have now successfully configured a desktop pool for Instant Clone virtual desktop machines, running Windows 10. In the next section, we are going to work through the steps to create a manual desktop pool.

Creating a manual desktop pool

In the previous sections, we have talked about creating automated desktop pools. Horizon View also has the ability to create desktop pools from already existing virtual desktop machines, or even physical desktop machines.

The process for creating manual desktop pools is not too dissimilar to the process we covered previously for automated desktop pools, so, in the following section, we will create a manual pool and highlight where the process differs:

1. From a workstation, open a browser and enter the address details of the View Connection server. In the example lab, the address of the connection server is `https://hzn7-cs1.pvolab.com/admin`. Don't forget the `/admin` at the end; otherwise, you will end up on the **Horizon Client** page.
2. You will now see the View Administrator login screen. Log in using the administrator account.
3. Once logged in, from the Horizon View administrator, click to expand the **Catalog** option, and then click on **Desktop Pools**. Then, from the **Desktop Pools** pane that is now displayed, click the **Add...** button.
4. You will now see the **Add Desktop Pool** screen, starting with the **Type** section where we select which type of desktop pool you want to create. In this example, we are creating a manual pool.
5. Click the radio button for **Manual Desktop Pool** (1) as shown in the following screenshot:

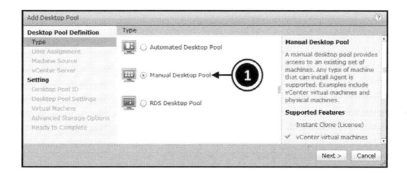

[507]

6. Now click the **Next >** button to continue.
7. You will now see the **User Assignment** screen. Select whether or not you want a dedicated assignment with an automatic assignment or a floating assignment. In the example lab, we are going to click the radio button to select the option for **Dedicated**, and also check the box for **Enable automatic assignment**.
8. Click the **Next >** button to continue.
9. Next, you will see the **Machine Source** screen as shown in the following screenshot:

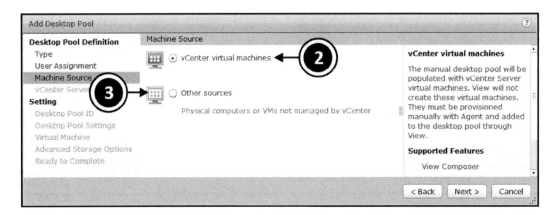

10. On this configuration screen, there are two options. The first is the option to select virtual desktop machines that are managed by vCenter but are not built using some form of cloning technology. As the virtual desktop machine we are going to use resides on the vCenter server, then in the example lab, click the radio button for **vCenter virtual machines** (2).
11. The second option is for **Other sources** (3). This option is for non-vCenter-managed desktops that you want users to connect to using Horizon View. An example of this may be something such as a blade- or rack-mounted workstation machine that resides in the datacenter and that you want users to connect to remotely using a protocol capable of the high-performance graphics. All you need do is ensure that the Horizon Agent is installed on these machines.

Chapter 9

12. Click the **Next >** button to continue.
13. You will now see the **vCenter Server** configuration screen. Select the example lab vCenter server by clicking on it and then click the **Next >** button to continue.
14. Next, you will see the **Desktop Pool ID** screen as shown in the following screenshot:

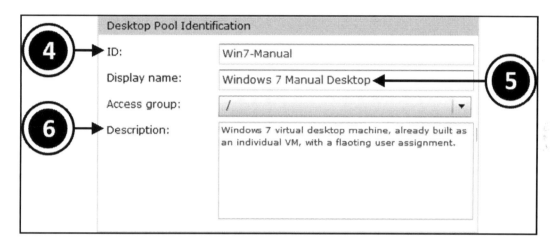

15. In the **ID** box (4), enter a name for this desktop pool. In the example lab, for this pool, we are going to call it `Win7-Manual`.
16. In the **Display name** box (5), enter a name for this desktop pool that the end users will see. In the example lab, we have called this `Windows 7 Manual Desktop`.
17. Finally, in the **Description** box (6), enter a description to describe the function of this desktop pool.
18. Click the **Next >** button to continue.
19. You will now see the **Desktop Pool Settings** screen. Complete the configuration details as per your required settings and then click the **Next >** button to continue.

[509]

20. The next section to configure is for the **Virtual Machine**, where we add the virtual desktop machines that we want to include as part of this desktop pool, as shown in the following screenshot:

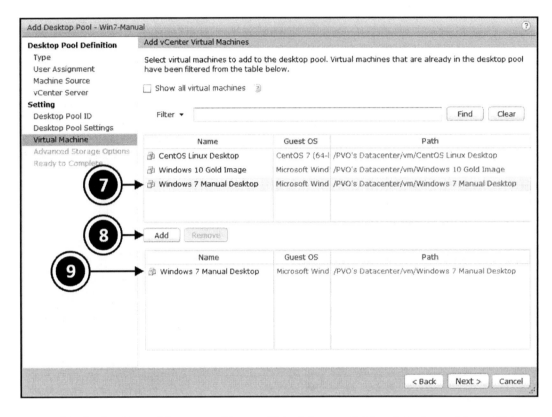

21. In the first table, you will see a list of the available virtual machines. This table does not include any virtual desktop machines that are already part of another desktop pool.
22. Click and highlight the virtual desktop machine you want to include in the desktop pool. In the example lab, this virtual desktop machine is called `Windows 7 Manual Desktop` (**7**).
23. Now click the **Add** button (**8**).
24. You will now see the virtual desktop machine has been added to the table at the bottom, meaning that it has been selected and added to the desktop pool (9). If you wanted to remove it, then simply click and highlight the machine in the lower table and click the **Remove** button.
25. Click the **Next >** button to continue.

26. You will now see the **Advanced Storage Options** configuration screen. Leave the default settings and then click the **Next >** button to continue.
27. Finally, you will now see the **Ready to Complete** screen. Review your configuration settings, and then click the **Finish** button to create the desktop pool.
28. You will now see that the pool has been created as shown in the following screenshot:

You have now successfully configured a manual desktop pool using an existing, pre-built virtual desktop machine running Windows 7.

Now that we have a number of desktop pool configured, and virtual desktop machines created, in the next section, we are going to work through the steps to entitle end users to desktop pool.

Adding end user entitlements

Now that you have created a number of desktop pools that contain virtual desktop machines, the next step is to allow the users to have access to the pools and virtual desktop machines.

We are going to look at how to entitle end users, first using Horizon View Administrator, and then using the new Horizon Console web-based client.

Adding user entitlement using the Horizon View Administrator Classic console

To entitle end users to desktop pools using Horizon View Administrator, we are going to follow the steps described:

1. From a workstation, open a browser and enter the address details of the View Connection server. In the example lab, the address of the connection server is https://hzn7-cs1.pvolab.com/admin. Don't forget the /admin at the end; otherwise, you will end up on the Horizon Client page.
2. You will now see the **View Administrator** login screen. Log in using the administrator account.
3. Once logged in, from Horizon View Administrator, click on **Users and Groups** (1) from the **Inventory** pane on the left-hand side as shown in the following screenshot:

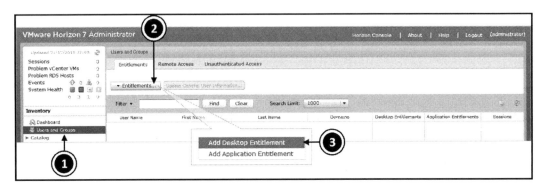

4. Now click the **Entitlements...** button (2). From the drop-down menu options, click on **Add Desktop Entitlement** (3). You will now see the **Add Desktop Entitlement** as shown in the following screenshot:

Chapter 9

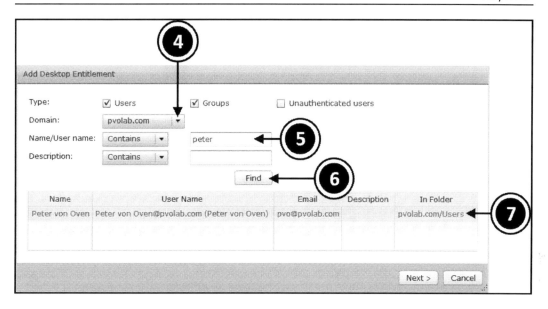

5. On this screen, we can search for, and add users from Active Directory. The first option is for **Type**. You have the option of searching for **User**, **Groups**, or **Unauthenticated users**. Check the relevant box for the type of search.

6. Next, you can select the domain in which you want to search. In the **Domain** box, click the down-arrow (**4**) and select the relevant domain from those that are listed. In the example lab, we are going to choose pvolab.com from the list.

7. You can then choose to search for either a name or username or by description. You also have the option of the criteria on which to filter using **Contains**, **Starts with**, or **Is exactly**. In the example lab, we are going to search for a specific user so in the **Name/User name** box, select **Contains** from the drop-down, and then type in the username peter and then click the **Find** button.

8. The results are shown in the table below. In the example lab, you will see the details for the user entered (**7**).

Configuring and Managing Desktop Pools - Part 2

9. Once you have completed adding user and group entitlements, you want to add the desktop pool then click the **Next >** button. You will now see the **Select the desktop pools to entitle** screen as shown in the following screenshot:

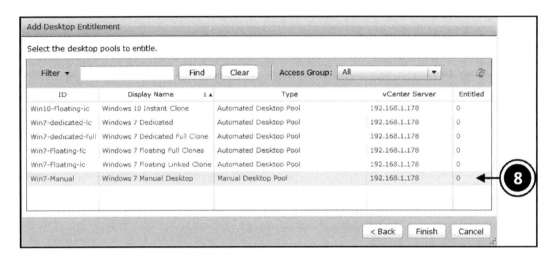

10. In the example lab, click and highlight the entry in the table for **Win7-Manual** (8). If you want to entitle this user to more than one desktop pool, you can press and hold the *Ctrl* key while clicking on the pool you want to entitle them to.
11. Once you have finished adding users and desktop pools, click the **Finish** button.
12. You will now return to the **Users and Groups** screen, which now shows the entitled user(s) as shown in the following screenshot:

[514]

Chapter 9

An alternative way of entitling users to a desktop pool is to do it from the **Desktop Pools** screen as shown in the following screenshot:

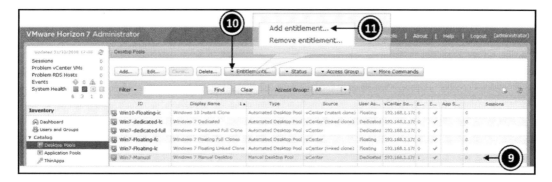

13. Highlight the desktop pool you want to entitle users to. In the example lab, we will use the Windows 7 manual pool again, so click and select **Win7-Manual** (9) from those listed in the table.
14. Then click the **Entitlements...** button (10), and then from the menu options, select **Add entitlement...** (11). You will now see the **Add Entitlements** box as shown in the following screenshot:

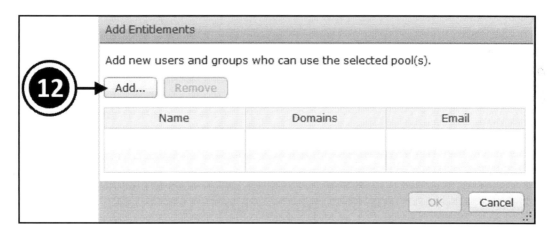

[515]

15. Now click the **Add...** button (**12**).
16. You will now see the **Find User or Group** box, the same box as the **Add Desktop Entitlement** in point 4. Enter the users and/or groups you want to entitle to the desktop pool and then Click **OK**. Then, on the **Add Entitlements** box, click **OK** again to complete entitling users to the desktop pool.

There is one other final way to demonstrate entitling users to desktop pools, which we have seen already when we created the desktop pools. This is the option on the **Ready to Complete** screen as shown in the following screenshot:

Click the **Entitle users after this wizard finishes** box (**12**), and once you complete the desktop pool configuration, the **Add Desktop Entitlement** will automatically be displayed.

You have now successfully entitled users to a desktop pool. If you were now to log in to Horizon View as a user that is entitled to a desktop pool, you would now see that the pool is available to select and connect to from Horizon Client. We will look at connecting to the virtual desktop machines in more detail in Chapter 12, *Horizon Client Options*.

In the next section, we are going to look at how to entitle users from the new Horizon console.

Adding user entitlement using the new Horizon console

In this section, we are going to repeat the previous task, but this time using the Horizon Console to configure the user entitlements, following the steps described:

1. From a workstation, open a browser and enter the address details of the View Connection server. In the example lab, the address of the connection server is https://hzn7-cs1.pvolab.com/admin.

2. You will now see the View Administrator login screen. Log in using the administrator account.
3. Once logged in, from Horizon View Administrator, click on the option for Horizon Console as shown in the following screenshot:

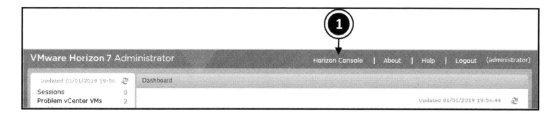

4. Alternatively, you can navigate your browser directly to the Horizon console using the connection server URL `https://hzn7-cs1.pvolab.com/newadmin`. Then log in using the administrator account.
5. You will now see the Horizon console screen.
6. From the menu options on the left-hand side of the screen, click on **Users and Groups** (2) as shown in the following screenshot:

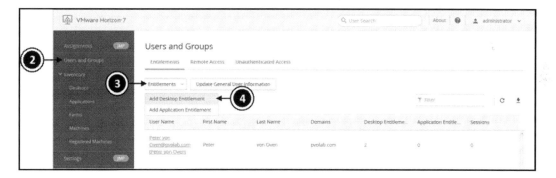

7. The **Users and Groups** screen is now displayed. Click on the **Entitlements** button (3), and then from the drop-down menu options, select **Add Desktop Entitlement** (4).

Configuring and Managing Desktop Pools - Part 2

8. You will now see the **Add Desktop Entitlement** screen and the first of the configuration options for **User** as shown in the following screenshot:

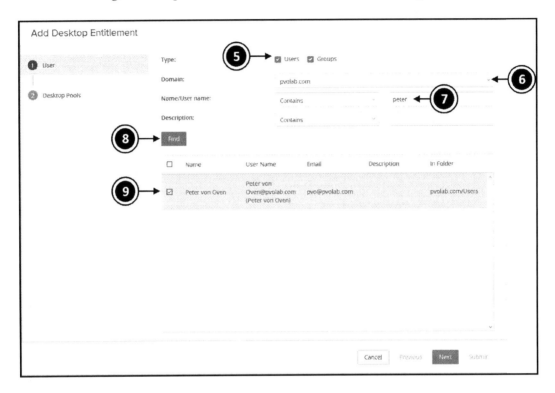

9. First of all, select whether or not you want to entitle individual **Users** or **Groups** (from AD) by checking the relevant box (**5**).
10. Next, in the **Domain** box, click the drop-down arrow (**6**) and select the domain where the user or group resides. In the example lab, this is the `pvolab.com` domain.
11. You then have the option to search for the user or group, either by name or by description. In this example, we are going to search for a username, so in the **Name/User name** box, we are going to type the first part of the username, which is `peter`. We are also going to select the filter option for **Contains**.

12. Now click the **Find** button (8).
13. The results of the search are then displayed. You will see that our user has been found so check the box (9) to select the user and then click **Next** to continue.
14. You will now see the **Desktop Pools** configuration option where we select which desktop pool the user will have access to as shown in the following screenshot:

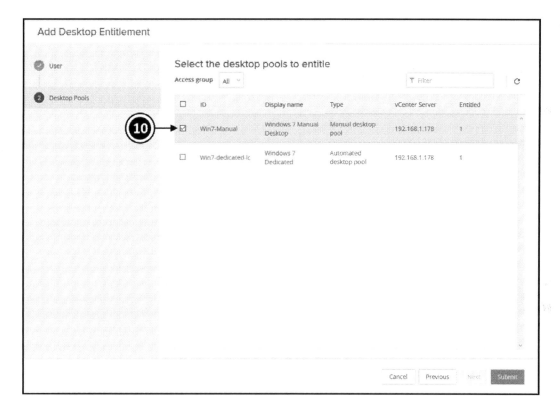

15. Check the box for the desktop pool you want to entitle this user to. In the example lab, this is the Windows 7 manual desktop pool, so check the box for **Win7-Manual** (10).
16. Click the **Submit** button to complete the entitlement configuration.

17. You will now return to the **Users and Groups** screen where you will see that the user has been entitled to the desktop pool. You will see in the **Desktop Entitlements** column of the table that this particular user is actually entitled to two desktop pools as shown in the following screenshot:

You have now successfully entitled a user to a desktop pool using the Horizon console.

In the next section of this chapter, we are going to take a closer look at some of the management tasks required in managing Linked Clone desktop pools.

Managing Linked Clone desktop pools

With a Linked Clone desktop pool, once you create and entitle your desktop pool, your desktops will be created, first by creating the replica and then by creating the Linked Clones virtual desktop machines. There are a number of management tasks that you will need to perform, which we will cover in this section. Before performing any of these, it's always worth checking the status of the desktop pool first:

1. To do this, from the Horizon View Administrator dashboard screen, under the **Inventory** section in the left-hand pane, expand the **Catalog** section and then click on **Desktop Pools** (1). You will now see the following screenshot:

Chapter 9

2. From the list of desktop pools displayed, you can now select one by clicking on it. In the example lab, we are going to select the Linked Clone desktop pool, so click on the entry for Win7-Floating-lc (2). You will now see the following screenshot:

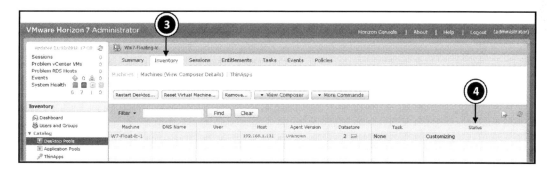

3. From the tabs across the top, click the **Inventory** tab (3). You can then check the **Status** of the desktop pool (4).

In total, there are 24 different statuses that get reported on for the Linked Clone virtual desktop machines. You can see a breakdown of all the statuses taken from the Horizon View documentation:

- **Provisioning**: The virtual machine is being provisioned.
- **Customizing**: The virtual machine in an automated pool is being customized as per the configuration.
- **Deleting**: The virtual machine is marked for deletion, but is not yet deleted. Once the process has completed, then it will be deleted.
- **Waiting for Agent**: The View Connection server is waiting to establish communication with the Horizon Agent running on a virtual desktop machine in a manual pool.

[521]

- **Maintenance mode**: The virtual machine is in maintenance mode. This means it is unavailable and therefore end users cannot log in or use the virtual desktop machine.
- **Startup**: The Horizon agent has started on the virtual desktop machine, but other required services such as the display protocol are still in the process of starting up.
- **Agent disabled**: This state can occur in two cases. First, in a desktop pool with the **Delete or refresh machine on logoff** or the **Delete machine after logoff** setting enabled, a desktop session is logged out, but the virtual machine is not yet refreshed or deleted. Second, the View Connection server disables the Horizon agent just before sending a request to power off the virtual desktop machine. This state ensures that a new desktop session cannot be started on the virtual desktop machine
- **Agent unreachable**: The View Connection server cannot establish communication with the Horizon agent running on a virtual desktop machine.
- **Invalid IP**: The subnet mask registry setting is configured on the virtual desktop machine, and no active network adapters have an IP address within the configured range.
- **Agent needs reboot**: A View component was upgraded, and the virtual desktop machine must be restarted to allow the Horizon agent to operate with the upgraded component.
- **Protocol failure**: A display protocol did not start before the Horizon agent startup period expired.
- **Domain failure**: The virtual desktop machine encountered a problem reaching the domain. The domain server was not accessible, or the domain authentication failed.
- **Already used**: In a desktop pool with the **Delete or refresh machine on logoff** or **Delete machine after logoff** setting enabled, there is no session on the virtual desktop machine, but the session was not logged off. This could occur should a virtual desktop machine shut down unexpectedly or if the end user resets the machine in mid-session.
- **Configuration error**: The display protocol is not enabled.
- **Provisioning error**: An error occurred during provisioning.
- **Error**: An unknown error occurred in the virtual desktop machine.
- **Unassigned user connected**: A different user who is not the assigned user is logged into a virtual desktop machine in a dedicated desktop pool.

- **Unassigned user disconnected**: A user other than the assigned user is logged in and disconnected from a virtual machine in a dedicated desktop pool.
- **Unknown**: The virtual desktop machine state is unknown.
- **Provisioned**: The virtual desktop machine has been built but is powered off or suspended.
- **Available**: The virtual desktop machine is powered on and ready for an end user to connect to it.
- **Connected**: The virtual desktop machine already has a user session running and is connected to the Horizon client.
- **Disconnected**: The virtual machine is already being used in a session, but it is disconnected from the Horizon client device.
- **In progress**: The virtual machine is in a transitional state during a maintenance operation.

There are also a number of tasks you can complete on each virtual desktop machine within the desktop pool. By right-clicking on any desktop listed in the table, you are able to undertake any of a number of tasks on that given desktop. You have the following options as shown in the following screenshot:

These options are described in more detail in the following list:

- **Restart Desktop**: Restarts that particular virtual desktop machine.
- **Reset Virtual Machine**: Will complete a hard reset on the desktop and could be used in the case of a system lockup. This will also reset the virtual desktop machine back to the original snapshot state.
- **Remove**: Will remove the virtual desktop machine from the pool.
- **Refresh**, **Recompose**, and **Rebalance**: This options have been described in Chapter 2, *Understanding Horizon 7 Architecture and Components,* and can be completed here on an individual desktop basis rather than performing them on the entire pool. We will look at these in more detail in the next section.
- **Cancel task**: Cancels any outstanding task on the individual virtual machine.
- **Assign User**: Can be used to allocate a desktop to a specific user.
- **Unassign User**: Removes a user from being entitled to this desktop this allocation.
- **Enter Maintenance Mode**: Places the desktop in a state where users cannot be allocated to the desktop or connect to it while maintenance is carried out.
- **Exit Maintenance Mode**: Returns the desktop to the pool.
- **Disconnect Session**: Disconnects the currently connected user from the pool without logging them off.
- **Logoff Session**: Logs the user off.
- **Send Message**: Sends a message to any given user.
- **Export table contents**: Exports a copy of the table containing the virtual desktop machine details as a CSV file.
- **Refresh table contents**: Updates the table with the latest information.

In the next section, we are going to look at a couple of the more common, Linked Clone specific tasks for managing the desktop pools, starting with recomposing a desktop pool.

Recomposing a Linked Clone desktop pool

One of the more common tasks you are likely to perform is to recompose a desktop pool to update the operating system or applications in the base image or, alternatively, to add new applications. It's always recommended to have test pools available for you to test updates prior to sending them out to your end users.

In this example, we are going to recompose one of the example desktop pools, but you could also perform a recompose operation on an individual virtual desktop:

1. To recompose a desktop pool, from the Horizon View Administrator dashboard screen, under the **Inventory** section in the left-hand pane, expand the option for **Catalog**, and then click on **Desktop Pools**. Double-click on the desktop pool on which you want to perform the recompose operation. In the example lab, we are going to select the Linked Clone desktop pool called `Win7-Floating-lc`. You will now see the details of the desktop pool in the **Summary** tab of the chosen desktop pool as shown in the following screenshot:

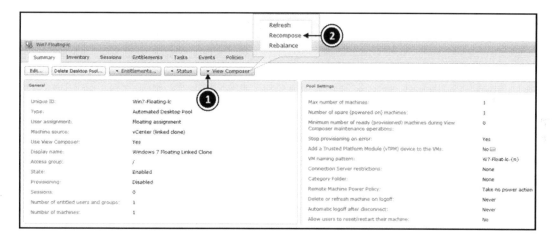

2. Click the **View Composer** button (1), and then from the menu options displayed, click on **Recompose** (2).

3. You will now see the **Recompose** screen and the **Image** option as shown in the following screenshot:

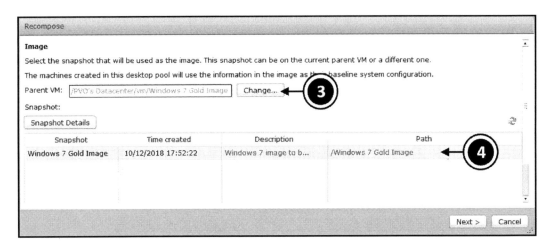

4. Here, you have the option to change the parent VM by clicking the **Change...** button (3). You can then select a new parent VM to recompose from. You would then see the snapshots that are associated with the newly selected parent VM in the table (4), from where you would then click it to select it.
5. You can just select a new snapshot of the current image. This would reflect an updated version of the existing image that you then created a new snapshot from. To do this, again click the snapshot you want to use (4).
6. Click **Next >** to continue.

7. You will now see the **Scheduling** screen where you can configure the time of the recompose operation, and what happens if users are connected at the time of the recompose. This is shown in the following screenshot:

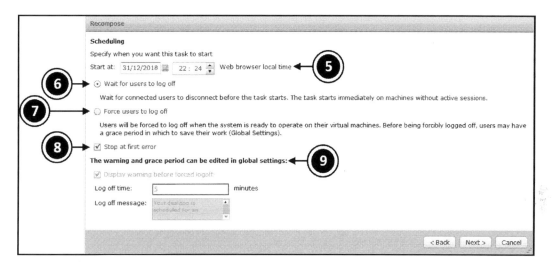

8. The first option is to set the date and time that you want the recompose operation to start (**5**).
9. Next, you have the option to wait until users log off before the recompose starts. To enable this option, click the radio button for **Wait for users to log off** (**6**). Or you can click the radio button for **Force user to log off** (**7**), which will forcibly log users off. However, they may be given a grace period before actually being logged off to allow them to save any work.
10. You then have the option to check the box for **Stop at first error** (**8**). Check this to stop the recompose if there are any errors. This would prevent rebuilding all the virtual desktop machines in the pool if there are any problems.

Configuring and Managing Desktop Pools - Part 2

11. If we just refer back to the force users to log off option, you can also configure a grace period before they are logged off. This can be edited in the **Global Settings** section as shown in the following screenshot:

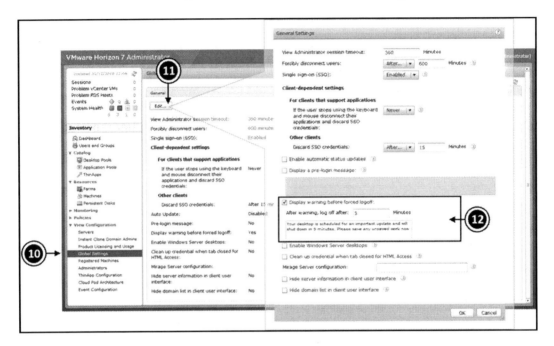

12. To edit the global settings, from the **Inventory** pane on the left-hand side, expand out the option for **View Configuration**, and then click on **Global Settings** (10). Then click on **Edit...** (11), and in the **General Settings** box, scroll down to the highlight section (12). You can then configure the message and the grace period.
13. On the **Recompose** screen, now click **Next >** to continue.
14. You will now see the **Ready to Complete** box as shown in the following screenshot:

15. Check the configuration settings and then click the **Finish** button.
16. The recompose operation will now start depending on the start time configured and whether to wait for users to log off.

You have now successfully performed a recompose operation on one of the Linked Clone desktop pools in the example lab. In the next section, we will look at the refresh operation.

Refreshing a Linked Clone desktop pool

Another task you are likely to perform is to refresh a desktop pool. By carrying out a refresh of the Linked Clone virtual desktops or desktop pools, you are effectively reverting them back to their initial state, when the original snapshot was taken after they had completed the customization phase. Only the operating system disk is refreshed and no other disks are affected:

1. To recompose a desktop pool, from the Horizon View Administrator dashboard screen, under the **Inventory** section in the left-hand pane, expand the option for **Catalog**, and then click on **Desktop Pools**. Double-click on the desktop pool on which you want to perform the refresh operation. In the example lab, we are going to select the Linked Clone desktop pool called `Win7-Floating-lc`. You will now see the details of the desktop pool in the **Summary** tab of the chosen desktop pool.

Configuring and Managing Desktop Pools - Part 2

2. Click the **View Composer** button, and then from the menu options displayed click on **Refresh**.
3. You will now see the **Scheduling** screen where you can configure the time of the recompose operation, and what happens if users are connected at the time of the refresh. This is shown in the following screenshot:

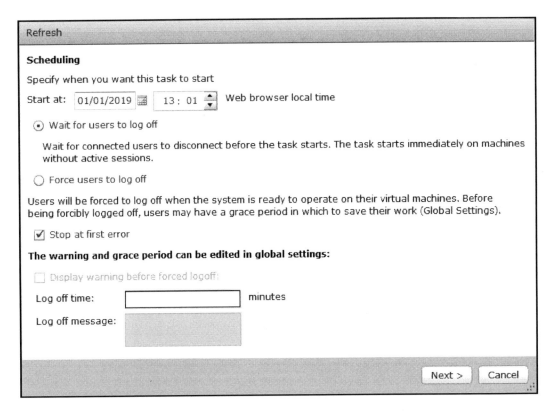

4. Click the **Next >** button to continue.

5. You will now see the **Ready to Complete** box as shown in the following screenshot:

6. Check the configuration settings and then click the **Finish** button.
7. The refresh operation will now start depending on the start time configured and whether to wait for users to log off.

You have now successfully performed a refresh operation on one of the Linked Clone desktop pools in the example lab. In the next section, we will look at the rebalance operation.

Rebalancing a Linked Clone desktop pool

The final task you will perform is to rebalance a desktop pool. The rebalance operation in View Composer is used to evenly distribute the Linked Clone virtual desktop machines across multiple datastores in your environment.

Configuring and Managing Desktop Pools - Part 2

You would perform this task if one of your datastores was becoming full while others have ample free space:

1. To rebalance a desktop pool, from the Horizon View Administrator dashboard screen, under the **Inventory** section in the left-hand pane, expand the option for **Catalog**, and then click on **Desktop Pools**. Double-click on the desktop pool in which you want to perform the rebalance operation. In the example lab, we are going to select the Linked Clone desktop pool called `Win7-Floating-lc`. You will now see the details of the desktop pool in the **Summary** tab of the chosen desktop pool.
2. Click the **View Composer** button, and then from the menu options displayed, click on **Rebalance**.
3. You will now see the following information box:

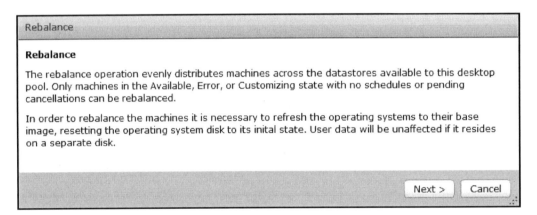

4. Click the **Next >** button to continue.
5. You will now see the **Scheduling** screen where you can configure the time of the rebalance operation, and what happens if users are connected at the time of the rebalancing. This is the same screen as we have seen previously for the refresh and recompose operations.
6. Click the **Next >** button to continue.
7. You will now see the **Ready to Complete** box as shown in the following screenshot:

Chapter 9

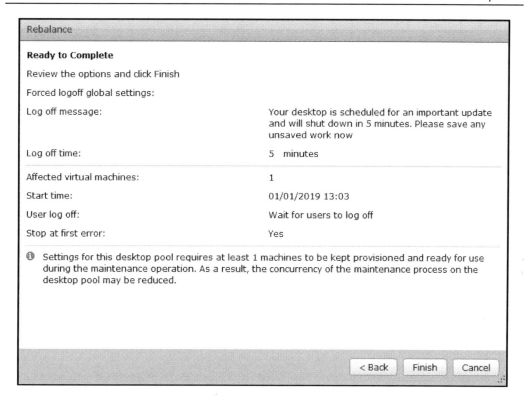

8. In the **Ready to Complete** box, this time you will see the logoff message that will be displayed to the users. There is also an important information box at the bottom regarding the desktop pool settings and the number of virtual desktop machines available in the desktop pool during the rebalance operation.
9. Check the configuration settings and then click the **Finish** button.
10. The rebalance operation will now start depending on how you configured the start time and whether to wait for users to log off.

You have now successfully performed a rebalance operation on one of the Linked Clone desktop pools in the example lab. In the next section, we will look at managing some of the additional disks that are created by View Composer.

Managing persistent disks

In the previous section, we discussed View Composer's operations, which are all about managing the OS side of what gets created for the virtual desktop machines. In this section, we are going to look at how to manage the non-OS disks or the persistent disk.

A persistent disk can be configured on a dedicated virtual hard disk per user, which will allow you to preserve user data and settings between recompose operations and more. There are a number of tasks that can be undertaken with regard to persistent disk management.

You are able to detach the virtual disk from a dedicated desktop. The main use case for this could be due to the end user leaving the company, and so the desktop is no longer needed but the data needs to be kept for compliance or audit reasons. It could also be because there is an issue with the desktop and you need to recreate it afresh without losing the user's data. Equally, you can attach an existing persistent disk to a virtual desktop machine in order to access the files and data stored on it. In the next sections, we are going to work through both attaching and detaching a persistent disk.

Detaching a persistent disk

In the first instance, let's look at how you would detach a persistent disk from a user's virtual desktop machine, following these steps:

1. From a workstation, open a browser and enter the address details of the View Connection server. In the example lab, the address of the connection server is `https://hzn7-cs1.pvolab.com/admin`.
2. You will now see the View Administrator login screen. Log in using the administrator account.
3. You will now see the Horizon View Administrator dashboard screen.

4. From Horizon View Administrator, click to expand the **Catalog** option from the **Inventory** on the left-hand side. From there, click on **Desktop Pools** (1), as shown in the following screenshot:

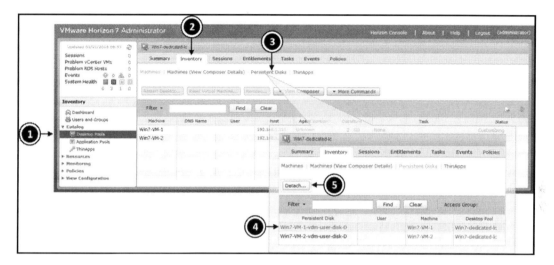

5. Next, click on the **Inventory** tab (2). You will now see a table listing the virtual desktop machines within the desktop pool, along with a number of clickable options across the top.
6. Click on the **Persistent Disks** option (3).
7. The table view then switches to detail the persistent disks attached to these virtual desktop machines. Click and select one of the disks. In this example, we will select **Win7-VM-1-vdm-user-disk-D** (4).
8. Now click the **Detach...** button (5). The disk is now detached and is available as a standalone disk that can be attached to another virtual machine. The use case for this could be for keeping a user's data should they leave your organization and you need to keep their data for compliance purposes or to share it with other users.

There is also another way to detach a persistent disk as described in the following steps:

1. Once logged in to the Horizon View Administrator, from the dashboard, click to expand the resources option from the **Inventory** on the left-hand side. From there, click on **Persistent Disks** (6), as shown in the following screenshot:

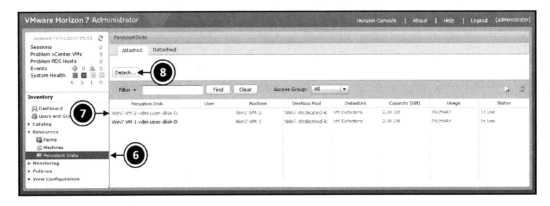

2. You will now see the table detailing the persistent disks attached to these virtual desktop machines. Click and select one of the disks. In this example, we will select **Win7-VM-2-vdm-user-disk-D** (7).
3. Now click the **Detach...** button (8). The disk is now detached.

In the next section, we are going to work through the reverse and show you how to attach a persistent disk.

Attaching a persistent disk

To attach a persistent disk to a users virtual desktop machine, follow these steps:

1. From a workstation, open a browser and enter the address details of the View connection server. In the example lab, the address of the connection server is https://hzn7-cs1.pvolab.com/admin.
2. You will now see the View Administrator login screen. Log in using the administrator account.
3. You will now see the Horizon View Administrator dashboard screen.

Chapter 9

4. From Horizon View Administrator, click to expand the resources option from the **Inventory** on the left-hand side. From there, click on **Persistent Disks** (1), as shown in the following screenshot:

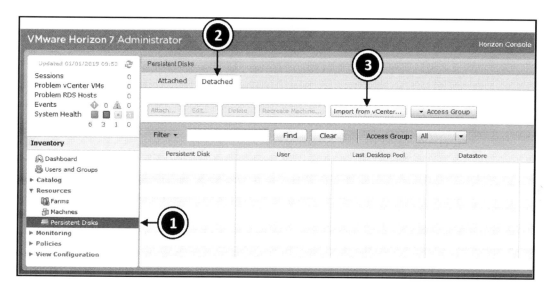

5. Now click on the **Detached** tab (2). If you already had a number of detached disks, then you would see them listed in the table. In the example lab, we don't have any, but if we did, you would click the entry for the persistent disk from the list, and then click on the **Attach...** button.
6. The next step is to select a Linked Clone virtual desktop machine to which to attach the persistent disk, select the **Attach as a secondary disk** option, and then click **Finish**.
7. The disk will now be made available on the virtual desktop machine you selected.

 You cannot attach a persistent disk that is stored on a non-VMware Virtual SAN datastore to a virtual desktop machine that is stored on a VMware Virtual SAN datastore. Also, you need to ensure that the virtual desktop machine you are attaching the persistent disk to uses the same operating system as the virtual desktop machine in which the persistent disk was created.

[537]

Configuring and Managing Desktop Pools - Part 2

You also have the option to import an existing disk direct from vCenter. To do this, follow these steps:

1. Click the **Import from vCenter...** button (3) as shown in the previous screenshot. You will now see the **Import Persistent Disk from vCenter** configuration box as shown in the following screenshot:

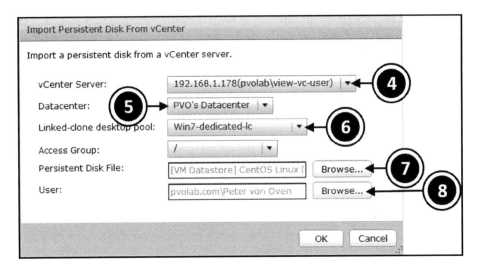

2. First, in the **vCenter Server** box, click the drop-down arrow and select the vCenter server from the list shown that contains the virtual disk you want to import. In the example lab, this is shown by the IP address `192.168.1.178`. You will also see that it shows the vCenter user account.

3. Next, select the datacenter from the **Datacenter** box (5) by clicking the drop-down arrow and selecting the datacenter where the virtual disk resides. In the example lab, this is the **PVO's Datacenter** option.

4. Now, in the **Linked-clone desktop pool** box, click the drop-down arrow (6) and select the desktop pool of where the virtual disk resides. In the example lab, this is the desktop pool called `Win7-dedicated-lc`.

5. Next, you need to choose the **Persistent Disk File**. Click the **Browse...** button (7). You will now see the **Select Datastore Path** configuration box as shown in the following screenshot:

Chapter 9

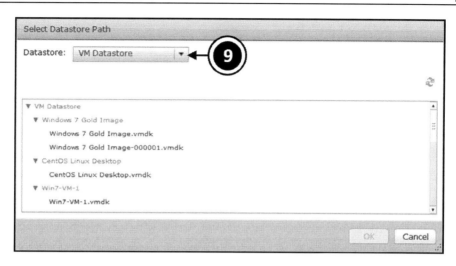

6. From the **Datastore** box, click the down-arrow (**9**), and from the list, choose the datastore on which the persistent disk resides. In the example lab, this is the datastore called **VM Datastore**.

7. Then, from the list, navigate to the virtual disk you want to import and click the **OK** button.

8. You will now return to the **Import Persistent Disk from vCenter** configuration box. The final thing to configure is the **User** option.

9. Click the **Browse...** button (**8**). You will now see the select datastore path configuration box as shown in the following screenshot:

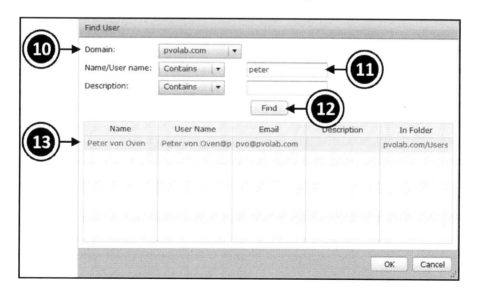

10. In the **Domain** box **(10)**, click the drop-down arrow and select the domain in which the user resides. In the example lab, this is the `pvolab.com` domain.
11. Next, in the **Name/User name** box **(11)**, type in the username of `Peter` and ensure that you select **Contains** from the drop-down menu for the filter.
12. Now click the **Find** button **(12)**.
13. In the table, you will now see the results displayed. Click and select the relevant user **(13)** and then click **OK**.
14. You will now return to the **Import Persistent Disk from vCenter** configuration box.
15. Click **OK** to complete the configuration. The disk will now be attached to a virtual desktop machine in the selected desktop pool when the associated user logs on.

You have now successfully attached a persistent disk to an existing virtual desktop machine.

Reviewing the infrastructure post-deployment

So, with the desktop pools created and the virtual desktop machines built and running, now is a good time to go back and review the infrastructure to check that everything is running as expected before you start adding end users and allowing them to log in. This is just to make sure your sizing of resources is as you expected it to be, but it also gives you another opportunity to tweak anything before it's too late and you have live users logged in.

Ideally, you should compare the assessment data with the current data from your environment. Back in `Chapter 3`, *Design and Deployment Considerations*, we looked at Liquidware Stratusphere as a solution for this, as not only will it give us the assessment data, it will also provide data on the infrastructure performance and will be useful in the next section when we come to fine-tuning the end user experience.

This will allow you to measure CPU, memory, and network performance so you can quickly understand the resources being used and identify any potential bottlenecks.

Summary

In this, the second part of Chapter 8, *Configuring and Managing Desktop Pools - Part 1*, we looked at how to create floating desktop pools, and then we looked at how to entitle end users to have access to the desktop pools and the virtual desktop machines in the pool. We looked at doing this from the View Admin console and also from the new Horizon Console.

Then, we went on to look at some the of the more common pool management tasks, particularly when it came to managing Linked Clone desktop pools.

We finished the chapter by looking at how to review your environment once you complete the initial deployment.

10
Fine-Tuning the End User Experience

So far, we have built our Horizon View infrastructure, deployed and optimized our virtual desktop OS, and configured our user entitlements by means of creating Horizon View desktop pools. This means that our end users can now access their virtual desktop machines.

In this chapter, we will look at how to fine-tune the end user experience, by which we mean how the desktop will perform, and determine the features that will be made available to the users.

We have already talked about optimizing the virtual desktop OS and how we can tune the OS so that it acts like a virtual desktop machine. Now we will talk about fine-tuning and configuring things such as the delivery protocol, as well as enabling and disabling certain features and functions related to how an end user interacts with their virtual desktop machine. By this, we mean configuring things such as whether or not you can cut-and-paste text between the endpoint device running the client and the virtual desktop machine.

These configuration options are all centrally deployed and managed using the Active Directory Group Policy.

In this chapter, we will cover the following topics:

- Configuring and preparing **Active Directory** (**AD**) for tuning virtual desktop machines
- Configuring Horizon AD policies
- Installing the PCoIP tuning tool to configure and tune the delivery protocol
- Tuning the virtual desktop for optimum performance

Fine-Tuning the End User Experience

Configuring and preparing AD

The behavior of a virtual desktop machine and how a user interacts with it is governed by an AD policy. As we mentioned previously, this policy configures things such as a graphics experience and cut-and-paste options.

To make life easier, the templates for these policies have already been created and are shipped as part of the Horizon View software that was downloaded as part of the software downloads in Chapter 4, *Installing and Configuring Horizon 7 - Part 1*, and can be found in the ZIP file named VMware-Horizon-Extras-Bundle-4.9.0-9539668.

The first thing we need to do is unzip this file and save it to the shared software folder on the file server. You will see that it contains 15 Administrative Template (ADMX) files, as shown in the following screenshot:

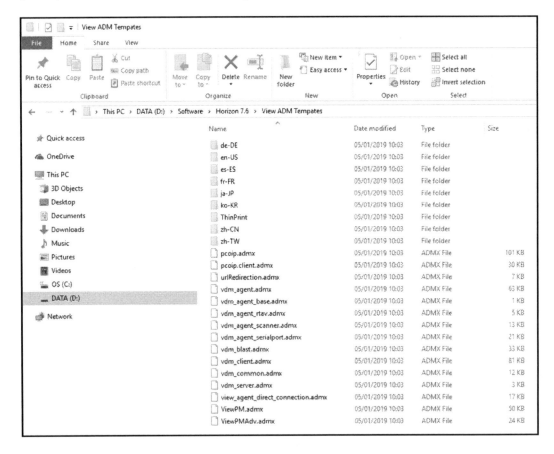

In the next section, we will look at the AD ADMX and ADML templates and how to import them.

Importing and applying Horizon View ADMX templates

Now that you have unzipped the template files, they can be imported. Since we are using AMDX/ADML templates and Windows Server 2016, the import process is as simple as copying the files into the central location on the domain controller. The same would apply to Windows Server 2019. There are two sets of files to copy, that is, the `ADMX` files and the `ADML` files:

1. First, copy all of the Horizon `ADMX` files to the domain controller in the `C:\Windows\PolicyDefinitions` folder, as shown in the following screenshot:

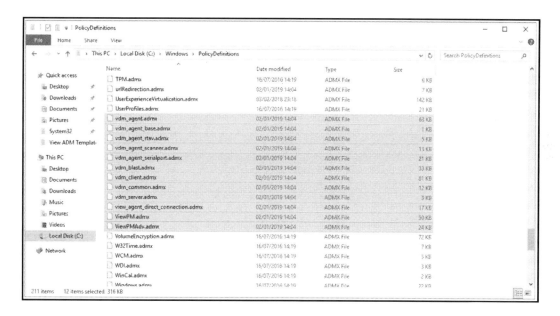

Fine-Tuning the End User Experience

2. Next, copy the Horizon `ADML` files to the domain controller in the `C:\Windows\PolicyDefinitions\en-US` folder, as shown in the following screenshot:

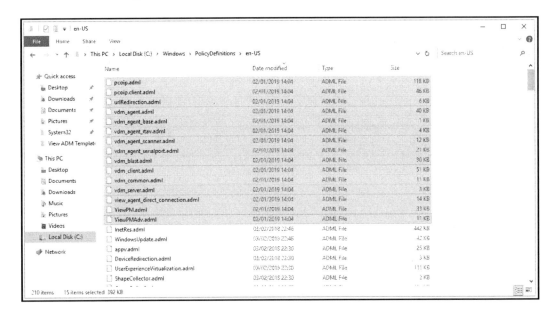

In the next section, we will look at the AD OU requirements for the deployment of virtual desktop machines and the things you need in place before you can configure and tune your environment.

Creating an organizational unit (OU)

The first thing you need to do is create an **organizational unit** (OU) for your virtual desktop machines. It's a best practice to have a separate OU for virtual desktop machines to ensure that you don't end up applying the wrong policies to them, such as those that are used for your physical machines, which could potentially contain components that may impact performance and vice versa. You don't want to apply VDI-based policies to the physical desktop estate.

Depending on your own environment, you may want to create an OU for different use cases, for example, you may want a different OU for each different department within your organization. This would then allow you to apply different VDI-based policies to each OU. For example, a particular department might use high-end graphics, which would mean that PCoIP will be configured to deliver that richer experience over that of a standard office user, or it could be a policy specific to LAN users, where the policy governs the behavior based on the available bandwidth.

In the example lab, we will create an OU called `Horizon View Desktops` on the domain controller, as shown in the following screenshot:

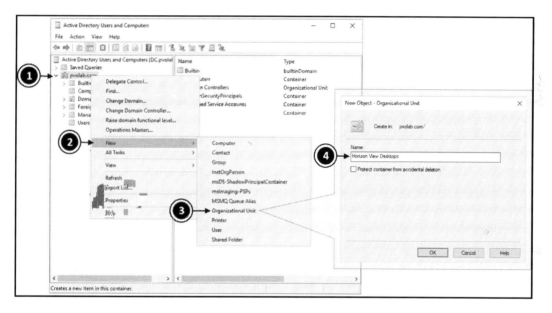

To configure the policy, follow these steps:

1. From the **Active Directory Users and Computers** configuration screen, click on highlighted domain `pvolab.com` (**1**) and then right-click.
2. From the contextual menu that you will now see, move your mouse down to hover on **New** (**2**), and then from the next contextual menu, move the mouse and click on **Organizational Unit** (**3**).

3. In the **New Object - Organization Unit** box, type in the specified name to call this OU. In the example lab, we have named it **Horizon view Desktops (4)**.
4. Click **OK**.
5. You will now return to the **Active Directory Users and Computers** screen, where you will see that the new OU has been added.

Next, we will create the policy to link to this new OU so that we can apply the Horizon-specific virtual desktop machines to it.

Creating Group Policy Objects (GPO) for Horizon View

Now that you have created an OU for your virtual desktop machines, you can create group policy objects to link to that OU. In the example lab, the policy is called **Horizon View Virtual Desktop Policy**:

1. To start the configuration, double-click on the **Windows Administrative Tools** icon to launch the admin tools. You will now see the **Windows Administrative Tools** screen being displayed.
2. From this screen, scroll down and then double-click on the option for **Group Policy Management**. You will now see the **Group Policy Management** screen, as shown in the following screenshot:

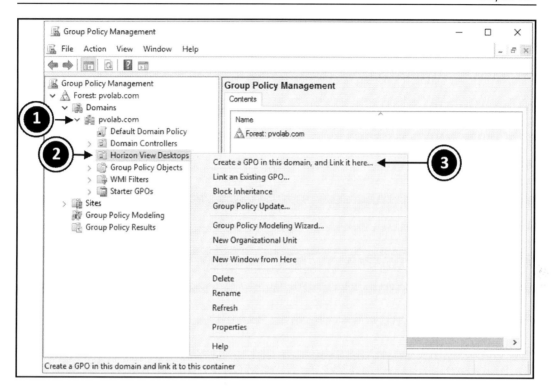

3. Expand the folders for Forest:pvolab.com (**1**), Domains, and pvolab.com. Click and highlight the Horizon View Desktops OU (**2**), and then right-click on it.
4. From the contextual menu that appears, click the option for **Create a GPO in this domain, and Link it here…** (**3**).

Fine-Tuning the End User Experience

5. You will now see the **New GPO** dialog box, as shown in the following screenshot:

6. In the name box, type in the name for this policy. In the example lab, we have called this `Horizon View Virtual Desktop Policy`.
7. Click **OK**.
8. You will now return to the **Group Policy Management** screen, which will show the newly created policy, as shown in the following screenshot:

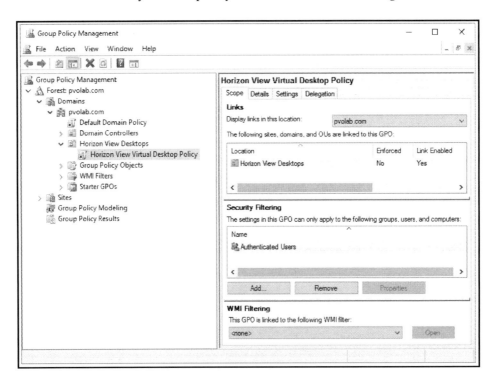

Chapter 10

Now, if we edit the newly created `Horizon View Virtual Desktop Policy`, you will see the new Horizon-specific policy options listed:

1. To edit the policy, from the **Group Policy Management** screen, click and highlight the `Horizon View Virtual Desktop Policy` (**1**).
2. Right-click and from the contextual menu that appears, click **Edit...** (**2**), as shown in the following screenshot:

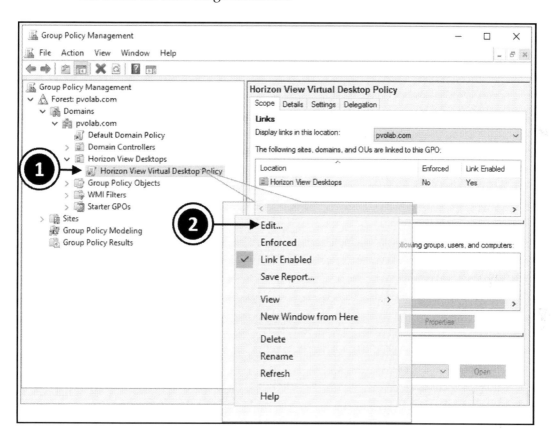

Fine-Tuning the End User Experience

You will now see the **Group Policy Management Editor** screen with the VMware Horizon-specific policies outlined:

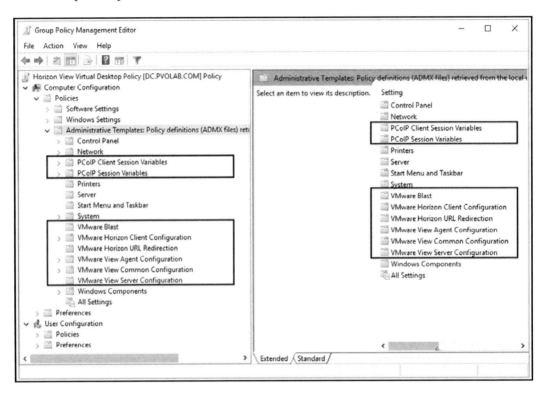

In the example lab, we are going to add all the policy templates to the one policy, just to show the various options that are available. In your environment, and depending on your design, you may want to create different policies and apply different templates to different policies. You may even want to create different OUs as well. Maybe this will be on a departmental basis or for different use cases, as we have previously mentioned. This is the recommended approach as it makes troubleshooting and the management of policies much easier.

Before we look at each of the individual policy options, in the next section, we will complete one final AD configuration task: to configure the loopback policy.

Chapter 10

Enabling the loopback policy

In a VDI model, and particularly with floating desktop assignments, you will have multiple users accessing the same desktop. For any configuration changes that a user makes to one of the virtual desktop machines apply to all of the users that use that machine, we need to enable the loopback processing feature. This is particularly important if you are using virtual desktop machines in a kiosk type environment. To configure loopback mode, complete the following steps from the Group Policy Management Editor screen:

1. Launch the **Group Policy Management Editor** screen, as shown in the following screenshot:

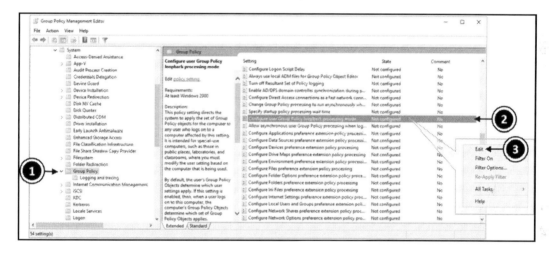

2. Under the **Computer Configuration** section, expand the folders for `Policies`, `Administrative Templates: Policy definitions`, and `System`.
3. Highlight `Group Policy` (**1**). You will now see the policy options listed in the right pane.
4. Scroll down to **Configure user Group Policy loopback processing mode** (**2**). Click to select it and then right-click.
5. From the contextual menu that appears, click the **Edit** option (**3**).

[553]

Fine-Tuning the End User Experience

6. You will now see the **Configure user Group Policy loopback processing mode** configuration screen, as shown in the following screenshot:

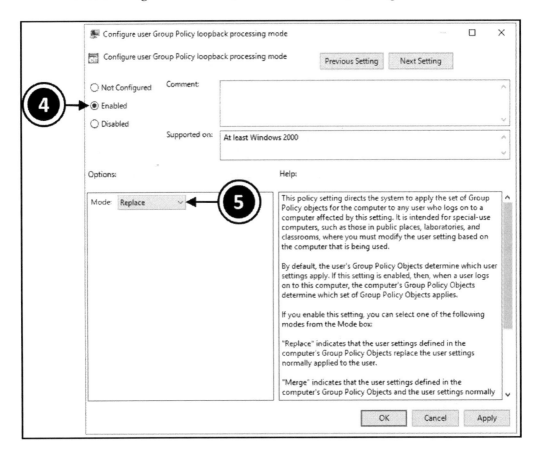

7. Click the radio button for **Enabled (4)** to enable the policy within the **Horizon View Virtual Desktop Policy**. You then have the option to configure the **Mode** operation.
8. Click the drop-down arrow **(5)** and select the option for **Replace**.

With the **Replace** option, the user policy is applied, which is associated with the computer. Any other user policies are ignored. Choosing the **Merge** option means that the policies that are applied are both the user and the computer-related policies, where the computer policy wins in the event of a conflict.

Chapter 10

We have now successfully completed the main admin tasks in configuring AD. In the next section, we are going to take a look at the different policy settings that are available with the Horizon View admin templates.

Configuring Horizon View policy settings

In this section, we are going to walk through all the different configurable policy options for the Horizon View ADMX templates that were added to AD. This section will act as a reference guide that shows all the different policy settings that you can configure.

PCoIP Client Session Variables

The first set of policy settings are for `PCoIP Client Session Variables`. To view the different policy settings, under **Computer Configuration**, expand the options for `Policies` and `Administrative Templates: Policy definitions`, and then click on `PCoIP Client Session Variables`, as shown in the following screenshot:

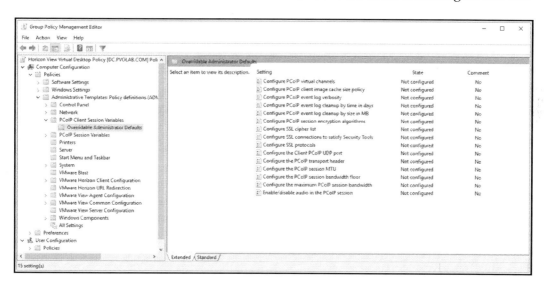

You will see a folder called `Overridable Administrator Defaults`, which contains the different settings. These settings control the behavior of the PCoIP protocol from the client session. To edit a setting, double-click the setting you want to configure, and then, ensuring it is enabled, configure the relevant setting.

[555]

Fine-Tuning the End User Experience

As an example, we have used the **Configure PCoIP virtual channels** to demonstrate this. From the **Group Policy Management Editor** screen, double-click the **Configure PCoIP virtual channels** setting, as shown in the following screenshot:

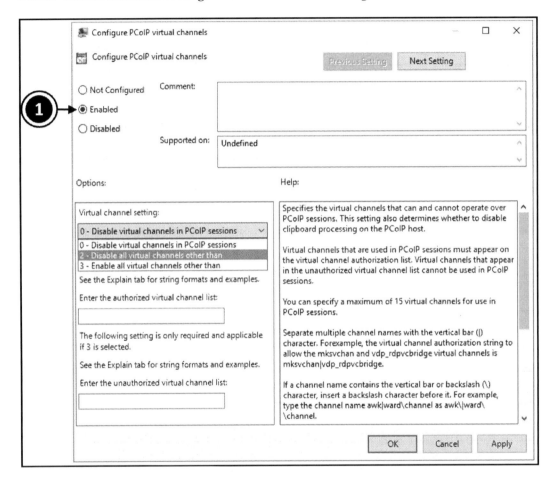

To configure the policy, follow these steps:

1. To enable the policy settings, click the radio button for **Enabled (1)**.
2. You can then choose your settings in the **Options** section on the left-hand side of the screen. On the right-hand side of the screen, you will see a description of the various options that are available in the **Help** section.
3. Click **Apply** to save the setting.
4. Now, click **OK** to exit, or **Next Setting/Previous Setting** to work through the other policy settings.

Let's now look at policy settings that define how the PCoIP session behaves.

PCoIP Session Variables

The next set of policy settings are for `PCoIP Session Variables`, which define how PCoIP behaves during a desktop session, as shown in the following screenshot:

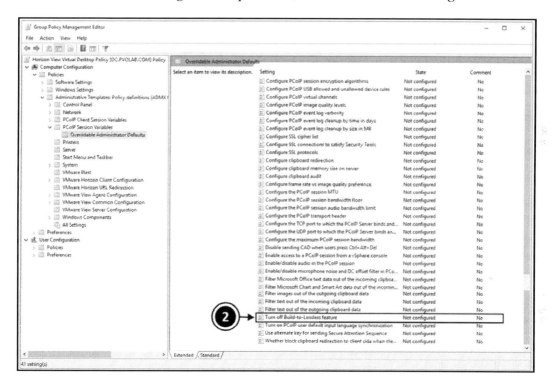

We have highlighted a particular setting on this screen, and that is the **Turn off Build-to-Lossless feature** setting (**2**).

The reason to quickly highlight this setting is for anyone that has used previous versions of View. Before View 6, the default option for PCoIP build-to-lossless was that it was enabled, meaning that you will need more bandwidth for that level of image detail. From View 6 onward, the default setting is for build-to-lossless to be set to be disabled.

The next set of policy settings are for controlling the VMware Blast protocol, should you use that instead of PCoIP.

Fine-Tuning the End User Experience

VMware Blast

The next set of policy settings are for configuring the `VMware Blast` delivery protocol, which allows you to define how the protocol behaves, as shown in the following screenshot:

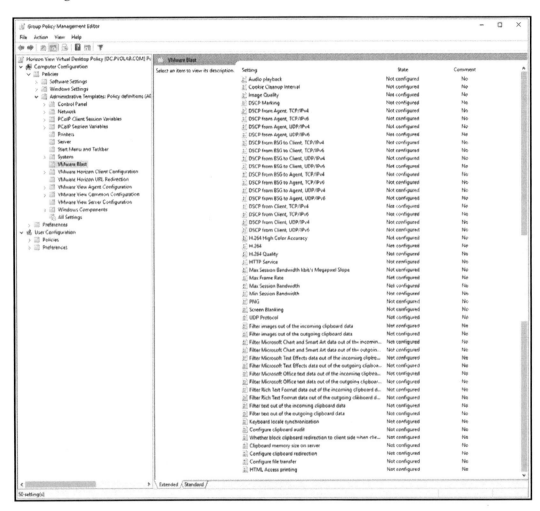

Chapter 10

The next set of policy settings are for configuring the `VMware Horizon Client Configuration`.

VMware Horizon Client Configuration

The next set of policy settings are for configuring the `VMware Horizon Client Configuration`, which defines the behaviour of the Horizon Client, as shown in the following screenshot:

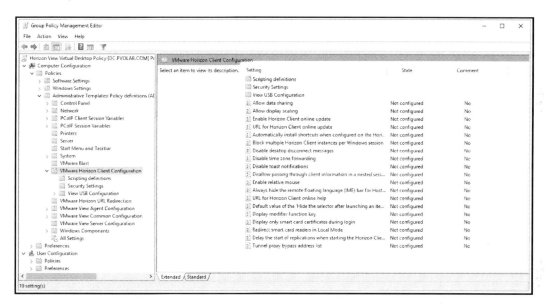

Under this particular set of configuration options, you can see that there are a number of policy settings under the main subject heading. However, there are also a number of subfolders, also containing a number of settings, which we will list in the following sections.

Scripting definitions

In the `Scripting definitions` subfolder, you will find the following policy settings for scripting definitions:

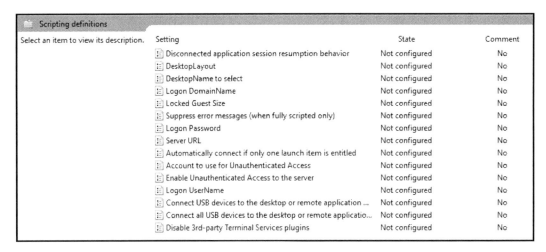

Next, we have the **Security Settings** configuration options.

Security Settings

In the `Security Settings` subfolder, you will find the following policy settings for managing the security settings around SSL and certificate management:

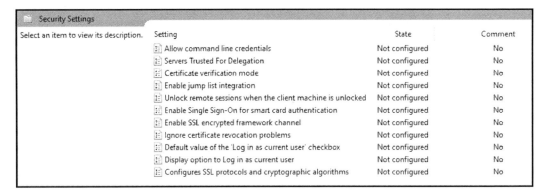

Next, we have the USB configuration options.

View USB Configuration

In the `View USB Configuration` folder, as well as the settings in the root of the folder, there is also a subfolder containing additional settings, as shown in the following screenshot:

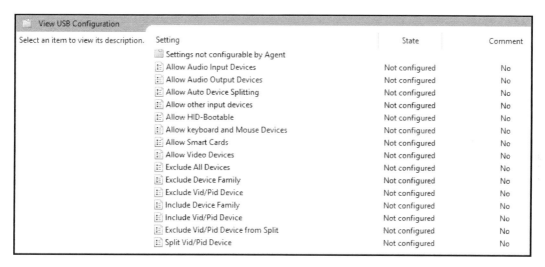

The policy settings in the `Settings not configurable by Agent` folder are shown in the next section.

Settings not configurable by Agent

The policy settings in the `Settings not configurable by Agent` folder are shown in the following screenshot:

We have now outlined all of the policy settings that are covered under the VMware Horizon Client Configuration section. The next set of options are for URL redirection, which is covered in the next section.

Fine-Tuning the End User Experience

VMware Horizon URL Redirection

In the `VMware Horizon URL Redirection` folder, you will find the policy settings for managing the URL redirection feature, as shown in the following screenshot:

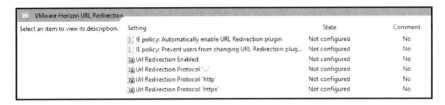

In the next section, we are going to look at the configuration options for the View Agent.

Horizon View Agent Configuration

In the `VMware View Agent Configuration` folder, you will see that there is only one policy setting in the root of the folder. The rest are all divided into subfolders, as shown in the following screenshot:

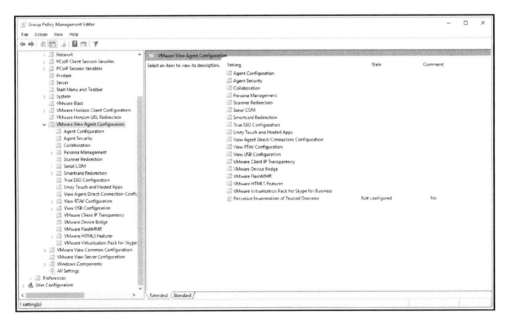

Chapter 10

In the next section, we will take a look at the policy setting options in the `VMware View Agent Configuration` subfolders, starting with `Agent Configuration`.

Agent Configuration

In the `Agent Configuration` folder, you will find the policy settings for the Agent Configuration, as shown in the following screenshot:

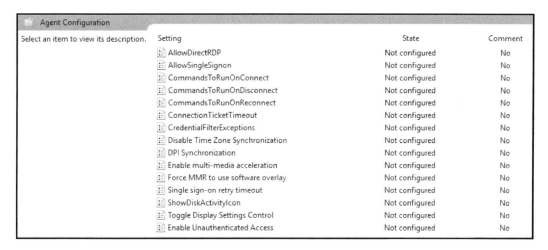

In the next section, we will take a look at the policy setting options in the `Agent Security` subfolder.

Agent Security

In the `Agent Security` subfolder, you will find the policy settings, as shown in the following screenshot:

In the next section, we will take a look at the policy setting options in the `Collaboration` subfolder.

[563]

Collaboration

In the `Collaboration` subfolder, you will find the policy settings, as shown in the following screenshot:

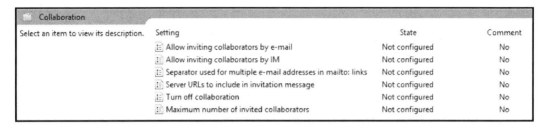

In the next section, we will take a look at the policy setting options in the `Persona Management` subfolder.

Persona Management

In the `Persona Management` subfolder, you will see that the policy settings are in further subfolders, as shown in the following screenshot:

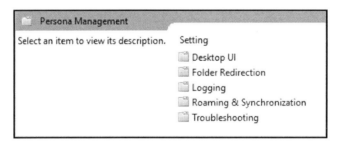

We will cover the policy settings in these subfolders in the following sections.

Chapter 10

Desktop UI

In the `Desktop UI` subfolder, you will find the policy settings, as shown in the following screenshot:

In the next section, we will take a look at the policy setting options in the `Folder Redirection` subfolder.

Folder Redirection

In the `Folder Redirection` subfolder, you will find the policy settings, as shown in the following screenshot:

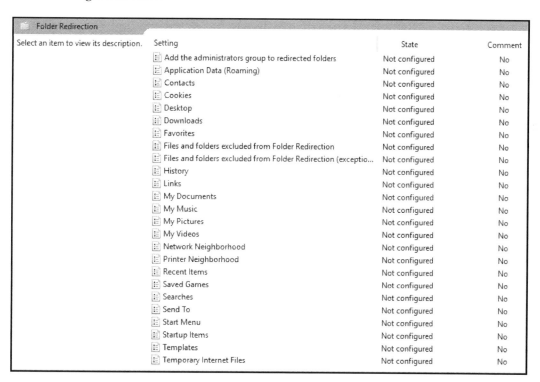

Fine-Tuning the End User Experience

In the next section, we will take a look at the policy setting options in the Logging subfolder.

Logging

In the `Logging` subfolder, you will find the policy settings, as shown in the following screenshot:

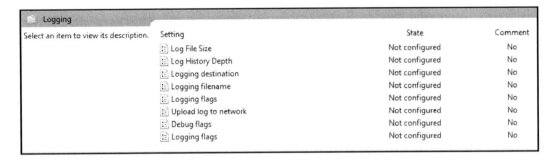

In the next section, we will take a look at the policy setting options in the `Roaming & Synchronization` subfolder.

Roaming and Synchronization

In the `Roaming & Synchronization` subfolder, you will find the policy settings, as shown in the following screenshot:

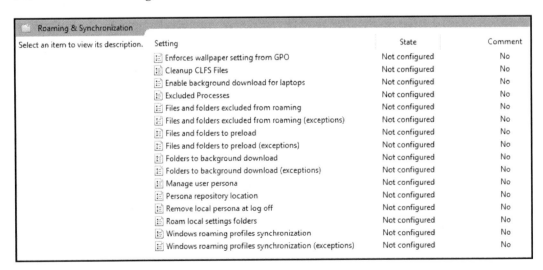

In the next section, we will take a look at the policy setting options in the `Troubleshooting` subfolder.

Troubleshooting

In the `Troubleshooting` subfolder, you will find the policy settings, as shown in the following screenshot:

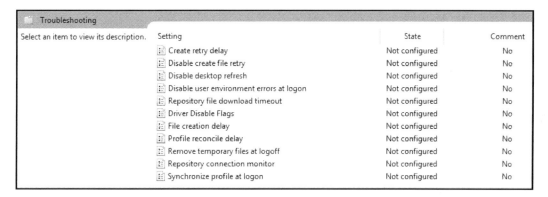

In the next section, we will take a look at the policy setting options in the `Scanner Redirection` subfolder.

Scanner Redirection

In the `Scanner Redirection` subfolder, you will find the policy settings, as shown in the following screenshot:

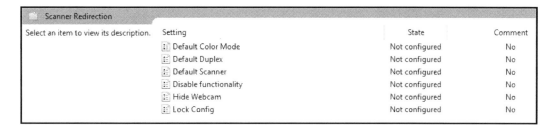

In the next section, we will take a look at the policy setting options in the `Serial COM` subfolder.

Serial COM

In the `Serial COM` subfolder, you will find the policy settings, along with another subfolder, as shown in the following screenshot:

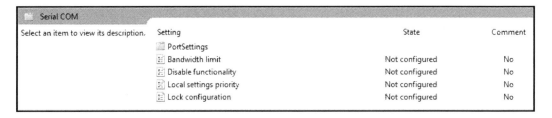

In the next section, we will take a look at the policy setting options in the `PortSettings` subfolder.

PortSettings

In the `PortSettings` subfolder, you will find the policy settings, as shown in the following screenshot:

In the next section, we will take a look at the policy setting options in the `Smartcard Redirection` subfolder.

Smartcard Redirection

In the `Smartcard Redirection` subfolder, you will see that there are no actual settings, and just another subfolder, as shown in the following screenshot:

Chapter 10

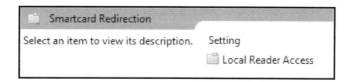

In the next section, we will take a look at the policy setting options that are in the `Local Reader Access` subfolder.

Local Reader Access

In the `Local Reader Access` subfolder, you will find the policy settings, as shown in the following screenshot:

In the next section, we will take a look at the policy setting options in the `True SSO Configuration` subfolder.

True SSO Configuration

In the `True SSO Configuration` subfolder, you will find the policy settings, as shown in the following screenshot:

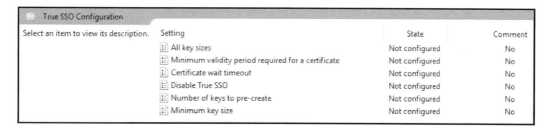

[569]

In the next section, we will take a look at the policy setting options in the `Unity Touch and Hosted Apps` subfolder.

Unity Touch and Hosted Apps

In the `Unity Touch and Hosted Apps` subfolder, you will find the policy settings, as shown in the following screenshot:

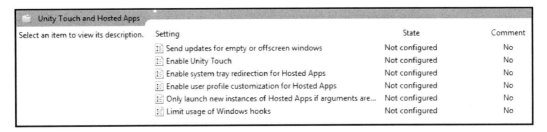

In the next section, we will take a look at the policy setting options in the `View Agent Direct-Connection Configuration` subfolder.

View Agent Direct-Connection Configuration

In the `View Agent Direct-Connection Configuration` subfolder, you will find the policy settings, as shown in the following screenshot:

Chapter 10

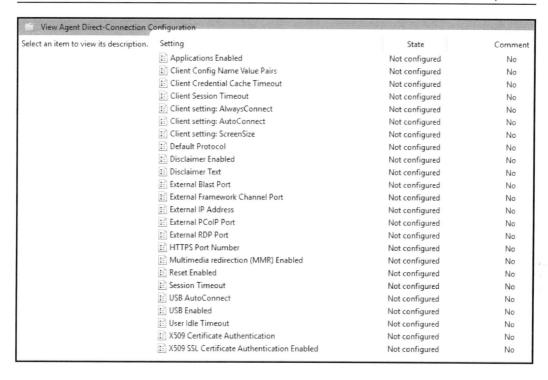

In the next section, we will take a look at the policy setting options in the View RTAV Configuration subfolder.

View RTAV Configuration

In the View ATV Configuration subfolder, you will find a single policy setting and another subfolder, as shown in the following screenshot:

Fine-Tuning the End User Experience

In the next section, we will take a look at the policy setting options in the `View RTAV Webcam Setings` subfolder.

View RTAV Webcam Settings

In the `View RTAV Webcam Settings` subfolder, you will find the policy settings, as shown in the following screenshot:

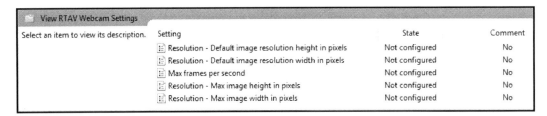

In the next section, we will take a look at the policy setting options in the `View USB Configuration` subfolder.

View USB Configuration

In the `View USB Configuration` subfolder, you will find the policy settings, as shown in the following screenshot:

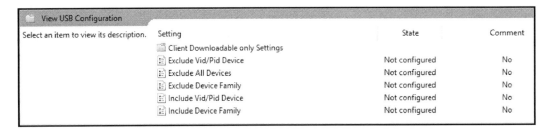

In the next section, we will take a look at the policy setting options in the `Client Downloadable only Settings` subfolder.

Client Downloadable only Settings

In the `Client Downloadable only Settings` subfolder, you will find the policy settings, as shown in the following screenshot:

Chapter 10

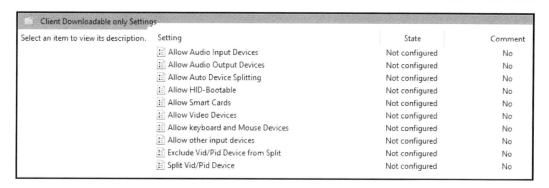

In the next section, we will take a look at the policy setting options in the `VMware Client IP Transparency` subfolder.

VMware Client IP Transparency

In the `VMware Client IP Transparency` subfolder, you will find the policy settings, as shown in the following screenshot:

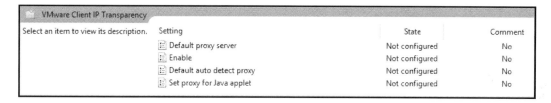

In the next section, we will take a look at the policy setting options in the `VMware Device Bridge` subfolder.

VMware Device Bridge

In the `VMware Device Badge` subfolder, you will find the policy settings, as shown in the following screenshot:

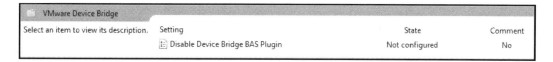

In the next section, we will take a look at the policy setting options in the `VMware Flash MMR` subfolder.

[573]

Fine-Tuning the End User Experience

VMware Flash MMR

In the VMware Flash MMR subfolder, you will find the policy settings, as shown in the following screenshot:

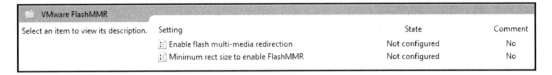

In the next section, we will take a look at the policy setting options in the VMware HTML5 Features subfolder.

VMware HTML5 Features

In the VMware HTML5 Features subfolder, you will find two policy settings and two additional subfolders, as shown in the following screenshot:

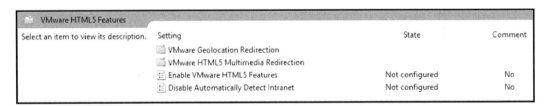

In the next section, we will take a look at the policy setting options in the VMware Geolocation Redirection subfolder.

VMware Geolocation Redirection

In the VMware Geolocation Redirection subfolder, you will find the policy settings, as shown in the following screenshot:

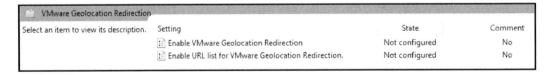

Chapter 10

In the next section, we will take a look at the policy setting options in the `VMware HTML5 Multimedia Redirection` subfolder.

VMware HTML5 Multimedia Redirection

In the `VMware HTML5 Multimedia Redirection` subfolder, you will find the policy settings, as shown in the following screenshot:

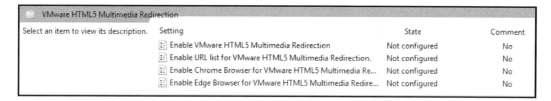

In the next section, we will take a look at the policy setting options in the `VMware Virtualization Pack for Skype for the Business` subfolder.

VMware Virtualization Pack for Skype for Business

In the `VMware Virtualization Pack for Skype for Business` subfolder, you will find the policy settings, as shown in the following screenshot:

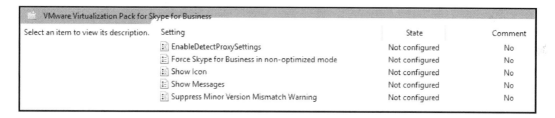

In the next section, we are going to return to the top-level policy folders and look at the `VMware View Common Configuration` policy setting configuration options.

[575]

VMware View Common Configuration

In the VMware View Common Configuration subfolder, you will find three policy settings and three subfolders, as shown in the following screenshot:

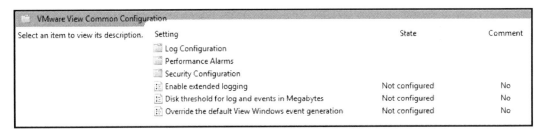

In the next section, we will take a look at the policy setting options in the Log Configuration subfolder.

Log Configuration

In the Log Configuration subfolder, you will find the policy settings, as shown in the following screenshot:

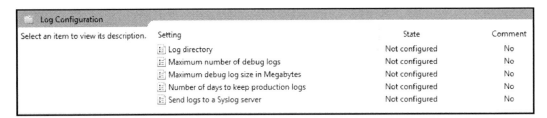

In the next section, we will take a look at the policy setting options in the Performance Alarms subfolder.

Performance Alarms

In the `Performance Alarms` subfolder, you will find the policy settings, as shown in the following screenshot:

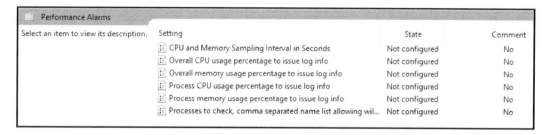

In the next section, we will take a look at the policy setting options in the `Security Configuration` subfolder.

Security Configuration

In the `Security Configuration` subfolder, you will find the policy settings, as shown in the following screenshot:

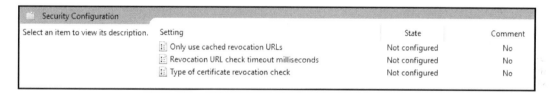

In the next section, we are going to return to the top-level policy folders and look at the final set of policy options for the `VMware View Server Configuration` policy setting configuration options.

VMware View Server Configuration

In the `VMware Viiew Server Configuration` subfolder, you will find the policy settings, as shown in the following screenshot:

VMware View Server Configuration			
Select an item to view its description.	Setting	State	Comment
	Enumerate Forest Trust Child Domains	Not configured	No
	Recursive Enumeration of Trusted Domains	Not configured	No
	Windows Password Authentication Mode	Not configured	No

We have now shown you all of the policy configuration options that are available from the VMware View ADMX templates. In the next section, we are going to look at a specific tool for tuning the PCoIP protocol, should you choose to use that particular protocol to deliver virtual desktop machines.

PCoIP tuning tool

The final thing we are going to cover in this chapter is how you can dynamically tune virtual desktop machines using the PCoIP tuning tool. You can download this tool from the following link: `http://tinyurl.com/ocqxykn`.

One of the things that this tuning tool enables is the ability to change settings on the fly rather than manually editing policies. This is convenient because, as you can see from the number of policies, there are a large number of different configurable options.

Once you have downloaded the tool, launch it on the virtual desktop machine you want to tune. It's probably worthwhile doing this on your parent image and with an end user so that you can not only get their feedback but also get their buy-in to the solution.

With the tool launched, you will see that there are a number of options to choose from:

- **Activate Profile**
- **Manage Profiles**
- **Clear Profile Settings**
- **Show Session Stats**
- **Show Session Health**

These options are shown in the following screenshot:

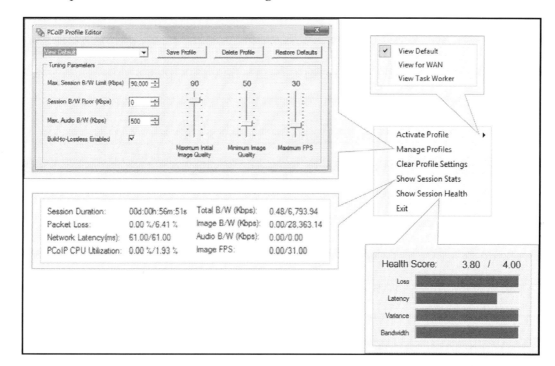

In the following sections, we will briefly cover what each option is used to configure.

Activate Profile

The Activate Profile settings allow you to activate one of the preset profiles. Each profile is based on a different use case, and three have already been built that you can choose from. There's one for a default user, one for a WAN-based user, and another for a task worker.

By selecting one of the preset profiles, the settings for things such as session bandwidth, image quality, or frame rate will be updated and changed to a setting that matches that particular use case.

> To activate a profile, you will need to reboot the virtual desktop machine.

Manage Profiles

The Manage Profiles option allows you to adjust the settings of a particular profile. You can dynamically change image quality, frames per second, bandwidth, and switch on build-to-lossless. You can choose from the pre-built profiles or create a new one and then save it.

Clear Profile Settings

Clear Profile Settings will clear the profile settings and restore them to their defaults.

Show Session Stats

The Show Session Stats option shows you real-time usage statistics for things such as bandwidth, frames per second, latency, and CPU utilization, allowing you to understand what a particular virtual desktop machine is consuming. By clicking this option, you effectively switch it on and it will appear on the desktop so that you can monitor it.

Show Session Health

As with the session stats option, by clicking this option, you effectively switch it on and it will appear on the desktop. It gives you a health score for the PCoIP session to give you an indication of where there might be a problem. For example, the latency score might be low, indicating a higher latency between the client and the virtual desktop.

For a more in-depth overview of performance, capacity planning, and troubleshooting, it's worth installing vRealize Operations for Horizon, which comes as part of the VMware Horizon enterprise edition product, or considering a third-party user experience monitoring tool such as Liquidware Labs Stratusphere UX.

Teradici support tools for PCoIP

In addition to the VMware and other third-party solutions, Teradici (the inventor of the PCoIP protocol) also have a number of tools to assist with the tuning experience, including a network bandwidth calculator and PCoIP statistics viewer.

To access the tools, go to the following link: http://tinyurl.com/qacpzr4.

> You will need to have a Teradici support account to access these tools, which you can create for free.

In the next section, we are going to look at monitoring the end user experience to ensure that it is running at its optimum.

Monitoring the end user experience

Once you have tuned the desktop's performance, you should consider deploying an end user experience monitoring solution to ensure that the initial experience and performance is maintained, and that the solution is running at its best.

We have already mentioned vRealize Operations for Horizon, but this tool is better for monitoring the infrastructure components rather than the end user experience.

Fine-Tuning the End User Experience

A more focused end user experience monitoring tool would be something such as Liquidware Stratusphere UX, which goes deeper into what the end user is doing, such as application launch times and applications crashes, and gives you a complete breakdown of the login process. An example of one of the many Stratusphere dashboards is shown in the following screenshot:

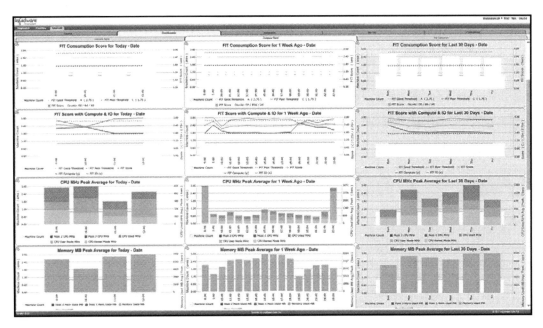

The other advantage of the Liquidware solution is that Stratusphere UX is based on the same solution that was used during the assessment phase. It therefore gives you the ability to compare your initial baseline assessment data (your starting point) with the production environment and easily demonstrate the improvements that are made as you migrate to a new environment.

For more information, visit `https://www.liquidware.com/products/stratusphere-ux`.

Summary

In this chapter, we have looked at how to start fine-tuning the performance of virtual desktop machines and the end user experience.

To do this, we have covered how to prepare AD with Horizon View-specific policies and administrative templates to define how the virtual desktop machines behave, as well as the overall end user experience.

We then went on to show each of the individual policy settings.

Finally, we looked at some of the many tools that are available to help with the tuning process, and how to monitor the user experience. Tools such as the PCoIP tuning tool and Liquidware Stratusphere and its Spotcheck feature were covered.

In the next chapter, we will look at how we can manage user profiles in a Horizon View environment using View Persona Management and VMware's **User Environment Management (UEM)**.

Section 3: Advanced Features, Troubleshooting, and Upgrading an Environment

In section 3, you will learn about the additional features of Horizon; published apps and desktops, and the just-in-time management platform. Then, we will cover troubleshooting and upgrading an existing environment.

The following chapters are included in this section:

Chapter 11, *Delivering Published Apps with Horizon 7*
Chapter 12, *Horizon Client Options*
Chapter 13, *Upgrading to a New Version of Horizon*
Chapter 14, *JMP and VMware Horizon 7 Deployment Considerations*
Chapter 15, *Troubleshooting*
Chapter 16, *What is New in Horizon 7*
Chapter 18, *Delivering Published Desktops with Horizon 7* (Online chapter)

11
Delivering Published Apps with Horizon 7

So far in this book, we have concentrated on the delivery of virtual desktop machines, but Horizon View also has the ability to deliver remote applications, or published applications, as they're more commonly known, as well as session-based desktops, all from the same platform. In this chapter, we are going to dive deeper into this feature, which is part of the Horizon Advanced Edition and above, and look at how Horizon View publishes an application directly into the Horizon View Client, without the need to launch a full virtual desktop machine.

A use case for this could be a call center worker who uses just a couple of different applications. It's far easier from a management perspective to just give them the applications they require rather than a full-blown virtual desktop. Another use case is the ability to launch applications using the View Client running on a device that wouldn't normally be able to run that application. For example, you could run the "real" version of Microsoft Word on your iPad using the Horizon View Client for iOS.

The infrastructure required for this is based on Microsoft **Remote Desktop Services (RDS)** running at the backend, with Horizon View acting as the broker to connect users with the applications or desktop sessions. As it's View-based, it uses the View protocols, such as PCoIP and Blast, as the delivery protocols, taking advantage of all the features the protocols have to offer, as we have discussed previously.

In this chapter, we will cover the following topics:

- Architectural overview
- RDSH sizing guidelines
- Installing and configuring View-hosted apps
- Installing the Horizon View Agent for RDSH
- Configuring published apps in the View Administrator
- Load-balancing published apps in Horizon View

Architectural overview

So, what does the architecture look like, and how does the hosted application feature work when compared to virtual desktop machine brokering? In terms of the architecture, delivering hosted applications is handled in pretty much the same way as virtual desktop machines are managed and brokered.

Horizon View acts as the broker, using the same Connection Server, but instead of brokering a virtual desktop machine that would be running on the ESXi host server, it is now brokering an application session that is running on a Microsoft Windows server, configured with the RDSH role and the applications installed on it.

The following diagram gives you a high-level outline of the architecture for delivering hosted applications:

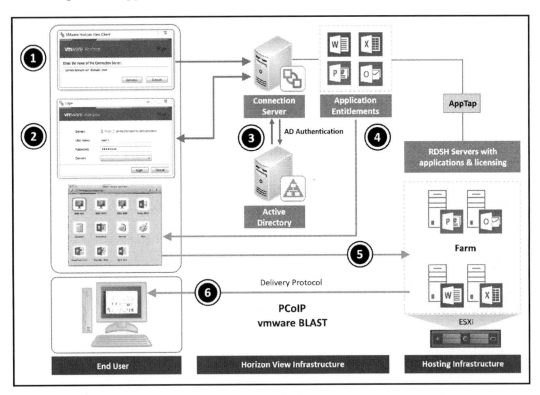

So, how does the hosted application feature work?

To begin with, as with connecting to a View delivered to the virtual desktop machine, you launch the View client and log in to the Connection Server. You enter the details of the View Connection Server you want to connect to (**1**), enter your **User name** and **Password** (**2**), and then authenticate against AD (**3**).

Once authenticated, the client sends a `<get-launch-items>` request to the Connection Server to request a list of all the entitled application sessions, applications, and desktops for that user. The response contains the following details:

- `<app-sessions>`, `<desktops>`, and `<applications>`
- Absolute paths to the icons

The client fetches any icons it doesn't have already cached via HTTPS using the paths that were provided by the Connection Server when it sent the response.

Access to icon **uniform resource identifiers** (**URIs**) needs to be authenticated. The Connection Server performs an entitlement check and only returns an icon if that user is entitled to at least one application that has an icon associated with it. For applications that don't have any icons, the client will provide a default icon.

A list of entitled desktop and application pools is then displayed to the end user in the View Client (**4**).

The end user then double-clicks on an application (or desktop) to launch it (**5**), the connection is made, and the application opens in a new window (**6**).

In the next section, we will take a deep dive into what happens during the connection process to connect the user to the application or desktop session they requested.

Application connection sequence

In this section, we are going to break down the connection sequence into three separate parts, showing the process flow of what happens when the user launches an application.

The process starts when the end user double-clicks to launch an application and is illustrated in the following diagram:

So, now we have a user that has made a request via the View Client to the Connection Server to launch an application.

The next phase of the connection process is for the Connection Server to talk to the Horizon Agent installed on the RDS host server.

The following diagram illustrates the next part of the process:

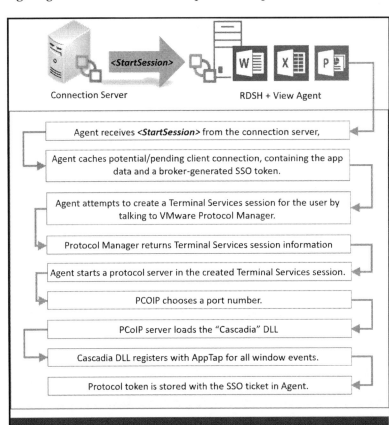

The next step in the connection process is to set up the secure connection to the **PCoIP Secure Gateway server (PSG)**.

A tunnel is set up by the View agent on the RDS server by talking to the PSG. The details of this connection are then forwarded, via the Connection Server, back to the client. This is pretty much the same way that this process works when connecting to a virtual desktop machine hosted on an ESXi host server.

This process is illustrated in the following diagram, along with the final part of the process, which is to log the end user in and then connect them to the application that they requested:

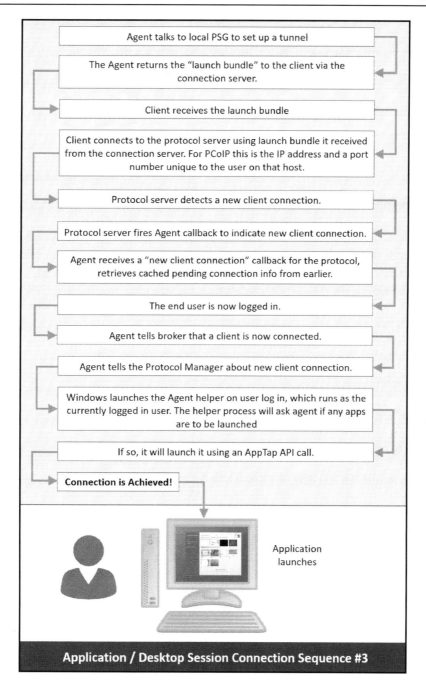

We have now covered a deep dive on how the process works for connecting the end user to their remote applications. In the next section, we are going to look at some of the specifics around the RDS roles in this environment, starting with sizing guidelines.

RDSH sizing guidelines

As with the sizing of View for virtual desktop machines, configuring the right specification for the RDSH servers is also key, and in a similar way in which we consider the desktop sizing, we are going to look at different user types.

The VMware recommendation for the user workloads and the memory requirements are shown in the following table:

	Memory	Use Case
User Workload Requirements	512 MB	Basic application user such as Microsoft Office applications and some web browsing
	768 MB	Running multiple Microsoft Office applications and light user of multi-media, and more intensive web browsing
	1 GB	Advanced application user running 3D-based applications and multi-media, and heavy web-browsing

For the total memory in each RDSH server, VMware recommends that a virtual machine configured as an RDSH server should be provisioned with 64 GB memory, and in terms of CPU requirements, the VMware recommendation is to create virtual servers for the RDSH roles and configure each one with four vCPUs. Make sure that you do not overcommit on the number of cores.

So, for example, if you had a virtual machine running as an RDSH server configured with 64 GB of memory, and had heavy users hosted on it, you would be able to host a maximum of 64 sessions on that server.

For the hardware configuration, let's say you had a physical ESXi host server, configured with a 2-socket CPU that had 12 cores, giving you a total of 24 cores.

This would allow a maximum of 6 RDSH servers as we are going to provision virtual machines for the RDSH role that each has 4 cores (24 cores/4 cores per server). That would mean that the physical server would also need to be configured with 384 GB of memory in total (64 GB x 6 RDSH host servers).

These figures are only guidelines and are based on some of the VMware-recommended best practices. It is always best to run an assessment on your environment to work out your optimum configuration.

In the next section, we are going to install and configure the View-hosted applications feature.

Installing and configuring View-hosted apps

We are now going to start the installation process, starting with configuring the server that is going to be used for hosting the remote applications, by adding the RDSH role to it. In the example lab, there is a Windows Server 2016 server ready built, called **RDSH-Apps**, to perform this role.

The installation and configuration process is pretty straightforward and can be summarized with the following schematic diagram:

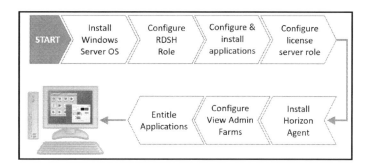

In the next sections, we are going to walk through this process in more detail, starting with configuring the RDSH role.

Configuring the RDS server role

The first thing that we are going to do is to configure the RDSH server role, and then configure this server to deliver the remote applications. In the example lab, the server we are going to configure is called **RDSH-Apps**. To configure the RDSH role, perform the following steps:

1. Open a console to the server, and then from the **Server Manager** and the **Dashboard** screen, click on **Add roles and features** (1), as shown in the following screenshot:

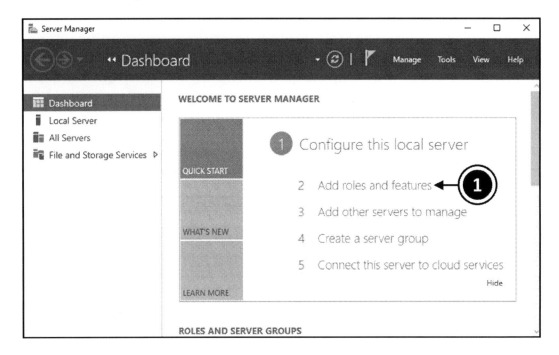

2. The first screen you will see is the **Before You Begin** screen, as shown in the following screenshot:

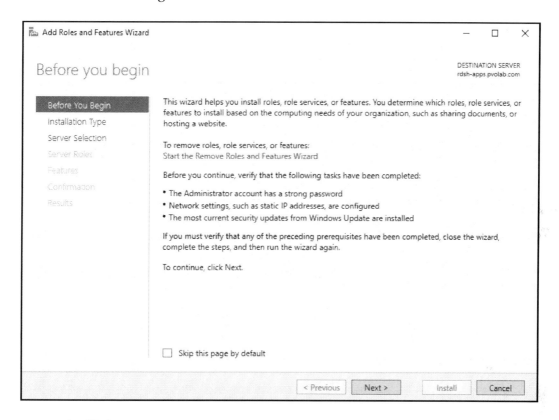

3. Click **Next >** to continue.

4. You will now see the **Select installation type** screen, as shown in the following screenshot:

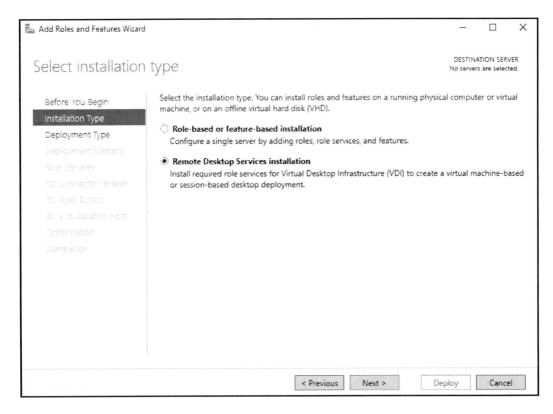

5. Click the radio button for **Remote Desktop Services installation**, and then click **Next >** to continue.

Chapter 11

6. You will now see the **Select deployment type** screen, as shown in the following screenshot:

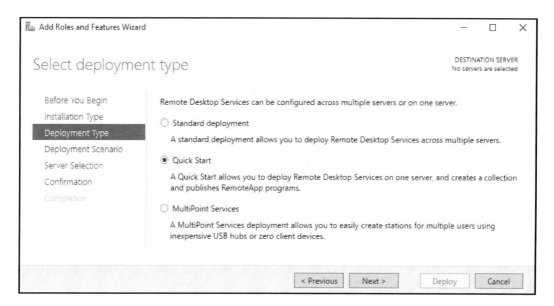

7. Click the radio button for **Quick Start**, and then click **Next >** to continue.
8. You will now see the **Select deployment scenario** screen, as shown in the following screenshot:

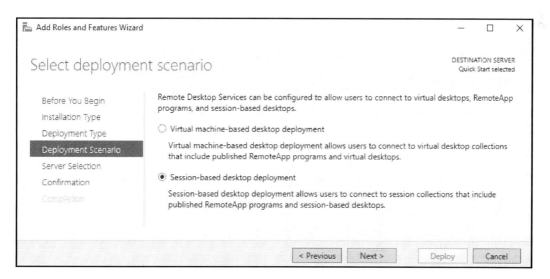

[597]

9. Click the radio button for **Session-based desktop deployment**, and then click **Next >** to continue.
10. You will now see the **Select a server** screen, as shown in the following screenshot:

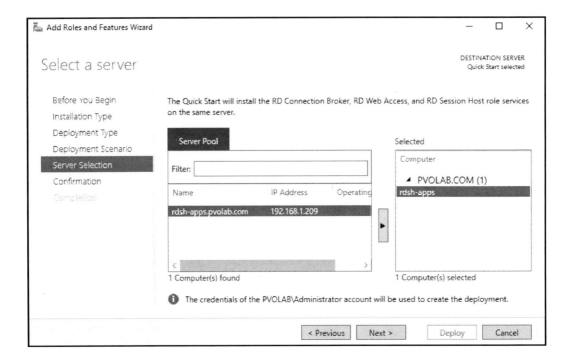

11. From the **Server Pool** box, click and highlight the server you want to install the RDSH role onto and click the arrow to add it to the **Selected** box. In the example lab, this is the server called `rdsh-apps.pvolab.com`.
12. Click **Next >** to continue.

Chapter 11

13. You will now see the **Confirm selections** screen, as shown in the following screenshot:

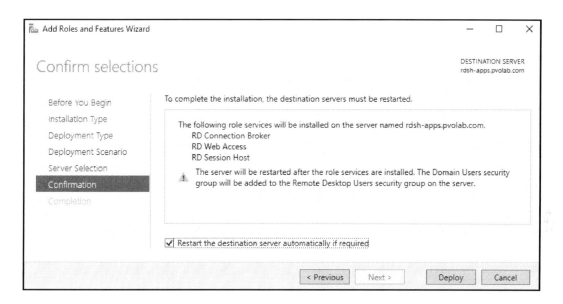

14. Check the services that are going to be installed, and then check the box to **Restart the destination server automatically if required**.
15. Click **Deploy** to start the installation.

16. You will now see the progress of the installation, as shown in the following screenshot:

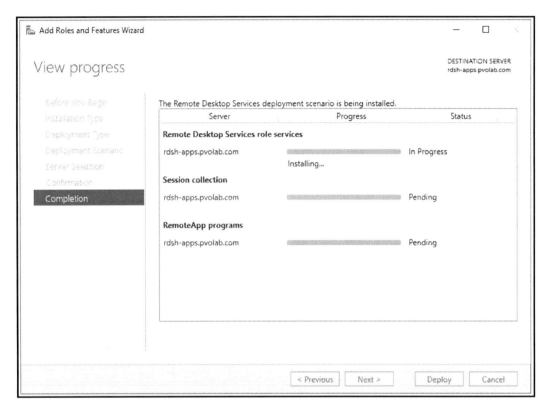

17. During the installation, the server will reboot. After rebooting, log back in and launch the Server Manager again to monitor the rest of the installation process.
18. Once the installation has completed, from the **Server Manager Dashboard**, you will now see that the **Remote Desktop Services** role has been added, as shown in the following screenshot:

Chapter 11

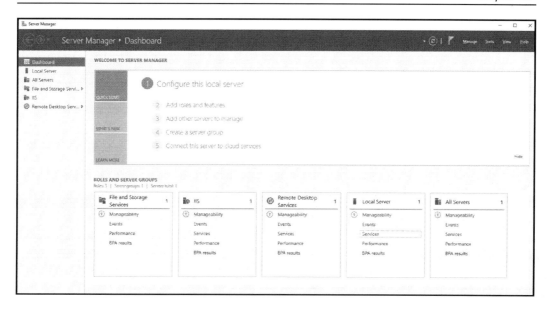

You have now successfully installed the RDS role.

 You will need to add and configure the Remote Desktop Licensing role on this server.

In the next section, we will configure some example applications that will be made available as remote applications.

Testing with the standard remote applications

The first applications we are going to configure for session-based remote access are those that are integrated into the Windows operating system and configured by default when you create the RDSH server role. These include applications such as Calculator and Notepad.

[601]

Delivering Published Apps with Horizon 7

We are going to test that these applications work as remote applications by first checking they have been configured, and then whether or not we can access them remotely, before configuring the Horizon View components and any additional applications:

1. From the **Server Manager Dashboard** screen, click on **Remote Desktop Services** (1), as shown in the following screenshot:

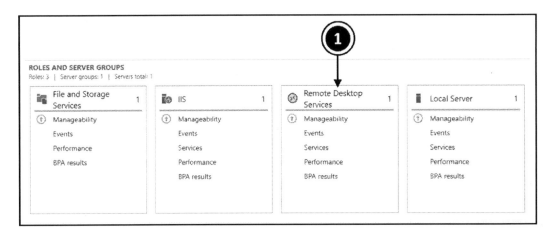

2. You will then see the list of servers that are configured with the RDSH role, as shown in the following screenshot:

3. Click to highlight the RDSH_APPS server, and then click on **QuickSessionCollection** (3).

Chapter 11

4. You will now see the **QuickSessionCollection** and **REMOTEAPP PROGRAMS** (4) boxes, as shown in the following screenshot:

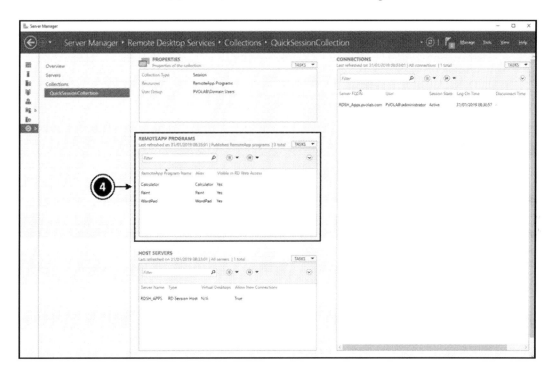

This will show WordPad, Paint, and Calculator listed as available remote applications.

So, now that the standard applications are available as remote sessions for end users, we are going to try connecting using the RD Web Access web portal to test that everything is working before continuing with the configuration. To do this, perform the following steps:

1. Open a browser from either your desktop or the server itself. It's best to test from a remote desktop rather than the server itself.
2. In the browser, type in the URL of the RDSH server. In the example lab, this address is `https://rdsh-apps.pvolab.com/rdweb`.

Delivering Published Apps with Horizon 7

3. You will then see the login screen, as shown in the following screenshot:

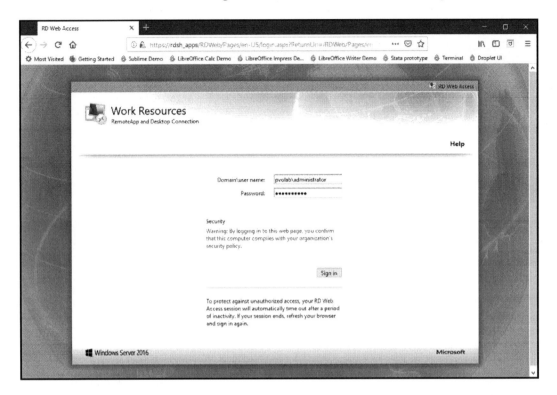

4. In the **Domain\user name** box, enter a username in the format of **Domain\user name**. So, for this example, we are logging in as the administrator using the format `pvolab\administrator`. Then enter the password.
5. Now click the **Sign in** button. You will now see the following **Work Resources** web page, which displays the available applications:

Chapter 11

To test that an application launches, double-click on it. In this example, we will launch the calculator. The calculator should then successfully launch, as shown in the following screenshot:

Now that everything is working and applications can be published and launched, in the next section, we are going to add some more applications.

Installing additional applications

In this section, we are going to install some additional application for remote access, starting with Microsoft Office 2016.

Installing applications is almost identical to installing applications on any other Windows operating system; however, there are a few subtle differences given that this is a remote session host server. We are going to quickly run through the process, as described in the following steps:

1. As we are going to install Microsoft Office 2016, the first thing to do is mount the ISO image containing the installer, as shown in the following screenshot:

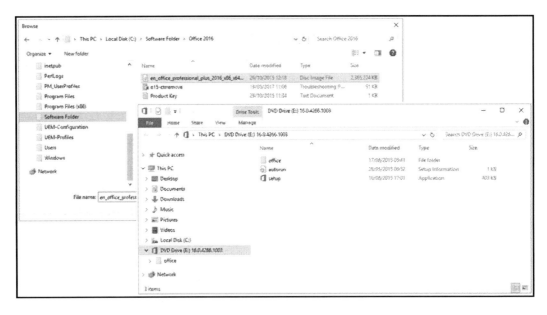

We can now move on to the actual installation process.

2. Open a console to the RDSH server on which you want to install the applications and open the **Control Panel,** as shown in the following screenshot:

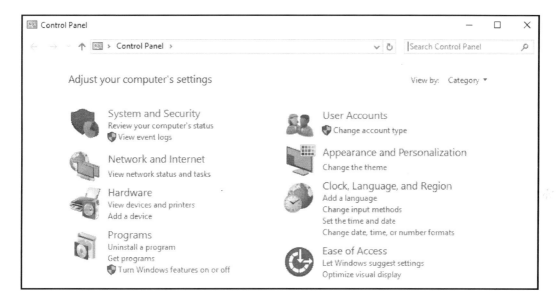

3. Click on **Programs**. You will now see the **Programs** dialog box, as shown in the following screenshot:

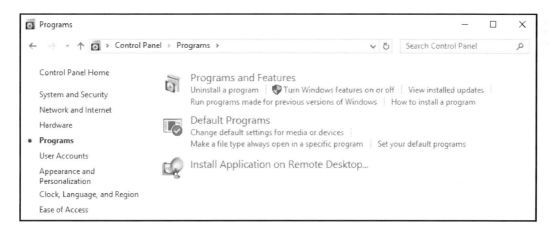

4. Click on **Install Application on Remote Desktop....**

5. You will now see the **Install Program From Floppy Disk or CD-ROM** dialog box, as shown in the following screenshot:

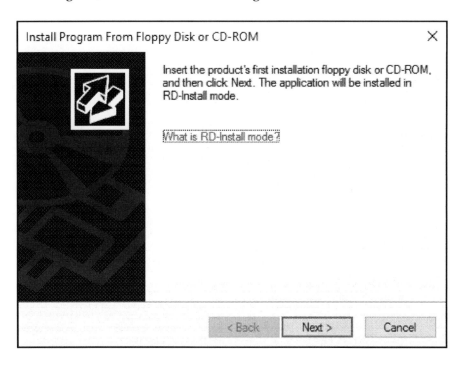

Before we continue, we are going to talk about how to install apps on an RDSH server. In this dialog box, it highlights something called the **RD-Install mode**; so, what does that mean?

To install an application on an RDSH host server, it needs to be switched into a special install mode called **RD-Install** to make sure that the applications are able to run in a multi-user environment.

Once you have installed the applications on the RDSH server, the server will then need to be switched back into what is called the execution mode, or **RD-Execute**, so that users can remotely connect to the server and the applications running on it.

This can also be done at the command line, using the following commands:

```
change user /install
change user /execute
```

You can check the current install mode of your RDSH server using the following command:

```
change user /query
```

The easiest way to install applications is by using the **Programs** option from the **Control Panel**, which is how we are going to do it in this example. This option takes you through the installation process by automatically switching the server to the RD-Install mode, installing the program, and switching the server back to the RD-Execute mode once finished. Let's continue with the installation:

1. Click **Next >** to start the installation.
2. You will now see that the **Run Installation Program** dialog box is displayed, as shown in the following screenshot:

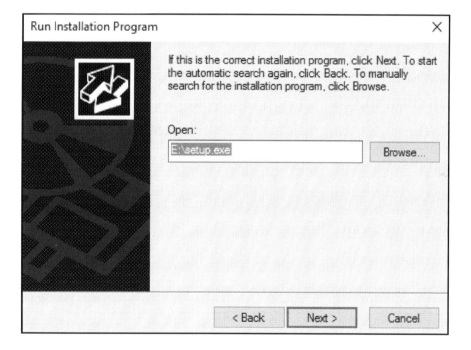

3. Click the **Browse...** button and then navigate to the installer for the app you want to install. In the example lab, this is the `setup.exe` file for Microsoft Office 2016 from the ISO image we mounted at the beginning of this section.
4. Now click **Next >** to continue.

5. The first thing you will see is the **Finish Admin Install** dialog box, as shown in the following screenshot:

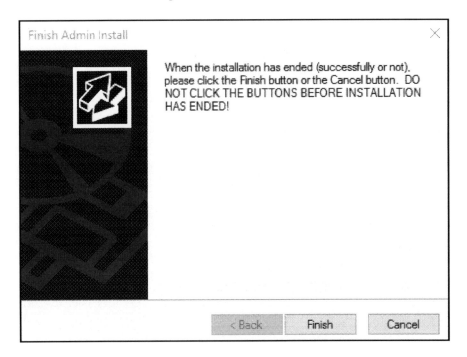

 Ignore this dialog box for now, and make sure that you **DO NOT** click the **Finish** button at this point. You need to complete the application installation first.

6. The installation of Office 2016 will now run, and you should install Office in exactly the same way as you would normally.
7. Once the installation is complete, return to the **Finish Admin Install** box and click on the **Finish** button.

Now Microsoft Office 2016 has been installed on the RDSH server, you need to go back and configure which of the individual Office suite applications are going to be made available to the users as remote applications. To do this, perform the following steps:

1. From the **Server Manager** dashboard screen, click on **Remote Desktop Services**.
2. Highlight the RDSH server you want to configure, and then click on **QuickSessionCollection** (1), as shown in the following screenshot:

- Scroll down to the **REMOTEAPP PROGRAMS** dialog box and then click the down arrow on the **TASKS** button in the top right of the screen, and then click **Publish RemoteApp Programs** (4).

Delivering Published Apps with Horizon 7

- You will now see the **Select RemoteApp programs** configuration screen, as shown in the following screenshot:

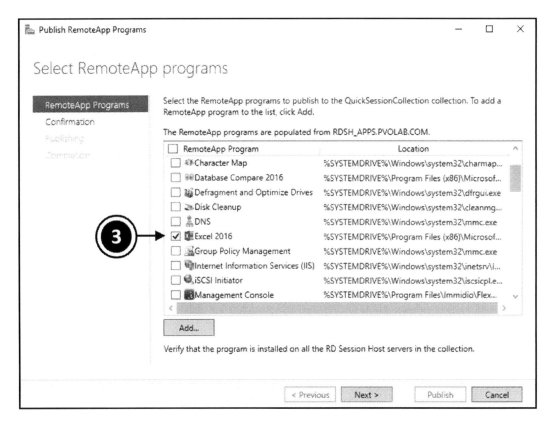

3. From here, you can select which applications you want to publish and make available remotely to your end users.
4. Check the boxes next to the applications you want to add (3). In the example lab, we are going to check the boxes for the following applications:
    - **Excel 2016**
    - **OneNote 2016**
    - **Outlook 2016**
    - **PowerPoint 2016**
    - **Publisher 2016**
    - **Word 2016**
5. From here, you can select which applications you want to publish and make available remotely to your end users.

6. Once you have selected all the applications you want to publish, click the **Next >** button.
7. You will now see the **Confirmation** box of the applications you selected, as shown in the following screenshot:

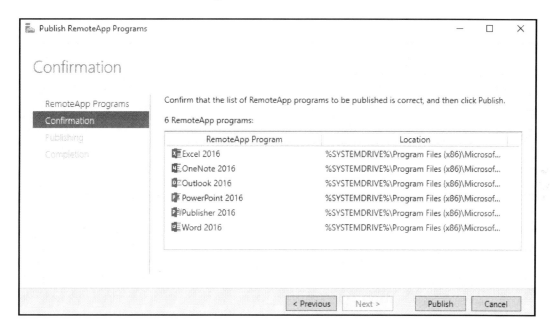

8. Now click the **Publish** button.
9. You will then see a progress bar, detailing the progress of the applications being published, as shown in the following screenshot:

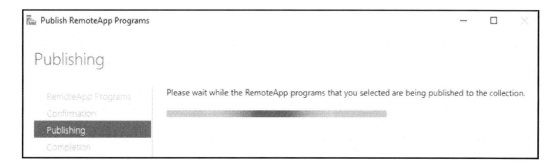

10. Once completed, you will now see the **Completion** screen, as shown in the following screenshot, detailing the applications that were successfully published:

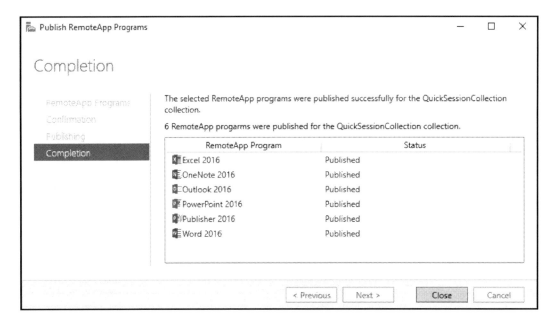

11. Click the **Close** button to complete the publishing process.

As previously, we are going to test that the applications are available from the web access portal. Open a browser and go to the following address: `https://rdsh-apps.pvolab.com/rdweb`.

Log in to the portal using the administrator account.

You will see the following screenshot from the RD web access portal, showing the newly published applications for Office 2016:

Chapter 11

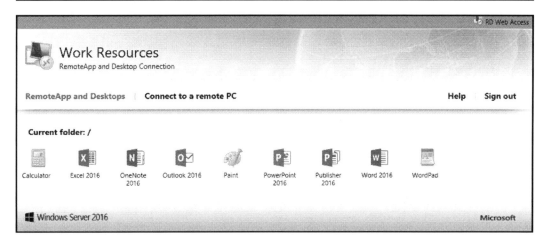

As you can see, the newly published Office applications are available to the end users. Double-click on one of them to test that it launches and, once happy it's working, then click on **Sign out** and close the web page.

In the next section, we are going to install the Horizon Agent on the RDSH server.

Installing the Horizon Agent for RDSH

In the next part of the process, we are going to install the Horizon View Agent onto the RDSH server. The agent is exactly the same agent as the one that you would install on virtual desktop machines and registers the RDSH with the Horizon Connection Server. To install the agent, perform the following steps:

1. Open a remote console to the RDSH server running the applications, navigate to the shared software folder, and then find the agent installer, as shown in the following screenshot:

Name	Date modified	Type	Size
View ADM Tempates	05/01/2019 10:03	File folder	
VMware OS Optimization Tool	07/12/2018 08:39	File folder	
VMware-Horizon-Agent-x86_64-7.6.0-9539447	02/11/2018 13:23	Application	225,043 KB
VMware-Horizon-Client-4.10.0-11021086	04/01/2019 16:51	Application	195,669 KB
VMware-Horizon-Connection-Server-x86_64-7.6.0-9823717	02/11/2018 13:26	Application	267,730 KB
VMware-Horizon-Extras-Bundle-4.9.0-9539668	04/12/2018 13:21	Compressed (zipp...	5,347 KB
VMware-Horizon-Persona-Management-x86_64-7.6.0-9539447	02/11/2018 13:25	Application	39,685 KB
VMware-Jmp-Installer-7.6.0-9823717	02/11/2018 13:28	Application	115,462 KB
VMware-viewcomposer-7.6.0-9491669	02/11/2018 13:27	Application	47,011 KB

2. Double-click to launch `VMware-Horizon-Agent-x86_64-7.6.0-9539447`. The seven-digit number at the end of the filename refers to the build version, and so you may have a different number, depending on the build version you are using.

3. You will now see the **Welcome to the Installation Wizard for VMware Horizon View Agent** dialog box, as shown in the following screenshot:

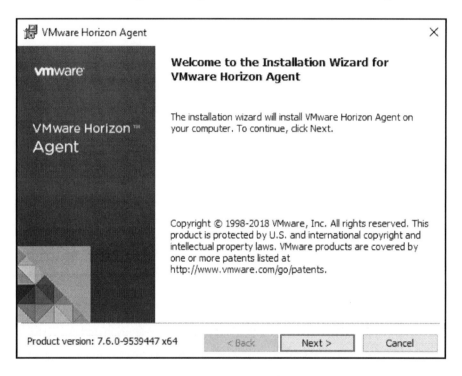

4. Click the **Next >** button to start the installation.

5. You will now see the **License Agreement** dialog box, as shown in the following screenshot:

6. Click the radio button for **I accept the terms in the license agreement**, and then click the **Next >** button to continue.

7. You will now see the **Network protocol configuration** screen, as shown in the following screenshot:

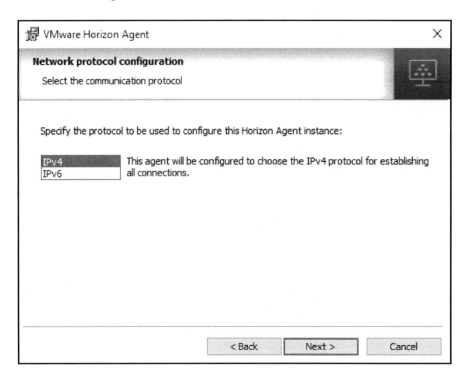

8. Click on **IPv4** and then click on the **Next >** button to continue the installation.

9. You will now see the **Custom Setup** screen, as shown in the following screenshot:

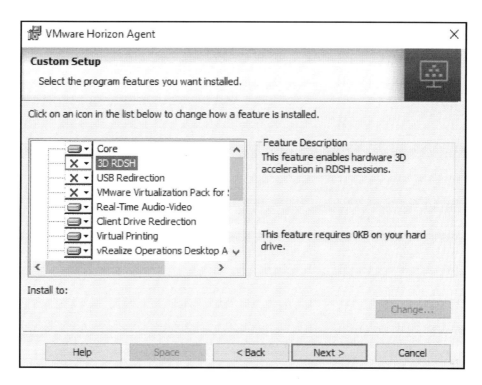

In the example lab, we are going to accept the default options; however, you can choose to install the 3D RDSH, USB Redirection, View Composer, and Flash Redirection options, should you want to.

As you can see, there are a number of features that can be installed as part of the View Agent installation. These are listed here:

- **Core**: Installs the core features required for RDSH
- **3D RDSH**: Enables 3D acceleration in RDSH sessions
- **USB Redirection**: Redirects USB devices from the client to the RDSH session
- **VMware Horizon View Composer Agent**: Allows RDS host servers to be built from a single parent image using linked clone technology to easily deploy the RDS server farm

- **Client Redirection**: Allows clients to share local drives with the RDS sessions (not supported when using IPv6)
- **Virtual Printing**: Allows printing from RDS sessions
- **vRealize Operations Desktop Agent**: Allows the management agent to be deployed for monitoring RDS sessions with vRealize
- **Flash Redirection**: Enables the Flash redirection feature with RDS sessions (note that this is currently a tech preview in this version of Horizon View)

10. Click the **Next >** button to continue the installation.
11. You will now see the **Register with Horizon 7 Connection Server** configuration screen, where we will configure the Horizon Agent to talk to the Connection Server. This allows the Connection Server to read the published applications list from the RemoteApp catalog and allows you to create application pools within View.
12. In the **hostname or IP address** box, enter the name of the Connection Server. In the example, this is `hzn7-cs1.pvolab.com`.
13. In the **Authentication** section, click the radio button for **Specify administrator credentials** and then in the **Username** box, enter the user account you want to use to connect to the Connection Server. In the example lab, this is **pvolab\administrator**.

Make sure you use the D**omain\user** format to enter the username, and also that the account has the correct privileges to access the Connection Server. You would typically use a service account for this.

14. In the **Password** box, type in the password for the account, as shown in the following screenshot:

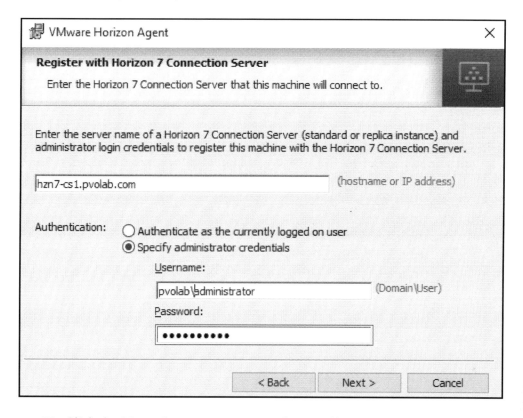

15. Click the **Next >** button to continue the installation.
16. You will now see the **Ready to Install the Program** screen. Click the **Install** button to start the installation process.
17. Once successfully installed, you will see the **Installer Complete** screen.
18. Click **Finish** to quit the installation.
19. You will then be prompted to reboot the server. Click **Yes** to reboot.

 One of the most common reasons that the installation of the View agent fails is down to the configuration of the RDSH server. More often than not, there are no sound drivers loaded on the Windows Server running the RDSH role. If this is the case, then the installation of the agent will fail and automatically roll back. If that happens, it is worth checking this first.

Delivering Published Apps with Horizon 7

We have now completed the first part of the Horizon View configuration. In the next step of the process, we will turn our attention to the View Administrator and configure the application pools.

Configuring published apps in the View Administrator

The next stage in the installation and configuration process is performed using the View Administrator console and, like a standard View setup, involves creating pools and entitlements. However, rather than creating pools for virtual desktop machines, this time we are going to configure application pools.

Before we do any of that, the first thing we need to do is to set up a farm that contains the newly built RDSH server. To do this, perform the following steps:

1. Open a browser and connect to the View Administrator. In our example lab, the address for the View Administrator is `https://hzn7-cs1.pvolab.com/admin/`.
2. Log in to the View Administrator using the administrator account and password.
3. You will now see the View Administrator **Dashboard**, as shown in the following screenshot:

4. Expand the arrow for **Resources** from the **Inventory** pane on the left, and then click on **Farms** (1).
5. Now click the **Add...** button (2).
6. You will now see the **Add Farm** configuration screen, as shown in the following screenshot:

7. In the **Type** section, click the radio button for **Manual Farm**.
8. Click the **Next >** button to continue.

Delivering Published Apps with Horizon 7

9. You will now see the **Identification and Settings** configuration screen, as shown in the following screenshot:

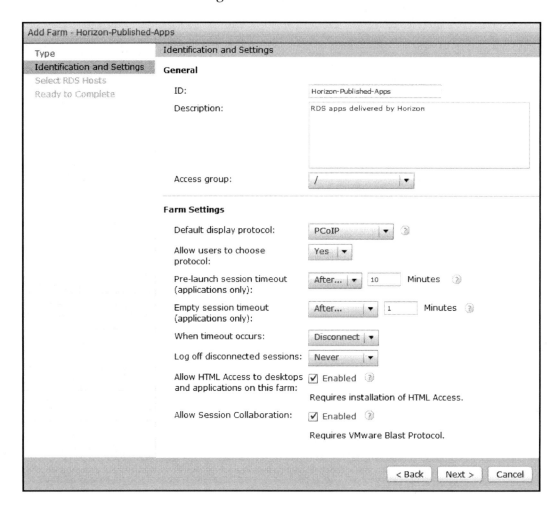

You need to fill the details, as shown here:

1. In the **ID** box, enter an ID for the farm that will be used by View to identify it. In the example lab, this is called `Horizon-Published-Apps`.

You cannot use spaces for the ID, only letters (upper and lowercase), numbers (0-9), and – (minus) or _ (underscore) characters.

2. In the **Description** box, enter an optional description for the farm and then, from the **Access Group** dropdown, select an access group if you have one.
3. Next, under **Farm Settings**, set the **Default display protocol** to PCoIP and from the **Allow users to choose protocol** dropdown, select **Yes**.
4. In the **Pre-launch session timeout**, leave this as the default setting of `10` minutes. Pre-launch allows apps to load ahead of a user clicking to launch it. This option configures a timeout.
5. In the **Empty session timeout,** enter a time after which the session should timeout when not being used, and then in the **When timeout occurs** box, from the drop-down menu, select what happens at timeout. In the example lab, this is set to disconnect the user from the session.
6. The next option is whether or not to **Log off disconnected sessions**. This option will log off any disconnected sessions. In the example lab, this is set to **Never** happen.
7. Check the **Enabled** box to allow **HTML access to desktops and applications on this farm**.
8. Finally, check the box for **Allow Session Collaboration**. This only works when you connect using the Blast protocol.
9. Once you have completed the configuration options on this screen, click the **Next >** button to continue.

10. You will now see the **Select RDS Hosts** configuration screen from where you select which hosts are going to participate in this farm, as shown in the following screenshot:

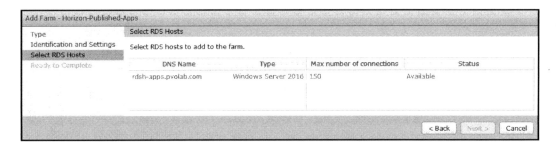

10. Click and select the `rdsh-apps.pvolab.com` server entry and then click the **Next >** button.
11. You will now see the **Ready to Complete** screen, as shown in the following screenshot:

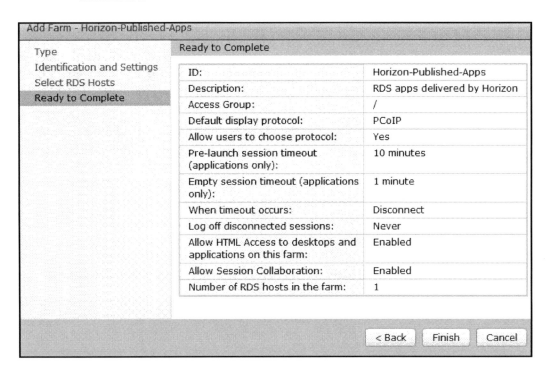

12. Check that the settings you have entered are correct, and then click the **Finish** button.

You have now successfully created a new farm configuration for the hosted applications, as shown in the following screenshot:

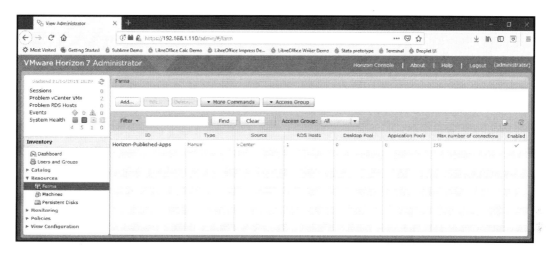

You will also see in the **RDS Farms** section in the **System Health** box on the View Administrator Dashboard that the farm name, **Horizon-Published-Apps**, and the server name, rdsh-apps.pvolab.com, are now listed, along with a green box to show they are working correctly:

In the next section, we are going to create an application pool.

Creating an application pool for published apps

In this section, we are going to create an application pool. This allows you to create a pool that contains a number of different applications. You may want to create application pools to reflect different departments, for example. To configure an application pool, perform the following steps:

1. From the View Administrator, expand the arrow for **Catalog** from the **Inventory** pane on the left, and then click on **Application Pools** (1), as shown in the following screenshot:

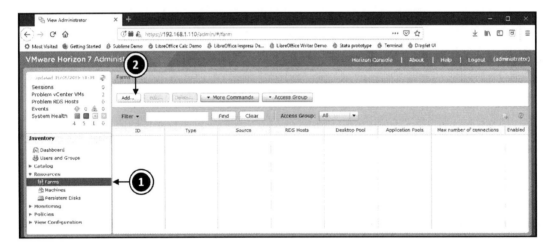

2. Now click on the **Add...** button (2).

3. You will now see the **Add Application Pools** configuration screen, as shown in the following screenshot:

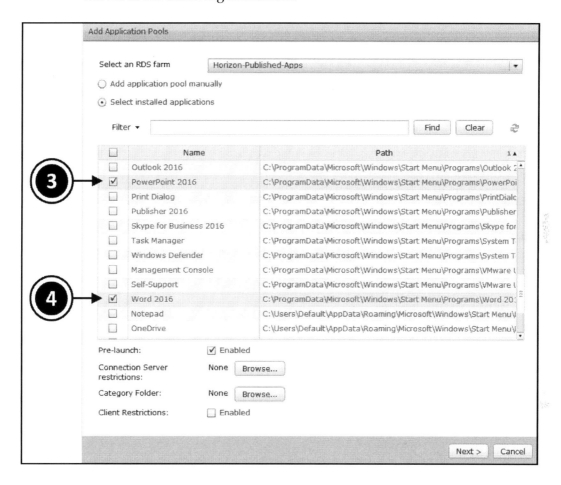

4. From the **Select an RDS farm** drop-down menu, select the farm that we created previously for our published applications. In the example lab, select the farm called **Horizon-Published-Apps** from the menu.
5. Next, click the radio button for **Select installed applications**. This will automatically list all the applications that are installed on that particular RDSH server. There is also the option to add an application pool manually.

6. From the list of applications, check the box for the applications you want to add to the application pool. In the example, we have selected **PowerPoint 2016 (3)** and **Word 2016 (4)**, as well as Calculator, Paint, Excel 2016, Publisher 2016, and Outlook 2016.
7. You then have the option to check the **Pre-Launch** box. That means the applications in the pool are launched and ready when the end users click on them to speed up launch times.
8. The next option is for **Connection Server restrictions**, which allows you to configure tags for which Connection Servers you can connect with.
9. Finally, you can configure the **Category Folder,** which allows you to add a shortcut on the end user's device.
10. When you have selected all the required applications, click the **Next >** button to continue.
11. You will now see the **Edit ID and Display Name** screen. Here, you can choose to edit the ID and the display name for the applications if you want to. This is shown in the following screenshot:

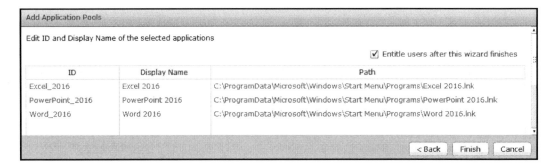

12. Also, check the **Entitle users after this wizard finishes** box to automatically launch the user entitlement configuration, which we will complete in the next section.
13. Click the **Finish** button to complete the configuration. You will then see that the application pool has been created.

Chapter 11

Now that you have your application pool all set up and ready to go, the next step is to entitle end users to the pool and allow them to launch applications.

Entitling users to application pools

In the previous section, we checked the **Entitle users after this wizard finished** box, which means that you will now see the **Add Entitlements** configuration screen, as shown in the following screenshot:

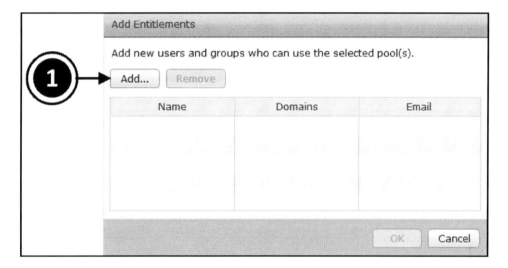

Now perform the following steps to add entitlements:

1. Click the **Add...** button (1).
2. You will now see the **Find User or Group** configuration screen, as shown in the following screenshot:

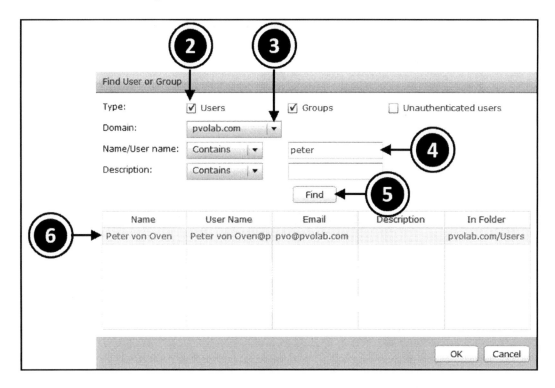

3. In the **Type** section, ensure that the **Users** box (2) is ticked.
4. From the **Domain** drop-down menu (3), select the domain that contains the user you want to entitle. In the example lab, this is the `pvolab.com` domain.
5. In the **Name/User name** box (4), enter the details of the user you want to entitle. In the example lab, we are going to entitle the user called `Peter von Oven`, so type the first part of the username, in this case, `peter`, into the box and then click the **Find** button (5) to search for the user in the domain.

6. Once found, the user and their details will be displayed in the table. Select the user by clicking on the entry in the table to highlight and select the user.
7. Click **OK** to continue.
8. You will now return to the **Application Pools** screen, detailing the applications published, as shown in the following screenshot:

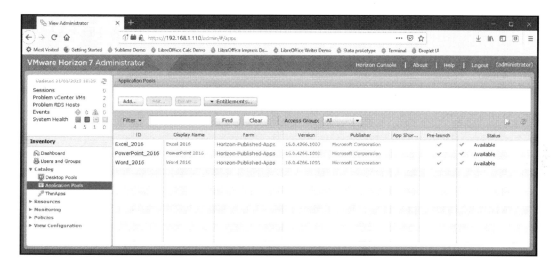

As a final check, we are going to launch the Horizon Client, log in as the entitled user, and then launch one of the published applications using the Horizon Client, to test that everything works.

 Make sure you are using the latest version of the Horizon Client, version 3.0 and above. Older versions will still work with VDI desktops, but will not show the published applications.

To test the functionality, complete the following steps:

1. Launch the VMware Horizon Client and make sure that you have added the address of the Connection Server. We will cover the Horizon View Client in `Chapter 12`, *Horizon Client Options*.

2. In the example lab, we are connecting to the `hzn7-cs1.pvolab.com` Connection Server, as shown in the following screenshot:

3. Double-click on the `hzn7-cs1.pvolab.com` icon in the VMware Horizon Client.
4. You will then see the **Login** box, as shown in the following screenshot:

5. In the **User name** box, enter the username for the user that is entitled to the application pool. In the example lab, the **User name** for the user `Peter von Oven` is `pvo`.
6. In the **Password** box, enter the password for the username.
7. In the **Domain** box, ensure the correct domain is selected from the drop-down menu. In the example lab, this is the **PVOLAB** domain.
8. Now click the **Login** box.
9. Once authenticated, the Horizon Client will connect to the application pool and display the available applications, as shown in the following screenshot:

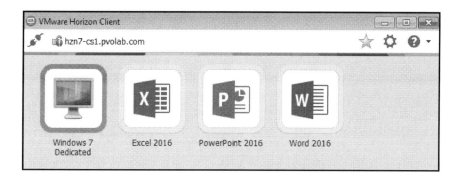

10. Double-click on any of the applications to ensure that they launch correctly.

You have now successfully installed, configured, and delivered a Vieww-hosted applications environment. In this example, we have deployed a single RDSH server to host remote applications; however, in a production environment, you are more likely to have multiple servers in a farm.

In the final section of this chapter, we are going to look how you load-balance the session connections across multiple host servers in a farm.

Load-balancing published apps in Horizon View

The next thing we are going to cover is how the Connection Broker decides which of the RDS host servers in the farm that is running the requested application is actually going to deliver the application. There are two options for configuring load balancing.

For the first option, there is no real complicated science behind the load balancing from a Horizon View perspective. It is purely based on how many sessions are available on any given RDSH server. So, that means when a user logs in and launches a published application, the application is delivered from the server that has the highest amount of free sessions available; that is, the one that is least busy.

This is illustrated in the following diagram:

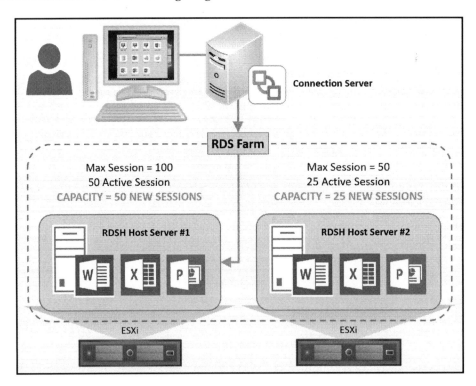

This first option works fine, but how does it know what each session is consuming in terms of resources? A particular host may well have enough capacity for additional sessions based on the number of sessions it has free, but what if the sessions it's already hosting are consuming vast amounts of resources?

This is where the second option comes in, as it uses more in-depth information to place sessions, which is based on measuring the CPU and memory utilization of each host rather than the number of free sessions.

To enable this load-balancing method, there are a number of manual steps you need to complete, as we will now describe.

First of all, this method is based on executing scripts, and therefore you need to ensure that those scripts are stored on each RDS host server in the farm. You can create your own scripts; however, there are a couple of example scripts that ship as part of the View Agent installation. You will find them in the following folder once the View Agent has been installed (View Agent installation was covered earlier on in this chapter):

```
C:\Program Files\VMware\VMware View\Agent\scripts
```

You will then see the two example scripts, as shown in the following screenshot:

Delivering Published Apps with Horizon 7

As the names suggest, one script monitors CPU utilization and the other monitors memory utilization. Each script monitors its respective component and returns the following values to make the decision on placing sessions:

- 0: For utilization > 90%
- 1: For utilization > 75%
- 2: For utilization > 25%
- 3: For utilization > 25%

Let's now configure the CPU script for use in the example lab by completing the following tasks. The first of these is to enable the View Script Host service. To do this, perform the following the steps:

1. Open a console to the RDSH host server, RDSH-Apps, and from the desktop of the server, launch a RUN command.
2. In the **Open** box, type services.msc and click **OK** to launch the **Services** management screen. You will now see the **Services** screen, as shown in the following screenshot:

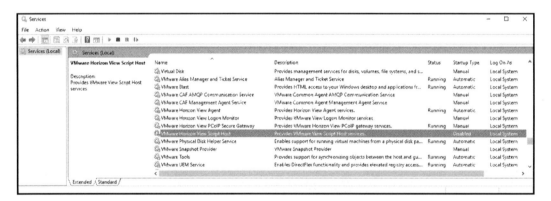

3. Scroll down until you find the entry for **VMware Horizon View Script Host**. Click on it to highlight it, and then right-click.
4. From the contextual menu that is now displayed, click **Properties**.

Chapter 11

5. You will now see the **VMware Horizon View Script Host Properties** screen, as shown in the following screenshot:

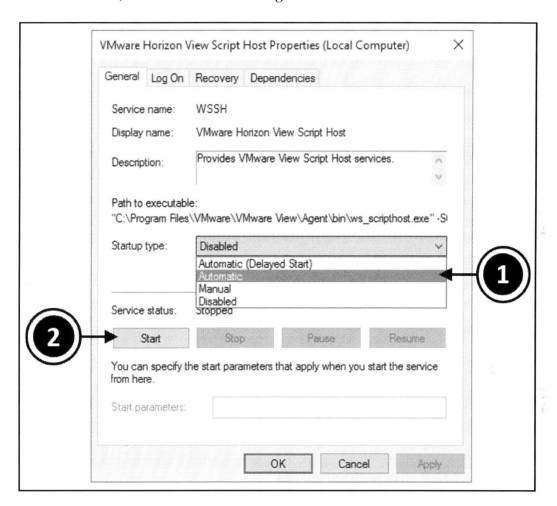

Delivering Published Apps with Horizon 7

6. In the **Startup type** box, from the drop-down menu (**1**), select the option for **Automatic,** so that this service starts when the server boots.
7. Next, click the **Apply** button.
8. Finally, click the **Start** button (**2**) to start the service. You should now see that the service is running, as shown in the following screenshot:

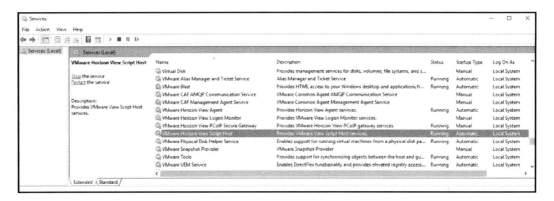

Once completed, close the **Services** management screen. The next step is to add the script details to the registry of the server. To do this, perform the following steps:

1. Open a console to the RDSH host server, RDSH-Apps, and from the desktop of the server, launch a RUN command.
2. In the **Open** box, type regedit and click **OK** to launch the registry editor.
3. Once the registry editor has launched, navigate to the following path:

```
Computer\HKEY_LOCAL_MACHINE\SOFTWARE\VMware, Inc.\VMware VDM\ScriptEvents\RdshLoad
```

Chapter 11

4. You will now see the following screen:

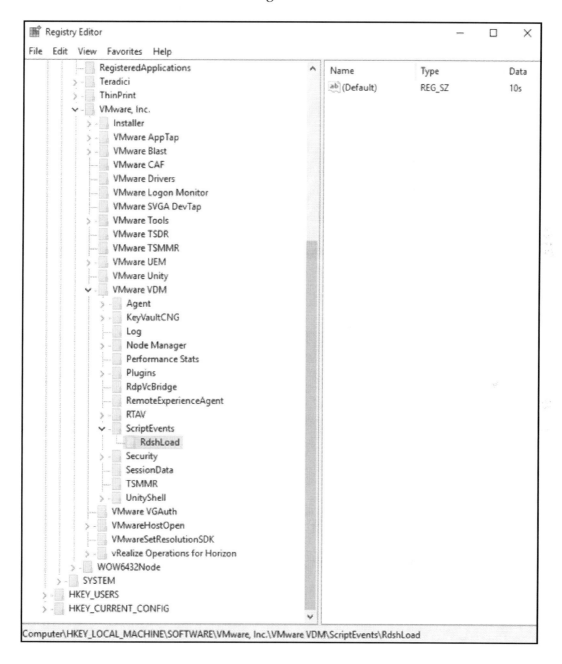

5. Now right-click in the right-hand side pane and, from the contextual menu displayed, click on **New** (3), and then select the option for **String Value** (4), as shown in the following screenshot:

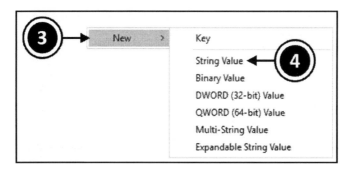

6. You will now be able to enter a new string value. In the example lab, this is called cpuutilisation (5) to reflect the script that will be run, as shown in the following screenshot:

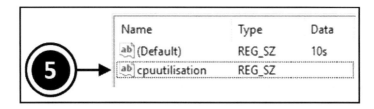

7. Next, you need to edit the newly created string value and enter a value.

8. To do this, highlight the cpuutilisation entry (6), right-click and from the contextual menu, and click the option for **Modify…** (7), as shown in the following screenshot:

Chapter 11

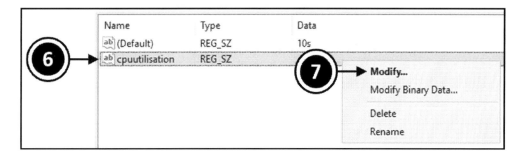

9. You will now see the **Edit String** box, as shown in the following screenshot:

10. In the **Value data,** box enter the path to the script. In the example lab, this path is `C:\Program Files\VMware\VMware View\Agent\scripts\cpuutilisation.vbs`.
11. Click **OK**.
12. You will now see that the script has been added, as shown in the following screenshot:

13. Exit the registry editor.

As you have changed the properties of the VMware Horizon Agent, you will need to restart this service for the changes to be applied. To do this, perform the following steps:

1. Launch a RUN command.
2. In the **Open** box, type service.msc and click **OK** to launch the **Services** management screen, as shown in the following screenshot:

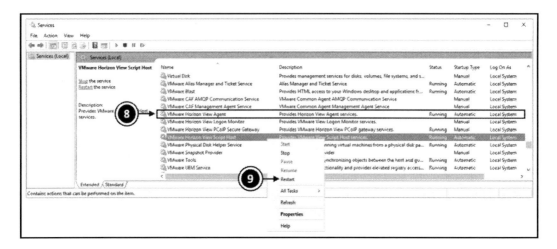

3. Scroll down until you find the entry for **VMware Horizon View Agent** (8).
4. Click on it to select it, right-click, and, from the contextual menu, select the **Restart** option (9) to restart the service.
5. Once the service has restarted, you can close the **Services** management screen.

You have now completed the configuration steps for load balancing and this will now be calculated based on CPU utilization. You can check that this is working by performing the following:

1. From the View Administrator Dashboard, navigate to the **System Health** box.
2. Then expand the options for **RDS Farms** and the farm for **Horizon-Published-Apps**. Now click on the RDSH-Apps.pvolab.com server. You will see the following screen:

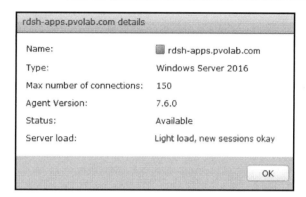

You will see that at the bottom of the box, there is a **Server load** option now shown. This is being measured from the script, and as you can see, currently, the CPU load is light and new sessions are able to be resourced by this particular server.

Click **OK** to close the box. You have now successfully configured the optional load-balancing feature.

Summary

In this chapter, we have discussed how to deliver remote/published applications with the Horizon published applications feature. We started off by looking at the architecture and took a deep dive into how it works, before walking through the installation and configuration process of both the Microsoft RDSH components and the Horizon View components needed to make it work.

We then configured an RDS farm and an application pool, and then entitled a test user to the pool. Finally, to check that everything was working, we logged in as the user and tested the environment by launching a remote application.

In the final section, we looked at how to configure load balancing in a View published application environment.

In the next chapter, we are going to look at how we apply the same methodology to deliver session-based or published desktops.

12
Horizon Client Options

In this chapter, we will discuss how an end user can connect to their virtual desktops and published applications using the various Horizon Client options that are available. We will also cover the different types of hardware-based endpoint devices that exist. The job of the client is to receive and display the screenshots of virtual desktop machines and the published applications on the end users' devices and then send the keystrokes and mouse movements back. These are the keystrokes and mouse movements from the end users client device, that get sent across the network back to the virtual desktop session.

We will discuss each of the available client options and why you would choose one over the other, based on the use case at hand. So, let's start by looking at the software-based client options.

In this chapter, we will cover the following topics:

- VMware Horizon Clients
- Hardware clients
- Accessing the desktop using a browser

VMware Horizon Clients

To get the best user experience, a user should connect to their virtual desktop machine from their client device using a piece of software called the Horizon View Client. The Horizon View Client is installed onto the local client device and allows users to communicate with the View Connection Server, allowing them to authenticate, select a desktop or application from a desktop pool they are entitled to, and then establish the connection between the client and the virtual desktop machine.

In the more recent versions of Horizon, the software client has been unbundled from the major View releases, which means that the client downloads are updated more often and you don't have to wait for the next release of View. This reflects the fast pace at which new devices come to the market.

There are a number of different platform versions available, depending on the endpoint device you choose to use. In this section, we are going to give you a high-level overview of each of the available versions, along with any specific requirements.

You can download the different Horizon Clients by going to `http://www.vmware.com/go/viewclients`.

Horizon Client for Windows

The Horizon Client for Windows allows you to access your Windows virtual desktops and View-hosted applications from a Windows-based device and delivers the best possible user experience over either a LAN or a WAN connection.

The following screenshot shows Horizon Client version 5.0 for Windows, which now has the same look and feel as Workspace ONE, connected to the example lab. You can see that there are two desktop pools available: one for published desktops and one for Windows 7 virtual desktop machines, along with a number of published apps:

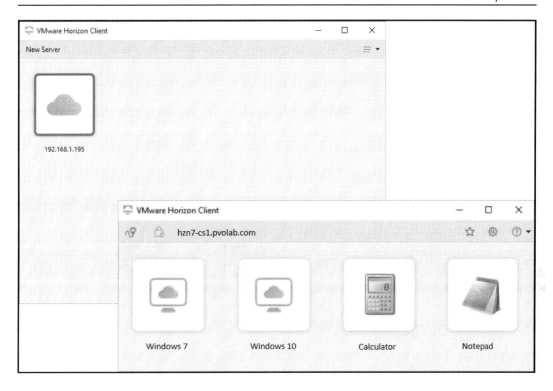

The latest version of the Horizon Windows Client has the following new features:

- **Support for up to six monitors**: It allows virtual desktop machines and published apps to run across six screens.
- **Use published applications in multi-session mode**: When multi-session mode is enabled for a published app, you can use multiple sessions of that particular published app when you log on to the Connection Server using different endpoint devices and clients. For example, if you open a published app in multi-session mode on client A, and then open exactly the same published app on client B, the published app remains open on client A and a new session of the published app opens on client B.
- **TLS v1.0 is disabled**: TLS v1.0 is no longer supported.

- **Clipboard audit feature enhancements**: The Horizon Agent can be configured to log information about copy and paste activity in a virtual desktop machine. A Horizon administrator can now configure the clipboard audit feature to record information about data that is copied from the client machine to the agent machine, about data that is copied from the agent machine to the client machine, or about data that is copied in both directions. This feature requires Horizon Agent 7.7.
- **Select specific monitors to display published applications**: If you have three or more monitors, you can select the monitors on which to display published applications.
- **Geolocation redirection feature enhancements**: You can now use the geolocation redirection feature with Google Chrome. To use this feature, a Horizon administrator must enable the VMware Horizon Geolocation Redirection Chrome plugin on the agent machine.
- **VMware Virtual Print Redirection feature**: With the VMware Virtual Print Redirection feature, you can print to a virtual printer or USB printer that is attached to the client system from a remote desktop or published application. This feature requires Horizon Agent 7.7.
- **Drag and drop files and folders**: You can drag and drop files and folders between the client system and Windows remote desktops and published applications. This feature requires Horizon Agent 7.7.
- **Share Linux remote desktops**: You can now use the Session Collaboration feature to share Linux remote desktops.
- **Support for Virtual Printing on physical RDS host machines**: The Virtual Printing feature for published desktops and published apps is now supported on physical RDS host servers. This feature requires Horizon Agent 7.7.
- **Allow High-Efficiency Video Decoding (HEVC) with VMware Blast**: When you allow HEVC for VMware Blast sessions, performance and image quality is improved if the client machine has a GPU that supports HEVC decoding.

For more information about the features in the latest Horizon Windows Client, you can read the release notes at the following link: https://docs.vmware.com/en/VMware-Horizon-Client-for-Windows/index.html.

The latest Horizon Client, version 4.10, requires the following Windows operating systems:

- 32-bit or 64-bit Windows 10, Home, Pro, Enterprise, or **Internet of Things (IoT)** Enterprise (up to 1809)
- 32-bit or 64-bit Windows 8, 8.1, or 8.1 Pro, Enterprise, or Industry Embedded
- 32-bit or 64-bit Windows 7 SP1, Home, Enterprise, Ultimate, or Professional edition
- Windows Server 2008 R2
- Windows 2012 Server R2

There is also a specific version of the Horizon Client for the Windows 10 **Universal Windows Platform (UWP)**.

This version of the Horizon Client is supported with the latest maintenance release of Horizon 6 version 6.2.x and later releases.

The Horizon Client requires a valid SSL certificate for connections to the View Connection Server. You will also need to enter the **Fully Qualified Domain Name (FQDN)** for the View Connection Server, and not use its IP address when entering the address of the Connection Server in the Horizon Client.

In the next section, we are going to look at the Android agent.

Horizon Client for Android

The Horizon Client for Android-based devices, like the Windows client, allows you to access your Windows virtual desktops and published applications from an Android tablet or smartphone device.

The client software can also be downloaded as an app from the Google Play Store at https://play.google.com/store/apps/details?id=com.vmware.view.client.androidhl=en-GB.

The following screenshot shows the Horizon Client for Android. Here, you can see the login screen running on an Android smartphone. The middle section shows a Windows 10 VDI desktop, along with the Unity Touch Sidebar, so that you can access features such as settings, mouse, and disconnect.

Horizon Client Options

The Unity Touch sidebar makes it easy to browse, search, open, and close Windows applications and files. It also helps to you switch between running applications. All of this can be done without using the Windows start menu or task bar:

The Horizon Client supports native Android gestures for quick and easy navigation around the desktop. When working on a Windows desktop, the full-screen touchpad feature lets you touch anywhere on the screen to move the mouse pointer around the Windows virtual desktop.

The latest version of the Horizon Android Client has the following new features:

- **It has a new User Interface**: The look and feel has been brought into line with Workspace ONE, including a new Horizon logo.
- **Use published applications in multi-session mode**: When multi-session mode is enabled for a published app, you can use multiple sessions of that particular published app when you log on to the Connection Server using different endpoint devices and clients. For example, if you open a published app in multi-session mode on client A, and then open exactly the same published app on client B, the published app remains open on client A and a new session of the published app opens on client B.

- **Create a virtual smart card for smart card authentication**: You can create a virtual smart card to use when you log in to a server and connect to a remote desktop. With a virtual smart card, you do not need to connect a traditional smart card reader to the client device. One virtual smart card can hold multiple certificates.
- **TLS v1.0 is disabled**: TLS v1.0 is no longer supported.

For more information about the features in the latest Horizon Android Client, you can read the release notes at the following link: `https://docs.vmware.com/en/VMware-Horizon-Client-for-Android/index.html`.

The latest Horizon Client, version 5.0, requires the following Android versions:

- Android 5.0 (Lollipop)
- Android 6.0 (Marshmallow)
- Android 7.0 and 7.1 (Nougat)
- Android 8.0 and 8.1 (Oreo)
- Android 9.0 (Pie)

It also runs on both ARM and x86 architectures. In the next section, we will look at the iOS client.

Horizon Client for iOS

The Horizon Client for iOS allows you to access your Windows virtual desktop from an iOS-based device such as an iPhone or iPad.

Horizon Client Options

The following screenshot shows the iOS Horizon Client 5.0:

The Horizon Client for iPad and iPhone supports native iPad and iPhone gestures for quick and easy navigation around your desktop.

As with the Android client, the whole full screen touchpad feature lets you touch anywhere on the screen so that you can move the mouse pointer around the Windows virtual desktop.

The Unity Touch sidebar makes it easy to browse, search, open, and close Windows applications and files, and switch between running applications, all without using the Windows start menu or taskbar.

The client software can also be downloaded as an app from the iTunes Store at
`https://itunes.apple.com/gb/app/vmware-horizon-client/id417993697?mt=8`

With the latest version of the Client (version 4.10), there are a number of new features:

- **New user interface:** The iOS Horizon Client has an upgraded, modern user interface.
- **Windows 10 Continuum support**: A remote desktop can adjust its user interface between desktop mode and tablet mode automatically when an iPad or iPhone is disconnected or reconnected to a Bluetooth or dock keyboard.
- **Use published applications in multi-session mode**: When the multi-session mode is enabled for a published app, you can use multiple sessions of that particular published app when you log on to the Connection Server using different endpoint devices and clients. For example, if you open a published app in multi-session mode on client A, and then open exactly the same published app on client B, the published app remains open on client A and a new session of the published app opens on client B.
- **TLS v1.0 is disabled**: TLS v1.0 is no longer supported.
- **RTAV support for camera redirection**: It uses a real-time audio-video feature when redirecting a camera.
- **Screen rotation in presentation mode**: It allows the screen to be rotated when running in presentation mode.

For more information about the features in the latest Horizon iOS Client, you can read the release notes at the following link: https://docs.vmware.com/en/VMware-Horizon-Client-for-iOS/index.html.

The latest Horizon Client, version 4.10, requires the following iOS versions:

- iOS 10.x
- iOS 11.x
- iOS 12.x

This version of the Horizon Client is supported with the latest maintenance release of Horizon 6 version 6.2.x and later releases.

In the next section, we will look at the Horizon Client for Linux.

Horizon Client for Linux

The Horizon Client for Linux allows you to access your Windows virtual desktop from a PC or laptop that's running Linux as the OS:

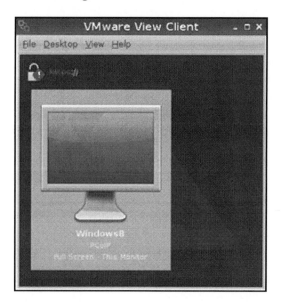

With the latest version of the Client (version 4.10), there are a number of new features:

- **Support for Windows Server 2019**: Microsoft Windows Server 2019 is now supported as an RDS-hosted server for remote desktop and published application sessions.
- **Support for PIV Smart Cards**: PIV smart card authentication and redirection support is now available.
- **TLS 1.0 support discontinued**: Support for TLS 1.0 has been discontinued, beginning with this release.
- **Serial port redirection for RDS-hosted desktops in nested mode**: The serial port redirection feature is now supported in published applications that are launched from Horizon Client inside RDS-hosted desktops (nested sessions). Horizon Agent 7.7 and Horizon Client 4.10 or later must be installed in the RDS-hosted desktops. The number of concurrent users is limited in a nested mode scenario.

- **Support for virtual printing on physical RDS host machines**: You can now use the Virtual Printing feature for published desktops and published apps that are hosted on RDS host servers that run on physical servers.
- **Multi-session mode support**: You can use multiple instances of the same published application on different client devices when multi-session mode is enabled for a published application.
- **Logging copy and paste activity**: You can enable the clipboard audit feature in Horizon Client to record information about clipboard data that is copied from the Horizon Agent machine to the Linux client machine. This feature requires Horizon Agent 7.7.
- **Support for Workspace ONE mode**: From Horizon 7 version 7.2, a Horizon administrator can enable Workspace ONE mode for a Connection Server instance. You will be redirected to the Workspace ONE portal if you use the Horizon Client for Linux to connect to the Workspace ONE mode enabled server. This portal will help you launch your entitled desktops and applications.

For more information about the features in the latest Horizon Linux Client, you can read the release notes at the following link: `https://docs.vmware.com/en/VMware-Horizon-Client-for-Linux/index.html`.

Horizon Client for Linux 4.10 is supported on the following operating systems when you use the VMware installer that's provided:

- Ubuntu 16.04 (32-bit)
- Ubuntu 16.04 and 18.04 (64-bit)
- Red Hat Enterprise Linux 6.10 (32-bit)
- Red Hat Enterprise Linux 6.10 and 7.5 (64-bit)

This version of the Horizon Client is supported with the latest maintenance release of 6.2.x and later releases. Published application support is only available on Horizon 6.0 (or later) servers.

In the next section, we will look at the Horizon Client for macOS.

Horizon Client for macOS

The Horizon Client for macOS X allows you to access your Windows virtual desktop machines and View hosted applications from an Apple Mac:

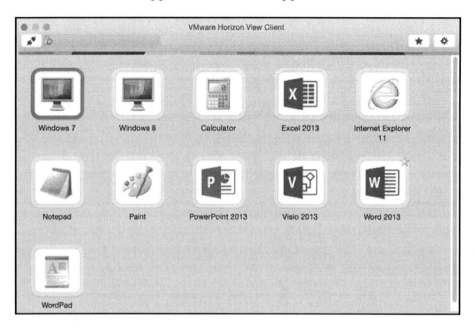

With the latest version of the Client (version 5.0), there are a number of new features:

- **macOS Mojave (10.14) support**: You can install Horizon Client for Mac on a macOS Mojave (10.14) system.
- **Show category folders for published applications in the Applications folder**: When Horizon Client for Mac is configured to run published applications from the Applications folder, you can enable the **Allow automatic shortcuts from the server** setting to make category folders that have been configured for published applications appear in the Applications folder.
- **Use published applications in multi-session mode**: When multi-session mode is enabled for a published app, you can use multiple sessions of that particular published app when you log on to the Connection Server using different endpoint devices and clients. For example, if you open a published app in multi-session mode on client A, and then open exactly the same published app on client B, the published app remains open on client A and a new session of the published app opens on client B.

- **TLS v1.0 is disabled**: TLS v1.0 is no longer supported.
- **Collect support data**: You can collect support data to help VMware troubleshoot problems with Horizon Client for Mac. To use this feature, click on the option for **VMware Horizon Client | About VMware Horizon Client** and click on **Collect Support Data**. Horizon Client saves log files in a ZIP file in the Desktop folder.
- **Use ActivClient middleware with smart card redirection**: You can install ActivClient 7.x middleware on Windows 10 virtual desktops and ActivClient 6.2.x middleware on Windows 7 virtual desktops.
- **Share Linux remote desktops**: You can now use the Session Collaboration feature to share Linux remote desktops.
- **Support for Virtual Printing on physical RDS host machines**: The Virtual Printing feature for published desktops and published apps is now supported on physical RDS host servers. This feature requires Horizon Agent 7.7.

Support for **dark mode** has also been added, as shown in the following screenshot:

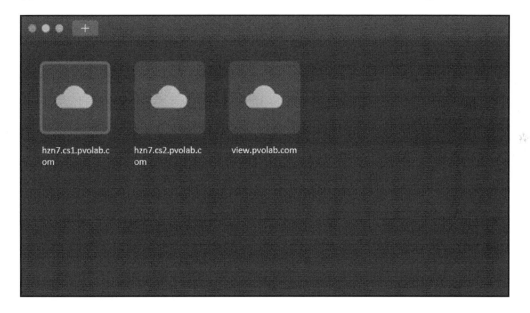

For more information about the features in the latest Horizon Linux Client, you can read the release notes at the following link: https://docs.vmware.com/en/VMware-Horizon-Client-for-Mac/index.html.

Horizon Client Options

Horizon Client for Linux 4.10 is supported on the following operating systems when you use the provided VMware installer:

- macOS Sierra (10.12)
- macOS High Sierra (10.13)
- macOS Mojave (10.14)

This version of the Horizon Client is supported with the latest maintenance release of Horizon 6 version 6.2.x and later releases.

In the next section, we will look at the Horizon Client for Chrome OS.

Horizon Client for Chrome OS

The final client is for Chrome OS-based devices such as Chromebooks. The Horizon View Client for Chrome OS X allows you to access your Windows virtual desktop machines and View hosted applications from a Chrome OS-based device:

With the latest version of the Client (version 4.10), there are a number of new features:

- **Chromebook's camera support**: The Real-Time Audio-Video feature supports Chromebook cameras with remote desktops and apps. This works with apps such as Skype, WebEx, and Google Hangouts.
- **SHA-256 support**: Chrome OS client now supports security using the 256-bit Secure Hash Algorithm.
- **There's OpenSSL 1.0.2l support**.
- **File transfer support is available for published apps**.

For more information about the features in the latest Horizon Chrome OS Client, read the release notes at the following link: `https://docs.vmware.com/en/VMware-Horizon-Client-for-Chrome/index.html`.

Horizon Client for Chrome OS 4.7 is supported on the following operating systems when you use the provided VMware installer:

- Chromebook with Chrome OS, stable channel, ARC version 41.4410.244.13 or later

This version of the Horizon Client is supported with the latest maintenance release of Horizon 6 version 6.x and later releases.

In the next section, we will look at some of the hardware-based options that you can choose from.

Hardware clients

One of the things we hear a lot from speaking with customers is that the endpoint device is irrelevant when you're connecting to a virtual desktop machine as it's just a dumb device to access the infrastructure and display my desktop screen, so that means I can buy the cheapest device possible and that will be fine, right?

The correct answer is that it depends on the use case for the users and what their requirements in terms of features and functionality are. Then, you can choose the most suitable endpoint device for them to connect from.

The other confusion that seems to be out there is whether there is a difference between a thin client and a Zero Client, and is there actually a difference at all?

In this section, we are going to cover the different types of hardware clients that are available, explain what each one is, and the best one to choose for a specific use case.

Thin clients

A thin client is a hardware endpoint device that's used to connect to the network and deliver a remote desktop/application session. Unlike a traditional PC that has its own memory, storage, and computing power to run applications on its own, complete with a full-blown OS and applications installed locally, a thin client has a cut-down OS, minimal CPU, memory, and often no storage and relies on the computing power of the servers running in the data center to do all of the processing. In this case, the thin client is used as a means to display the server's content to the end user.

Typically, a client device will have just enough processing power and resources to access and use the computing resources of the server. They have little or no storage (just enough to host their own internal OS) and more importantly no moving parts, which means they don't go wrong very often. Due to the reduced CPU and memory capacity, a thin client will draw a fraction of the power that a PC would normally need, meaning that thin clients should be cheaper to run and manage, and they have longer life cycles.

One thing they do have in common with a PC is that they have an operating system. A thin client will have its own local operating system installed, typically embedded on a flash card, and would be running the vendor's own cut-down version of a Linux distribution such as Dell Wyse ThinOS or Microsoft Windows Embedded. In addition, it would be running the appropriate client software to connect to the appropriate virtual desktop infrastructure, such as a Horizon Client with PCoIP to connect to VMware View-based virtual desktops and hosted apps, and the Citrix Receiver to connect to a Citrix-based infrastructure, and so on. Usually, a thin client will have all of the connection options installed, giving you the choice and flexibility to connect to different infrastructures.

Now, this is where you need to make the right choice regarding a device, as the operating system will be embedded onto the device. As we mentioned previously, the use case for the user will typically dictate the type of device. For example, if you are going to deploy unified communications with Microsoft Skype for Business, then you will need a Windows Embedded operating system, as it will more than likely require some of the Windows multimedia functionality. Always check before going off and buying the cheapest device.

There are also a couple of other points to bear in mind with thin clients. If the device is running on a local operating system, this will still need to be managed and maintained. The other consideration relates to licensing and the fact that you will need a Windows VDA license if you are connecting from a non-Windows device. This needs to be taken into account when looking at cost models and looking at TCO and ROI.

Zero Clients

A Zero Client performs the same functionality as a thin client; however, instead of an operating system, a Zero Client will have a highly tuned on-board processor that's been specifically designed for one of the VDI protocols (PCoIP, HDX, or RemoteFX). For example, the VMware View-based Zero Clients would use the onboard Tera2 hardware chipset such as a Dell Wyse 5030/7030 or a 10ZiG V1200-P. These devices are still small, light, have no moving parts, and consume minimal power, just like a thin client.

The decoding and display processes take place on the silicon of the Zero Client and are more efficient. Since they are a hardware-based solution, they deliver better performance than if you were to use a software client with a standard CPU and GPU. Zero Clients boot up in just a few seconds as there is no operating system to load. As such, they are far more immune to viruses and other malware as they have next to no storage or data stored on them. This decreases the overall downtime of the device, meaning there are very few failures, mainly due to the lack of moving parts. This increases productivity to the end user.

A Zero Client device does not require any major maintenance and it rarely needs any updates, that is, unless there is a remarkable change or improvement to the VDI protocol or a rare BIOS-related update.

There are a couple of things to watch out for. First is the licensing. Since these devices are not running on an operating system, you need to look at VDA licensing for using a non-Windows device. The final thing is that, if you change your VDI infrastructure from PCoIP to a new protocol, then the device cannot be used with a different protocol, so you lose the flexibility that you get with a thin client. However, you will get much better performance.

Repurposed PCs (software-defined thin clients)

It is also possible to repurpose existing physical PCs so that they can be used as thin clients. There are a number of ways to achieve this, but you must ensure it is simple for the user to use and does not confuse the usage between a virtual desktop machine and the physical desktop machine that is sitting in front of them.

There are a couple of ways to do this. First is to use a local policy or group policy to lock down the Windows PC and change the shell to the Horizon Client only. The second is to use a third-party solution, such as the market leading ThinKiosk solution from ThinScale.

The ThinKiosk solution enables any Windows-based endpoint device to be repurposed into a centrally managed, secure, Windows-based thin client. For end users, it delivers an intuitive and familiar-looking user interface with a secure workspace environment that it can access remote or local resources from. It's an ideal solution for migrating to VDI, as you can continue to use local apps and resources while maintaining security. This also means that you won't be held back when moving to VDI due to the apps not working in virtual environments and newer operating systems. When it comes to security, ThinScale's Secure Remote Worker solution allows an end user to launch an app that is essentially a temporary, secure, workspace environment that runs on any Windows device and is designed to allow home and remote workers to use their own devices:

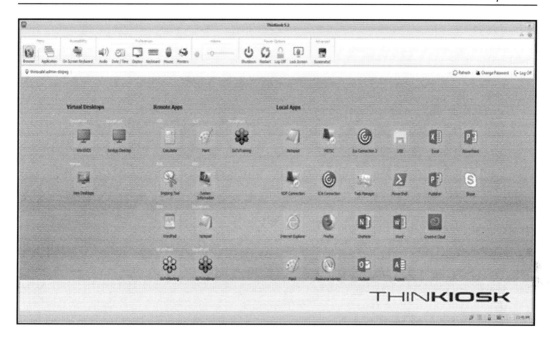

There are other solutions on the market that deliver this repurposing approach, but by using a Linux-based OS, these can add additional costs of management, and don't always offer the best levels of compatibility and functionality.

Accessing the desktop using a browser

In the previous sections, we talked about either using a software-based or hardware-based client to access our virtual desktop, but there is also a third method: using an HTML5-enabled browser on any device. The key use case for using this method is when installing client software on an endpoint device is not possible. For example, you might have a bring-your-own-device policy where end users don't want to install client software, or you might want to use a public-facing endpoint in a hotel lobby where the device is locked down and you cannot install the client software.

This is where this use case comes in, allowing you to access your virtual desktop machine using an HTML5-enabled web browser, which also requires no additional plugins or software to be downloaded and installed. The HTML desktop access is what is referred to as the VMware Blast protocol.

Horizon Client Options

To connect to your virtual desktop machine or View-hosted application using the browser, open the browser, and in the address bar, type the address of your Connection Server.

In the example lab, the address is `https://hzn7-cs1.pvolab.com`.

Before you access your virtual desktop machine, you will first see a web page that displays two different options. You have the choice of downloading the full version of the Horizon Client or you can continue and connect via HTML, as shown in the following screenshot:

Click on the link for **VMware Horizon HTML Access** from the left-hand side of the screen. You will now see the login box, as shown in the following screenshot:

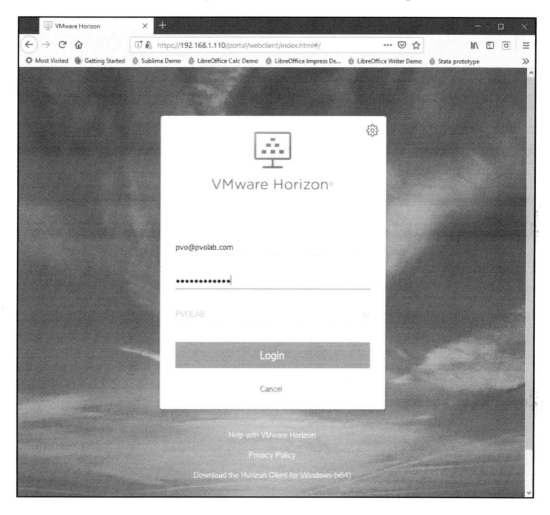

Type in the username and password, and then click on the **Login** button.

Horizon Client Options

You will now see the resources that the user is entitled to. In this example, a Windows 7 Dedicated desktop pool, along with Excel, PowerPoint, and Word, are delivered as Horizon published applications. This is shown in the following screenshot:

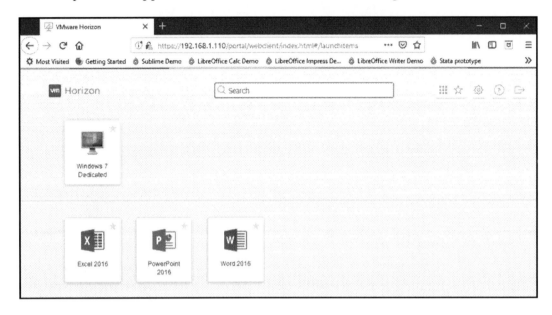

You can now click on the resource you want to run, which will then launch inside the browser.

With the latest version of the Client (version 4.10), there are a number of new features:

- **Full-screen mode support**: You can now display a remote desktop or published application in full-screen mode.
- **Support for multi-session modes**: When a multi-session mode is enabled for a published app, you can use multiple sessions of the same published app when you log on to the same server and app but from a different client device.
- **Enhanced copy and paste feature**: If you are using a Chrome or Firefox browser, you can now copy and paste directly from your local client system to a remote desktop or published application. Internet Explorer, Microsoft Edge, or Safari browser users must continue to use the copy and paste window.

For more information about the features in the latest Horizon Chrome OS Client, you can read the release notes at the following link: https://docs.vmware.com/en/VMware-Horizon-HTML-Access/4.10/rn/horizon-html-access-410-release-notes.html.

To use the HTML access feature, you need to run a supported browser. The browsers that are currently supported are as follows:

- Chrome 69, 70
- Internet Explorer 11
- Safari 12
- Firefox 62, 63
- Microsoft Edge 42, 44

You also need to make sure that you have enabled the desktop pool for HTML access and that you have the remote experience agent installed on the virtual desktop. Otherwise, you will not be able to access desktops or apps using the browser.

We have explored the various options for how an end user can connect to their virtual desktops and Horizon published applications.

Summary

In this chapter, we have taken a closer look at the available options for connecting to a virtual desktop machine or View hosted application from an endpoint device.

We discussed software-based clients, hardware-based clients, and the HTML access feature, and looked at the pros and cons of each type of access method and why you might choose one over the other.

In the next chapter, we will discuss how to upgrade from a previous version of Horizon View to the latest version.

13
Upgrading to a New Version of Horizon

In this chapter, we are going to cover the upgrade process and recommendations for upgrading your VMware View environment to the latest version, and, in this example, we will upgrade from Horizon 6 to Horizon 7. We will start by discussing the elements that need to be considered before undertaking the upgrade, how we undertake the upgrade to ensure there is minimum disruption to our users, and finally, the step-by-step process to completing the upgrade.

In this chapter, we will cover the following topics :

- Upgrading compatibility
- Upgrading Horizon Composer
- Upgrading the Horizon View Connection Server
- Upgrading the View Security Server
- Upgrading Group Policy templates
- Upgrading the VMware Horizon Agent
- Upgrading the Horizon Client

Upgrading compatibility

Before undertaking any upgrades, you should start off by reading the release notes and the upgrade guide for Horizon View. With a number of interdependent components, you not only need to check the compatibility between the different versions of these components, but also ensure that you undertake the upgrade in the correct order to minimize the risk of failure and disruption to our users.

Upgrading to a New Version of Horizon

In this section, we are going to look at compatibility, starting with which versions you are able to upgrade to Horizon 7. The following list shows the different versions:

- The latest maintenance release of Horizon View 5.3
- The latest maintenance release of VMware Horizon 6.0 (with View)
- The latest maintenance release of VMware Horizon 6 version 6.1
- The latest maintenance release of VMware Horizon 6 version 6.2

You also need to check compatibility between the different View Components and whether Horizon 7 works with earlier versions of these components. By components, we mean the Connection Server, the Security Server, and so on.

The following table demonstrates version compatibility:

Component	Connection Server	Security Server	View Composer	Horizon Agent	Horizon Client
Connection Server 7.0	Only during upgrade	Pair before upgrade	☒	Only during upgrade	☑
Security Server 7.0	☒	N / A	☒	Only during upgrade	☑
View Composer 7.0	Only during upgrade	Only during upgrade	N / A	Only during upgrade	N / A
Horizon Agent 7.0	Only during upgrade	☒	☒	N / A	Only during upgrade
Horizon Client 4.0	☑	☑	☑	☑	N / A

(Earlier Versions of ....)

As such, the process by which the upgrade needs to take place is as follows:

- View Composer upgrade
- View Connection Server upgrade
- View Security Server upgrade
- Upgrading group policies
- Upgrading vCenter (if required)
- Upgrading ESXi hosts and virtual machine hardware/tools (if required)
- Upgrading Horizon Agents
- Recomposing desktop pools

You will also need to think about the impact of any upgrade that may need to be undertaken on your end users. For example, you wouldn't want to upgrade a View Connection Server in the middle of a working day, with potentially thousands of users connected to it. You would normally schedule any upgrades to take place out of hours, or at least ensure that each View Connection Server is removed from the load balancer the night before the planned upgrade.

You could decide to build new Connection Servers with the latest Horizon version, rather than upgrading the existing Connection Servers, and then simply point users to the new servers and then remove the old Connection Servers once completed.

The first component we are going to look at upgrading is the View Composer.

Upgrading Horizon Composer

In the first part of the process, we are going to upgrade the View Composer Server.

Before you begin the upgrade

There are a couple of prerequisites you need to have completed before starting the upgrade of the View Composer. You need to perform the following steps prior to commencing with the upgrade:

1. Check the prerequisites with the VMware Horizon View installation guide to ensure all components to be upgraded meet the minimum requirements for resources, operating system, and applicable database versions.
2. If your View Composer Server is installed on a virtual machine, snapshot the virtual machine before starting.
3. Back up your vCenter and View Composer databases.
4. Back up the folder containing the SSL certificates on your View Composer Server. Certificates can be found in the following folder:
   `%ALLUSERSPROFILE%\Application Data\VMware\VMware VirtualCenter`
5. Document the IP address and hostname of your vCenter Server.
6. Ensure the usernames and passwords are documented for the accounts used to access your composer database.

Upgrading to a New Version of Horizon

With the prerequisite tasks completed, the next step is to disable provisioning. To do this, perform the following steps as:

1. Log in to the View Administrator, expand out the **Catalog** option, and click on **Desktop Pools** (1).
2. Now, click and highlight the desktop pool you want to disable (2), right-click, and, from the contextual menu, select **Disable Provisioning...** (3), as shown in the following screenshot:

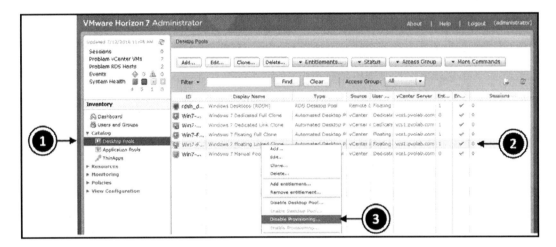

3. You will now see the following message displayed:

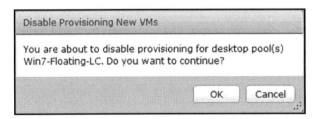

4. Click the **OK** button to disable provisioning. You will need to disable provisioning for all desktop pools that are going to be affected by the View Composer upgrade. This prevents any new desktops from being provisioned during the upgrade.
5. Next, you need to modify any desktop pools that are set to refresh upon logging off to ensure that they are set to never refresh.

Chapter 13

6. To do this, from the **Catalog** option, click on **Desktop Pools** (4), and then click and highlight the desktop pool you want to edit (5), right-click, and, from the contextual menu, select **Edit...** (6), as shown in the following screenshot:

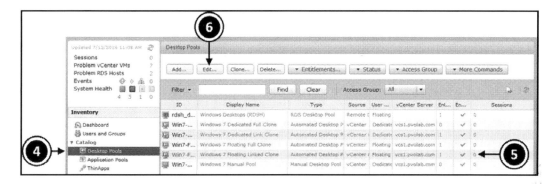

7. You will now see the **Edit Win7-Floating-LC** dialog box, as shown in the following screenshot:

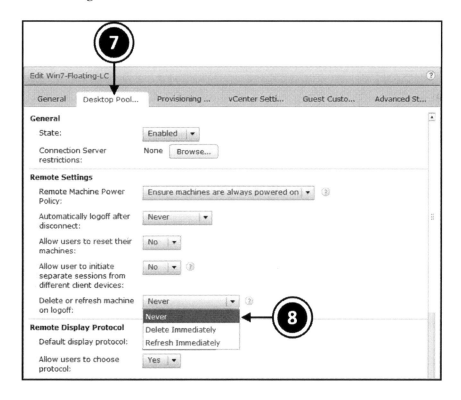

[675]

8. Click the **Desktop Pool...** tab (7), and then, from the **Delete or refresh machine on logoff** section, from the drop-down menu, select the option for **Never** (8).
9. Click the **OK** button to save the changes and close the dialog box.

You are now ready to complete the upgrade process, which we will cover in the next section.

Completing the View Composer upgrade

Once you have completed all the prerequisites, and have planned the upgrades so as to have the minimal impact on your end users, you are able to start the upgrade. The next stage is to install the new version of the Horizon Composer software.

We are not going to cover this, as it's exactly the same process as we covered back in `Chapter 4`, *Installing and Configuring Horizon 7 - Part 1*, in the *Installing and Configuring Horizon View* and the *Horizon Composer Installation Process* sections, with the slight difference being that you need to uninstall the old version first. Once uninstalled, you can follow the instructions in that section, remembering that you have already set up the database details, so all you need to do is enter the DSN details you already created when prompted to do so.

Verifying the upgrade

Now that the upgrade has completed, the next stage is to check that everything is back up and running. The first thing we will check is to make sure that the Horizon Composer service is running by performing the following steps:

1. First, from the Horizon Composer Server, launch a services console by opening a **Run** dialog box and typing `services.msc`.

Chapter 13

2. In the **Services** screen, scroll down and check that the **VMware Horizon 7 Composer** service is running, as shown in the following screenshot:

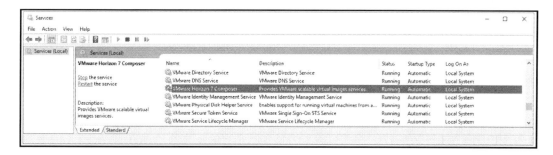

3. The second check is to run through the View Composer verification process.
4. From the View Administrator, click on **Servers** (**1**), and then highlight the vCenter server you want to verify (**2**), as shown in the following screenshot:

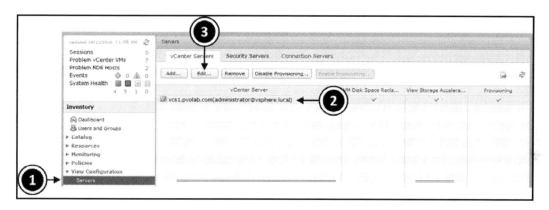

5. Now, click the **Edit...** button (**3**).

[677]

Upgrading to a New Version of Horizon

6. You will now see the **Edit vCenter Server** dialog box, as shown in the following screenshot:

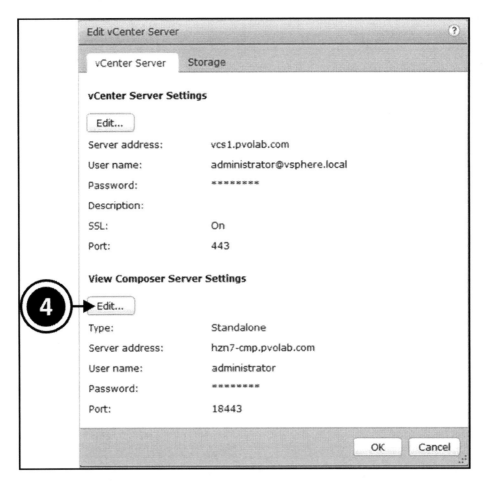

7. In the **View Composer Server Settings** section, click the **Edit...** button (4).

8. You will now see the **View Composer Server Settings**, as shown in the following screenshot:

9. In the **Domains** section at the bottom, click the **Verify Server Information** button (5).

Upgrading to a New Version of Horizon

10. You will now see the **Domains** section populated, along with the desktop pool information, as shown in the following screenshot:

11. Click the **OK** button to close the dialog box.

You have now successfully completed the upgrade procedure for the Horizon Composer Server. Obviously, if you are using multiple composer servers, you will need to repeat these steps on all your Horizon Composer servers.

Upgrading the Horizon View Connection Server

You are now in a position to move on to upgrading all the View Connection Servers within your infrastructure.

Before you begin the upgrade

There are a couple of prerequisites you need to have completed before beginning the upgrade of the View Connection Server:

1. Check the prerequisites with the VMware Horizon View installation guide to ensure all components to be upgraded meet the minimum requirements for resources, operating system, and so on.
2. If your View Connection Server is installed in a virtual machine, snapshot the virtual machine. Please note that if you need to recover this snapshot, you will first need to uninstall any replicated Connection Servers before reverting the master to the snapshot.
3. Ensure that your documentation is up to date, including pool configuration, global configuration settings, IP addresses, batch files, SQL credentials for the event database, and load balancer configuration.

Use the vdmexport.exe command-line utility to back up the existing configuration help within the LDAP database. From the command line, run the following command:

```
vdmexport > {backup location\filename.ldf}
```

Completing the Connection Server upgrade

Once you have completed all the prerequisites, and have planned the upgrades so as to have the minimal effect on your end users, you are able to start the upgrade.

The next stage is to install the new version of the View Connection Server software.

Upgrading to a New Version of Horizon

We are not going to cover this, as it's exactly the same process as we covered in back in Chapter 4, *Installing and Configuring Horizon 7 - Part 1*, the *Installing and Configuring Horizon View* and the *Horizon Composer Installation Process* sections, with the slight difference being that the old version gets uninstalled first. Follow the instructions in that section to install the Connection Server software.

Once the installation has finished and the server has rebooted, you should be able to see that the upgrade has completed successfully by accessing the View Administrator. To do this, click on **Servers** (1) and then click the **Connection Servers** tab (2). You can then check the version number for the associated **Connection Server** (3), as shown in the following screenshot:

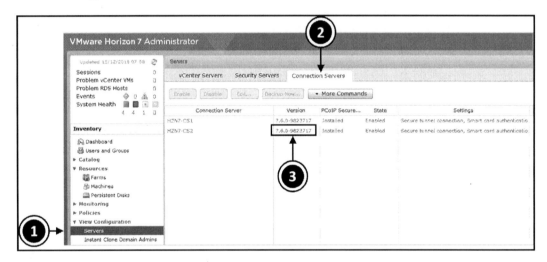

You have now successfully completed the upgrade procedure for the View Connection Server. Obviously, if you are using multiple **Connection Servers**, you will need to repeat these steps on all your View Connection servers.

Alternative View Connection Server upgrade method

There may be a situation where you decide to upgrade View Connection Servers by adding new Horizon 7 Connection Servers to your existing Horizon Connection Servers, and then remove the old Connection Servers from the configuration when you are ready to do so. We aren't going to cover the procedure for the installation of the new replica View Connection Servers here, as this is extensively covered in Chapter 4, *Installing and Configuring Horizon - Part 1*, but it is important to understand how to remove the old View Connection Servers correctly, by performing the following steps.

Once you have installed the new version of the Connection Server, and are ready to remove your first old version Connection Server, you will need to ensure that the View Connection Server to be removed has been removed from any load balancers and is no longer in use by the users; in other words, nobody is connected to it.

Then, launch the **Programs and Features** configuration screen from the control panel, as shown in the following screenshot:

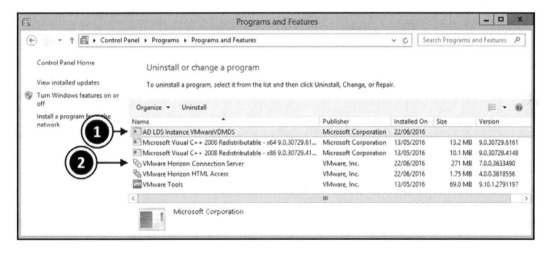

You will then need to uninstall the **AD LDS Instance VMwareVDMS** (1) and the **VMware Horizon Connection Server** (2) from the View Connection Server you want to remove.

Upgrading to a New Version of Horizon

Once you have completed the uninstall, you will need to connect to all of your remaining Connection Servers, open a command line, and run the following command:

```
"C:\Program Files\VMware\VMware View\Server\tools\bin\vdmadmin.exe" -S
-r -s server_name
```

This removes this Connection Server entry from the other Connection Servers. You will then get confirmation of the scheduled removal of the server from the configuration, and the server will no longer be displayed in the View Administrator screen.

The process described is also the same process you would use to upgrade a replica server, as, essentially, a replica server is just a Connection Server.

Upgrading the View Security Server

The next step in upgrading your Horizon View environment is to upgrade the Security Servers that are used to enable external users to connect to their desktops. Bear in mind that this won't be added to your domain, so you will need to log in using local credentials.

Before you begin the upgrade

There are a couple of prerequisites you need to have completed before starting the upgrade of the View Security Server.

By default, since View 5.3, traffic between the Security Server and Connection Server is governed by IPSEC rules. When you complete an upgrade of a View Security Server, these rules will need to be recreated, and if the existing rules still exist, this will fail.

As such, VMware has built-in functionality to clear the IPSEC rules prior to the upgrade being started. To do this, perform the following the steps:

1. From the View Administrator screen, click on **Servers** (1), and then the **Security Servers** tab (2), as shown in the following screenshot:

Chapter 13

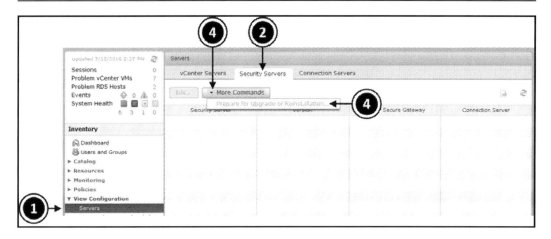

2. Now, highlight the Security Server and click the dropdown for **More Commands** (3).
3. Select the **Prepare for Upgrade or Reinstallation...** option (4).

Once you have completed this action, the Security Server is no longer able to communicate with the Connection Server, so ensure this is only completed as part of planned maintenance to the Security Server, so as to avoid disruption, since external users may now be unable to log in and connect to a virtual desktop machine.

Completing the View Security Server upgrade

Once you have completed all the prerequisites, and have planned the upgrades, so as to have the minimal effect on your end users, you are able to start the upgrade by uninstalling the current version of the Security Server using the **Add and Remove Programs** configuration on the server running the current version. Once removed, you can now proceed and install the new version.

Before you actually install the new version of the Security Server, you first need to set the pairing password. To do this, perform the following the steps:

1. From the View Administrator console, select **Servers,** and then click on the **Connection Servers** tab.
2. Select your View Connection Server, and then click on the **More Commands** button.
3. Select the option for **Specify Security Server Pairing Password...**

[685]

4. You will now see the **Specify Security Server Pairing Password** dialog box.
5. Type in a password, and then confirm it by typing it in again. If you need to extend the length of time the pairing password is valid for then you can enter a new time in the **Password timeout** box.
6. Click the **OK** button to continue.

For more detailed information on this process, please refer back to the installation of the Security Server in Chapter 5, *Installing and Configuring Horizon 7 - Part 2*.

The next stage is to install the new version of the View Security Server software.

We are not going to cover this, as it's exactly the same process as we covered in Chapter 4, *Installing and Configuring Horizon 7 - Part 1*, in the *Installing and Configuring Horizon View* and the *Horizon Composer Installation Process* sections. Follow the instructions in that section to install the Security Server software.

Once the installation has completed and the server rebooted, you should be able to see that the upgrade has completed successfully by logging in to the View Administrator console, navigating to the **Servers** section, and then clicking on the **Security Servers** tab and checking the version number for the Security Server you just upgraded.

Upgrading group policy templates

As part of new Horizon versions, there will be a number of new features, some of which will be controlled via Group Policy. Therefore, you will need to upgrade the Group Policy Administrative templates to the latest version when upgrading to a new version of Horizon View. This is easily achieved through the Group Policy Object Editor on your domain controllers.

We are not going to cover the process on how to do this, as it has been extensively covered in Chapter 10, *Fine-Tuning the End User Experience*.

 One thing to be aware of is that any policy changes can affect end users, and some policies may have been deprecated and other new ones added. It's worth creating a new GPO for any new versions so that you can roll back to the previous one if users start to report any issues.

In the next section, we are going to look at upgrading the Horizon Agent.

Upgrading the VMware Horizon Agent

Upgrading the Horizon Agent is probably one of the simplest tasks of the upgrade process. You are going to need to upgrade the agents in all of your golden images and then, if you are using Linked Clones, recompose the desktop pools.

With non-persistent desktops, this is a relatively simple task of upgrading the agent, taking a new snapshot, and recomposing all the pools. With persistent desktops, you may need to take further consideration of the effect of recomposing the pool, or, alternatively, look at manually upgrading the agent on each virtual desktop machine, or deploy an applications deployment tool.

You also need to consider that the Horizon Agent may be installed on an RDSH host server used for delivering desktop sessions and View hosted applications. For this, you will need to schedule time where you can take host machines out of the farm in order to perform the upgrade.

We are not going to go through the Horizon Agent installation process, as this has been covered previously in Chapter 7, *Building and Optimizing the Virtual Desktop OS*.

Upgrading the Horizon Client

There is no built-in method to upgrade the Horizon Clients automatically, unless, of course, you use something like Microsoft SCCM to deploy software automatically.

If you are running thin clients as end user devices for your users, the upgrade procedure is usually easily managed with the management software that comes with the thin clients.

If you are using re-provisioned PCs, or maybe laptops, to connect to the Horizon View environment, you are going to need to either manually update the client, direct your users to do so, or use a third-party software deployment tool to complete the upgrade.

For those users who are using BYOD, or any other type of non-corporate device, then they will have to rely on the device stores to alert them to the fact that a new version is available. However, you will need to make sure that any new client version that a user does install will still be compatible with your Horizon infrastructure.

Summary

In this chapter, we have covered the process of upgrading your VMware Horizon View environment to a newer version, walking through what you need to do for each of the individual infrastructure components. The actual upgrade process itself is relatively easy, but you must take the time to check and complete the prerequisites first. You also need to keep in mind the importance of planning the update, so as to minimize the effect on your end users.

14
JMP and VMware Horizon 7 Deployment Considerations

The VMware **Just-in-Time Management Platform (JMP)**, or VMware JMP, accelerates the composite desktop model, allowing all the component parts of the desktop, **operating system (OS)**, apps, user profiles, and data to be abstracted, managed, and delivered back to end users on demand. This allows you to deliver a truly stateless desktop environment.

In this chapter, we will introduce you to the VMware JMP, how it works, and how to configure it.

We will cover the following topics in this chapter:

- How does JMP work?
- VMware Workspace ONE
- VMware App Volumes
- Installing and configuring JMP

How does JMP work?

The VMware JMP brings together a number of VMware technologies to deliver this stateless desktop environment. The following diagram shows a high-level overview of the JMP components and how they fit together:

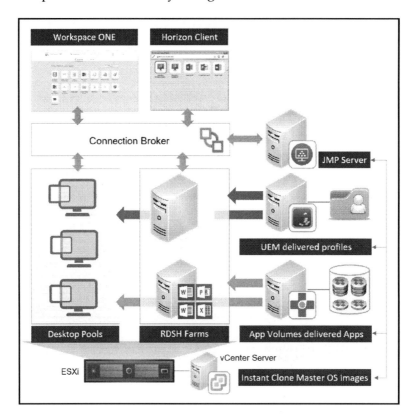

As you can see from the preceding diagram, the JMP solution is made up of a number of VMware technologies working together to deliver the desktop or app to the end user. These components are as follows:

- **Instant Clones**: Builds virtual desktop and RDSH server images on demand
- **VMware UEM**: Delivers the user profiles and policies to apps and desktops
- **VMware Workspace ONE**: Provides a workspace portal to access apps and desktops from (optional)
- **VMware App Volumes**: Delivers just-in-time apps to virtual desktops and RDSH servers

Before we continue, let's take a minute to describe what these technologies are in a bit more detail. We have already covered Instant Clones and VMware UEM, so we will start by giving you an overview of VMware Workspace ONE.

VMware Workspace ONE

VMware Workspace ONE is a management platform that allows IT admins to centrally control end users' mobile devices and cloud-hosted virtual desktops and applications from the cloud or from an on-premises deployment. It allows end users to access their corporate resources securely using smartphones, tablets, PCs, and laptops that are either personally owned or corporately owned.

It presents a user's apps in a single portal or workspace, along with a catalog of self-service apps that a user can access and entitle themselves to use – all under the control of the IT teams. Apps can be Software-as-a-Service-based, published, or mobile. End users can also access their virtual desktop machines from here. The following screenshot shows the launcher view of Workspace ONE:

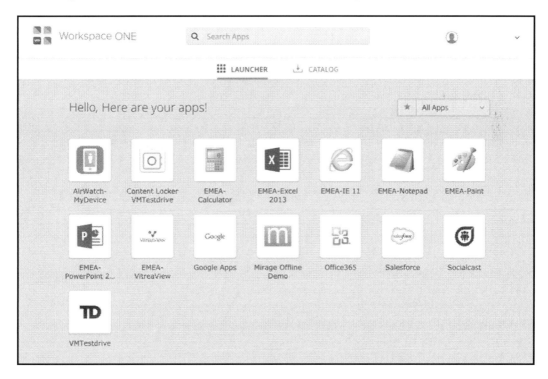

The Workspace ONE suite also includes VMware AirWatch, an **enterprise mobility management (EMM)** solution for checking and enrolling devices before delivering the workspace and the apps that are available to the end user. It also includes VMware Identity Manager vIDM to deliver single sign-on authentication to resources.

In the JMP scenario, Workspace ONE delivers a portal where end users can access desktops and apps that are delivered by Horizon and the JMP Server.

VMware App Volumes

The App Volumes solution came from an acquisition that VMware made in August 2014, when they acquired a startup company called CloudVolumes. The original CloudVolumes solution delivered a real-time application delivery engine for virtual and physical desktop environments.

In December 2014, CloudVolumes was rebranded and became what we now know as App Volumes, and was offered as part of the Horizon Enterprise edition.

So, what does App Volumes give you? At a high-level, App Volumes provides real-time application delivery and life cycle management solution that is used to deliver applications that you capture using the App Volumes provisioning process. The captured applications are then layered into the OS of your virtual and physical desktops. In a nutshell, App Volumes is an application layering solution.

But how is this different to the way a virtual desktop environment and app delivery works today? Even though in VDI, the desktop OS has been abstracted from the underlying hardware, the apps still remain tightly integrated into the OS. As we have already discussed this in Chapter 1, *Introducing VDI and VMware Horizon 7*, the ideal virtual desktop solution is to be able to deliver fully stateless desktops and have the elements of what makes up the full end user experience added on the fly.

Having a fully stateless desktop model provides the most cost-effective solution by making it easier to manage each component individually and also requires less infrastructure. Today, there are a number of tools that can take care of delivering the user personalization, user data, and user profile elements to the desktop, such as Liquidware ProfileUnity. However, apps are still delivered as part of the base OS image, or are delivered using an app publishing solution where the apps are actually running on a server in the datacenter.

App Volumes provides a layer of abstraction between the OS and the applications by delivering the applications in separate containers. These containers are called **AppStacks**, and integrate seamlessly by effectively layering the applications into the OS of the virtual desktop machine. The following diagram shows a comparison between the traditionally installed model versus the **App Volumes Agent** layered approach:

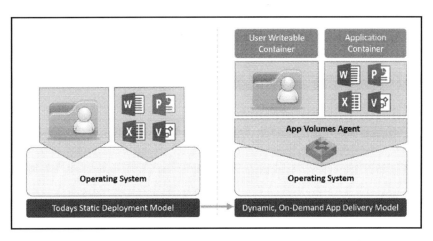

As well as the application containers, **App Volumes Agent** also provides the end user with their own container or virtual hard disk where they can install their own applications. This container is called a **Writable Volume**, and follows the end user when they log in to different virtual desktop machines, bringing all of their applications with them.

The following diagram illustrates the **App Volumes Agent** model, which has application containers (**AppStack**) and user writeable containers (**Writeable Volumes**):

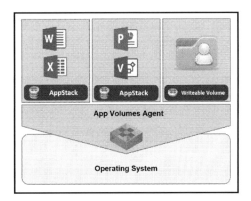

In the next section, we are going to take a look at how to build an AppStack and also how to deliver it to an end user.

How does App Volumes work? Step 1 – app capture

So, how does App Volumes work? The first thing you must do is create or capture an application that can be delivered by App Volumes. You start this process by installing the application on a virtual desktop machine, which is referred to as the provisioning machine. This provisioning machine is basically a vanilla installation of the OS, with no applications installed.

When you start the capture process, an empty VMDK file (App Volumes also supports VHD), called an AppStack, is mounted on the provisioning machine. Next, you start the application installation as you would do normally. All of the files associated with this application are then redirected to the AppStack or VMDK file.

This is shown in the following diagram:

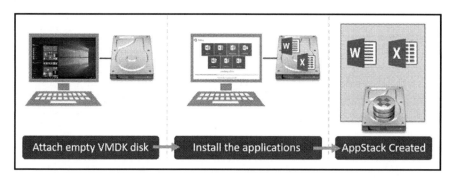

Once you have completed the capture process, the AppStack is set to read-only and is ready to be assigned to end users based on their Active Directory group membership. AppStacks can also be assigned to individual users or other groups.

How does App Volumes work? Step 2 – app delivery

Once you have your AppStacks created, you can now deliver them to the end users. AppStacks are assigned based on Active Directory membership. An **App Volumes Agent** runs on their virtual desktop machine and mounts the virtual hard disk that contains the captured application. The agent "layers" in the applications files and settings, making the application appear as if it were fully integrated and installed locally, rather than running it from an additional drive. This is how applications are able to be delivered to a user in real-time, since **AppStack** can be assigned on the fly based on AD membership.

This is shown in the following diagram:

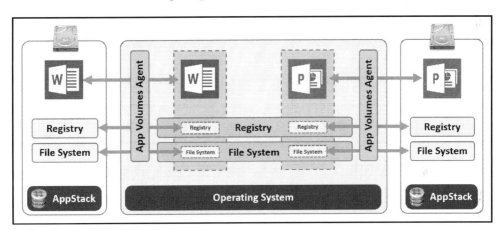

When an **AppStack** is unassigned from an end user, the virtual hard drive is simply unmounted, taking with it all of the application's files and settings, making the OS appear as though the application was never actually there!

This enables the delivery of applications to stateless virtual desktop machines, and in the case of JMP, delivers applications on demand as desktops are built and delivered to the end users.

Installing and configuring JMP

In this section, we are going to install and configure the Horizon JMP solution. The key part of the solution is to not only install the other VMware technology components, such as App Volumes, but to also install the JMP Server itself.

Before we start the installation process, we are going to discuss the requirements and prerequisites.

Prerequisites

There are a number of elements that need to be in place before you install the JMP software, both from the other components that are required to make the solution work, to the hardware and software requirements for JMP itself. Let's start by listing the other VMware solution components first.

VMware JMP component requirements

Supported versions of the VMware products that make up the JMP technology must be installed before you can start the installation of the JMP Server. These are required to utilize the JMP Integrated Workflow features. The following versions of the VMware products must be installed before you can install JMP Server:

- VMware Horizon 7 version 7.5 or later
- VMware App Volumes 2.14 or later
- VMware User Environment Manager 9.2.1 or later
- VMware Identity Manager 2.9.2 or later (for integration with VMware Workspace™ ONE™)

Next, we will look at the hardware requirements to run the JMP Server.

VMware JMP hardware requirements

To install the JMP Server, you need either a physical or virtual server that's configured with the following setup:

- 4 CPUs or vCPUs
- 8 GB memory (4 GB for POC)
- 100 GB disk space (25 GB for POC)

Next, we will look at the software and database requirements for running the JMP Server.

VMware JMP software requirements

The JMP Server needs to be installed on one of the following Windows Server operating systems:

- Windows Server 2008 R2 SP1 64-bit Standard, Enterprise, or Datacenter
- Windows Server 2012 R2 64-bit Standard or Datacenter
- Windows Server 2016 64-bit Standard or Datacenter

You will also need a SQL database that's using one of the following versions:

- SQL Server Express 2014 64-bit (for POC deployments)
- SQL Server 2012 (SP1, SP2, SP3, and SP4) 64-bit Standard and Enterprise
- SQL Server 2014 (SP1 and SP2 with CU7 or later) 64-bit Standard and Enterprise
- SQL Server 2016 (SP1 with CU6 or later)

You will need to ensure that the SQL Server logins and permissions have been configured for the JMP Server host and Windows user account that you plan to use to install the JMP Server.

Now that we have covered the prerequisites and other requirements, we can start the installation of the JMP Server.

Installing the JMP Server

In this section, we are going to install the JMP Server.

JMP and VMware Horizon 7 Deployment Considerations

To install the JMP Server, navigate to the location of the installer file. In the example lab environment, this is the shared folder on the domain controller, as shown in the following screenshot:

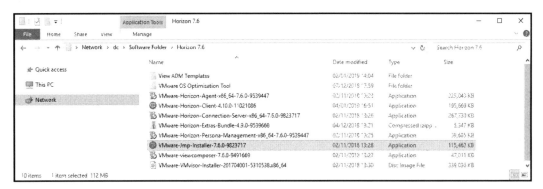

Double-click the `VMware-Jmp-Installer-7.6.0-9823717` file to launch the installer. The installer will launch and you can complete the installation steps as described. We will also provide them here for clarity:

1. You will see the **Welcome to the InstallShield Wizard for VMware just-in-Time Management Platform (JMP) Server** screen.
2. Click **Next >** to continue.
3. Then, you will see the **VMware End User License Agreement** screen.
4. Click the radio button for **I accept the terms in the license agreement**, and then click **Next >** to continue.
5. Next, you will see the **Allow HTTP Traffic on Port 80** screen. By default, port 443 (HTTPS) is used, but if you want to use port 80, then check the box for **Allow HTTP**.
6. Click **Next >** to continue.

7. You will now see the **Database Server for JMP Server Platform Services** screen, as shown in the following screenshot:

8. In the **Database server that you are connecting to** box, enter the details of the SQL Server. Alternatively, you can click the **Browse...** button and select it from the list of servers that are displayed.
9. Next, click the radio button for either **Windows authentication** or **Server authentication**. For server authentication, you then need to enter the **Login ID** and the **Password** for the account you want to use, and for **Windows authentication**, it will use the credentials of the currently logged in user. If you use this option then ensure that the account has the appropriate permission levels.
10. In the **Name of database catalog** box, enter the name of the SQL database that you have set up for JMP. Alternatively, you can click the **Browse...** button and select the database from the list of databases that are displayed.

11. You then have the option to check the **overwrite existing database** checkbox. If you are installing additional JMP Servers, then ensure that this box is unchecked as checking it will overwrite an existing database should the installer find one.
12. Finally, to ensure secure communication between the JMP Server and the SQL server, check the **Enable SSL** box.

> When the **Enable SSL** box is checked, you need to ensure that the TLS/SSL certificate that's used on the SQL Server is imported into the Windows local certificate store on the JMP Server. If you have not done this, then the JMP Server installation process will fail.

13. Click **Next >** to continue.
14. You will now see the **Ready to Install Program** screen.
15. Click **Finish** to complete the installation.

The next step is to ensure that the time is synchronized between the JMP Server and the Horizon Connection Server.

Syncing the time with Horizon Connection Server

The time on both the Horizon Connection Server and JMP Server hosts must be synchronized so that the authentication process between the two servers works successfully.

When you access the JMP Integrated Workflow features using the Horizon Console, the JMP Server authenticates the token it receives from Horizon Connection Server, which in turn returns a token to the JMP Server. If the time between the two host servers is not in sync, then the Horizon Connection Server will reject the token and the JMP Integrated Workflow features won't be available from the Horizon Console.

Since these servers are virtual machines, the easiest way to deploy this is via the ESXi host server. You can do this by configuring the **Time Configuration** option to point to a **Network Time Protocol** (**NTP**) client.

On each of the virtual machines, open a command prompt, and then from the `c:\program files\VMware\VMware Tools` directory, run the following command:

`VMwareToolboxCmd.exe timesync enable`

In the next section, we are going to configure the JMP Server and the other solution components to work together by using the Horizon Console.

Adding JMP Server and its components to Horizon

The first thing to note is that JMP can only be configured using the new Horizon Console and not by using the View Admin console. To configure this, follow these steps:

1. To start the configuration and add the other components together, log in to the Horizon Console using `https://hzn7-cs1.pvolab.com/newadmin`.
2. You will then see the login screen, as shown in the following screenshot:

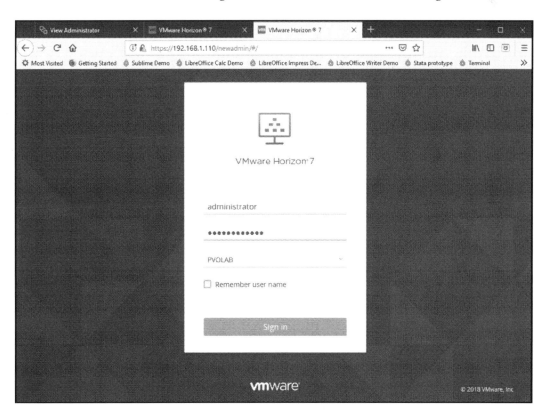

JMP and VMware Horizon 7 Deployment Considerations

3. Enter your username and password. Ensure that the correct domain has been selected from the drop-down box and then click **Sign in**.
4. You will now see the dashboard screen, as shown in the following screenshot:

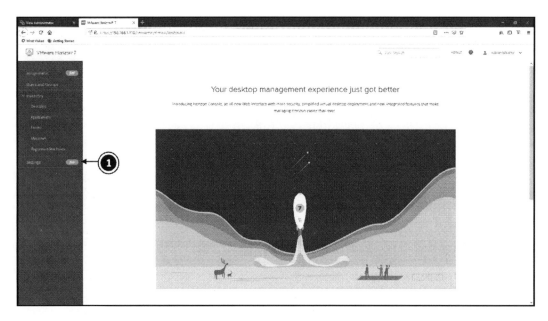

5. Click on **Settings JMP (1)**.

Chapter 14

6. You will now see the **JMP Settings** screen, as shown in the following screenshot:

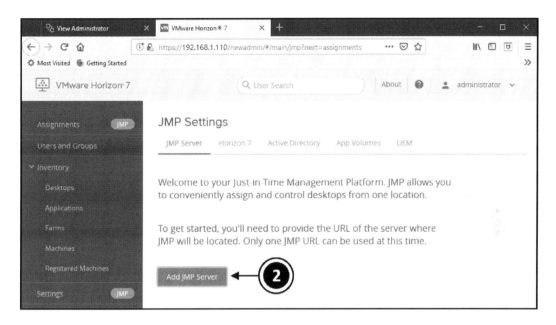

7. The first thing you need to do is add the JMP Server. To do this, click **Add JMP Server** (2).
8. You will now see the **Add JMP Server** screen, as shown in the following screenshot:

JMP and VMware Horizon 7 Deployment Considerations

9. In the **JMP Server URL** box, enter the address for the JMP Server. In the example lab, this is `https://jmp.pvolab.com`.
10. Click **Save** to continue.
11. You will now return to the **JMP Settings** screen, which now shows that the **JMP Server** has been validated and added, as shown in the following screenshot:

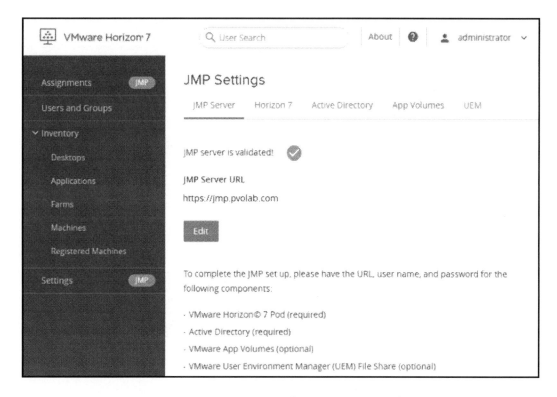

12. Next, we are going to move on to the Horizon 7 configuration and add the Horizon Connection Server. You will now see the following screenshot:

Chapter 14

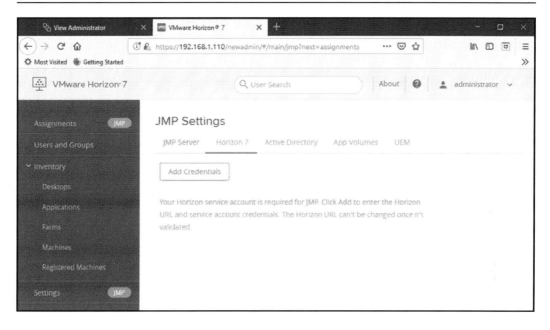

13. Click the **Add Credentials** button.
14. You will now see the **Edit Horizon** configuration screen, as shown in the following screenshot:

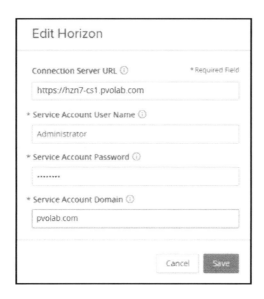

JMP and VMware Horizon 7 Deployment Considerations

15. In the **Connection Server URL** box, enter the address to the Connection Server. In the example lab, this is `https://hzn7-cs1.pvolab.com`.
16. In the **Service Account User Name**, enter the username that is used for the Horizon View service account, and in the **Service Account Password** box, enter the password for the account.
17. Finally, in the **Service Account Domain** box, enter the domain name. In the example lab, this is the `pvolab.com` domain.
18. When you have completed the configuration details, click **Save** to continue.
19. Next, we are going to configure **Active Directory**, as shown in the following screenshot:

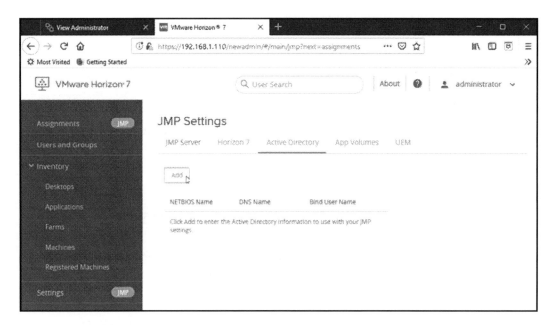

20. Click the **Add** button.

[706]

21. You will now see the **Add Active Directory** configuration screen, as shown in the following screenshot:

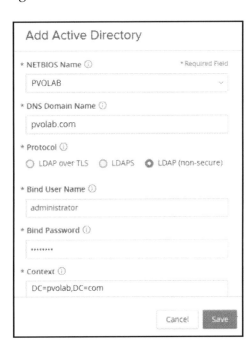

22. In the **NETBIOS Name** box, enter the NETBIOS name for the domain. In the example lab, this is `PVOLAB`.
23. Then, in the **DNS Domain Name** box, enter the name of the domain. In the example lab, this is `pvolab.com`. Then, click the radio button to choose the protocol. In the example lab, we are going to select **LDAP (non-secure)**.
24. In the **Bind User Name**, enter a user that has access to Active Directory and can create machine and user accounts, and then in the **Bind Password** box, enter the password for this user account.
25. Finally, in the **Context** box, enter the details in the format `DC=`. In the example lab, this would be `DC=pvolab,DC=com`.
26. When you have completed the configuration details, click **Save** to continue.

JMP and VMware Horizon 7 Deployment Considerations

27. Next, we are going to configure **App Volumes**, as shown in the following screenshot:

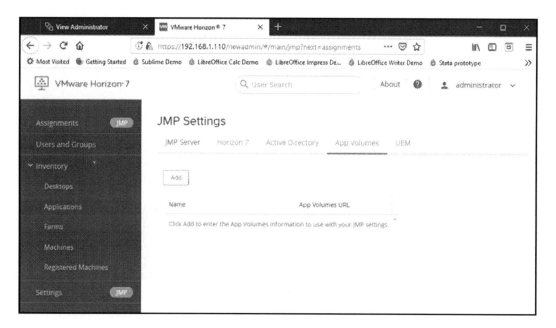

28. Click the **Add** button.
29. You will now see the **Add App Volumes Instance** configuration screen, as shown in the following screenshot:

30. In the **Name** box, enter the name of the **App Volumes** instance.
31. Next, in the **App Volumes Server URL** box, enter the address to the App Volumes Server. In the example lab, this is `https://app-vol.pvolab.com`.
32. In the **Service Account User Name**, enter the details of the service account that's used to manage the App Volumes server, and in the **Service Account Password** box, enter the password for the service account.
33. Finally, in the **Service Account Domain** box, enter the name of the domain for the service account.
34. When you have completed the configuration details, click **Save** to continue.
35. Next, we are going to configure the final component, **UEM**, as shown in the following screenshot:

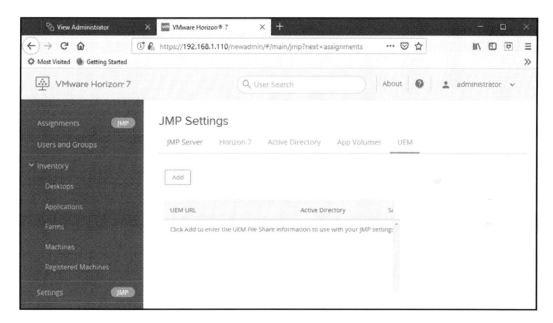

36. Click the **Add** button.
37. You will now see the **Add UEM File Share** configuration screen, as shown in the following screenshot:

38. In the **File Share UNC Path** box, enter the path details to the **UEM** configuration share. In the example lab, this is on the domain controller, and so the path is `\\dc\uem-configuration`.
39. In the **User Name** box, enter the details of a user that has access to the shared folder, and in the **Password** box, enter the password for this account.
40. Finally, in the **Active Directory** box, enter the domain details.
41. When you have completed the configuration details, click **Save** to continue.

You have now successfully configured the JMP Server settings. In the next section, we are going to look at configuring JMP assignments.

Chapter 14

JMP assignments

Now that we have completed the setup and configuration of the JMP Server and the other components, we can now create the JMP assignments. A JMP assignment brings together the end users, Instant Clone virtual desktop pools, applications (App Volumes AppStacks), and user profiles and settings (VMware UEM). To create the assignment, follow these steps:

1. Log in to the Horizon Console using `https://hzn7-cs1.pvolab.com/newadmin`.

> As with the previous configuration steps, JMP assignments can only be configured using the new Horizon Console.

2. You will then see the login screen. Log in using the administrator account and password.
3. Once you're logged in, click on **Assignments JMP (1)** in the top left of the screen, as shown in the following screenshot:

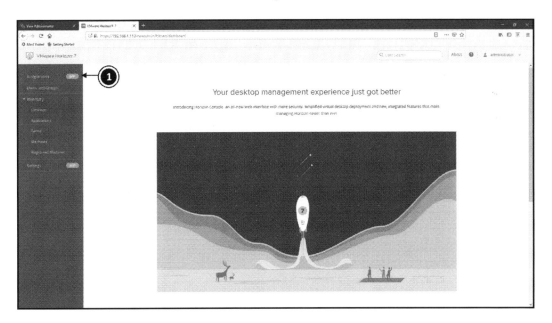

4. You will now see the **JMP Assignments** screen.
5. Click the **New** button. You will now see the **New Assignment** screen.
6. Enter the details of either a user or group that you want to assign the desktop workspace to. These users and groups are selected from the domain details that were entered during the configuration process. In the search box, start typing in the user or group name. The matching names will appear in the results box.
7. Select the user or group you want to assign and then click **Next** to continue.
8. You will now see the **Desktops** configuration screen, where you choose the desktop pool to include in the JMP assignment. Select the desktop pool from the table of those shown (read from the Connection Server), and then click **Next**.
9. In the next screen, you can choose which applications you want to include in the JMP assignment. These applications are the **AppStacks**, which are displayed and available from the configured App Volumes server. Select the apps from those displayed in the table and then click **Next** to continue.
10. You will now see the **User Environment** configuration screen. The settings on this screen are automatically pulled from the **UEM** server that was configured in the previous section.
11. The first setting on the screen is for **Disable UEM Settings** and is a simple on or off switch. Switching this to on means that none of the UEM settings will be applied to this assignment. If you have this set to **No** and you click on **Skip** in the settings page, then be aware that all settings will be applied to the assignment. You will also see a list of the settings displayed in a table on the screen. You can check individual settings if you want to apply them to this assignment.
12. Click **Next** to continue.
13. You will now see the **Definitions** configuration screen. In the **Name** box, enter a name for this JMP assignment, and optionally, enter a description. A default assignment name is automatically added.
14. Then, in the **AppStack Attach** box, from the drop-down menu, select how you want the AppStacks to be attached to the virtual machines. You can choose either **On next login** or **Immediately**.
15. Click **Next** to continue.
16. You will now see the **Summary** screen.
17. If you are happy with your configuration, then click **Submit**.
18. You will now return to the **JMP Settings** screen where you will see that the assignment is shown as **Pending**. Once the assignment is loaded, the status will change to **Success**.

You have successfully configured a JMP assignment. When an end user next logs in to a desktop in the desktop pool that's been configured as part of the assignment, the virtual desktop machine will be created from an Instant Clone. The apps will be delivered via an App Volumes AppStack and the user's profile and personal data will be delivered via VMware UEM.

Summary

In this chapter, we have taken a closer look at the just-in-time management platform and how it delivers all the component parts that make up the desktop back to the end users on demand. JMP is made up of a number of different VMware technologies: Instant Clones to build the virtual desktop machines, App Volumes to deliver applications as app layers (AppStacks), and VMware UEM to deliver the unique end user elements such as profiles and user-authored data. Optionally, the desktops and apps can be made available from the Workspace ONE portal.

Using this approach allows you to deliver truly stateless virtual desktop machines on demand.

In the next chapter, we are going to look at some of the tips for troubleshooting an environment.

15
Troubleshooting

As you must be aware by now, a successful VDI, or end-user computing project, is made up of multiple components, and its success comes down to delivering a good user experience. It's not just about whether the infrastructure is working or not. As such, it is important to have a well-defined methodology, and the tools to be able to adequately diagnose and fix issues within your environment. In this chapter, we are going to cover some of the troubleshooting techniques, and other methods for monitoring the end user experience within Horizon View.

Essentially, we are going to look at troubleshooting from two angles, reactive and proactive, covering the following topics:

- General troubleshooting tips
- Troubleshooting Horizon View issues
- vRealize Operations for Horizon
- Liquidware Stratusphere UX

We are also going to use Liquidware Stratusphere UX to highlight some of the key elements to look at when troubleshooting and monitoring your environment.

General troubleshooting tips

In the first section of this chapter, we are going to briefly look at some general troubleshooting tips. We will start with looking at what the end users are reporting as issues. Is it down to a particular app or desktop configuration? If it is a performance-related issue, we need to be able to correlate that back to the supporting infrastructure components, such as which server their desktop or apps are running on, so that we can isolate host resource issues, such as a slow network or slow disk.

Look at the bigger picture

Quite often, when there are issues, it is the VDI solution that automatically gets the blame. This is because it is a new deployment, and end user perception is that, because the desktop is running remotely, then it is to blame. You need to remember that the Horizon View technology is just one component in the overall infrastructure, along with the desktop that the user is utilizing. Just because the desktop is sitting within a VDI environment doesn't always mean it's a View issue. It could well be a desktop, network, or application issue, which would have occurred in a physical environment too.

When a user reports an issue, or you notice an issue within the infrastructure, you will need to think logically as to which component within the infrastructure is going to be the likely cause, and where you are going to start your troubleshooting journey. Maybe it is a storage issue, or even a Windows issue, and it has got nothing to do with VDI at all!

Is the issue affecting more than one user?

A good place to start examining any issues within your environment is by finding the answers to the following questions: who is experiencing the issue? Has more than one user reported the same issue? If you try and recreate the issue, do you get the same results? Can another user, with the same permissions and the same resources, recreate the issue?

If you find that the issue is really only related to a single user, then consider what the issue is that they are experiencing. For example, you can ask the following questions:

- What device are they connecting from?
- What connection protocol are they connecting over, and have they tried a different protocol?
- Could it be a bandwidth or connection reliability issue?
- Could a port be blocked?
- Do they have specific application or permission requirements?
- Are they entitled the correct pools?

If you believe that the issue has something to do with their desktop, then maybe consider refreshing it. This is the beauty of VDI; you could simply rebuild a new desktop, and not spend hours trying to troubleshoot and fix application or OS issues if a simple refresh could resolve it.

If the issue is affecting more than one user, check whether a fix could be applied to the base image, and then be rolled out to your desktop pools to simplify the process of resolving the issue.

Performance issues

This is probably one of the widest subject areas to look at when troubleshooting your View environment. Performance issues could relate to so many areas, aspects, and also (in some cases) be based on a personal opinion.

When a user reports performance issues

If your users are reporting poor performance, then ask them to try and be more specific, rather than them just saying "it's slow". Is it taking a long time to log in, or is it an application that is taking longer than expected to load? Keep a log of the issue, along with the time and date that the issue occurred, or if it's an ongoing issue.

Ask the users the following when the issue occurs:

- How are they measuring the performance?
- What time of the day do they experience the problem?
- Are they doing something specific when they experience the problem?
- Are they connecting from somewhere specific, or from a specific device, when they have the issue?

Wherever possible, try to visit the end user and understand their issue first-hand. This will enable you to the get to the bottom of the issue with ease. Hopefully, as we discussed in Chapter 3, *Design and Deployment Considerations*, you will have engaged the end users early, and they will be positive and on board with the overall solution and willing to help.

Troubleshooting

Using Liquidware Stratusphere, you could also look at the baseline for when this user was on-boarded, and then look at the trend information. This will help you identify any changes to the environment, and you would also know what else was happening at the time they experienced the issue. An example of this is shown in the following screenshot:

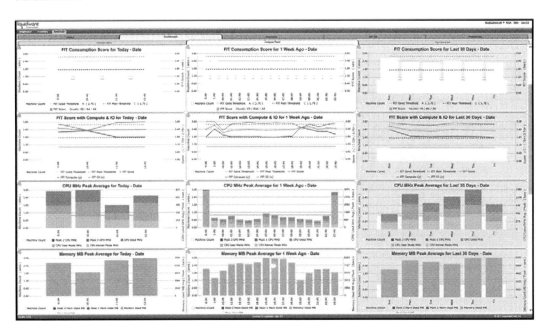

Liquidware Stratusphere showing trend information

Non-VDI related issues

Performance issues on a desktop can be caused by many factors, regardless of whether they are virtual or physical desktops. Common areas for consideration include the following:

- Extended login times
- Application crashes
- Long application load times
- OS crashes
- Poor application performance
- Permission errors

As we just mentioned, many of these issues can, and will, occur whether the desktop is virtualized or not, but, in the virtualized environment, any type of issues that arise will be easier to resolve. For example, if you find you are getting OS or application crashes, consider patching these elements to the latest updates and recomposing the image for all users. This could take a lot longer, and be a lot more difficult, with a physical desktop estate.

Maybe login times or application load times are suffering due to a CPU performance issue. The following screenshot shows the output of the login monitoring feature of Liquidware Stratusphere:

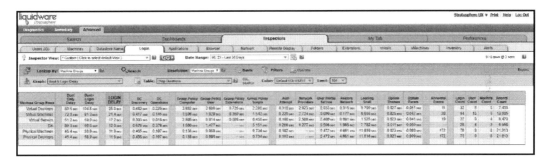

Monitoring feature of Liquidware Stratusphere

With each individual virtual desktop machine, you can drill down into each process and service running on it, allowing you to see things such as how long the process took to load, as well as any other dependencies that process has. This is invaluable information when troubleshooting login issues, and particularity when migrating from physical desktops to virtual desktops and identifying services that should not be used in virtual environments, yet still exist and cause issues in virtual desktops.

With physical desktops, you would be stuck with the hardware unless you replace or upgrade the constrained components, but in a VDI environment you can consider tweaking the spec at a push of a button, as long as you have the underlying resources.

The important point to understand is that generic desktop issues will still exist regardless, and so, it is recommended to use the VDI platform to your advantage to help resolve these. We have worked with so many organizations that have deployed VDI and have it running in production, and once the solution is implemented they tend to forget about generic desktop support and spend far too much time digging deep into the VDI architecture infrastructure looking for faults, when the answer maybe a simple Windows OS or application issue.

Troubleshooting

Bandwidth, connectivity, and networking

Any networking-related issues can often be the most difficult to get to the bottom of. Wherever possible, ensure that you work closely with your networking team to ensure there is suitable end-to-end monitoring in place.

While your users are connecting on a LAN, you would hope there would be plentiful bandwidth, latency would be low enough, and therefore connectivity would be reliable. If you are struggling on a LAN, consider the following:

- Has anything on the network changed?
- Is the user connecting via a wired or wireless network?
- Have you configured PCoIP for QoS on your switches?
- Is the network currently reliable?
- Are you seeing any dropped packets between any of the following?
    - Clients to the core switching
    - Clients to servers
    - Clients to VDI desktops
- Is the latency as expected?
- Even on the LAN in larger environments, bandwidth could be an issue—have you considered the sum of the bandwidth required from your client devices to VDI desktops?
- Are you routing between networks? Do the routers work at a suitable level of performance?
- Are the load balancers sized correctly for your environment?

When your users are connecting over a WAN, it can sometimes be more difficult to troubleshoot or guarantee connection quality.

For remote or branch offices, ensure that the internet connection is suitably sized; wherever possible, ensure that you have configured QoS for the PCoIP protocol from end to end, and ensure that you have suitably configured the PCoIP policy to cope with the reduced bandwidth.

When troubleshooting issues, investigate the relevant logs on the client and on the View Connection Servers, as well as any intermediary components, such as the load balancers and routers.

The following list contains some of the more common faults that a user will report:

- **Black screens**: This is commonly caused by ports blocking the PCoIP Protocol somewhere in the chain. Check that the PCoIP port are open; namely, port `4172`.
- **Disconnections**: High latency and dropped packets will cause the users to be disconnected from their desktops. Ensure that you allow enough time for users to reconnect before refreshing desktops.
- **Poor resolution images**: Due to the nature of the protocol if there is low bandwidth, users may complain about low-quality images. Consider limiting the image build options in the user policy.

The following screenshot shows an example of information for the PCoIP protocol recorded by Liquidware Stratusphere UX:

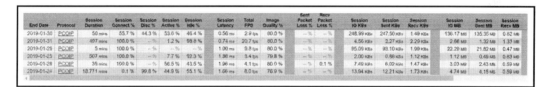

PCoIP protocol

In the next section, we are going to look at compute resources.

Compute resources

CPU and memory issues on your host servers can adversely affect the end user experience. As with most technical solutions, we recommend that, while you are going through your initial testing and rolling out, you document your baseline for key performance characteristics, such as CPU and memory utilization, and deeper metrics such as CPU-ready times.

With this baseline information in your toolkit, it is easier to compare the performance before the issue occurred to what you are seeing now. This will help to try and pinpoint what could be causing the problem. Likewise, using technology such as vRealize Operations for Horizon will help you understand performance utilization over time. You could use a third-party product such as Liquidware Stratusphere. Stratusphere provides the baseline metrics (measured during the assessment phase), as well as the current user experience, allowing you to quickly identify what changed, and what is causing the issue.

Troubleshooting

Within your VDI infrastructure, you don't want to be experiencing any memory overcommits. You need to consider how much memory is allocated to your virtual desktops, as well as the total memory within your hosts. Ideally, you want to ensure that your total allocated memory is less than the total in your host servers. Don't forget that should one of the host servers fail, you will still need to supply the required memory resource.

If you are experiencing performance issues related to memory or CPU, check whether memory is being swapped by any of the virtual desktop machines. Check whether there is any ballooning within the environment. Understand what your CPU-ready characteristics are. The acceptable CPU-ready figures within your VDI environment will vary based on the environment and users. Generally speaking, you are going to want to keep CPU-ready below 5% per allocated CPU, with 10% at peak. Anything over these numbers would indicate that the host server is being overloaded, and will impact the performance of the CPU and lead to slow performance of the virtual desktop machines. The following screenshot shows an example of CPU monitoring and, in particular, the CPU-ready time:

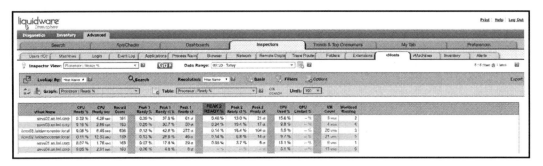

CPU monitoring and CPU-ready time

It can be very easy when growing your VDI solution from the initial design to forget to sanity-check these metrics and keep an eye on them as you grow, and, all of a sudden, you may find you have a compute performance issue.

Disk

As we have previously mentioned, the disk solution deployed is a key component for a successful VDI deployment. You need to be able to keep an eye on the disk performance, which is key to avoiding issues in the future.

How much latency is acceptable within your environment is going to very much depend on the users. Also consider what will happen as you scale up the solution. While we may say that disk latency of less than 25 ms is generally acceptable, it doesn't mean that a user who has been using a desktop with sub-25 ms latency would even notice if, all of a sudden, they were experiencing 25 ms latency or more.

Your storage vendor will likely have their own toolset to manage and monitor the performance; however, the following screenshot shows an overview of storage IOPS performance on a per-host basis:

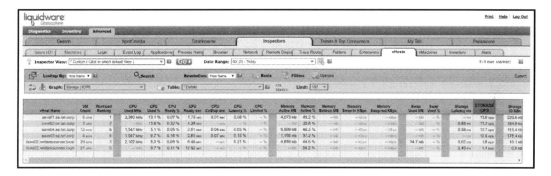

Overview of storage IOPS performance

Having covered some of the general troubleshooting tips around the infrastructure components, in the next section, we are going to look at Horizon View-specific issues.

Troubleshooting Horizon View issues

There are a number of components that we have discussed throughout this book that make up your Horizon View infrastructure, and while they are generally very reliable, they can of course fail at some point, with serious knock-on effects. Wherever possible, you should be ensuring that your Horizon environment is highly available, and where this may not be possible, then ensure that the components are sufficiently monitored using components such as vRealize Operations for Horizon, or, as we have used in the example lab, a third-party monitoring solution such as Liquidware Stratusphere.

Horizon View general infrastructure issues

The first port of call when troubleshooting your Horizon View infrastructure should be the event log within the Horizon View Administrator console. You can quickly and easily access the event log by clicking alerts in the top left-hand corner of the screen, as shown in the following screenshot:

Event log within the Horizon View Administrator console

You should also utilize the dashboard view in the View Administrator to get a quick overview to understand the health of your environment. This screen will show you the health of all the key components within your infrastructure, such as vCenter, Hosts, View Connection Servers, View Security Servers, Desktops, RDS Hosts and Datastores.

This is a great resource to start troubleshooting infrastructure issues within your Horizon View environment.

You should also not forget the simplest of troubleshooting steps when experiencing issues with your Horizon View Infrastructure:

- Are all the servers, desktops, hosts, and so on, contactable on the network?
- Are all the required services started?
- Is there sufficient free space on all servers?
- Is the memory and CPU maxed out?
- Have you checked all the events logs?

Consideration also needs to be given to the backend database systems, and the effect that would be felt if they were to go offline. Ensure your SQL solution is reliant and the same as all other components. If you are having issues with maybe your vCenter or View Composer, ensure you check the SQL Server for the following:

- Are there sufficient resources?
- Are the services started?
- Are the correct ports open?
- Is there enough free disk space for the database and logs?

View infrastructure component issues

Of course, there may be issues that arise that are outside those that we have discussed so far. Horizon View has its own integrated system health monitoring and, as such, reports errors relating to Horizon View-specific issues, allowing administrators to quickly pinpoint issues easily. Unfortunately, sometimes the corrective actions can be quite cumbersome and manual to implement.

Issues you may see that require specific corrective actions are as follows:

- Manual removal of a View Connection Server or Security Server after loss of a component or OS corruptions
- Manual removal of VDI desktops or whole pools
- Recovery of Horizon View from a backup
- Recovery of a persistent disk from a backup
- Persistent disks running out of space for users

We aren't going to cover all the specific corrective actions for all of these processes here, as we could write an entire book to do them justice, but there are some great **knowledge-base (KB)** articles already available on VMware's KB site at http://kb.vmware.com.

One issue that we will cover briefly, and one that does come up fairly often, is with the View Composer database, and inconsistencies in the database that lead to provisioning errors. VMware has a tool to address database errors called the **ViewDBChk** tool, which we will cover in the next section.

Troubleshooting

Fixing View Composer issues with the ViewDBChk tool

A provisioning error can occur when there are inconsistencies between the LDAP, vCenter Server, and View Composer databases, and are often caused by editing virtual desktop machines directly in the vCenter Server inventory, or restoring a virtual desktop machine from a backup.

The ViewDBChk tool allows View administrators to scan for machines that cannot be provisioned, and also allows you to remove invalid database entries. This then allows the Connection Server to be able to re-provision desktops without any errors.

You will find this in the `View` folder that gets created at install time. The folder can be found by navigating to the following path:

`C:\Program Files\VMware\VMware View\Server\Tools\bin`

The tool is command-line-driven, and has a number of parameters for each of the functions you can perform. These are listed in the following table:

Command Parameter	Output / Result
`--findDesktop`	Finds a desktop pool
`--enableDesktop`	Enables a desktop pool
`--disableDesktop`	Disables a desktop pool
`--findMachine`	Finds a machine
`--removeMachine`	Removes a machine from a desktop pool. Before removing a machine, ViewDbChk prompts the user to disable the desktop pool. After removing the machine, ViewDbChk prompts the user to re-enable the desktop pool.
`--scanMachines`	Searches for machines that are in an error or cloneerror state or have missing virtual machines, lists the problem machines grouped by desktop pool, and gives the option to remove the machines. Before removing a machine, ViewDbChk prompts the user to disable the desktop pool. After removing all erroneous machines in a desktop pool, ViewDbChk prompts the user to re-enable the desktop pool.
`--help`	Displays the syntax of ViewDbChk
`--desktopName desktop_name`	Specifies the desktop pool name
`--machineName machine_name`	Specifies the machine name
`--limit maximum_deletes`	Limits the number of machines that ViewDbChk can remove. The default is 1.
`--force`	Forces machine removal without user confirmation
`--noErrorCheck`	Forces the removal of machines that have no errors
`--verbose`	Enables verbose logging

Table showing parameters for each of the functions

For example, to run the command to remove a machine from a desktop pool, at the command prompt, type the following command:

```
ViewDbChk --removeMachine --desktopName
```

In the next section, we are going to look at some of the additional tools available for monitoring and managing the environment.

vRealize Operations for Horizon

vRealize Operations for Horizon is available as part of Horizon Enterprise or as a separate product. Where vRealize Operations differs from most monitoring tools is in its analytics engine. Most monitoring tools are based around setting thresholds for key values, such as CPU, or memory consumed. The issue with these kinds of alarms is that simply stumbling over a threshold value doesn't mean there is necessarily an issue. Sometimes, it is within the normal parameters of the applications in use, or potentially, the problem could be one of the resources not being consumed when it should be.

With the analytics engine included within vRealize Operations, it is able to learn and understand what the normal working parameters of your environment are. From this, it is then able to alert you when an error occurs that falls outside these parameters. It is also able to track growth and consumption over time to preempt an issue prior to it occurring.

vRealize Operations for Horizon should be installed, where possible, at the beginning of your project. vRealize Operations is deployed simply via a single virtual appliance, or vApp, and when deployed and configured, it starts listening and learning about your environment.

There are three key metrics tracked with vRealize Operations, which are health, risk, and efficiency:

- Health reports on the current health status of your environment. Items that could affect health are high packet loss, component failure, and disk capacity at a critical level, among others.
- Risk indicates an issue within your environment that, if left unattended, could very well become an issue to the health of your environment.

Troubleshooting

- Efficiency reports on considerations, such as overprovisioning, which, if rectified, could help you get more out of your environment to maximize the investment. An example of this is VMs with overprovisioned CPU or memory.

The following screenshot shows an end user experience dashboard, highlighting CPU usage:

End user experience dashboard

vRealize Operations for Horizon also includes specific features to ensure you fully understand the health of your Horizon View environment, including the full visibility of the PCoIP protocol as well as integration for health monitoring with the View Connection Server, View Security, and more.

The analytics engine of vRealize Operations will learn your environment and understand what is normal, raising alarms based on dynamic thresholds for your environment rather than meaningless static thresholds.

Within vRealize Operations, it also incorporates a smart alerts feature that allows you to quickly understand the root cause of an issue within your infrastructure, and the recommended remediation actions to resolve the issue.

There are also a number of third-party tools and solutions that go beyond the monitoring of the environment. One of those tools is Liquidware's Stratusphere solution, which we will discuss in the next section.

Liquidware Stratusphere UX

Liquidware Stratusphere UX is more than just a monitoring tool. In fact, it is more of a user life cycle management tool, and has played a part throughout the deployment we have covered throughout this book. We first used the output from Stratusphere UX when we assessed our current environment to provide us with an overview of the resources being used, but also to give us a baseline to work from as we deployed Horizon.

We then used this baseline to assist in tuning the end user experience as we on-boarded users and built our gold images to ensure that the end users were running at their most optimal levels of performance.

Finally, Stratusphere can be used as a diagnostic tool to aid the IT support team to get to the root cause of an issue quickly. IT can quickly understand where the issue lies, providing a detailed analysis of a single user, single machine, or single application, allowing an end-to-end view of a user's virtual desktop session, where it's hosted, and what resources it's consuming, helping to identify issues quickly.

As you will have seen in the previous sections and the screenshots, Liquidware Stratusphere can easily help monitor and manage your environment.

Getting further help

There are a number of resources available if you are struggling to get to the bottom of an issue with Horizon View. First and foremost, we recommend logging a call as early as possible with VMware Support to get the best assistance possible to resolve your issue. You could also try the various blogs and posts from the VMware EUC community.

There is also the VMware Community, which has a wealth of resources available at `https://communities.vmware.com`.

Troubleshooting

Finally, and possibly the most useful resource, is the VMware Knowledge Base, as we mentioned previously in this chapter. At the time of writing this, there are 300 specific support topics related to Horizon View, including video how-to guides alongside step-by-step resolution guides.

Summary

In this chapter, we have covered some of the methods and areas to consider when troubleshooting issues within your Horizon View environment. Consideration should be given to the bigger picture, ensuring you fully understand the issues the user is facing, and which area of the user's desktop experience could be causing these issues. Where possible, use monitoring tools such as vRealize Operations for Horizon to find the root cause of the problem. There are a number of areas within Horizon View you should check if you believe you have infrastructure problems. These include the dashboard and the event log within the Horizon View Administrator.

Finally, we covered getting further help from the VMware Knowledge Base.

We have now reached the end of this book, and by reaching this point, you should now have a greater understanding of the architecture of the Horizon Suite and how to design your end user computing solution. You should also understand the stages and details involved with rolling out Horizon View for your users, including installing the various components, and configuring, designing, and building the desktop images and pools. You will have learned about the various methods to layer your applications to your desktops, using technology such as ThinApp, RDSH-published applications, and App Layers.

Designing and rolling out any end user computing solution to any organization is a task that must be undertaken with care and understanding for the users, and we hope the topics that we have covered within this book will better equip you for your tasks ahead.

16
What is New in Horizon 7

Since I started writing this book, VMware has released version 7.7 and 7.8 of Horizon.

These new releases adds a number of updated features and expanded support, which we will discuss in this chapter. We will also discuss platform and infrastructure changes.

Operating system and infrastructure updates

In the latest Horizon 7 version releases, VMware has added support for newer operating systems, virtual infrastructures, and other software applications. These are as follows:

- Support for Windows Server 2019 (including RDSH support)
- Support for VMware vSphere 6.7 Update 1
- Support for VMware vSAN 6.7 Update 1
- The ability to upgrade the Horizon Cloud Connector (used for VMware on AWS)
- Support for IPv6 with the VMware virtualization pack for Skype

There have also been a number of improvements and new features when using VMware Cloud on AWS to run Horizon. These are as follows:

- The minimum size cluster has now been reduced to 3
- Support for vSphere stretched clusters
- Support for NSX-T and VMware vSAN datastore encryption
- Support for Horizon 7 Enterprise Edition, adding VMware UEM, VMware App Volumes, and VMware Instant Clone
- Support for running Linux desktops

In the next section, we are going to look at some new management features.

Horizon management updates

In this book, we have used a mixture of both the original View Administrator and the new Horizon Console to manage our Horizon View environment. The main reason is that some management tasks and features don't exist in the new Horizon Console.

Horizon console updates

In this release, VMware has added some new functionality into the new Horizon Console. These features are as folllows:

- Managing manual desktop pools.
- Managing Linked Clone desktop pools and Linked Clone persistent disks.
- The addition of a new **Connected User** column and an **Assigned User** column to make it easier to see who is connected to a virtual desktop machine. This has also been added to the original View Administrator.

View Administrator updates

VMware has added some new functionality into the View Administrator management console. These features are as follows:

- VMware Unified Access Gateway is displayed on the system health dashboard.
- The Connection Server Pod name is now displayed in the browser, on the title bar.

Help Desk Tool updates

Finally, for the management updates, VMware has added some new functionality into the Help Desk Tool. An administrator now has the ability to end a running application process.

In the next section, we will look at scalability enhancements in Horizon 7, version 7.7.

Scalability

Along with the features that have been added to this latest 7.7 release, VMware has also enhanced the scalability of Horizon, adding support for larger deployments. These features are as follows:

- A single vCenter Server now has the ability to manage multiple pods when using the Cloud Pod Architecture.
- Support for up to 500 RDSH servers in a farm.
- vMotion support for Linked Clone and automated desktop pools with full virtual machines.
- vMotion support for Full Clone, Instant Clone, and Linked Clone virtual desktop machines that are configured to use vGPU.

In the next section, we are going to look at end user experience enhancements.

Enhancements to the end user experience

The end user experience is the key to a successful Horizon environment, and in this latest release VMware has added more features to improve the overall experience for the end user. These features are as follows:

- Physical PCs now support the Blast Extreme protocol.
- Blast Extreme HEVC (H.265) video encoding support. This doubles the data compression rate but maintains the quality. NVIDIA GRID is not a requirement for this feature.
- Support for copying and dragging and dropping files and folders for Client Drive Redirection.
- Virtual Print feature added. This allows printing to any printer on the end user's Windows client. This feature also supports client printer redirection and location-based printing.
- Administrators can specify whether users can open multiple instances of the same application.
- Users can assign RDSH-published apps when using Windows clients.
- Hybrid login feature now supports app access for unauthenticated users.

In the final section, we are going to look some enhancements added to Linux-based virtual desktop machines.

Linux virtual desktop machine updates

Linux is becoming more popular as the operating system for virtual desktop machines. VMware continues to add features to bring it up to the same level as those features supported when using Windows desktops. Linux features now include the following:

- SLES 12x virtual desktop machines now support SSO
- SLED/SLES supports audio-in
- Support for Instant Clone floating desktop pools
- Session collaboration
- Instant Clone support for offline domain joins

Platform updates

With the platform updates, Horizon now supports newer operating systems, as detailed here:

- Connection server now supports Microsoft Windows Server 2019
- View composer now supports Microsoft Windows Server 2019
- Microsoft Skype for Business 2019 is now supported in a Horizon environment

In the next section, we are going to look at the Horizon Console updates.

Horizon Console updates

In the previous versions of Horizon, there were still a large number of management tasks and features that were still only available in the View Administrator Console. In this latest release, a lot of these features are now present in the new Horizon Console. These newly added features are listed here:

- Manage persistent disks in a Linked Clone environment
- Manage global policies

- Manage administrator access as well as role-based access
- Manage vCenter Server settings and Connection Server settings
- Manage Linked Clone and View Composer
- Manage Cloud Pod Architecture settings
- The ability to create shortcuts for RDSH published apps and desktops

In the next section, we are going to look at the scalability of Horizon.

Scalability

Cloud Pod Architecture now supports the following:

- 250,000 sessions
- 50 pods
- 10,000 sessions per pod
- 15 sites
- 7 connection servers per pod
- 350 total connection servers

In the next section, we are going to look at the improvements that occur when we deliver apps and desktops using RDSH.

RDSH improvements

The following features have been added to the RDSH feature of Horizon View for delivering published apps and desktops:

- The ability to configure the load balancing of desktop and app sessions using a graphical user interface instead of the manual scripted approach of previous versions
- Published apps and desktop support for configuring client restrictions for OUs

In the next section, we are going to look at a couple of new features that are supported if you use Horizon on VMware Cloud on AWS.

Horizon with VMware Cloud on AWS

If you are running your Horizon environment on VMware Cloud, which is running on AWS, then the following new features are supported:

- NSX-T on VMC now has Multi-vLAN support
- Support for AWS 1.6

In the next section, we are going to look at the Horizon Agent updates.

Horizon Agent updates

As well as the server-based components being updated, to take advantage of some of these new features, the Horizon Agent has also been updated to support multiple platforms. These are going to be discussed in this section.

Windows Agent

The Horizon Agent for Windows now includes the following features:

- URL content redirection rules using regular expressions
- Smart card authentication support for **Universal Windows Platform (UWP)** apps
- The help desk agent in now integrated as part of the Horizon Agent installation process
- VMware integrated printing finishing

To take advantage of these features, you will need to update the Horizon Agent that's running on your Windows virtual desktop machines or your gold images, which you will then need to redeploy.

Linux Agent

The Horizon Agent for Windows now includes the following features:

- HTML access for multi-screen deployments
- Session Collaboration read-only mode
- SLED 12.x expanded support when running a NVIDIA vGPU

- RHEL 7.1 and onward support for smart card redirection
- True **Single Sign-On (SSO)** expanded OS support
- Extended support for CentOS 7.6 and RHEL operating systems

To take advantage of these features, you will need to update the Horizon Agent that you're running on your Linux virtual desktop machines or your gold images, which you will then need to redeploy.

Horizon Client

As well as the updates to the infrastructure and virtual desktop machine agents, this latest release also includes and upgrades the Horizon Clients to version 5.0. The details of these new features can be found in `Chapter 12`, *Horizon Client Options*.

You will also see that there is a new logo, as shown here:

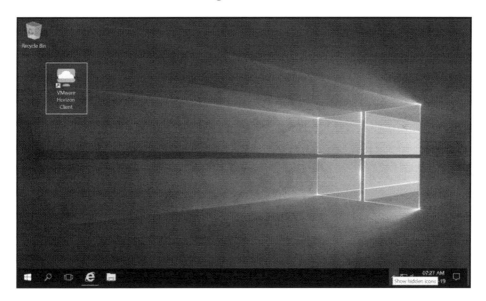

This logo is part of the redesign of the look and feel of Horizon to bring it more into line with the look and feel of the Workspace ONE solution.

Summary

In this chapter, we have briefly covered some of the new features that have been added to Horizon 7, version 7.7 and 7.8.

Full details of what's included can be found by taking a look at the following links:

```
https://docs.vmware.com/en/VMware-Horizon-7/7.7/rn/horizon-77-view-release-notes.html
```

```
https://docs.vmware.com/en/VMware-Horizon-7/7.8/rn/horizon-78-view-release-notes.html?hWord=N4IghgNiBcIOwDoAcIC+Q.
```

That now brings us to the end of this book, and I hope that you enjoyed reading about how the Horizon solution can benefit you and your organization, and that having followed the step-by-step example lab, you know have the knowledge to build your own Horizon environment.

Other Books You May Enjoy

If you enjoyed this book, you may be interested in these other books by Packt:

Mastering VMware vSphere 6.7 - Second Edition
Andrea Mauro, Karel Novak, Et al

ISBN: 978-1-78961-337-7

- Get a deep understanding of vSphere 6.7 functionalities
- Design a virtualization environment based on VMware vSphere 6.7
- Manage and administer a vSphere 6.7 environment and resources
- Get tips for the VCP6-DCV and VCIX6-DCV exams
- Implement different migration techniques across different environments
- Deploy and understand different concepts of VMware vSphere 6.7 lab

Implementing VMware Horizon 7.7 - Third Edition
Jason Ventresco

ISBN: 978-1-78961-784-9

- Work with the different products that make up VMware Horizon
- Implement a multi-site VMware Horizon Pod using the Cloud Pod Architecture feature
- Deploy and configure VMware Horizon's optional components
- Implement and maintain Microsoft RDSH, Horizon Linux, and Windows Desktop Pools and RDSH Application Pools
- Configure and manage Horizon remotely using PowerCLI
- Learn about the Microsoft Windows Group Policy templates for Horizon
- Understand how to manage the SSL certificates for each of the VMware Horizon components

Leave a review - let other readers know what you think

Please share your thoughts on this book with others by leaving a review on the site that you bought it from. If you purchased the book from Amazon, please leave us an honest review on this book's Amazon page. This is vital so that other potential readers can see and use your unbiased opinion to make purchasing decisions, we can understand what our customers think about our products, and our authors can see your feedback on the title that they have worked with Packt to create. It will only take a few minutes of your time, but is valuable to other potential customers, our authors, and Packt. Thank you!

Index

A

Active Directory (AD)
  about 171, 299, 543
  configuring 544
  DNS, requisite 181
  Group Policy Objects (GPO), creating for Horizon View 548, 550, 552
  Horizon View ADMX templates, applying 545
  Horizon View ADMX templates, importing 545
  IP addressing, requisite 181
  loopback policy, enabling 553, 555
  organizational unit (OU), creating 546
  Organizational Units (OUs) 180
  preparing 172, 544
  user accounts 173
  user accounts, used for viewing vCenter Server 173, 175, 176, 177, 178, 180
  View Composer user account 180
Active Directory Application Mode (ADAM) 52
Active Management Technology (AMT) 337
antivirus software
  for virtual desktops 71
application pools
  creating, for published apps 628, 629, 631
  users, entitling to 631, 633, 635
AppStacks 693
assessment, project definition
  about 100
  applications 103
  department champions 105, 106
  desktop analysis tools 101, 103
  floor walks 105
  interviews 105
  performance 104
  user experience 101, 103
  user experience, ending 105
  users tasks 103
automated desktop pools
  about 404
  dedicated, Full Clone desktop pools, creating 472, 473, 476, 478, 480, 482, 484
  dedicated, Linked Clone desktop pools, creating 405
AWS
  Horizon, running with VMware Cloud 736

B

backup
  about 157
  options 157
bandwidth 720
Blast Extreme
  about 77
  connection process, working 79
  features 78
  using 82
block architecture 117, 118, 119, 120, 121, 122
Brokerless View 35
browser
  used, for accessing desktop 665, 667, 669

C

Capital expenditure (CAPEX) 17
Certificate Authority (CA) 40, 268
Certificate Revocation Lists (CRL) 316
client software
  download link 651, 654
cloning 44
Cloud Pod Architecture
  about 122, 123
  configuring 246, 248, 249

initializing 247, 250
second pod, connecting 251, 252, 253, 254
users, entitling 254, 255, 256, 258, 259, 260
compatibility
  upgrading 671, 673
components, View architecture
  about 32
  Horizon View Connection Server 32
  Horizon View enrolment server 39
  Horizon View replica server 37
  Horizon View security server 36
  True SSO 39
  VMware Unified Access Gateway 41, 42
composite desktop
  applications 156
  base layer 156
  user environment management 156
  user profiles 156
compute resources 721
configuration maximums 138
connectivity 720
Content Based Read Cache (CBRC) 46, 442

D

delivery protocols, virtual desktop machine
  about 72
  Blast Extreme 77
  PCoIP 72
  Remote Desktop Protocol (RDP) 80
delta disk 49
department champions 106
design specifics, Horizon View
  about 134
  configuration maximums 138
  networking 138, 140
  Remote Desktop Session Host (RDSH),
    design considerations 142, 143, 144
  vCenter Servers 136
  View Composer 136
  View Connection Server 135
  View Enrolment Server 136
  View Replica Server 135
  View Security Server 135
  VMware Access Point 137
Desktop as a Service (DaaS) 35

desktop design considerations
  about 149
  composite desktop, building 155
  Full Clone 153
  host server's CPU requisite, sizing to run
    virtual desktops 150
  host server's memory requisite, sizing to run
    virtual desktops 153
  Instant Clone 153
  Linked Clone 153
  persistent, versus non-persistent 154
  pool design 149
  virtual desktop machines, sizing 150
desktop pools
  automated desktop pool 404
  Horizon Console method 450, 452, 454,
    456, 458, 460, 463, 465, 468, 470
  manual desktop pool 404
  RDS desktop pool 404
  setting up, Horizon View Administrator
    Console used 406, 407, 409, 410, 412
  types 403
desktop
  accessing, browser used 665, 667, 669
device splitting 68
differential disk 49
disaster recovery
  about 157
  options 157, 158, 159
disk 723
Distributed FileSystem Replication (DFSR) 159
Dynamic Virtual Channels (DVC) 93

E

End User Computing (EUC) 11
end user experience
  enhancing 733
  features 733
  monitoring 581
end-user entitlements
  adding 511
  adding, Horizon console used 516, 518, 520
  adding, Horizon View Administrator Classic
    console used 514, 516
  adding, Horizon View Administrator console

used 512
Enrollment Agent (Computer) certificate 318
Enrollment Server
   installing 244, 245, 246
enterprise mobility management (EMM) 692
ESXi host servers
   configuring 261, 263
   CPU, overcommitting 126
   CPU, requirements 126
   CPU, sizing 127
   graphics 128
   memory resources, overcommitting 126
   memory, requirements 126
   memory, sizing 127
   networking 128
   storage 129
   storage capacity 129, 130, 131
   storage performance 131, 132, 133, 134
example lab environment
   about 169
   requisite 170, 172
example solution scenario
   about 160
   desktop blocks, sizing 164, 165
   desktop pool design 163
   management blocks, sizing 167
   network, requisite 167
   network, sizing 167
   storage requisite, sizing 166
   user requisite 161

F

Flex+ 64
fling 371
floating, full-clone desktop pool
   creating 492, 494, 495
floating, instant clone desktop pools
   creating 496
floating, linked clone desktop pools
   creating 488, 489, 491, 492
full clone 45
fully qualified domain name (FQDN) 651

G

GPU-enabled virtual desktop machine
   creating 379
GPU-enabled virtual desktops
   configuring 260
graphics cards
   reference 88
Graphics Processing Unit (GPU) 75
graphics, Horizon View Hardware
   vDGA 86
   Virtual Graphics Processing Unit (vGPU) 88
   vSGA 83, 84
Group Policy Objects (GPO)
   creating, for Horizon View 548, 550, 552
group policy templates
   upgrading 686
group policy, infrastructure design
   functionality 146
   lockdown 147
   management 147
   performance 147

H

hardware clients
   about 661
   repurposed PCs (software-defined thin
      clients) 664, 665
   thin clients 662
   Zero Client 663
High Definition Experience (HDX) 81
Horizon 7
   download link 172
Horizon Advanced Edition 24
Horizon Agent
   for Linux 736
   for Windows 736
   installing 389, 390, 392
   installing, on virtual desktop machine 364,
      366, 370
   updates 736
Horizon Android Client, features
   about 652
   reference 653
Horizon Apps Advanced 25

Horizon Apps Standard 25
Horizon architecture
  overview 31
Horizon Chrome OS Client
  features 661
  features, reference 661, 669
Horizon Client
  about 95, 737
  upgrading 687
Horizon Console
  about 450
  updates 734
Horizon Enterprise Edition 24
Horizon for Linux 23
Horizon iOS Client
  features 655
Horizon Linux Client
  features 656
  features, reference 657
  for Chrome OS 660, 661
  for macOS 658
Horizon macOS Client, features
  reference 659
Horizon macOS Client
  features 658
Horizon management updates
  about 732
  console updates 732
  Help Desk Tool updates 732
  View Administrator updates 732
Horizon Standard Edition 23
Horizon View Administrator Console
  Adobe Flash settings 420, 422, 424, 425
  Advanced Storage Options 442, 444, 445, 447, 449
  Desktop Pool Sizing 426, 428, 429, 430, 432
  general settings 412, 414
  Remote Desktop Protocol settings 417, 418, 420
  remote settings 414, 415, 416, 417
  using 406, 407, 409, 410, 412
  vCenter Settings 432, 434, 435, 436, 438, 439, 440, 441
Horizon View ADMX templates

applying 545
  importing 545
Horizon View Agent Configuration
  about 562
  Agent Configuration 563
  Agent Security 563
  Collaboration 564
  Persona Management 564
  Scanner Redirection 567
  Serial COM 568
  Smartcard Redirection 568
  True SSO Configuration 569
  Unity Touch and Hosted Apps 570
  View Agent Direct-Connection Configuration 570
  View RTAV Configuration 571
  View USB Configuration 572
  VMware Client IP Transparency 573
  VMware Device Bridge 573
  VMware Flash MMR 574
  VMware HTML5 Features 574
  VMware View Common Configuration 576
  VMware View Server Configuration 578
Horizon View Agent
  features 619
  installing, for RDSH server 615, 617, 620, 622
Horizon View Composer Server
  about 136
  installing 182, 183
  installing, on vCenter Server 191, 192, 193, 195, 197, 198, 200, 202, 203, 204, 205, 206
  SQL Server, configuring for 183, 185, 186, 188, 189, 190
  upgrade, completing 676
  upgrade, verifying 676, 679, 680
  upgrading 673
  upgrading, prerequisites 673, 675
Horizon View Composer
  about 44
Horizon View Connection Server
  about 32, 135
  alternative upgrade method 683, 684
  configuring 214, 215
  hardware, requisites 35

installing 206, 207, 208, 209, 210, 211, 212, 214
installing, on operating systems 36
license, adding 216, 217, 218
requisites 35
upgrade, completing 681
upgrading 681
upgrading, prerequisites 681
vCenter Server, adding to View Administrator 219, 220, 221, 222, 224, 226
View events database, configuring 226, 227, 228
working 32, 33, 34
Horizon View enrolment server 39
Horizon View Enrolment Server 136
Horizon View Hardware
 graphics 82
Horizon View issues
 infrastructure component issues, viewing 725
 infrastructure issues 724
 troubleshooting 723, 729
 View Composer issues, fixing with ViewDBChk tool 726
Horizon View pod 117, 118, 119, 120, 121, 122
Horizon View policy settings
 configuring 555
 Horizon View Agent Configuration 562
 PCoIP Client Session Variables 555, 557
 PCoIP Session Variables 557
 VMware Blast 558
 VMware Horizon Client Configuration 559
 VMware Horizon URL Redirection 562
Horizon View replica server
 about 37
Horizon View Replica Server
 about 135
 installing 230, 231, 232, 233, 234
Horizon View replica server
 working 38
Horizon View Security Server
 about 135
Horizon View security server
 about 36
Horizon View Security Server
 upgrade, completing 685
 upgrading 684
 upgrading, prerequisites 684
Horizon View security server
 working 37
Horizon View
 about 267
 configuring, for GPU-enabled virtual desktops 260
 design specifics 134
 Group Policy Objects (GPO), creating for 548, 550, 552
 load balancing published apps 644
 load, balancing between View Connection Servers 140, 141
 load-balancing published apps 636, 638, 640, 642
 SSL certificates, installing for 269
 True SSO, setting up 298
 vSphere, designing for 124, 125
Horizon
 deploying, benefits 16, 17
 platform updates 734
 running, with VMware Cloud on AWS 736
 vRealize Operations 727, 728
host server's CPU requisite
 heavy user 152
 light user 151
 medium user 152
hosted applications
 architectural overview 588, 589
 connection sequence 589, 590
hosted virtual desktop (HVD) 12
HZN7-CERTS 269
HZN7-CS1 323
HZN7-ENROL 318

I

ICA protocol 81
Independent Computing Architecture (ICA) 80
infrastructure design
 about 144
 antivirus 146
 database, requirements 144
 file servers 144

group policy 146
IP addressing 145
Key Management Server (KMS) 147
infrastructure post-deployment
  reviewing 540
infrastructure updates 731
Input/Output Operations Per Second (IOPS) 46
instant clone desktop pool
  creating 498, 500, 501, 503, 505, 506
instant clone domain administrator
  configuring 496
instant clones
  about 59
  benefits 62
  building process 61
Internet of Things (IoT) 651
iOS Horizon Client
  features 655

J

Java Message Service (JMS) 120
JMP Server
  adding, to Horizon 701, 703, 705, 707, 709, 710
  components, adding to Horizon 701, 703, 705, 707, 709, 710
  installing 697, 699
  time, syncing with Horizon Connection Server 700
Just-in-Time Management Platform (JMP)
  about 689
  assignments 711, 713
  configuring 696
  installing 696
  prerequisites 696
  working 690, 691

K

Key Management Server (KMS) 147

L

Lightweight Directory Access Protocol (LDAP) 38
Linked Clone desktop pool
  managing 520, 521, 523, 524
  persistent disks, managing 534
  rebalancing 531, 533
  recomposing 525, 526, 529
  refreshing 529, 531
linked clone
  about 44, 45, 47
  creating 49
  disk 49
  disposable disk 50
  features 54
  functionality 54
  internal disk 51
  operations, rebalancing with View Composer 58, 59
  persistent disk 49
  user data disk 49
  virtual desktop machine, creating 52
  virtual desktop machine, customizing 53, 54
  virtual desktop machine, provisioning 52
  virtual desktop machine, recomposing 54, 56
  virtual desktop machine, refreshing 56, 58
  working 47, 48, 52
Linux virtual desktop machine updates 734
Linux
  features 734
  virtual desktop machine, creating 388
Liquidware Stratusphere UX 729
load-balancing published apps
  in Horizon View 636, 638, 640, 642, 644
loopback policy
  enabling 553, 555

M

manual desktop pool
  creating 507, 508, 510, 511
Microsoft Deployment Toolkit (MDT) 336
Microsoft Management Console (MMC) 285
Microsoft Skype
  disadvantages 93

N

Network Load Balancing (NLB) 140
network ports, in VMware Horizon 7
  reference 80
networking 138, 140, 720

non-persistent desktops 42, 43
Non-VDI related issues 718

O

Open Virtualization Format (OVF) 159
operating system (OS)
　installing, on virtual desktop machine 357
　updates 731
operational expenditure (OPEX) 17
optimization tool
　download link 371
organizational unit (OU)
　creating 546

P

PCI pass-through 87
PCoIP Client Session Variables 555, 557
PCoIP protocol tools
　reference 581
PCoIP Secure Gateway server (PSG) 590
PCoIP session handshake 76
PCoIP Session Variables 557
PCoIP tuning tool
　about 578
　Activate Profile settings 579
　Clear Profile Settings 580
　Manage Profiles option 580
　Show Session Health option 580
　Show Session Stats options 580
　Teradici, support tools 581
PCoIP
　about 72
　connection process, working 76
　host rendering 73
　image quality, controlling 74
　multi-codec, using 74
　networking, capabilities 74
　offloading, with Teradici PCoIP Hardware
　　Accelerator 75
　Teradici host, card for physical PCs 76
　using 81
performance issues
　about 717
　user reports 717
persistent desktops 42, 43

persistent disks
　attaching, to users virtual desktop machine
　　536, 538, 539, 540
　detaching, from users virtual desktop
　　machine 534, 536
　managing 534
Persona Management
　Desktop UI 565
　Folder Redirection 565
　Logging 566
　Roaming and Synchronization 566
　Troubleshooting 567
physical-to-virtual tool (P2V) 336
pilot
　about 110
　deploying 112
　infrastructure, designing 111
　reviewing 112
　testing 112
post-optimization tasks 375
prerequisites, Just-in-Time Management
　Platform (JMP)
　about 696
　VMware component 696
　VMware hardware 696
　VMware software 697
printing 148
product editions, VMware Horizon 7
　about 23
　comparison 26
　Horizon Advanced Edition 24
　Horizon Apps Advanced 25
　Horizon Apps Standard 25
　Horizon Enterprise Edition 24
　Horizon for Linux 23
　Horizon Standard Edition 23
　overview 26
　user licensing models 27
production environment
　designing 113
project definition
　assessment 100
　business case, building 100
　business drivers, identifying 99
　phase 99

success criteria, defining 106
Proof of concept (POC) 109
Proof of technology (POT) 108, 109
published apps
  application pool, creating for 628, 629, 631
  configuring, in View Administrator 622, 625, 627
  users, entitling to application pools 631, 633, 635

R

RD-Execute 608
RD-Install 608
RD-Install mode 608
RDS server role
  configuring 594, 596, 598, 601
RDSH server
  Horizon Agent, installing for 615, 617, 620, 622
  sizing guidelines 592
RDSH-Apps 593
Real-Time Audio-Video (RTAV)
  about 94
  issue 94
  issue, solving 94
remote access
  additional applications, installing 606, 607, 608, 611, 612, 615
Remote Desktop Connection 80
Remote Desktop Protocol (RDP)
  about 80
  using 81
Remote Desktop Services (RDS) 15, 587
Remote Desktop Session Host (RDSH)
  design considerations 142, 143, 144
  improvements 735
root CA
  installing 269, 270, 272, 274
  post-deployment configuration tasks 274, 276, 278, 279, 280, 282, 284

S

scalability 733, 735
Secure Sockets Layer (SSL) certificates
  installation, for Horizon View
    on View Connection Server 285, 286, 288, 289, 290, 291, 293, 294
  post-certificate enrollment configuration tasks 294, 295, 296, 298
  root CA, installing 269, 270, 272, 274
Secure Sockets Layer (SSL) certificates
  about 267
  for Horizon View 268
  installing, for Horizon View 269
SecureSecure Sockets Layer (SSL) certificates
  installation, for Horizon View
    on View Connection Server 287
Security Assertion Markup Language (SAML) 40
Security Server
  installing 234
  software, installation 237, 239, 240, 241, 242, 243, 244
  View Administrator, preparing for 235, 236, 237
Serial COM
  PortSettings 568
server-based computing (SBC)
  versus Virtual Desktop Infrastructure (VDI) 14, 16
Service Provider License Agreement (SPLA) 19
Simple Device Orientation (SDO) 368
Simple Object Access Protocol (SOAP) 204
Single Sign-On (SSO) 737
SIP stack 92
Smartcard Redirection
  Local Reader Access 569
SQL Server
  configuring, for View Composer database 183, 185, 186, 188, 189, 190
standard remote applications
  testing with 601, 603, 605
Stratusphere UX
  reference 582
System Center Configuration Manager (SCCM) 336

T

technology decisions

about 113
conclusions 116
preparing, for production 117
use case example scenario 114, 116
use case example scenarios 114, 115
Teradici 72
Teradici PCoIP Hardware Accelerator 75
thin client 662
ThinApp application virtualization
    about 69
    working 69, 70
ThinScale's ThinIO
    reference 47
troubleshooting
    bandwidth 720
    compute resources 721
    connectivity 720
    disk 722
    issue affecting 716
    networking 720
    Non-VDI related issues 718
    performance issues 717
    tips 715
    VDI solution 716
True SSO
    about 39, 267
    AD, preparing for 299, 301, 302, 303
    certificate template, creating for 303, 304, 306, 307, 308, 309, 310, 311, 312, 313
    certificate template, issuing 313, 314, 315, 317
    configuring, on Connection Server 330, 331, 332, 333
    Enrollment Agent (Computer) certificate, deploying 318, 319, 320, 321, 323, 324, 325, 327, 329, 330

U

unified communications support
    about 90, 91
    for Microsoft Skype 92, 93
    working 92
uniform resource identifiers (URIs) 589
Universal Windows Platform (UWP) 651, 736
URL Content Redirection 95

USB devices
    filtering 68
    managing 67
    multi-function, managing 68
use case example scenarios, technology decisions
    about 114, 115, 116
    solution recommendation 114, 115, 116
User Datagram Protocol (UDP) 74
User Environment Manager (UEM) 29
user requisite, example solution scenario
    application developers 161
    contractors 162
    engineering 162
    office workers 162
    sales 162

V

vCenter Server
    about 136
    adding, to View Administrator 219, 220, 221, 222, 224, 226
View Administrator
    about 214
    published apps, configuring in 622, 625, 627
    vCenter Server, adding 219, 220, 221, 222, 224, 226
View Composer Array Integration (VCAI) 47, 132
View Connection Server
    SLL certificate, installing on 291
    SSL certificate, installing on 285, 286, 287, 288, 289, 290, 293, 294
View hosted applications
    configuring 593
    installing 593
View Interpod API (VIPA) 123
View Persona Management (VDI) 29
View Persona Management
    about 62
    benefits 63
    user profiles, managing in 63
    using 66
View RTAV Configuration
    View RTAV Webcam Settings 572

View Storage Accelerator (VSA) 46, 131
View USB Configuration
  client downloadable only Settings 572
view-events 226
ViewDBChk tool 725
virtual CPUs (vCPUs) 127
Virtual Dedicated Graphics Acceleration (vDGA)
  about 19, 83, 86
  graphics cards 88
  virtual desktops 87
Virtual Desktop Customization 447
virtual desktop images
  building, best practice 336
Virtual Desktop Infrastructure (VDI)
  about 11, 12
  high-level architecture, working 12, 13, 14
  history 18, 20
  versus server-based computing (SBC) 14, 16
virtual desktop machine
  antivirus software 71
  applications, installing for parent image 364
  BIOS, updating 354, 356, 357
  container, creating 339, 341, 342, 343, 344, 346, 347, 349, 350, 352
  container, creating in GPU-enabled 379, 382
  container, creating in Windows 10 376, 378
  container, creating in Windows 7 353, 354
  creating, with GPU-enabled 379
  creating, with Linux 385, 388
  creating, with Windows 10 375
  creating, with Windows 7 338
  delivery protocols 72
  GPU-enabled desktop build, completing 385
  guest-operating system, optimizing 371, 373, 392
  Horizon Agent, installing 364, 366, 370, 389, 390, 392
  Linux build, completing 388
  operating system, installing 357, 358
  operating system, installing for GPU-enabled desktop 383
  pool design 393
  post-optimization tasks 375
  preparing, for delivery 393
  printing from 67

snapshot, creating for instant clones 398
snapshot, creating for linked clones 394, 395, 397
template, creating for full clones 398, 399, 400
VMware Tools, installing 358, 359, 360, 362, 363
Virtual Graphics Processing Unit (vGPU)
  about 83, 88
  virtual desktops 90
Virtual Profiles 62
Virtual SAN (VSAN) 19
Virtual Shared Graphics Acceleration (vSGA)
  about 19, 83, 84
  graphics cards 85
  virtual desktops 85, 86
VMDirectPath I/O pass-through 87
VMware Access Point 137
VMware App Volumes
  about 692, 694
  application, capturing 694
  AppStacks, delivering 695
  working 694, 695
VMware Blast 558
VMware Cloud
  with, Horizon running on AWS 736
VMware Horizon 7
  about 20
  product editions 23
  timeline 20, 21, 22
VMware Horizon Agent
  upgrading 687
VMware Horizon Client Configuration
  about 559
  scripting definitions 560
  security settings 560
  Settings not configurable by Agent 561
  View USB Configuration 561
VMware Horizon Clients
  about 648
  download link 648
  features 649
  for Android 651, 653
  for iOS 653, 654
  for Linux 656, 657

   for Windows 648, 651
   reference 650
VMware Horizon components 30
VMware Horizon URL Redirection 562
VMware HTML5 Features
   VMware Geolocation Redirection 574
   VMware HTML5 Multimedia Redirection 575
VMware Identity Manager (VIDM) 39
VMware Optimization Tool 371
VMware UEM
   about 64, 65, 66
   using 66
VMware Unified Access Gateway 41, 42
VMware View Common Configuration
   about 576
   Log Configuration 576
   Performance Alarms 577
   Security Configuration 577
VMware View Server Configuration 578
VMware Windows Operating System
    Optimization Tool Guide
   reference 374

VMware Workspace ONE 691, 692
VMware
   history 18, 20
Voice over IP (VoIP) 74
vRealize Operations
   for Horizon 727, 728
vShield Endpoint 71
vSphere, designing for Horizon View
   about 124, 125
   configuration maximums 125
   ESXi host servers 126

W

Windows 10
   build, completing 378
   virtual desktop machine, creating 375
Windows 7
   virtual desktop machine, creating 338
Writable Volume 693

Z

Zero Client 663

Printed in Poland
by Amazon Fulfillment
Poland Sp. z o.o., Wrocław